THE WORKS OF JOHN MILTON

JOANNIS MILTONI

Angli

PRO POPULO ANGLICANO

DEFENSIO

Contra *Claudii Anonymi*, aliàs *Salmasii*,
Defensionem REGIAM.

LONDINI,
Typis *Du Gardianis.* Anno Domini 1651.

THE WORKS OF JOHN MILTON

VOLUME VII

NEW YORK

Columbia University Press

1932

PRINTED IN THE UNITED STATES OF AMERICA
BY THE PRINTING HOUSE OF WILLIAM EDWIN RUDGE, INC.
MOUNT VERNON, NEW YORK

CONTENTS

JOANNIS MILTONI ANGLI
PRO POPULO ANGLICANO DEFENSIO

CONTRA CLAUDII ANONYMI, ALIÀS SALMASII

DEFENSIONEM REGIAM

JOANNIS MILTONI

ANGLI

Pro Populo Anglicano Defensio

CONTRA

CLAUDII ANONYMI, ALIÀS SALMASII

Defensionem Regiam.

PRÆFATIO.

TAMETSI vereor, si in defendendo Populo Anglicano tam sim profusus verborum, vacuus rerum, quàm est plerisque visus in defensione regia Salmasius, ne verbosissimi simul et ineptissimi defensoris nomen meritus esse

5 videar, tamen cùm in mediocri quavis materia tractanda nemo sibi adeò properandum esse existimet, quin exordio saltem aliquo pro dignitate suscepti à se operis uti soleat, id ego in re omnium ferè maxima dicenda si non omittam, neque nimis perstringam, spero equidem, duas propemodùm res, quas

10 magnopere vellem, assecuturum me esse: alteram, ut causæ huic nobilissimæ, et seculorum omnium memoriâ dignissimæ nulla ex parte, quantum in me est, desim; alteram, ut reprehensam in adversario futilitatem et redundantiam, devitâsse tamen ipse nihilo minus judicer. Dicam enim res neque

15 parvas, neque vulgares; Regem potentissimum, oppressis legibus, religione afflicta, pro libidine regnantem, tandem à suo

JOHN MILTON

AN ENGLISHMAN HIS

Defence of the People of England

AGAINST

CLAUDIUS ANONYMOUS, ALIAS SALMASIUS

his Defence of the King

PREFACE.

IF I be as copious of words and empty of matter in my Defence of the People of England as most men think Salmasius has been in his Defence of the King, I fear that I shall apparently have deserved to be called a defender at
5 once wordy and silly. Yet no man thinks he must make such haste, even in handling any ordinary subject, as not to employ an opening worthy of its importance. In handling well-nigh the greatest of all subjects, then, if I neither omit an introduction, nor overdo it, I am in hopes of attaining two things,
10 both of which I earnestly desire: the one, that I be nowise wanting, as far as in me lies, to this cause, most renowned and most worth the remembrance of all the generations of men; the other, that I myself be yet deemed to have avoided the silliness and verbosity which I blame in my antagonist.
15 For I shall relate no common things, or mean; but how a most puissant king, when he had trampled upon the laws, and

populo, qui servitutem longam servierat, bello victum; inde
in custodiam traditum; et cùm nullam omnino meliùs de se
sperandi materiam vel dictis vel factis præberet, à summo
demùm regni Concilio capite damnatum; et pro ipsis Regiæ
5 foribus securi percussum. Dicam etiam, quod ad levandos
magna superstitione hominum animos multum contulerit,
quo jure, præsertim apud nos, judicatum hoc atque peractum
sit; meosque cives fortissimos et integerrimos, deque universis
orbis terrarum civibus ac populis egregiè meritos ab impro-
10 bissimis maledicorum, sive nostratium, sive exterorum ca-
lumniis, tum imprimis ab hujus inanissimi Sophistæ male-
dictis, qui pro duce et coryphæo cæterorum se gerit, facilè de-
fendam. Quæ enim ullius regis alto solio sedentis majestas
unquam tanta eluxit, quanta tum Populi Anglicani effulgebat,
15 cùm excussa illa veteri superstitione, quæ diu invaluerat, ipsum regem, seu potiùs de rege hostem, qui solus mortalium
impunitatem sibi divino jure vendicabat, suis legibus irreti-
tum judicio perfunderet; et quo is quemcunque alium supplicio affecisset, eodem sontem ipsum afficere non vereretur?
20 At quid ego hæc tanquam populi facta prædico; quæ ipsa per
se penè vocem edunt, et præsentem ubique testantur Deum?
Qui, quoties suæ sapientissimæ menti complacitum est, super-

stricken down religion, and was ruling at his own lust and
wantonness, was at last subdued in the field by his own
people, who had served a long term of slavery; how he was
thereupon put under guard, and when he gave no ground
5 whatever, by either word or action, to hope better things of
him, was finally by the highest council of the realm condemned to die, and beheaded before his very palace gate. I
shall likewise relate (which will much conduce to the easing
men's minds of a great superstition) under what system of
10 laws, especially what laws of England, this judgment was
rendered and executed; and shall easily defend my valiant and
worthy countrymen, who have extremely well deserved of all
subjects and nations in the world, from the most wicked
calumnies of both domestic and foreign railers, and chiefly
15 from the reproaches of this utterly empty sophister, who sets
up to be captain and ringleader of all the rest. For what king's
majesty high enthroned ever shone so bright as did the
people's majesty of England, when, shaking off that age-old
superstition which had long prevailed, they overwhelmed
20 with judgment their very king (or rather him who from their
king had become their enemy), ensnared in his own laws him
who alone among men claimed by divine right to go unpunished, and feared not to inflict upon this very culprit the same
capital punishment which he would have inflicted upon any
25 other.

Yet why do I proclaim as done by the people these actions,
which themselves almost utter a voice, and witness everywhere the presence of God? Who, as often as it hath seemed

bos et effrænatos reges, supra humanum modum sese efferentes, solet deturbare, et totâ sæpe cum domo funditus evertit.
Illius nos manifesto numine ad salutem et libertatem propè
amissam subitò erecti, illum Ducem secuti, et impressa passim
5 divina vestigia venerantes, viam haud obscuram, sed illu-
strem, illius auspiciis commonstratam et patefactam ingressi
sumus. Hæc ego omnia dignè satis explicare, et quod omnes
fortasse gentes legant atque ætates, monumentis tradere, si
diligentiâ solùm meâ, cujusmodicunque est, meis tantùm viri-
10 bus sperem me posse, frustra sim. Quæ enim oratio tam augu-
sta atque magnifica, quod tam excellens ingenium huic oneri
subeundo par esse queat, ut cùm illustrium virorum aut civitatum res gestas vix reperiatur tot seculis qui luculentè possit
scribere, confidat quisquam hæc, non hominum, sed omnipo-
15 tentis planè Dei gloriosè et mirabiliter facta ullis se verbis aut
stylo assequi posse? Quod quidem munus ut susciperem, tametsi summi in republica nostra viri sua authoritate perfece-
runt, mihique hoc negotium datum esse voluerunt, ut quæ
illi, Deo ductore, magna cum gloria gesserant, ea, quod certè
20 proximum est, contra invidiam et obtrectationem, quas in res
ferrum et apparatus belli nihil potest, alio genere armorum
defenderem, quorum ego quidem judicium magno mihi or-
namento esse existimo, me scilicet eorum suffragiis eum esse

good to his infinite wisdom, useth to cast down proud unbridled kings, puffed up above the measure of mankind, and
often uprooteth them with their whole house. As for us, it
was by His clear command we were on a sudden resolved
5 upon the safety and liberty that we had almost lost; it was He
we followed as our Leader, and revered His divine footsteps
imprinted everywhere; and thus we entered upon a path not
dark but bright, and by His guidance shown and opened to
us. I should be much in error if I hoped that by my diligence
10 alone, such as it is, I might set forth all these matters as worthily as they deserve, and might make such records of them as,
haply, all nations and all ages would read. For what eloquence can be august and magnificent enough, what man has
parts sufficient, to undertake so great a task? Yea, since in so
15 many ages as are gone over the world there has been but here
and there a man found able to recount worthily the actions of
great heroes and potent states, can any man have so good an
opinion of himself as to think that by any style or language of
his own he can compass these glorious and wonderful works
20 —not of men, but, evidently, of almighty God?

Yet such is the office which the most eminent men of our
commonwealth have by their influence prevailed upon me to
undertake, and have wished this next best task assigned to me
of defending their deeds from envy and calumny, against
25 which steel and the furniture of war avail not—of defending,
I say, with far other arms and other weapons, the works which
under God's guidance they had gloriously wrought. Their
decision, certainly, I count a great honor to myself—that they

præ cæteris, qui hanc patriæ meæ fortissimis liberatoribus
haud pœnitendam operam navarem, quin et ipse ab ineunte
adolescentiâ iis eram studiis incensus, quæ me ad optima quæque si minùs facienda, at certè laudanda incitatum ferebant,
5 his tamen diffisus adminiculis ad divinam opem recurro:
Deumque Opt. Max. donorum omnium largitorem invoco,
ut quàm prosperè quámque piè nostri illi ad libertatem claris-
simi duces regios fastus, et dominatum impotentem acie fre-
gerunt, dein memorabili tandem supplicio extinxerunt, quam-
10 que facili nuper negotio unus de multis ipsum regem veluti ab
inferis resurgentem, inque illo libro post mortem edito novis
argutiis, et verborum lenociniis populo se venditantem redargui atque summovi, tam nunc feliciter tamque verè declama-
toris hujus exotici petulantiam et mendacia refellam atque di-
15 scutiam. Qui alienigena cùm sit, et, quamvis id millies neget,
Grammaticus, non eâ tamen stipe contentus, quam hoc nomine
meretur, magnus ardelio esse maluit; non reipub. solùm immi-
scere se ausus, sed etiam alienæ: cum neque modestiam, neque
judicium, neque aliud quicquam afferat, quod oporteret sanè
20 tantum arbitrum, præter arrogantiam et Grammaticam. Et
sanè hæc quæ jam Latinè utcunque scripsit, si inter Anglos,
et nostro sermone protulisset, vix esset, credo, qui de responso
laborandum esse judicaret; sed partim trita, et refutationibus
jam crebris explosa negligeret, partim tyrannica et fœda, vilis-
25 simo quovis mancipio vix ferenda, quamvis ipse regias secutus

voted me, before all others, the one to render this never-to-be-regretted assistance to the valiant liberators of my country; and indeed from my youth upward I had been fired with a zeal which kept urging me, if not to do great deeds myself, at
5 least to celebrate them. Yet, mistrusting these advantages, I have recourse to the divine assistance, and pray the great and holy God, dispenser of all gifts: Even as successfully and piously as those our glorious guides to freedom crushed in battle the royal insolence and tyranny uncontrolled, and then
10 at last by a memorable punishment utterly ended them; even as easily as I, singlehanded, lately refuted and set aside the king himself when he, as it were, rose from the grave, and in that book published after his death tried to cry himself up before the people with new verbal sleights and harlotries; so,
15 I pray, may I now as auspiciously and as truly refute and demolish this outlandish rhetorician's wanton lies.

Foreign born as he is, and (though he deny it a thousand times) a mere grammarian, yet, not satisfied with the grammarian's dole, he has chosen to mind everybody's business,
20 and has presumed to mix in an affair of state, a foreign state at that, though he brings to the task neither moderation nor understanding nor anything else that so grand a judge would surely need, save his presumption and his grammar. Indeed if he had published here, and in English, the same things as
25 he now has writ in Latin (such as it is) I think scarce any man would have thought it worth while to return an answer to them, but would partly despise them as common, and exploded over and over already, and partly (even one who sided

partes, aversaretur. Nunc cùm inter exteros, et nostrarum
rerum penitùs ignaros grandi paginâ turgescat, sunt illi quidem, qui res nostras perperam intelligunt, edocendi; hic suo
more, (quandoquidem tantâ maledicendi aliis libidine fertur)
5 suo inquam more ac modo erit tractandus. Quod siquis miretur fortè, cur ergo tam diu intactum et ovantem, nostroque
omnium silentio inflatum volitare passi simus, de aliis sanè
nescio, de me audacter possum dicere, non mihi verba aut
argumenta, quibus causam tuerer tam bonam, diu quærenda
10 aut investiganda fuisse, si otium et valetudinem (quæ quidem
scribendi laborem ferre possit) nactus essem. Quâ cum adhuc
etiam tenui admodum utar, carptim hæc cogor, et intercisis
penè singulis horis vix attingere, quæ continenti stylo atque
studio persequi debuissem. Unde hoc si minùs dabitur, cives
15 meos præstantissimos, patriæ conservatores digno laudum
præconio celebrare, quorum immortalia facinora jam toto
orbe claruerunt, defendere tamen, et ab hujus importuni literatoris insolentia, et professoriæ linguæ intemperiis vindicare
haud mihi difficile futurum spero. Pessimè enim vel natura
20 vel legibus comparatum fuisset, si arguta servitus, libertas
muta esset; et haberent tyranni qui pro se dicerent, non haberent qui tyrannos debellare possunt: miserum esset, si hæc
ipsa ratio, quo utimur Dei munere, non multò plura ad homines conservandos, liberandos, et, quantum natura fert, inter

with the king) abhor them as foul despotic maxims, hardly
to be endured by the most worthless of slaves. But as he un-
dertakes to puff his portentous sheet among outsiders, who are
quite ignorant of our affairs, they, who thus get an utterly
5 false notion of them, certainly ought to be fully informed;
and he, who is so very forward to speak ill of others, should
be treated in his own kind.

If haply anyone wonder why, then, we all have suffered
him so long to strut unharmed, swollen in triumph at our
10 silence, I know not what others may say, but for myself I can
boldly declare that I had neither words nor arguments long
to seek for the defence of so good a cause, had I but found
leisure, and such health as could bear the toil of writing. Yet
as I still possess but slender strength, I am forced to write by
15 piece-meal, and break off almost every hour, though the subject be such as requires unremitted study and attention. If for
this reason it be not given me to clarion with right heraldry,
befitting their praises, those glorious fellow-citizens of mine,
their country's saviors, whose deathless deeds already ring
20 round the world, yet I hope it will not be difficult for me to
defend, at least, and justify them, against the impertinence
of this bore of a pedant, and the squallings of his professorial
tongue. Nature and laws would be in ill case if slavery were
eloquent, and liberty mute; if tyrants should find defenders,
25 and they that are potent to master and vanquish tyrants should
find none. And it were deplorable indeed, if the reason mankind is endued withal, which is God's gift, should not furnish
more arguments for men's preservation, for their deliverance,

se æquandos, quàm ad opprimendos et sub unius imperio
malè perdendos argumenta suppeditaret. Causam itaque pul-
cherrimam hac certâ fiduciâ læti aggrediamur, illinc fraudem,
fallaciam, ignorantiam, atque barbariem, hinc lucem, veri-
5 tatem, rationem, et seculorum omnium optimorum studia
atque doctrinam nobiscum stare.

Agè nunc jam, satìs præfati, quoniam cum criticis res est,
tam culti voluminis titulum imprimis, quid exponat, videamus: *Defensio regia pro Carolo I. ad Car. II.* Magnum sanè
10 præstas, O quisquis es! patrem defendis ad filium: mirum ni
causam obtineas. Verùm ego te falso aliàs sub nomine, nunc
sub nullo latitantem, Salmasi, ad alia voco subsellia, ad alios
judices, ubi tu illud euge et soph*ω̃*s, quod in palæstra tua lite-
raria captare miserè soles, fortasse non audies. Sed cur ad re-
15 gem filium defensio hæc regia? non opus est tortore, confi-
tentem habemus reum; *Sumptibus* inquit *Regiis:* O te venalem oratorem et sumptuosum! Siccine defensionem pro Carolo patre, tuâ sententiâ, rege optimo, ad Carolum filium
regem pauperrimum noluisti nisi sumptibus regiis? Sed ve-
20 terator etiam haud irridiculus esse voluisti, qui *regiam defen-*
sionem dixeris; non enim ampliùs tua quam vendidisti, sed
legitimè jam *regia defensio* est; centenis nimirum Jacobæis

and, as much as the nature of the thing will bear, for their equality, than for their oppression and utter ruin under one man's dominion. Let me therefore enter upon this noble cause with cheerfulness grounded upon the assurance that on the
5 other side are cheating, and trickery, and ignorance and out-landishness, and on my side the light of truth and reason, and the practice and theory of the best historic ages.

So much by way of introduction. And now, since our af-fair is with critics, let us consider first the title of this choice
10 volume. What does it say? "A Royal Defence for Charles the First, to Charles the Second." You undertake a wonderful piece of work, whoever you are—to plead the father's cause before his own son: a hundred to one but you carry it! But, Salmasius, though you hide from legal process as you for-
15 merly did under an assumed name, and do now under no name at all—I yet summon you to appear before another tri-bunal and before other judges, where perhaps you shall not get those "Bravo's" and "Hear Hear's" which you are wont to hanker after so desperately in your classroom. But why this
20 royal defence dedicated to the king's own son? We need not put him to the torture; he confesses: "At the king's expense," says he. Mercenary and costly advocate! so you would not write a defence for Charles the father, whom you pretend to have been the best of kings, to Charles the son, the most indi-
25 gent of kings, but it must be at the king's own expense? You old rogue, in calling it the "*King's* Defence" you certainly contrived not to have yourself laughed at; for, as you have sold it, 'tis no longer yours, but lawfully the *King's* indeed,—

empta, ingenti pretio ab egentissimo rege: Non enim ignota
loquimur; novimus qui illos aureos domum attulit tuam, qui
crumenam illam tessellis vitreis variatam; novimus qui te
avaras manus porrigentem vidit, in speciem quidem ut Sacel-
5 lanum Regis missum cum munere, re vera ut ipsum munus
amplecterere; et una tantùm mercede accepta totum penè
Regis ærarium exinanires. Sed eccum ipsum, crepant fores,
prodit histrio in proscenium.

Date operam, et cum silentio animadvertite,
10   Ut pernoscatis quid sibi Eunuchus velit.

Nam quicquid est, præter solitum cothurnatus incedit. *Hor-*
ribilis nuper nuntius aures nostras atroci vulnere, sed magis
mentes perculit, de parricidio apud Anglos in persona Regis
sacrilegorum hominum nefaria conspiratione admisso. Pro-
15 fectò nuntius iste horribilis aut machaeram multo longiorem
ea quam strinxit Petrus habuerit oportet, aut aures istæ auri-
tissimæ fuerint, quas tam longinquo vulnere perculerit: nam
aures non stolidas ne offendisse quidem potuit. Ecqua enim
vobis fit injuria, ecquis vestrûm læditur, si nos hostes et per-
20 duelles nostros, sive plebeios, sive nobiles, sive reges morte
multamus? At ista mitte, Salmasi, quæ ad te nihil attinent:
ego enim de te etiam *horribilem* habeo quem mittam *nun-*
tium; quique omnium Grammaticorum et Criticorum aures,
modò teretes habeant et doctas, atrociori vulnere si non per-

yea, bought for one hundred Jacobuses, a great sum to get
from a needy King. I speak not of things unknown: I know
who took those gold-pieces to your house in that beaded
purse; I know who saw you reach out your greedy hands
5 under pretence of embracing the king's chaplain who brought
the gift, but in fact to hug the gift itself, and by taking this
single fee almost to empty the king's treasury.

But here comes the man himself; the door creaks; enter
the actor.

10   In silence now and with attention wait,
          That ye may learn what th' Eunuch has to prate.

For whatever's the matter with him, he struts on with heroics
more than usual stilted. "A horrible message has lately struck
our ears, but our minds more, with a heinous wound concern-
15 ing a parricide committed in England in the person of a king,
by an execrable conspiracy of sacrilegious men." Surely that
horrible message must either have had a much longer sword
than the one that Peter drew, or those ears must have been
exceeding long-eared ears, that it could wound at such a dis-
20 tance; for it could not so much as in the least offend any ears
but dull ones. What harm is it to you foreigners—are any of
you hurt by it—if we amongst ourselves put our own enemies,
our own traitors, to death, be they commoners, noblemen, or
kings? Salmasius, you had better mind your own business;
25 for *I* have "a horrible message" to send about *you,* and I shall
be surprised if it strike not with a more heinous wound all
grammarians' and critics' ears, so these be but refined and

culerit, mirabor; *de parricidio* apud Hollandos *in persona*
Aristarchi, *nefaria* Salmasii barbarie *admisso:* te magnum scilicet Criticum *sumptibus regiis* conductum, ut defensionem
regiam scriberes, non solùm putidissimo exordio, præficarum
5 funebribus nugis et næniis simillimo, nullius, non fatui, mentem miseratione permovisse, sed primâ statim clausulâ risum
penè legentibus multiplici barbarismo excitâsse. Quid enim,
quæso, est *parricidium in persona Regis admittere,* quid *in
persona Regis?* quæ unquam latinitas sic locuta est? nisi ali-
10 quem nobis forte Pseudophilippum narras, qui personam
Regis indutus, nescio quid parricidii apud Anglos patraverit;
quod verbum verius opinione tua ex ore tibi excidisse puto.
Tyrannus enim, quasi histrionalis quidem rex, larva tantùm
et persona Regis, non verus Rex est. Cæterùm ob hujusmodi
15 noxas Gallicolatinas, quibus passim scates, non tam mihi,
neque enim est otium, quàm ipsis tuis Grammatistis pœnas
dabis; quibus ego te deridendum et vapulandum propino. Hoc
multo atrocius; quod à summis Magistratibus nostris de Rege
statutum est, id *sacrilegorum hominum nefariâ conspiratione*
20 admissum ais. Tune furcifer potentissimi nuper regni, nunc
reipub. eo potentioris acta et consulta sic nominas? quorum
de factis ne Rex quidem ullus ut quicquam gravius pronun-

learned: "Of a parricide committed in Holland in the person of Aristarchus by the abominable barbarism of Salmasius": to wit, that you, a great critic, hired forsooth, at a king's expense to write a king's defence, did with a sickening ex-
5 ordium, most like the trumpery doleful wailings of hired mourner-women, not only fail to move with pity the mind of any but a fool, but by the end of your first sentence instantly provoke, in those who had scarce read it, laughter at your manifold barbarisms. For, pray what is "parricidium in per-
10 sona regis admittere"? What is "in persona regis"? What Latinity ever used such diction?—as it were a murder committed in the mask or disguise of a king! Unless maybe you are telling us of some sham Philip—some Perkin Warbeck—who by *impersonating* a king did in a way perpetrate
15 parricide in England. This word, methinks, you have spoken better than you knew. For a tyrant is no real king; he is but a player-king, the mere mask and spectre of a king. At all events, for such Frenchified Latin blunders as this, with which you abound, you shall be punished not by me, for I
20 have no time, but by your own fellow-grammarians; to them I turn you over to be laughed and flogged out of court—and much good may it do them.

Far more heinous is it, that what was decreed by our supreme magistracy to be done to the king should be said by
25 you to have been done "by an execrable conspiracy of sacrilegious men." Rogue, is it thus you name the acts and decrees of our late most potent realm and present yet more potent commonwealth, concerning whose deeds no king, even,

tiaret, aut scriptum ederet, adduci adhuc potuit. Meritò itaque
amplissimi Ordines Hollandiæ, liberatorum olim patriæ vera
progenies, defensionem hanc tyrannicam, populorum omnium libertati pestilentissimam edicto suo tenebris damnâ-
5 runt; cujus et ipsum authorem omnis libera Civitas suis pro-
hibere finibus, aut ejicere deberet: eáque præcipuè quæ tam
ingratum támque tetrum reipublicæ hostem suo stipendio
alit; cujus ille reipublicæ haud secus atque nostræ, fundamenta ipsa atque causas oppugnat; necnon utramque unâ et
10 eâdem operâ labefactare et subruere conatur; præstantissi-
mósque illic Libertatis vindices nostrorum sub nomine male-
dictis proscindit. Reputate jam vobiscum illustrissimi Fœderatorum Belgarum Ordìnes, et cum animis vestris cogitate,
quis hunc regiæ potestatis assertorem ad scribendum impu-
15 lerit, quis nuper apud vos regiè se gerere incœperit, quæ consilia, qui conatus, quæ turbæ denique per Hollandiam secutæ
sint, quæ nunc essent, quàm vobis parata servitus, novusque
dominus erat, atque illa vestra tot annorum armis atque labo-
ribus vindicata libertas, quàm prope extincta apud vos nunc
20 fuisset, nisi opportunissimâ nuper temerarii juvenis morte re-
spirâsset. Sed pergit iste noster ampullari, et mirabiles tragœ-
dias fingere, *Quoscunque infandus hic* parricidialis nimirum
barbarismi Salmasiani *rumor attigit, haud secús ac si fulmine*

could hitherto be brought to utter or publish aught more abusive?

Rightly, then, have the High and Mighty States of Holland, true offspring of the ancient liberators of their country, 5 by their edict damned to darkness this defence of tyranny, most noxious to the liberty of all peoples. As for the author, him every free state ought to keep out of its bounds, or cast out; especially the state which supports and subsidizes so ungrateful and so foul an enemy of the republic. That republic's 10 foundations and causes he attacks precisely as he attacks ours; by one and the same effort, in fact, he strives to undermine them both, and make them totter to their fall; and under our names foully maligns the most eminent champions of liberty there. Consider with yourselves, most illustrious States General of the United Netherlands, and bethink you who it was 15 that moved this assertor of kingly power to write; who it was that lately began to king it among you; what counsels were taken, what attempts made, what tumults at length ensued throughout Holland; to what pass things might have been 20 brought by this time—how slavery and a new master were made ready for you, and that liberty of yours, vindicated by so many years' war and toil—how near spent it had now been among you, had it not recovered breath again of late by the exceeding timely death of a rash young man.

25 But that fellow of ours goes on with his bombast, play-acting strange tragedies: "Whomsoever this dreadful news reached"—the news, doubtless, of Salmasius's parricidal barbarism—"suddenly, as if they had been scorched by light-

afflati essent, derepente his arrectæque horrore comæ et vox faucibus hæsit. Quod nunc primitùs auditum discant Physici comas fulmine arrectas. Verùm quis hoc nescit, viles et imbelles animos, magni cujuspiam facinoris vel rumore obstu-
5 pescere; quódque priùs fuerunt, tum se maximè stipites indicare? Alii *lacrymas non tenuerunt,* mulierculæ credo aulicæ, aut siqui his molliores; inter quos et ipse Salmasius novâ quâdam metamorphôsi Salmacis factus est; et fonte hoc suo lacrymarum fictitio, et nocte parato viriles animos emollire
10 conatur. Moneo itaque et cavere jubeo,

> *— infamis ne quem malè fortibus undis*
> *Salmacis enervet.*
> *— ne vir cùm venerit, exeat inde*
> *Semivir, et tactis subitò mollescat in undis.*

15 *Fortiùs verò* inquit *animati* (nam fortes puto et animosos ne nominare quidem nisi putidè potest) tantâ *indignationis flammâ exarserunt, ut vix se caperent.* Furiosos illos non flocci facimus; vera fortitudine suíque compote istos minaces pellere, et in fugam vertere consuevimus. *Nemo certè non*
20 *diras imprecatus est tanti sceleris authoribus.* Vox tamen, ut tu

ning's flash, 'Up on end stood their hair in horror, and voice in their throat stuck.'" Something hitherto unheard of for natural philosophers to learn—that to be struck by lightning makes hair stand on end! But who knows not that base and
5 coward minds do get thunderstruck even at the mere noise of any great deed soever, and then most unmistakably show themselves for the blockheads they have been all along? Some, he says, "could not but weep"— some *petites femmes,* I suppose, and *cortegiane,* or others yet more sentimental,—
10 among whom, indeed, Salmasius himself has by a modern metamorphosis turned into Salmacis, and in this his counterfeit fountain of night-lucubrated tears, attempts to emasculate manly courages. I give warning therefore, and bid beware

Lest ill-reputed Salmacis with wave
15 Of evil power some victim shall unman;
Who, though a man he came, yet thence shall go
Hermaphrodite, and at the water's touch
Swift grow effeminate.

"In fact, the more bravely couraged," he says (for I sup-
20 pose he cannot even name the brave and courageous without nauseous affectation), "burned with such a flame of indignation that they could hardly control themselves." For such madmen we care not a rush, but have a way of driving off your blustering bullies, and routing them with that true
25 courage which does control itself.
"Surely not one but invoked curses upon the authors of so horrible a villainy." Yet, you were just saying, their voice in

modò aiebas, *faucibus hæsit;* atque hæsisset utinam in hunc
usque diem, si de nostris duntaxat perfugis hoc vis intelligi,
quod nos etiam pro comperto habemus, nihil illis crebrius in
ore esse, quàm diras et imprecationes omnibus bonis abomi-
5 nandas quidem, non tamen metuendas. De aliis credibile vix
est, cùm supplicii de rege sumpti fama illuc pervenisset, repertum in libero præsertim populo fuisse ullum, tam ad servitutem natum, qui nos dicto læderet, aut factum nostrum
crimini daret; immo potiùs omnes bonos omnia bona dixisse;
10 quinetiam Deo gratias egisse, qui exemplum justitiæ tam illustre et excelsum ediderit, quodque cæteris regibus tam salu-
tari documento esse possit. Istos itaque *feros ac ferreos cædem*
nescio cujus *miserabilem, ac mirabilem* plorantes, cum suo
tinnulo oratore, *post regium in orbe nomen natum notúmque,*
15 frigidissimo, etiam atque etiam plorare jubemus. At quis interim è ludo ferè puer, aut è cœnobio quovis fraterculus casum
hunc regis non multo disertiùs, immo Latiniùs hoc oratore
regio declamitasset? Verùm ego ineptior sim, si infantiam
hujus et deliramenta hunc in modum toto volumine accuratè
20 persequar; quod tamen libens facerem, (quoniam superbia
et fastidio, ut ferunt, supra modum turget) ni moli tanta libri
inconcinna atque incondita se protegeret, et veluti miles ille
Terentianus post principia lateret: callido sanè consilio, ut de-

their throat stuck. And as far as our exiles are concerned—if you mean them—would that it had stuck there even unto this day; for we have learned to a certainty that nothing is oftener upon their lips than curses and imprecations, to be by all good
5 men abhorred certainly, yet not feared. For the rest, it can scarce be believed that when news of the king's execution arrived, there was found, especially among a free people, anyone so much a slave by nature as to calumniate us or count our deed a crime; but rather that all righteous men said all was right-
10 eous—nay even thanked God for having published so high and shining an example of justice for so wholesome a lesson to the rest of the kings.

And so, to those "savage, sternly steeled and stony-hearted" persons who (he says) bewail the "miserable and amazing
15 marvellous murder" (whose, pray?), to them and their jingling spokesman, the dullest, surely, "since ever in the world the kingly name was native and known," I say: "Let them wail again! Let them wail again!" But meanwhile what boy just out of school, or what dear brotherkin from any
20 friary you like, could not have made a rhetorical exercise out of this royal fall more eloquently—yea, more Latinly—than this royal speechmaker?

It would surely be uncalled for were I carefully to follow up the man's babblings and ravings on the present scale through-
25 out his volume; yet I would do it willingly (for he swells, they say, with measureless pride and conceit) did he not shield himself behind the enormous ill-composed disordered bulk of his book, like Terence's soldier skulking behind the front

fessus singula notando etiam acerrimus quisque, tædio priùs conficeretur, quàm omnia redargueret. Nunc ejus quoddam specimen dare hac veluti prolusione duntaxat volui; et cordatis lectoribus à principio statim degustandum hominem
5 præbere, ut in hac paginæ unius promulside experiamur quàm lautè nos et luculenter cæteris ferculis accepturus sit: quantas ineptias atque infantias toto opere congesserit, qui tam densas, ubi minimè decuit, in ipsa fronte collocavit. Exinde multa garrientem, et scombris concionantem facilè præ-
10 tereo; ad nostras autem res quod attinet, haud dubitamus quin ea, quæ authoritate Parlamenti scripta publicè et declarata sunt, apud omnes bonos et prudentes exteros plus ponderis habitura sint, quàm unius impudentissimi homuncionis calumniæ et mendacia; qui ab exulibus nostris, patriæ hosti-
15 bus, pretio conductus, quolibet eorum dictante quibus operam suam locaverat, aut rumusculum spargente, falsissima quæque corradere, et in chartam conjicere non dubitavit. Utque plane intelligant omnes quàm non illi religio sit, quidlibet scribere, verum an falsum, pium an impium, haud alius mihi
20 testis adhibendus erit, quàm ipse Salmasius. Scribit is in *Apparatu contra primatum Papæ, maximas esse causas cur ecclesia redire ab episcopatu debeat ad Apostolicam* presbyterorum

ranks;—and a clever plan too—that even the most energetic
might weary of marking all the details, and die of boredom
before he could refute them. Yet I did wish to give at least a
sample by way, so to speak, of the present curtain-raiser, and
5 offer on the spot to let my thoughtful readers taste the man at
the beginning, that by trying these *hors d'oeuvres* and *anti-
pasti* from a single page we may learn how splendidly he will
entertain us with the rest of his gorgeous dishes: how many
silly puerilities he will prove to have heaped together in his
10 whole work, who has put them so thick—where least seemly
—at its very head and front.

Thenceforward I gladly disregard his much-twaddling
harangues, predestined as they are to wrap up mackerels;
moreover, as far as concerns our affairs, we doubt not that
15 what has been published and proclaimed by authority of
Parliament shall have more weight with all right-minded and
judicious foreigners than the lies and slanders of one brazen
petit-monsieur who has been hired at a price by our exiles,
their country's enemies, and has unhesitatingly scraped to-
20 gether and written down utter lies, whenever anyone to whom
he has leased his pen spreads a bit of malicious gossip, and
gives him his orders.

That all may see clearly how it matters nothing to his conscience what he writes—true or false, holy or unholy,—I
25 shall have to call no other witness than Salmasius himself. In
his *Apparatus contra Primatum Papae* he writes: "The reasons why the church ought to return from Episcopacy to the
Apostolic institution" of Elders "are very strong: in Episco-

institutionem; longè majus ex episcopatu introductum in ecclesiam esse malum, quàm illa schismata quæ priùs metuebantur: Pestem illam quæ ex eo ecclesias invasit, totum ecclesiæ corpus miserabili tyrannide pessumdedisse; immo ipsos

5 *reges ac principes sub jugum misisse; Majorem in ecclesiam utilitatem redundaturam Hierarchiâ totâ extinctâ, quàm solo capite Papâ,* p. 196. *Posse episcopatum cum Papatu tolli cum summo bono ecclesiæ; sublato episcopatu ruere ipsum Papatum, super illo utpote fundatum,* p. 171. *Cur removeri de-*

10 *beat in illis regnis quæ jam Papatui renuntiârunt proprias habere causas. Cur ibi episcopatus retineatur se non videre; non integram videri reformationem quæ hac in parte imperfecta sit; nihil afferri posse rationis aut causæ probabilis, cur sublato Papatu retineri debeat aut possit episcopatus,* p. 197.

15 Hæc et multò plura cùm ante annos quatuor scripserit, tanta nunc vanitate et impudentia est, ut Parlamentum Angliæ graviter incusare hoc loco audeat, quòd episcopatum *non solum senatu ejiciendum, sed etiam penitus abjiciendum censuerint.* Quid? quòd ipsum etiam episcopatum suadet atque

20 defendit, iisdem usus argumentis et rationibus, quas libro illo priore magno impetu confutaverat; *necessarios* nempe *fuisse episcopos, et omnino retinendos, ne mille pestiferæ sectæ et hæreses in Anglia pullularent.* O vafrum et versipellem! adeóne te etiam in sacris non puduit desultorem agere, propè

pacy there was brought into the church an evil much greater than those schisms which used to be feared before: the plague which came out of it into the church struck down the whole body of the church beneath a vile despotism: nay, put even
5 kings and princes under the yoke: the church would profit more by the abolition of the whole hierarchy than by the abolition of its head only, the Pope (p. 196). That episcopacy and papacy together might be removed with the greatest benefit to the church: that, episcopacy once removed, papacy itself, as
10 founded thereon, would fall (p. 171). He considers that there are special reasons why it should be done away in those kingdoms which have already renounced papacy, and sees no reason why it should be retained there. That a reformation this part of which has been left unaccomplished seems incomplete:
15 that no jot of reason or probable cause can be adduced why, when Papal supremacy is got rid of, episcopacy ought to be kept, or can be" (p. 197).

But though he wrote all this and much more four years ago, yet now he is so false and so shameless that he dares in this
20 passage violently to reproach the Parliament of England for voting that Episcopacy was to be "not only turned out of the House of Lords, but cast off utterly." Yea, he even recommends and defends episcopacy itself by means of the same reasons and proofs which in that earlier volume of his he had
25 forcibly confuted—namely that "the bishops are necessary" forsooth, "and by all means to be kept, lest a thousand plaguy sects and heresies should burgeon out in England." Sly turncoat, are you not ashamed even in matters of religion to play

dixeram, ecclesiam prodere? cujus tu ideò sanctissima instituta tanto strepitu asseruisse videris, ut quoties tibi commodum esset, eo majore cum infamia ea ipsa ludificari atque
subvertere posses. Neminem hoc latet, cùm regni Ordines,
5 Ecclesiæ nostræ, ad exemplum cæterarum, reformandæ studio flagrantes, episcopatum funditùs tollere statuissent, primò
regem intercessisse, dein bellum nobis eâ potissimùm causâ
intulisse; quod ipsi tandem in perniciem vertit. I nunc, et te
defensorem regium esse gloriare, qui ut regem gnaviter de-
10 fendas, susceptam à temetipso ecclesiæ causam nunc palàm
prodis atque oppugnas: cujus gravissimâ quidem censurâ esses
notandus. De forma autem reipub. nostræ, quoniam tu Professor triobolaris et extraneus remotis capsulis atque scriniis
tuis nugarum refertissimis, quas meliùs in ordinem redegisses,
15 in aliena repub. satagere et odiosus esse mavis, sic breviter
tibi, vel cuivis potiùs te prudentiori respondeo; eam formam
esse quam nostra tempora atque dissidia ferunt; non qualis
optanda esset, sed qualem obstinata improborum civium discordia esse patitur. Quæ autem respublica factionibus labo-
20 rat, atque armis se tuetur, si sanæ et integræ tantùm partis rationem habet, cæteros sive plebeios sive optimates præterit aut

fast and loose, and—I had almost said—to betray the church, whose most holy ordinances you seem to have defended with so much noise for the very purpose of ridiculing and over-turning them with all the deeper ignominy whenever you
5 thought convenient?

Everybody knows that when the Houses of Parliament, ardently desiring to reform our church after the pattern of the rest of the churches, had resolved to abolish episcopacy, first the King vetoed the measure, and next, chiefly for that
10 reason, made war upon us—which at last proved his own undoing. Go now and brag that you defend a king, you, who, to do it to the hilt, now openly betray and attack what you were the very one to support—the cause of the church—and should undergo her heaviest reprimand.

15 To come back, however, to the constitution of the English Commonwealth. Forasmuch as you, a tuppenny-thrippenny outlandish pedant, neglect those desks and portfolios of yours, stuffed as they are with trumpery that you would do better to put in order,—since you, I say, choose instead to play the
20 hateful busybody in the public affairs of a nation not your own,—I give you, then, or, preferably some wiser man than you, this short answer. Our constitution is what the dissensions of our time will permit: not such as were to be desired, but such as the persistent strife of wicked citizens will suffer
25 it to be. But any state soever which in the throes of partisan strife takes up arms for safety, surely does full justice if it maintains relations with its sound and uncontaminated part alone, and expels or removes the rest, whether populace or

excludit, satis profectò æqua est; quamvis regem et proceres, suis ipsa malis edocta, ampliùs nolit. *Concilium* autem illud *supremum* quod insectaris, atque etiam *Concilii Præsidem,* næ tu ridiculus es; Concilium enim illud, quod somnias, non
5 est supremum, sed Parlamenti authoritate ad certum duntaxat tempus constitutum, quadraginta virorum ex suo ferè numero, quorum quilibet cæterorum suffragiis præses esse potest. Semper autem hoc usitatissimum fuit, ut Parlamentum, qui noster Senatus est, delectos ex suorum numero pau-
10 ciores, quoties visum erat, constitueret: iis unum in locum ubivis conveniendi, et veluti minoris cujusdam habendi Senatûs potestas delata est. Iisdem res sæpe gravissimæ, quo celeriùs et majore cum silentio transigerentur, commissæ atque creditæ; Classis, exercitus, ærarii cura aut procuratio,
15 quævis denique pacis aut belli munia. Hoc sive concilium nominetur, sive quid aliud, verbo fortè novum, re antiquum est; et sine quo nulla omninò Respub. rectè administrari potest. De regis autem supplicio, et rerum apud nos conversione mitte vociferari, mitte virus illud tuum acerbitatis evomere; donec
20 ista *quâ lege, quo jure, quo judicio* facta sint, te licèt repugnante, singulis capitibus ostendam, et pedem conferam. Si tamen instas *quo jure, quâ lege,* eâ, inquam, lege quam Deus ipse et natura sanxit, ut omnia quæ reipub. salutaria essent,

patrician,—even though, taught by its own sufferings, it thenceforth utterly refuses a King and a House of Lords.

How absurd of you to rail at our "Supreme Council" and even at a supposed "President of the Council"! For that Coun-
5 cil—figment of your dreams—is not supreme, but appointed by authority of Parliament, for a definite time only, of about forty of its members, anysoever of whom may by vote of the rest be president. It has always been, moreover, a well-established practice for Parliament, which is our Senate, to fix a
10 comparatively small number of its members, choose and appoint them, and delegate to them authority to meet anywhere, and to hold, as it were, a kind of smaller Senate. To these, often, weightiest matters were turned over and entrusted, to be despatched the more quickly and quietly: the manage-
15 ment or administration of the navy, the army, the treasury,— in fine, any and all business of peace or war. This body, call it "council" or anything else, may be new in name, but is ancient in substance; without it no commonwealth can be managed properly.
20 Moreover—about the king's execution and about our revolution,—stop your howling, stop that celebrated act of vomiting up the venom of your bitterness, till I fight you hand to hand, and despite your struggles show, chapter by chapter, "in accordance with what law, under what system of right,
25 in virtue of what judgment" (as you put it) these things were done. If you yet insist upon your "What right? What law?" —under that law, I say, which God himself and nature hath appointed, that all things for the safety of the commonwealth

legitima et justa haberentur. Sic olim sapientes tuî similibus responderunt. *Leges per tot annos ratas refixisse* nos criminaris; bonasne an malas non dicis; nec si diceres audiendus esses; nam nostræ leges Ole quid ad te? Utinam plures re-
5 fixissent tum leges tum leguleios; rectiùs sanè et rei Christianæ et populo consuluissent. Frendes quod *hæc, Manii, terræ filii, vix domi nobiles, vix suis noti licere sibi crediderint.* Meminisses quid te non solùm libri sacri, sed etiam Lyricus doceat:

10   *— Valet ima summis*
        Mutare, et insignem attenuat Deus
        Obscura promens. —

Sic etiam habeto; eorum quos tu vix nobiles esse aïs, alios nulli vestrarum partium vel generis nobilitate cedere; alios ex
15 se natos per industriam atque virtutem ad veram nobilitatem iter affectare, et cum nobilissimis quibusque posse conferri; se autem malle *filios terræ* dici, modò suæ, et domi strenuè facere, quàm sine terrâ et lare fumos vendendo quod tu facis, homo nihili et stramineus eques, in aliena terra dominorum

should be deemed lawful and righteous. Thus did wise men
aforetime answer such as you.

You charge us with "having abolished laws that had been
settled so many years," but you do not say whether they were
5 good or bad; nor, if you did, would you be entitled to a hearing; for our laws—Olus, what business are they of yours?
Would that they had abolished more of the laws as well as
more of the pettifogging lawyers: they would have had more
regard for the people, and for the cause of Christianity. You
10 gnash your teeth because "the Manii, sons of the soil, persons
scarce of the nobility at home, scarce known to their own
countrymen, should have believed themselves entitled to do
such things." You should have remembered what not only
Scripture but even the Lyrist teaches you:

15   God can highest with lowest interchange—
                Such is his might;
             Degradeth men of mark,
             But hidden fortunes dark
                Bringeth to light.

20   Take this, too: of those whom you call "scarce noble," some
are second to none of your land or kind in nobility; others,
being as it were their own ancestors, tread the path to true
nobility by way of industry and personal worth, and are com-
parable with any the noblest soever. They had rather be called
25 "sons of the soil," too (it being their *own* soil!), and to work
hard at home, than be, like you, a landless homeless worthless
straw-stuffed scarecrow-knight, selling smoke to stave off star-

nutu et stipendio famem tolerare: ab ista, mihi crede, pere-
grinatione ad agnatos potiùs et gentiles deducendus, nisi hoc
unum saperes, quod frivolas quasdam prælectiones et nuga-
menta scis tanta mercede apud exteros effutire. Reprehendis
5 quòd magistratus nostri *colluviem omnium Sectarum reci-*
piant; quid ni recipiant? quos ecclesiæ est è cœtu fidelium
ejicere, non magistratuum è civitate pellere; siquidem in leges
civiles non peccant. Primò homines ut tutò ac liberè sine vi
atque injuriis vitam agerent, convenere in civitatem; ut sanctè
10 et religiosè, in ecclesiam; illa leges, hæc disciplinam habet
suam, planè diversam: hinc toto orbe Christiano per tot annos
bellum ex bello seritur, quòd Magistratus et Ecclesia inter se
officia confundunt. Quapropter et Papisticam minimè tole-
ramus; neque enim eam tam esse religionem intelligimus,
15 quàm obtentu religionis tyrannidem pontificiam civilis potentiæ spoliis ornatam, quæ contra ipsum Christi institutum
ad se rapuit. *Independentes,* quales à te solo finguntur, nulli
apud nos unquam visi; præter eos duntaxat qui cùm classes et
synodos supra Ecclesiam quamque singularem esse non agno-
20 scant, eas omnes velut Hierarchiæ particulas quasdam, aut
certè truncum ipsum, eradicandas esse tecum sentiunt. Hinc
nomen Independentium apud Vulgus obtinuit. Quod restat

vation in a strange land at the beck and call, and in the pay, of masters. Take my word for it, you would soon be sent packing from your foreign tour back to your own kith and kin, but for your one accomplishment: you do know how to blab out
5 trumpery pamphlets among strangers—and what price to get for them.

You blame our magistrates because they "admit the off-scourings of all the sects." Why should they not admit them? It is for the church to expel them from the company of the
10 faithful, not for the magistrates to banish them the country, provided they break no civil law. To live safe and free, without suffering violence or wrong, to this end it was that men first entered into a polity; to live piously and religiously, into a church; the former has its laws, the latter its doctrine and
15 discipline, quite distinct; and it is because the Magistracy and the Church confuse their jurisdictions that for so many years war has sown a harvest of more war throughout all Christendom. This, too, is why we cannot endure Popery; for we perceive it to be not so much a religion as a pontifical despotism
20 decked out, under pretence of religion, with the spoils of civil power, which it has seized unto itself contrary to Christ's own precept.

As for "Independents," none such as are assumed by you (and you alone) have ever been seen among us; except in so
25 far as they recognize no assemblies or synods above each individual congregation, and feel, with you, that such should be uprooted as branches of the Hierarchy, or in fact its very trunk. From this the name of Independents has got popular currency.

video te id agere, ut regum omnium et Monarcharum non invidiam solùm, sed etiam bellum atrocissimum in nos concites. Olim rex Mithridates, quamvis causa dissimili, omnes reges in Romanos concitabat, eadem prope calumniatus; Romanis consilium esse, omnia regna subvertere, iis nulla humana neque divina obstare, à principio nihil nisi partum armis habuisse, latrones, regnorum maximè hostes; Hæc Mithridates regi Arsaci. Te verò in illa tua exedra infantissimè rhetoricantem quæ tanta fiducia provexit, ut ad bellum hortando, et licèt nolis videri, *classicum canendo,* ullum vel inter pueros regem commovere te posse animum induceres, isto præsertim ore tam exili et rancidulo, ut ne mures quidem Homericos, te buccinatore, bellum unquam ranunculis illaturos fuisse credam? Tantum abest ut metuam quid tu belli nobis aut periculi, homo ignavissime, apud exteros reges istâ tuâ rabidâ et insulsâ simul facundiâ conflare possis: qui ad illos, acsi *regum capita* quasi *pilas habeamus, de coronis quasi trocho ludamus, sceptra imperialia non pluris faciamus, quàm bacula morionum capitata,* lusoriè sanè nos defers. At tu interea, stultissimum caput, morionis ipse baculo dignissimus es, qui reges ac principes tam puerilibus argumentis ad bellum suaderi putes. Omnes deinde populos inclamas, dicto audientes

Your course is such, I see, as would in the future stir up against us, on the part of all kings and monarchs, not hatred merely, but cruelest war. King Mithridates of old tried to rouse all kings against the Romans—for a different reason, to
5 be sure, but by using almost the same slanders: that the Romans were planning to overturn all thrones; that they would allow nothing human or divine to stand in their way; that from the beginning they had never got anything but by violence; that they were a gang of robbers, enemies above all to
10 royal authority. So wrote King Mithridates to King Arsaces. But you, mouthing your unspeakable baby-rhetoric there in your classroom, what overweening self-assurance carried *your* mind to the point of supposing that you could rouse a king (even one still a boy) to war by your urging, and (though you
15 like not to be caught at it) by your "trumpeting the signal to join battle"?—especially with so foul a scrannel mouth that Homer's mice, had you been their bugler, would never, I do believe, have made war upon tadpoles!

Just as far am I from fearing any war or danger to us which
20 you, arrant coward, can blow up among foreign kings with your windy rush of raving yet insipid language. You tell tales of us—you must be joking—that we "toss kings' heads like balls, play hoop with crowns, and make no more of imperial sceptres than of fools' bauble-sticks with heads atop." You,
25 most foolish head, are yourself most fit to top a fool's bauble, when you fancy that kings and princes can by such childish reasonings be persuaded to war. Then you cry aloud to all nations, but they, I know full well, will never heed what you

tuo, sat scio, minimè futuros. Hibernorum etiam consceleratam illam ac barbaram colluviem regiis partibus in auxilium vocas. Quod unicum indicio esse potest quàm scelestus sis et væcors, quàm omnes pene mortales impietate, audacia, et
5 furore superes, qui devotæ gentis fidem atque opem implorare non dubites, cujus ab impiâ societate tot civium innocentissimorum sanguine perfusa etiam rex ipse aut abhorruit semper, aut abhorrere se simulavit. Et quam ille perfidiam, quam ille crudelitatem occultare, quantum potuit, atque ab se longè
10 removere summo studio contendit, eam tu, bipedum nequissime, quo minùs ultrò atque palàm suscipias, neque Deum neque homines vereris. Agedum; Hibernis igitur fautoribus ac sociis ad defensionem regis jam te accinge. Caves imprimis quod cauto mehercule opus erat, nequis te Tullio fortasse aut
15 Demostheni omnem eloquentiæ laudem præreptum ire suspicetur; et prædicis, *oratorio more non tibi agendum videri.* Næ tu haud stultè sapis, id quod non potes, non videtur tibi esse agendum; oratoriè autem ut tu ageres, quis, qui te satis novit, unquam exspectavit? qui nihil elaboratè, nihil distinctè,
20 nihil quod sapiat, in lucem emittere aut soles aut potes, sed veluti Crispinus alter, aut Tzetzes ille græculus, modò ut multum scribas, quàm rectè non laboras; neque si labores valeas. *Agetur,* inquis, *hæc causa toto orbe audiente, et quasi ad judicandum sedente.* Id adeò nobis pergratum est, ut ad-

say. Even those depraved and barbarous offscourings of Irish
you call to the aid of the King's party; and this one thing may
be taken as a measure of your wickedness and folly—how you
surpass almost all men in irreligion, impudence, and madness;
5 for you scruple not to beg the loyalty and aid of a nation accursed and set apart for destruction, from whose godless fellowship, stained with the blood of so many harmless citizens,
even the King himself always shrank in horror—or pretended
to shrink. That treachery he did all he could to cover up, and
10 strove with all his might to clear his skirts of that cruelty,
which you, most worthless of two-legged creatures, have not
respect enough for God or man to keep you from wilfully and
publicly adopting. Come on, then, gird up your loins to defend the King—with your Irish for claque and for company!
15 At the beginning you take care (by Jove, a necessary caution!) not to be suspected of a possible design to snatch away
all of Tully's or Demosthenes's oratorical laurels; you say in
your preface that you think it "not proper for you to behave
like an orator." Bright mind—to perceive that what you
20 cannot do is not proper for you to do! Who indeed that knows
you well ever looked to see you fill the rôle of orator?—you
who never do, and never can, produce anything rightly de-
veloped, anything clean-cut, anything that has gust or savor,
but—like a second Crispinus, or Tzetzes that decadent Greek
25 —so you write much, care not how well you write, nor if
you care, can do it.

"This cause," you say, "will be tried with the whole world
hearing, and, as it were, sitting in judgment." That is what

versarium non cerebrosum et imperitum, qualis tu es, sed
cordatum et intelligentem dari jam nobis optemus. Perorans
planè tragicus es, immo Ajax ipse Lorarius: *Horum ego in-*
justitiam, impietatem, perfidiam, crudelitatem proclamabo
5 *cœlo et terræ, ipsosque authores convictos posteris tradam,*
reósque peragam. O Flosculos! Túne igitur sine sale, sine
genio proclamator et rabula, bonis authoribus divexandis tantùm aut transcribendis natus, quicquam de tuo quod vivat
producere te putas posse? quem unà cum scriptis tuis futilissi-
10 mis abreptum ætas, mihi crede, postera oblivioni mandabit.
Nisi si defensio hæc regia suo fortasse responso aliquid debi-
tura est, ut neglecta jam pridem et consopita, in manus iterum
sumatur. Idque ego ab Illustrissimis Hollandiæ Ordinibus
peterem, ut eam è fisco protinus dimissam, neque enim The-
15 saurus est, pervagari quò velit sinant. Si enim qua vanitate,
inscitiâ, falsitate referta sit, planum omnibus fecero, quò la-
tiùs excurrit, eò arctiùs, meâ quidem sententiâ, supprimitur.
Jam nos, quemadmodum *reos peragat,* videamus.

CAPUT I.

20 QUONIAM tibi vano homini et ventoso multum
hinc forsitan superbiæ, Salmasi, multum spiritûs
accessit, magnæ scilicet Britanniæ regem fidei defensorem esse, te verò regis, ego quidem et illum regi titulum,

we like so well that we could wish unto ourselves an adversary not, like you, hot-headed and unskilled, but full of understanding and sagacity. You are quite the tragic hero—quite the Ajax-with-the-Whip, when you perorate: "These men's
5 injustice, impiety, perfidy, cruelty, I will cry out unto heaven and earth; themselves the perpetrators I will turn over to posterity convicted, and transfix the culprits." Ye Little Flowers of Rhetoric! And so, you senseless witless bawling pettifogger, born only to pick good writers to pieces or transcribe them, do
10 you really think yourself capable of writing anything that will live?—you whom posterity—take my word for it—will damn to oblivion with all your scribbled trumpery.—Except perhaps your Royal Defence shall turn out to be something beholden to my answer to it, and after long slumbering unread
15 be once more handled. And this I would petition of the most Illustrious States of Holland, that they would allow it to be straightway dismissed their Treasury—'tis no treasure!—and to wander whither it will. For if I shall have made clear to all what idle talk and ignorance and deceit it is stuffed with,
20 then the more widely it circulates, the more straitly, methinks, it is suppressed. And now let us see how he will "transfix" us "culprits."

CHAPTER I.

INFLATED empty man that you are, Salmasius, you were haply yet more puffed up at the King of Great
25 Britain's being Defender of the Faith, and your being Defender of the King. For my part, I think you deserve your

et hunc tibi jure pari ac merito concedam: cùm sanè rex fidem,
tu regem sic defenderis, ut causam uterque suam evertisse
potiùs videatur. Quod cum passim infrà, tum hoc primo capite
ostendam. Dixeras tu quidem præfationis paginâ duodecimâ,
5 *Ornari pigmentis rhetoricis tam bonam et justam causam non*
debere: nam simpliciter rem, ut gesta est, narrare, regem de-
fendere est. Quando igitur toto hoc capite in quo narrationem
illam simplicem futuram pollicitus eras, neque rem simpliciter, ut gesta est, narras, neque non pigmentis, quantum in eo
10 genere consequi potes, rhetoricis ornas, profectò vel tuo judicio si standum esset, causa regia neque bona neque justa erit.
Quanquam hoc cave tibi sumas quod dat nemo, posse te quicquam rhetoricè narrare; qui neque oratoris, neque historici,
immò ne causidici quidem partes narrando sustinere possis;
15 sed quasi circulator quispiam, arte circumforanea, magnam de
te in proœmio, velut in posterum diem, exspectationem conci-
tabas, non tam ut rem promissam tum demum narrares, quàm
ut pigmenta illa misera, et ampullas fuco refertas lectoribus
quàm plurimis divenderes. Nam *de facto dicturus tot novi-*
20 *tatum monstris te circundari ac terreri sentis, ut quid pri-*
mum exequaris, quid deinde, quid postremò, nescias. Hoccine est simpliciter narrare? dicam quod res est, tot tuorum
ipse mendaciorum monstris, primùm terreri te sentis, deinde
tot nugis, tot ineptiis levissimum illud caput non *circundari*

titles both alike; for the king so defended the faith, and you
have so defended him, that each of you seems rather to have
ruined his case; as I shall make appear throughout the whole
ensuing discourse, and particularly in this first chapter. You
5 told us on the twelfth page of your preface that "so good and
just a cause needed no rhetorical colouring, for simply to tell
the thing as it occurred was to defend the king." Yet in your
first chapter, in which you had promised us that your tale
would be plain, you neither tell the thing simply as it occurred,
10 nor abstain from adorning it with such rhetorical colors as you
can command; so that—to take your own view of it—the
king's cause will be neither good nor just.

Nevertheless, be careful not to attribute to yourself (what
nobody grants you) the ability to state the facts of a case as
15 a right orator ought; for you can play the part neither of an
orator nor of an historian, nor even of a hired partisan advocate. Like some itinerant hawker, instead, touting from fair
to fair, you in your preface kept raising great expectations of
next day's performance—not that you might at last relate the
20 facts you promised, but that you might peddle out to as many
readers as possible those your wretched bottlefuls of rhetoric-
paint and fustian dye. For "being now about to give us an
account of the matter of fact," you find yourself "encompassed and affrighted with so many monsters of novelty"
25 that you "know not what to say first, what next, and what
last." Is this your plain tale? I will tell you what is the matter
with you. First of all you find yourself affrighted at your own
monstrous lies, and next you find that empty head of yours not

solùm, sed circumagi, *ut quid primum, quid deinde, quid postremò* dicendum ullo tempore sit, non modò nunc *nescias,* sed nunquam antea non nesciveris. *Inter difficultates quæ occurrunt ad exprimendam tam incredibilis flagitii im-*
5 *manitatem hoc unum facile dictu suppetit, quod iterum iterumque repeti debet,* nempe *solem ipsum atrocius factum nunquam adspexisse alterum.* Multa sol aspexit, bone magister, quæ Bernardus non vidit. Solem autem iterum atque iterum repetas licebit, id tu quidem prudenter feceris, quod non
10 nostra flagitia, sed defensionis tuæ frigus vehementissimè postulabit. *Regum,* inquis, *origo cum sole novo cœpit.* Dii te, Damasippe, deæque solstitio donent, quo te calfacias, qui ne pedem sine *sole;* nequis fortasse te umbraticum doctorem esse dicat. At hercle etiam in tenebris es, qui jus patrium à regio
15 non distinguis: et cùm reges Patriæ Patres nominaveris, eâ statim metaphorâ persuasisse credis, ut quicquid de patre non negaverim, id continuò de rege verum esse concedam. Pater et rex diversissima sunt. Pater nos genuit; at non rex nos, sed nos regem creavimus. Patrem natura dedit populo, regem
20 ipse populus dedit sibi; non ergo propter regem populus, sed propter populum rex est; ferimus patrem, morosum etiam et durum, ferimus et regem; sed ne patrem quidem ferimus ty-

only "encompassed" but set awhirl with so many trifles and follies that what was fit to be said first, what next, what last, you not only do not know, but never did know.

"Amid the difficulties of expressing the heinousness of so
5 incredible a piece of impiety, this expression alone offers itself," you say, "which is easily said and must be oft repeated," to wit, "that the sun itself never beheld a more outrageous action." My good schoolmaster, the sun has beheld many things that Bernard never saw. Yet we are content you
10 should bring in the sun over and over, and you shall act wisely so to do, for it will be insistently required—not by our wickedness but by the frigidity of your defence. "The origin of kings," you say, "arose with the new-created sun." May the gods and goddesses, Damasippus, bless you with a solstice
15 to warm yourself withal, that cannot warm a foot enough to stir a foot without "the sun."

Perhaps you would avoid the imputation of being called a doctor that lounges in the shade. Alas, your shade is utter darkness! You make no difference betwixt a paternal power
20 and a regal; and, once you have called kings fathers of their country, fancy this metaphor so persuasive that whatever I would admit concerning a father I would at once grant true of a king. A king and a father are very different things. Our fathers begot and made us; our king made not us, but we him.
25 Nature gave the people fathers, but the people itself gave itself a king; so that the people is not for the king, but the king for the people. We bear with a father, as we do with a king, though he be harsh and severe; but we do not bear

rannum. Pater si filium interficit, capite pœnas dabit: cur non item rex eadem justissima lege tenebitur, si populum, id est filios suos, perdiderit? præsertim cùm pater, ut ne pater sit, efficere non possit, rex facilè possit, ut neque pater sit neque

5 rex. Quod si *de facti qualitate,* quod aïs, *inde* æstimandum est, tibi dico, peregrine, et rebus nostris alienissime, testis oculatus et indigena tibi dico; nos regem neque *bonum,* neque *justum,* neque *clementem,* neque *religiosum,* neque *pium,* neque *pacificum;* fed hostem prope decennalem; nec paren-

10 tem patriæ, sed vastatorem *de medio sustulisse. Solet hoc fieri,* fateris, inficias enim ire non audes, *sed non a reformatis, regi reformato.* Siquidem reformatus is dici potest, qui scriptis ad Papam literis, Sanctissimum appellaverat Patrem, qui Papistis æquior semper quàm Orthodoxis fuit. Talis cùm fuerit, ne

15 suæ quidem familiæ primus à reformatis est *de medio* sublatus. Quid? ejus avia Maria nonne à reformatis exuta regno solum vertere coacta est, supplicio demùm capitis affecta, ne Scotis quidem reformatis ægrè ferentibus? immo si operam contulisse dicam, haud mentiar. In tanta autem regum *refor-*

20 *matorum* paucitate, nihil hujusmodi accidisse, ut eorum aliquis morte plecteretur, non est quod miremur. Licere autem regem nequam, sive tyrannum regno pellere, vel supplicio quovis, prout meritus erit, punire (etiam summorum senten-

with even a father, if he be a tyrant. If a father murder his
child, he shall suffer capital punishment; and why should
not a king likewise be subject to the same most just law if he
have destroyed the people his children? Especially as a father
5 can never cease to be such, but a king can easily bring it to
pass that he shall be neither father nor king. If this "action"
of ours is to be considered "next" according to its "quality,"
as you call it, I who am an eye-witness and a native, tell
you, who are a foreigner and an utter stranger to our affairs,
10 that we "removed from among us" a king neither "good,"
nor "just," nor "merciful," nor "devout," nor "godly," nor
"peaceable," as you style him, but one who was an enemy to
us for almost ten years, and no father, but a destroyer of his
country.

15 You confess, for you dare not deny it, that "such things
have been practised, but not by Protestants upon a Protestant
king." As if he deserved the name of Protestant, who in a
letter to the Pope could give him the title of Most Holy
Father, and who was always more favorable to the papists
20 than to those of the right faith. And being such, he is not the
first, even of his own family, that has been removed "from
among us" by Protestants. What! Was not his grandmother
Mary deposed and banished and at last beheaded by Protestants, while not even the Scottish Protestants took it ill? Nay,
25 if I should say they were parties to it, I should not lie. There
being so few Protestant kings, no wonder it never happened
that one of them was put to death. But that it is lawful to
depose a wicked king or a tyrant, and to punish him accord-

tiâ Theologorum, qui ipsi reformandæ ecclesiæ authores fuere) aude tu modò negare. Concedis quam plurimos reges non siccâ morte periisse, hunc *gladio,* illum *veneno,* alium squalore *carceris,* aut *laqueo.* Omnium tamen hoc tibi miser-
5 rimum videtur, et monstri quiddam simile, regem in judicium adduci, *causam capitis dicere coactum, condemnatum, securi percussum.* Dic mihi, homo insipientissime, annon humanius, annon æquius, annon ad leges omnium civitatum accomodatius est, cujuscunque criminis reum in judicio si-
10 stere, suî defendendi copiam facere, lege condemnatum ad mortem haud immeritam ducere, ita ut damnato vel pœnitendi, vel se colligendi spatium detur, quàm statim ut prehensus est, indictâ causa pecudis in modum mactare? Quotusquisque est reorum, qui, si optio detur, non illo potiùs quàm
15 hoc modo puniri se maluerit? Quæ ratio igitur animadvertendi in populum moderatior in rege est habita, cur non eadem animadvertendi in regem moderatior in populo, et vel ipsi regi acceptior fuisse creditur? Tu secretò, et sine arbitris extinctum regem malebas, vel ut exempli tam boni salubritate
20 omnis memoria careret, vel ut facti tam præclari conscientia defugisse lucem, aut leges atque ipsam justitiam minimè sibi faventem habuisse videretur. Exaggeras deinde rem, quòd

ing to his deserts, nay, that this is the opinion of eminent divines who have been the very leaders in the late reformation, do you deny it if you dare. You admit that great numbers of kings have met a violent death, some "by the sword," some
5 "by poison," some in a filthy "dungeon," some "in a noose"; but for a king to be brought to trial, "to be put to plead for his life, to be condemned, and brought to the block"—this you think a more lamentable instance than all the rest, and make it a prodigious piece of impiety. Tell me, superlative fool,
10 whether it be not more humane, more just, more agreeable to the laws of all civilized states, to bring a criminal, be his offence what it may, before a court of justice, to give him the opportunity of defending himself, and if the law condemn him, then to put him to death as he has deserved, so as he may
15 have time to repent or to compose himself; than presently, as soon as ever he is taken, to butcher him like a sheep, without trial or hearing? Is there a malefactor in the world who if he might have his choice would not choose to be punished that way rather than this? And if that proceeding be accounted
20 the fairer of the two when used by king against subjects, why should it not be so counted when used by subjects against king? Nay, why should we not think that himself liked it better? You would have had him killed in secret, without witnesses, either that all history might lose the advantage of
25 so good an example, or that this glorious action might in supposed guilt seem to have shunned the light, as having no law or even justice on its side.

Next you aggravate the matter by telling us that it was not

neque per tumultum aut factionem optimatium, aut rebel-
lium furorem, sive militum sive populi; non odio, non metu,
non studio dominandi, non cæco animi impetu, sed consilio et
ratione meditatum diu facinus peregerint. O meritò quidem
5 te ex jurisconsulto Grammaticum! qui ab accidentibus causæ,
ut loquuntur, quæ per se nihil valent, vituperationes instituis,
cùm nondum docueris illud facinus in vitio an in laude ponen-
dum sit. Jam vide quàm in te facilè incurram. Si pulchrum
et decorum fuit, eò magis laudandi quod nullis affectibus
10 occupati, solius honestatis causâ fecerint; si arduum et grave,
quòd non cæco impetu, sed consilio et ratione. Quanquam
ego hæc divino potiùs instinctu gesta esse crediderim, quoties
memoriâ repeto, quàm inopinato animorum ardore, quanto
consensu totus exercitus, cui magna pars populi se adjunxerat,
15 ab omnibus penè regni provinciis una voce regem ipsum suorum omnium malorum authorem ad supplicium depoposcerit. Quicquid erat, sive magistratum, sive populum spectes,
nulli unquam excelsiore animo, et, quod etiam adversarii fatentur, sedatiore, tam egregium facinus et vel heroicis ætatibus
20 dignum aggressi sunt: quo non leges tantùm et judicia, dehinc mortalibus ex æquo restituta, sed ipsam justitiam nobili-

done in the uproar of party strife amongst our nobles, or in a
raging rebellion either of the people or of the army, or
through hatred or fear or ambition or blind precipitate rashness, but was long designed and thought upon, and accom-
5 plished deliberately. You did well from advocate to turn
grammarian! For from the accidents of a case, so to speak,
which in themselves sway neither one way nor another, you
inveigh against it before you have proved the deed itself
either good or bad. See how easily I refute you: if the deed
10 was well and seemly, they that did it deserve the greater praise
in that they were prepossessed with no passions, but did that
they did for virtue's sake; if it was difficult and grievous, the
greater praise for doing it not upon blind impulse but upon
deliberation and design. Though for my own part, when I
15 call to mind with how unexpected an importunity and fer-
vency of mind, and with how unanimous a consent, the whole
army and a great part of the people from almost every county
in the kingdom cried out with one voice for justice against
the king as the very author of all their calamities, I cannot but
20 think that these things were brought about rather by a divine
impulse. However that may be, whether we consider the
magistrates or the body of the people, no men ever undertook
with a loftier courage, and, as our adversaries themselves confess, with a more tranquil mind, an action so distinguished,
25 so worthy of heroic ages—an action whereby they ennobled
not only law and its enforcement, which thenceforth seem restored to all men equitably, but Justice's very self, and ren-

târunt, séque ipsâ illustriorem dehinc, séque ipsâ majorem post hoc insigne judicium reddiderunt. Jam tertiam prope hujus capitis paginam exantlavimus, nec tamen illa simplex narratio, quam promisit, usquam apparet. Queritur nos do-
5 cere, *quoties rex molestè et odiosè regnat, impunè posse regno exui: ab hac,* inquit, *doctrina inducti, si mille rebus meliorem regem habuissent, non ei vitam conservâssent.* Spectate hominis acumen; nam istuc aveo ex te scire, quo pacto hoc sequitur, nisi tu nobis concesseris, nostro rege mille
10 rebus meliorem molestè et odiosè regnare; unde in eum de-ductus es locum, ut hunc quem defendis, iis regibus qui mo-lestè et odiosè regnant mille rebus deteriorem facias; id est tyrannorum omnium fortasse immanissimum. Macti estote reges tam strenuo defensore. Nunc narrare incipit. *Torse-*
15 *runt eum variis crucibus.* Dic quibus. *De carcere in carcerem traduxerunt.* Nec injuriâ, quippe ex tyranno hostem bello captum. *Custodiis sæpe mutatis:* ne ipsæ mutarent fidem. *Libertatis interdum spe ostensa, interdum et restitutionis per pactionem.* Vide quàm non antea meditatum nobis fuerit,
20 quàm non *tempora et modos* diu captavimus regis abdicandi. Quas res ab eo tum propemodum victore multo antè postu-

dered her after so signal a judgment more glorious, more august, than even she had been before.

We have now toiled to the end of the third page of his first chapter, and have not yet the plain tale he promised us. He complains of our doctrine "that a king ruling burdensomely and odiously may lawfully be deposed: according to this," he says, "if they had had a king better in a thousand respects than the one they had, they would not have spared his life." Keen reasoner! I long to have you tell me how this follows, unless you allow that a king a thousand ways better than our king may rule burdensomely and odiously. So now you have brought yourself to a pass where you make out the king that you defend a thousand ways worse than kings whose government is burdensome and odious, that is, the most monstrous perhaps of all tyrants. Kings, I wish you joy of so brisk a defender!

Now his narrative begins. "They put him to several sorts of torments." Give instances. "They removed him from prison to prison"; and so they might lawfully, for from a tyrant he was become a public enemy taken in war. "Often changing his guards,"—lest his guards should change their fidelity. "Sometimes they gave him hopes of liberty—sometimes even of restoring him to his crown upon articles of agreement." It seems then the taking away his life was not done upon so long premeditation as he talked of before, and that we did not so long before lay hold on all "opportunities and means" to renounce our king. Those things that we demanded of him in the beginning of the war, when he had almost brought us

lavimus, quæ nisi concederentur, nulla libertas, nulla salus
populo speranda erat, easdem à captivo suppliciter, haud semel, immo ter et amplius petivimus; toties repulsam accepimus. Cùm nulla de rege spes reliqua esset, fit Parlamenti
5 consultum illud nobile, nequa deinceps ad regem postulata
mitterentur; non ex quo is tyrannus esse, sed ex quo insana-
bilis esse cœpit. Postea tamen quidam ex Senatorum numero
nova sibi consilia capientes, et idoneum tempus nacti, conditiones iterum regi ferendas decernunt; pari sanè scelere atque
10 dementiâ ac Romanus olim Senatus, reclamante Marco Tullio
et cum eo bonis omnibus, legatos decrevit ad Antonium: pari
etiam eventu, nisi Deo immortali visum aliter fuisset, illos in
servitutem tradere, nos in libertatem vindicare. Nam cùm rex
nihilo plus quàm antea concessisset, quod ad firmam pacem
15 et compositionem revera spectaret, illi tamen satisfactum sibi
à rege esse statuunt. Pars itaque sanior, cùm se remque publicam prodi videret, fidem fortissimi, et semper reipub. fidis-
simi exercitûs implorat. In quo mihi quidem hoc solùm occurrit quod nolim dicere, nostras legiones rectiora sensisse
20 quàm patres conscriptos; et salutem reipub. armis attulisse,
quam illi suis suffragiis propè damnaverant. Multa deinde

under—things the denial of which would cut our people off
from all hope of liberty and safety—those very things we
petitioned of him when he was our prisoner, petitioned humbly and submissively, not once or twice, but thrice and often-
5 er, and were as often denied. When we had now lost all hopes
of the king's complying with us, then was made that noble
order of Parliament that from that time forward there should
no articles be sent to the king; so that we left off not from the
time he began to be a tyrant, but from the time he began
10 to be incurable. Still, afterward some Parliament men set
upon a new project, and meeting with a convenient opportunity to put it in practice, passed a vote to send proposals once
more to the king. Their wickedness and folly nearest re-
sembles that of the Roman Senate, who, against the opinion
15 of Marcus Tullius and all honest men, voted to send ambassadors to Antony; and the event had been the same, but that
it pleased God Almighty to order it otherwise—to deliver
them into slavery, but to assert our liberty. For though the
king did not agree to anything that might conduce to a firm
20 peace and settlement more than he had before, they go and
vote themselves satisfied. Then the sounder part of the house,
finding themselves and the commonwealth betrayed, implore
the aid of the army, valiant and ever faithful to the commonwealth. Whereon I can observe only this, which yet I am
25 loath to utter: that our soldiers showed better judgment than
our senators, and saved the commonwealth by their arms,
when the other by their votes had almost ruined it.

Then he tells a long tale of woe in a lamentable strain,

flebiliter narrat, verùm tam inscitè, ut luctum emendicare, non commovere videatur. Dolet, quòd *eo modo, quo nullus unquam, rex supplicium capitis passus sit:* cùm sæpiùs affirmaverit, nullum unquam regem supplicium capitis omnino esse passum. Tune, fatue, modum cum modo conferre soles, ubi factum cum facto quod conferas non habes? *Supplicium,* inquit, *capitis passus est, ut latro, ut sicarius, ut parricida, ut proditor, ut tyrannus.* Hoccine est regem defendere, an sententiam de rege ferre, eâ sanè quæ à nobis lata est, multò severiorem? quis te tam subitò pellexit ut nobiscum pronuntiares? Queritur *personatos carnifices regi caput amputâsse.* Quid hoc homine facias? questus est suprà *de parricidio in persona regis admisso,* nunc in persona carnificis admissum queritur. Quid reliqua percurram, partim falsissima, partim frivola *de pugnis* et *calcibus* militum gregariorum, et licentiâ *spectandi cadaveris quatuor solidis taxatâ,* quæ frigidissimi literatoris inscitiam et pusillitatem animi clamitant; legentem certè neminem pilo tristiorem reddere possunt: satius meherculè fuisset Carolo filio, quemvis ex eo balatronum grege conduxisse, qui ad coronam in triviis elegidia cantant, quàm oratorem hunc, luctificabilem dicam, an perridiculum deplo-

but so senselessly that he seems rather begging his readers
please to be sorrowful than moving them to sorrow. It grieves
him "to think that the king should undergo capital punishment after such a manner as no other king had ever done"—
5 though he had often told us before that there never was a
a king that underwent capital punishment at all. Fool, are
you wont to compare manner with manner when you have
not fact to compare with fact? "He suffered death," says he,
"as a robber, as a murderer, as a parricide, as a traitor, as a
10 tyrant." Is this defending the king, or is it not rather giving
a more severe judgment upon him than the one we gave?
Who has so suddenly drawn you round to give sentence with
us? He complains "that masked executioners cut off the
king's head." What shall we do with this fellow? He com-
15 plained before of "a murder done in the mask of a king";
now he complains that it was done in the mask of an executioner.

It were to no purpose to take particular notice of every
false or silly thing he says. He tells stories of "buffetings and
20 kicks that were given by common soldiers, and how it cost
fourpence to see the dead body." These and such-like stories
betray the ignorance and small-mindedness of our poor
scholar, but are far from making any reader ever a whit the
sadder. To bewail his father's misfortunes the younger
25 Charles had done better, in good faith, to have hired one of
the mountebanks that chant their doleful ballads to the
crowd at a street corner, than this lamentable—shall I call

rando patris infortunio adhibuisse; tam insipidum et insul-
sum, ut ne ex lacrymis quidem ejus mica salis exiguissima
possit exprimi. Narrare jam desiit; et quid deinde agat, dictu
sanè difficile est; adeò lutulentus et enormis fluit; nunc fre-
5 mit, nunc oscitat, nullum quidlibet garriendi modum sibi
statuit, vel decies eadem repetendi, quæ ne semel quidem dicta
non sordescerent. Et certè nescio, an blateronis cujuspiam ex-
temporales quælibet nugæ, quas ille uno pede stans versiculis
fortè effudisset, non digniores multo fuissent quæ chartis illine-
10 rentur: usque eò indignissimas esse reor quibus seriò responde-
atur. Præterea quòd regem *religionis protectorem* laudat, qui
ecclesiæ bellum intulit, ut episcopos religionis hostes et tyrannos in ecclesia retineret. *Puritatem autem religionis* quî potuit is conservare, ab impurissimis episcoporum traditionibus
15 et cæremoniis ipse sub jugum missus? *Sectarum* verò, quibus
tu *sacrilegos suos cœtus tenendi licentiam* ais *dari,* quam ipsa
Hollandia non dat, errores velim enumeres: interim nemo te
magis sacrilegus, qui perpetuò maledicendi pessimam omnium licentiam tibi sumis. *Non poterant graviùs rempubl.*
20 *lædere quàm ejus dominum tollendo.* Disce verna, disce ma-
stigia, nisi dominum tollis, tollis rempublicam: privata res
est, non publica quæ dominum habet. *At pastores facinus*
eorum abominantes cum summa injustitia persequuntur.
Pastores illos nequis fortè nesciat quales sint, breviter dicam;

him?—or rather most laughable—orator, so flat and tasteless that his very tears want salt.

Now his narrative is done; and it is hard to say what he does next, his discourse runs so muddy and irregular. Now he
5 rages, then he gapes, and keeps no method in his chatter but to repeat the same things ten times over that could not but be disgusting said but once. Really I know not but that the trumpery stuff of any babbling *improvisatore,* rhymed extempore while he stands on one foot, were better worth daubing
10 paper withal; so far am I from thinking aught he says worthy of a serious answer.

I pass by his praising as "protector of religion" a king who chose to make war upon the church rather than part with those church tyrants and enemies of religion, the bish-
15 ops. How is it possible, moreover, for one to "maintain religion in its purity" that was himself a slave to those impure traditions and ceremonies of theirs? And pray tell what errors you ascribe to those our "sects, whose sacrilegious meetings," you say, "have a public license" which even Holland
20 grants not. Meanwhile no one is more sacrilegious than you, who take unto yourself—worst license of all—the license of incessant slander. "They could not wound the commonwealth more dangerously than by taking off its master." You menial slave, learn, while you wait the lash, that unless ye
25 take away the master, ye destroy the commonwealth, for 'tis a private wealth, not a common wealth, that owns a master. "They persecute most unjustly those pastors that abhor this deed of theirs." Lest it be not clear what pastors he means, I

iidem sunt qui regi resistendum armis esse, et verbo et scriptis
docuerant; qui omnes tanquam Merozum indesinenter exe-
crari non destiterant, quotquot huic bello aut arma, aut pecuniam, aut vires non suppeditâssent; quod illi non contra regem, sed contra tyrannum Saule quovis aut Achabo, immo
Nerone ipso Neroniorem susceptum esse in concionibus sacris
vaticinabantur. Sublatis episcopis et sacerdotibus, quos Plu-
ralistarum et non residentium nomine insectari vehementissimè solebant, in eorum amplissima sacerdotia, hic bina, ille
trina, quàm ocyssimè irruebant: unde suos greges quàm turpiter negligant pastores isti meritò egregii nemo non videt:
nullus pudor, nulla numinis reverentia dementes cupiditate
et furiatos cohibere potuit, donec pessimo ecclesiæ publico
eâdem ipsi infamiâ flagrarent, quam paulò antè sacerdotibus
inusserant. Nunc quòd avaritia eorum nondum satiata est,
quòd inquies ambitione animus turbas concire, pacem odisse
consuevit, in Magistratus qui nunc sunt, id quod priùs in
regem fecerant, seditiosè concionari non desinunt; regem scilicet pium crudeliter sublatum; quem modò ipsi diris omnibus devotum, omni authoritate regia spoliandum, et bello
sacro persequendum, in manus Parlamento, quasi divinitus,
tradiderant; sectas scilicet non exstirpari; quod certè à magistratibus postulare perabsurdum est, qui avaritiam et ambitionem, quæ duæ in ecclesia hæreses perniciosissimæ sunt, ex
ipsorum ordine pastorum ac tribu, nullo adhuc modo aut ra-

shall say briefly: they were those very men who by their writings and sermons justified taking up arms against the king;
who cursed without ceasing, as Deborah did Meroz, all such
as would not help this war with arms or men or money; who
5 kept preaching to their congregations that they were fighting
not against a king but against a greater tyrant than any Saul
or Ahab, nay, one that out-Nero'd Nero. As soon as the bishops and the priests, whom they used to rail at with the names
of pluralists and absentees, were taken out of their way, in-
10 stantly they jump, some into two, some into three, of their best
benefices; so that everybody knows how foully these herds-
men, so deservedly raised above the common herd, neglect
their own. Their wild covetousness brake through all re-
straints of modesty and religion, till they were branded before
15 the church (ill notoriety!) with the same infamy which they
had branded but a little before upon the priests. Their covetousness yet unsated, and their restless ambition grown accustomed to raise tumults and hate peace, they cease not to preach
up sedition against the government now established, as they
20 had formerly done against the king. He was a kindly king
cruelly murdered, they say—this king upon whom but just
now themselves had heaped all their curses, and delivered up
as by God's will to the Parliament, to be despoiled of his
royalty and pursued with a holy war. They now complain that
25 the sects are not extirpated: a most absurd thing to ask of the
magistrates, who never yet by any means or method have been
able to extirpate avarice and ambition—the two heresies that
are most calamitous to the church—out of the very order and

tione exstirpare valuerunt. Quas illi sectas apud nos insectantur, obscuras esse scio; quas ipsi sequuntur, famosas, et ecclesiæ Dei longè periculosiores; quarum principes Simon ille Magus et Diotrephes fuere. Hos tamen, nequissimi cùm sint,
5 adeò non persequimur, ut factiosis et res novas quotidie molientibus nimiùm indulgeamus. Offendit jam te Gallum et errabundum, quod Angli *suis molossis,* quæ tua canina facundia est, *ferociores,* nullam *legitimi successoris et hæredis* regni, nullam *natu minimi,* nullam *reginæ Bohemiæ* ratio-
10 nem habuerint. Tute respondebis tibi, non ego. *Ubi reipub. forma mutatur ex monarchica in aliam, non datur successio inter differentis regiminis curatores;* Apparat. de primatu. *Minima,* inquis, *regni unius pars* hæc omnia *per tria regna* effecit: et digni quidem, si hoc verum esset, quibus in cæteros
15 imperium sit, viris in fœminas. *Isti sunt, qui regimen regni antiquum in alium qui à pluribus tyrannis teneatur, mutare præsumpserunt;* rectè quidem illi et feliciter; quos tu reprehendere non potes, quin simul fœdissimè barbarus et solœcus sis non moribus solùm, sed syntaxi etiam, grammaticorum
20 opprobrium. *Angli maculam hanc nunquam deleverint.* Immo tu, licèt omnium literatorum litura ipse sis, et verè macula, Anglorum tamen famam et sempiternam gloriam nunquam

estate of the ministers themselves. For the sects which they inveigh against, there are obscure ones, I know; but their own sects are notorious, and much more dangerous to the church of God: their heresiarchs were Simon Magus and Diotrephes.

5 Yet are we so far from persecuting these men, though they are pestilent enough, that, though we know them to be ill-affected to the government, and plotting change, we allow them but too much liberty.

You, vagabond Frenchman, seem displeased that "the 10 English, more fierce and cruel than their own mastiffs," as your barking eloquence has it, "have no regard to the lawful successor and heir of the crown, and take no care of the king's youngest son, or of the Queen of Bohemia." You, not I, shall answer yourself. "When the frame of a government is changed 15 from a monarchy to any other, the succession is not granted among the new-modellers" (*Apparatus de Primatu Papae*). "The great change throughout three kingdoms," you say, "was brought about by a small minority in one of them." If so, that small minority were worthy to have dominion over 20 the rest, as men over women. "These are they that presumptuously took upon them to change the ancient government of the realm into one held by many tyrants"—and well and auspiciously too! You cannot find fault with them without being a filthy barbarian and solecist, as well in morals as in syntax— 25 you shame of all grammarians. "The English will never be able to wash out this stain." Nay, you, though a blot and stain to all learned men, were never yet able to stain the renown and everlasting glory of the English nation, that with so great

valueris commaculare. Qui tantâ animi magnitudine, quanta omni memoriâ vix audita est, non hostes tantùm armatos, sed hostiles intus, id est, superstitiosas vulgi opiniones eluctati atque supergressi, Liberatorum cognomen posthac per omnes
5 gentes in commune sibi pepererunt: populariter id ausi, quod apud alias nationes heroïcæ tantùm virtutis esse existimatur. *Reformati et antiqui Christiani* quid hac in parte fecerint, aut facturi fuissent, tum respondebimus, cùm de jure tecum suo loco agetur; ne tuo vitio laboremus, qui gerrones omnes et
10 Battos loquacitate vincis. Quæris quid sis in nostra causa *Jesuitis* responsurus. Tuas res age transfuga; pudeat te facinorum tuorum, quando ecclesiam tui pudet; qui primatum Papæ, et episcopos tam jactanter modò et ferociter adortus, nunc episcoporum assecla factus es. Fateris *aliquos reformatorum,* quos
15 non nominas (ego tamen nominabo, quoniam tu eos *Jesuitis longè pejores esse* aïs, Lutherum nempe, Zuinglium, Calvinum, Bucerum, Paræum cum aliis multis) docuisse, *amovendum esse* tyrannum: *quis autem sit tyrannus ad judicium sapientum, et doctorum se retulisse. Isti verò qui? an sapien-*
20 *tes, an docti, an virtute nobiles, an nobilitate illustres?* Liceat, quæso, populo, qui servitutis jugum in cervicibus grave sentit, tam sapienti esse, tam docto, tamque nobili, ut sciat quid ty-

a resolution as we hardly find the like recorded in any history, struggled with, and overcame, not only their enemies in the field, but the hostile — that is, superstitious — persuasions of the common people, and won for themselves in general
5 amongst all posterity the name of Deliverer: the body of the people having undertook and performed an enterprise which in other nations is thought to proceed only from the magnanimity peculiar to heroes.

What "the Protestants and primitive Christians" did or
10 would do upon such an occasion, I will tell you hereafter, when we come to debate the merits of the cause; not to be guilty of your fault, who outdo in prolixity all the babbling Battuses. You wonder how you shall be able to answer all the Jesuits in our behalf. Mind your own business, renegade, and
15 be ashamed of your own actions, for the church is ashamed of you, who, though but of late you so boastfully and fiercely attacked the Pope's supremacy and the bishops, are now yourself become the bishops' sycophant. You confess that "some Protestants have asserted it lawful to depose a tyrant," and you do
20 not name them; but I will, because you say "they are far worse than the Jesuits." They are no other than Luther, and Zwingli, and Calvin, and Bucer, and Pareus, and many besides. "The question, though, who shall be accounted a tyrant," you say, "they have referred to the judgment of learned men and
25 wise. But what for men were these? Were they wise men, or learned? Were they anywise remarkable for either virtue or nobility?" A people that has felt the yoke of slavery heavy on its neck may well be allowed to be wise and learned and noble

ranno suo faciendum sit, etiamsi neque exteros, neque grammaticos sciscitatum mittat. Tyrannum autem fuisse hunc non Angliæ solùm et Scotiæ Parlamenta cùm verbis tum factis disertissimis declaraverunt, sed totus ferè utriusque regni po-
5 pulus assensus est; donec episcoporum technis et fraudibus in duas postea factiones discessit. Quid si Deus, quemadmodum eos qui lucis evangelicæ participes fiant, ita eos qui decreta ejus in reges hujus mundi potentissimos exequantur, non multos sapientes aut doctos, non multos potentes, non multos no-
10 biles esse voluit? ut per eos qui non sunt, aboleret eos qui sunt; ut ne glorietur caro coram eo. Tu quis es qui oblatras? an doctus? qui spicilegia, qui lexica et glossaria ad senectutem usque trivisse potiùs videris, quàm authores bonos cum judicio aut fructu perlegisse; unde nil præter codices, et varias
15 lectiones, et luxatum et mendosum crepas; doctrinæ solidioris ne guttulum quidem hausisse te ostendis. An tu sapiens? qui de minutiis minutissimis rixari, et mendicorum bella gerere soles, qui nunc astronomis, nunc medicis in sua arte credendis imperitus ipse et rudis convitia dicis; qui, siquis tibi voculæ
20 unius aut literulæ in exemplari quovis abs te restitutæ gloriolam præripere conaretur, igni et aquâ, si posses, illi interdiceres? Et tamen stomacharis, et tamen ringeris, quòd omnes te Grammaticum appellant. Hamondum nuper regis hujus

enough to know what should be done to its oppressor, though it send not to ask either foreigners or grammarians. But that this man was a tyrant not only the Parliaments of England and Scotland have declared by actions and words the clearest, but
5 almost all the people of both nations assented to it—till by the tricks and artifices of the bishops they were divided into two factions. For the execution of His decrees upon the most potent kings of this world, what if it has pleased God to choose such men as He chooses to be made partakers of the light of
10 the Gospel? "Not many wise or learned, not many mighty, not many noble; that by those that are not He might bring to naught those that are; that no flesh glory in His presence."

And who are you to scold at this? A learned man?—you that even unto your old age seem rather to have turned over
15 phrase-books and lexicons and glossaries than to have perused good authors with judgment or profit; so that you prate of naught but manuscripts and various readings and dislocated passages and scribal errors, but show that you have drunk never the least drop of more substantial learning. A wise
20 man?—you that use to carry on your beggarly disputes about the meanest trifles? You that being altogether ignorant in astronomy and physic, yet are always reviling astronomers and physicians who should be trusted in their own faculties? You that if any one should offer to deprive you of the vain glory of
25 having corrected or supplied the least word or letter in any copy you have criticised, would ban him, if you could, with the ban of fire and water? And yet you snarl in anger because everybody calls you a grammarian! In some trumpery book

Sacellanum imprimis dilectissimum in libro quodam nuga-
torio nebulonem appellas, quòd is te Grammaticum appella-
visset: idem, credo, esses ipsi regi convitium facturus, et defensionem hanc totam retractaturus, si Sacellani sui de te judi-
5 cium approbâsse audivisses. Jam vide quàm te Anglorum
unus, quos tu *fanaticos, indoctos, obscuros, improbos* vocitare
audes, contemnam et ludibrio habeam, nam nationem ipsam
Anglicanam de te quicquam publicè cogitare curculiunculo,
indignissimum esset; qui sursum, deorsum, quoquoversum
10 versatus et volutatus, nihil nisi grammaticus es: immo quasi
Deo nescio cui votum ipso Mida stultiùs nuncupâsses, quicquid attrectas, nisi cùm solœcismos facis, Grammatica est.
Quisquis igitur *de fæce illa plebis,* quam tu exagitas, (illos
enim verè optimates nostros, quorum sapientiam, virtutem
15 et nobilitatem facta inclyta satis testantur, non sic dehone-
stabo, ut te illis, aut tibi illos componere velim) quisquis, inquam, de fæce illa plebis hoc tantummodò sibi persuaserit,
non esse se regibus natum, sed Deo et patriæ, multo sanè te
doctior, multo sapientior, multo probior, et ad omnem vitam
20 utilior existimandus erit. Nam doctus ille sine literis, tu lite-
ratus sine doctrina, qui tot linguas calles, tot volumina per-
curris, tot scribis, et tamen pecus es.

of yours you call Dr. Hammond, who was lately this king's best beloved chaplain, *knave,* for no other reason than because he had called you grammarian. And you would have been as ready to throw the same reproach upon the king himself, I do 5 believe, and to withdraw this whole Defence, if you had heard that he had approved his chaplain's judgment of you.

Take notice now how much I, a single one of those Englishmen that you have the impudence to call "madmen, unlearned, ignoble, wicked," slight and despise you; that the 10 English nation in general should take any public notice of such a worm as you would be an infinite undervaluing of themselves. For whichever way you turn and twist you roundabout and upside down and inside out, you are a grammarian and nothing but a grammarian; nay, as if you had made to 15 some god or other a foolisher wish than Midas's, whatever you touch—except when you make blunders—*is* grammar. Whosoever therefore he be, though from among "those dregs of the common people" that you are so hard upon (as for those men of eminency amongst us whose great actions evidence 20 their wisdom and nobility and virtue, I will not disgrace them so much as to compare you with them or them with you),— whosoever, I say, among those dregs of the common people has but made this principle his own, that he was not born for kings, but for God and his country, should be deemed far 25 more learned and honest and wise than you, and every way of greater use in the world. For he is learned without letters, while you are lettered without learning,—you that understand so many languages, turn over so many volumes, write so many screeds, and yet are but a sheep when all is done.

CAPUT II.

QUOD argumentum pro se *indubitatum* esse, supe-
riore capite perorans dixerat Salmasius, *rem ita
se habere ut creditur, cùm omnes unanimiter
idem de ea sentiant,* quod tamen is *de facto* falsissimè affirma-
5 bat, id ego nunc, de jure regio disceptaturus, potero in ipsum
verissimè retorquere. Cùm enim regem definiat, *cujus suprema est in regno potestas, nulli alii nisi Deo obnoxia, cui
quod libet licet, qui legibus solutus est,* siquidem id definiri
dicendum est, quod infinitum in terris ponitur, evincam ego
10 contrà, non meis tantùm, sed vel ipsius testimoniis et rationibus, nullam gentem aut populum, qui quidem ullo numero
sit, nam omnem penetrare barbariam necesse non est, nullam,
inquam, gentem istiusmodi jura aut potestatem regi concessisse, *ut legibus solutus esset, ut quod libet liceret, ut omnes
15 judicaret, à nemine judicaretur;* nec verò quenquam cujuscunque gentis tam servili ingenio exstitisse puto, præter unum
Salmasium, qui tyrannorum immania quæque flagitia, regum
jura esse defenderit. Eorum plerique apud nos, qui regi maximè favebant, ab hac tam turpi sententia semper abhorruere;
20 quinetiam ipse, nondum pretio corruptus, his de rebus longè
aliter sensisse aliis jampridem scriptis facilè deprehenditur.
Adeò ut hæc non ab homine libero in libera civitate, nedum in

CHAPTER II.

IN winding up his first chapter Salmasius urged as "irrefragable" the argument that "a thing really is as it is believed to be, when all men unanimously agree in thinking it so." This argument, when applied, as he was then 5 applying it, "to matter of fact," is an utter fallacy; nevertheless I, that am now about to discourse matter of law—the right of kings—shall be able to turn it upon himself with full truth. He defines a king (if that may be said to be defined which he makes infinite) to be "a person in whom resides the supreme 10 power of the kingdom; who is answerable to God alone; who is permitted to do whatever he lists; who is loosed from the law." I will undertake to demonstrate, not by my own reasons and authorities alone, but even by his, that there never was a nation or people of any account (for to ransack all the 15 uncivilized parts of the world were to no purpose) that ever allowed it to be their king's right or power "that he should be loosed from the law, do what he pleased, and judge all, but be judged of none." Nor can I think that, save Salmasius alone, there ever was any one of any nation so slavish in spirit as 20 to assert the outrageous enormities of tyrants to be the rights of kings. Those amongst us that were the greatest royalists always abhorred this base opinion; nay, even Salmasius himself in some earlier writings of his—before he was bribed— was evidently of quite another mind. Insomuch that these 25 doctrines, so slavish in nature and spirit, seem to have been penned not by a free man in a free State, much less in the most

Repub. nobilissimâ, et Batavorum Academiâ celeberrimâ, sed
in ergastulo quovis aut catastâ, tam servili ingenio atque animo scripta esse videantur. Etenim, si quicquid regi libet, id
jure regio licitum erit, quod teterrimus ille Antoninus Cara-
5 calla, ab Julia noverca per incestum persuasus, non statim
ausus est credere, nemo profectò est, aut unquam fuit, qui tyrannus dici debeat. Cùm enim divina omnia atque humana
jura violavit, nihilo tamen minùs rex, jure regio insons erit.
Quid enim peccavit homo æquissimus? jure suo usus est in
10 suos. Nihil rex tam horrendum, tam crudele, támque furio-
sum committere in suos potest, quod præter jus regium fieri
quispiam possit queri aut expostulare. Hoc *tu jus regium à
jure gentium, vel potiùs naturali originem habere* statuis bel-
lua? Quid enim hominem te dicam, qui in omne hominum
15 genus, adeò iniquus et inhumanus es? quique omnem gentem
humanam Deo simillimam sic deprimere atque dejicere conaris, ut quos nunc superstitio, nunc scelus aut ignavia quorundam, aut denique perfidia tam feros atque immites dominos gentibus imposuit, eos à natura matre mitissimâ compa-
20 ratos atque impositos esse doceas. Quâ tu nefariâ doctrinâ
multo jam ferociores factos, non solùm ad proterendos omnes
mortales, et posthac miseriorem in modum conculcandos im-
mittis, sed jure naturali, jure regio, ipsis etiam populi legibus

excellent Dutch Republic and at its University of most renown, but at some prison-house or auction-block of slaves.

If whatever a king has a mind to do, the right of kings will bear him out in (a lesson that the hideous tyrant Antoninus
5 Caracalla, though his stepmother Julia taught it him through incest with herself, yet could not at once accept) then there neither is nor ever was anyone that deserved the name of tyrant. For though he has broken all the laws of God and man, yet the king shall be innocent none the less by the law of
10 kings. Excellent man—what wrong has he done? He has but used his own right upon his own subjects. No king can perpetrate upon his subjects an outrage so frightfully, so madly cruel, as anyone can remonstrate or complain that it exceeds the king's right.

15 Dare you assert that this "law of kings arises from the law of nations, or rather that of nature," you beast? Why should I call you a man, who to the human race are so unjust, so inhuman?—who endeavor so to bear down and vilify all mankind (made after the image of God) as to assert and
20 maintain that those fierce merciless masters whom the fanaticism of some, or crime, or cowardly indifference, or even treachery, has inflicted upon nations, are provided and appointed by Nature herself, that mild and gentle mother of us all. By which pestilent doctrine of yours having rendered
25 them far more fierce and fell, you not only incite them to tread down all poor mortals, and to trample the wretches under foot in the bargain, but endeavor with the law of nature, the law of kings, nay the very laws of the people, to arm them

in populum armare, quo nihil simul stultius et sceleratius esse
potest, contendis. Dignus profectò qui, contrà atque olim
Dionysius, ex grammatico tyrannus ipse sis; non quo tibi in
alium quemvis detur illa regia licentia malè faciendi, sed illa
5 altera malè pereundi; quâ solâ, ut inclusus ille Capreis Tiberius, à temetipso perditus quotidie te sentias perire. Verùm jus
illud regium paulò accuratiùs quale sit consideremus. *Sic*
Oriens totus, inquis, *judicavit, sic Occidens.* Non reponam
tibi quod Aristoteles et Marcus Cicero, authores, si qui alii,
10 cordatissimi, ille in Politicis, hic in oratione de Provinciis
scripsit, Gentes Asiaticas facilè servitutem pati, Judæos autem
et Syros servituti natos fuisse: fateor paucos ferè libertatem
velle, aut eâ posse uti, solos nempe sapientes, et magnanimos;
pars longè maxima justos dominos mavult, sed tamen justos;
15 injustos et intolerabiles ferendi, neque Deus unquam universo
generi humano tam infensus fuit, neque ullus unquam populus tam ab omni spe et consilio derelictus, ut necessitatem hanc
atque legem omnium durissimam in se atque in suos liberos
ultrò statuerit. Profers imprimis *verba regis in Ecclesiaste sa-*
20 *pientiâ clari.* Nos itaque ad legem Dei provocamus, de rege
posteriùs videbimus; cujus exinde sententiam rectiùs intelligemus. Audiatur ipse Deus, Deut. 17. *Cùm ingressus fueris*
in terram, quam Jehova Deus dat tibi, et dices, statuam super

against the people: the extreme at once of folly and of wickedness. As Dionysius of old from a tyrant became a schoolmaster, so you from a grammarian deserve to become a tyrant; that you may have—not that royal right to live an evil
5 life, but that other—to die an evil death; whereby, like
Tiberius shut up in Capri—yourself the author of your own
ruin—you shall feel yourself perish daily.

But let us look a little more narrowly into this right of kings
that you talk of. "This," you say, "was the sense of the eastern
10 and of the western part of the world." I shall not answer you
with what Aristotle in the *Politics* and Cicero in the oration
De Provinciis (both as trustworthy authorities as any we
have) have writ, viz. that the people of Asia easily submit to
slavery, but the Syrians and Jews are actually born to it. I con-
15 fess there are but few, and those men of great wisdom and
courage, that are either desirous of liberty or capable of using
it. Far the greatest part of the world prefers just masters—
masters, observe, but just ones. As for masters unjust and
unbearable, neither was God ever so much an enemy to man-
20 kind as to constrain our submission to them, nor was there
ever any people so destitute of all sense and sunk into such
depth of despair as of its own accord to impose so cruel a law
upon itself and its posterity.

You produce first "the words, in Ecclesiastes, of the king
25 illustrious for his wisdom." So we too appeal to God's law;
of the king we will consider hereafter, whose opinion we shall
thence better understand. Let God Himself be heard, Deut.
17. "When thou art come into the land which the Lord

me Regem sicut omnes gentes quæ sunt circa me: Quod ego
omnes velim etiam atque etiam animadvertant, teste hìc ipso
Deo, penes populos omnes ac nationes arbitrium semper fuisse
vel eâ, quæ placeret, formâ reipub. utendi, vel hanc in aliam
5 mutandi: de Hebræis disertè hoc dicit Deus, de reliquis haud
abnuit: deinde formam reipub. monarchiâ perfectiorem, ut
sunt res humanæ, suique populi magis ex usu Deo visam esse:
cùm hanc ipse formam instituerit; monarchiam non nisi serò
petentibus, idque ægrè concesserit. Sin regem planè vellent,
10 ut ostenderet Deus id se liberum Populo reliquisse, ab uno an
à pluribus respub. administraretur, modò justè; regi etiam fu-
turo leges constituit, quibus cautum erat, ut *ne multiplicet sibi
equos, ne uxores, ne divitias;* ut intelligeret nihil ipsi in alios
licere, qui nihil de se statuere extra legem potuerit. Jussus
15 itaque est *omnia legis illius præcepta,* etiam sua manu perscri-
bere; perscripta *observare; ne efferatur animus ejus præ fratribus suis.* Ex quo perspicuum est, regem æquè ac populum
istis legibus astrictum fuisse. In hanc fermè sententiam scripsit Josephus, legum suæ gentis interpres idoneus, in sua repub.
20 versatissimus, mille aliis tenebrionibus Rabbinis anteponen-

thy God giveth thee, and shalt say, I will set a king over me, like as all the nations that are about me." Which passage I could wish all men would consider again and again, for here it appears by God's own witness that all nations and peoples

5 have always possessed free choice to erect what form of government they will, and also to change it into what they will. This God affirms expressly concerning the Hebrews, and of other nations denies it not. A commonwealth, moreover, in the opinion of God, was, under human conditions, a more

10 perfect form of government than a monarchy, and more useful for His own people; for He himself set up this government, and could hardly be prevailed withal a great while after, and at their own importunate desire, to let them change it into a monarchy. But were they to insist upon a king, then

15 God, to show that He had left the people their choice to be governed by a single person or by more, so they were justly governed, prescribed laws for the king, though still but in prospect, whereby he was forbidden "to multiply to himself horses and wives, or to heap up riches." This was to make him

20 understand that outside the law no power over others was his, who concerning his very self could take no action outside the law. He was commanded therefore to transcribe with his own hand "all the precepts of the law," and, having writ them out, to "observe and keep them, that his mind might not be

25 lifted up above his brethren." Whence it is evident that as well the prince as the people was bound by those laws.

To this effect writes Josephus, a qualified interpreter of the laws of his nation, excellently versed in the Jewish polity, and

dus: Antiquitat. lib. 4, Ἀριστοκρατία μὲν οὖν κράτιστον, etc. *Optimum est,* inquit, *optimatium regimen; nec vos alium reipub. statum requiratis; satis enim est Deum habere præsidem. Attamen si tanta vos regis cupido ceperit, plus legibus*
5 *et Deo tribuat is, quàm suæ sapientiæ; prohibeatur autem, si potentior fieri studet, quàm rebus vestris expedit.* Hæc et plura Josephus in istum Deuteronomii locum. Alter Philo Judæus, gravis author, Josephi coætaneus, legis Mosaïcæ studiosissimus, in quam universam diffusa commentatione scripsit, cùm
10 in libro de creatione Principis hoc caput legis interpretatur, non alio pacto regem legibus solvit, atque hostis quilibet solutus legibus dici possit. τοὺς ἐπὶ λύμῃ καὶ ζημίᾳ τῶν ὑπηκόων, etc: *qui,* inquit, *ad perniciem et detrimentum populi magnam sibi acquirunt potentiam, non reges sed hostes appellandi*
15 *sunt; ea facientes, quæ hostes nulla pace reconciliandi faciunt; nam qui per speciem gubernandi faciunt injuriam, apertis hostibus pejores sunt; hos enim facile est propulsare, illorum autem malitia haud facilè detegitur.* Detecti igitur, quid obstat quo minùs hostium loco habendi sint? Sic libro secundo Al-
20 legoriarum Legis, *rex et tyrannus contraria sunt;* et deinde, *rex non imperat tantùm, sed paret.* Vera sunt ista, dicet aliquis; regem oportet quidem leges, ut qui maximè, observare; verùm si secùs fecerit, quâ lege puniendus? eâdem, inquam, lege quâ cæteri; exceptiones enim nullas reperio. Sed nec de

preferable to a thousand obscure rabbins, *Antiquities,* Book 4. "An aristocracy is the best form of government; wherefore seek ye not any other; it is enough to have God for your ruler. But if so huge desire of a king have seized you, let him yield
5 to the laws and to God more than to his own wisdom; and let him be restrained if he offer at more power than is proper to your affairs." Thus, in part, Josephus upon this passage in Deuteronomy.

Another solid authority, Josephus's contemporary Philo
10 Judaeus, one very studious in the law of Moses, upon the whole of which he wrote an extensive commentary, when in his book concerning the creation of the king he interprets this chapter of the law, releases the king from the law no otherwise than as an enemy may be said to be so released. "They," says he, "that
15 acquire great power to the prejudice and destruction of their subjects should be named not kings but enemies, for their actions are those of an irreconcilable enemy. Nay, they that under a show of government commit usurpation are worse than open enemies. The latter we may easily ward off, but the
20 wicked craft of the former is not always easy to discover." Once discovered, then, why should they not be dealt with as enemies? In the second book of the *Allegories of the Law,* "A king," says he, "and a tyrant are contraries." And a little after, "A king not only commands, but also obeys."
25 'All this is very true,' someone will say; 'a king ought to observe the laws most exactly, but if he will not, what law is there to punish him?' The same law, I answer, that there is to punish all others; I find no exception. There is no express

Sacerdotibus, sed nec de infimis quidem magistratibus puniendis lex ulla scribitur; qui omnes, cùm de iis puniendis nulla
lex scripta sit, pari certè jure et ratione possent impunitatem
scelerum omnium sibi vendicare; quam tamen neque eorum
5 quispiam vendicavit, neque quenquam iis arbitror idcirco esse
daturum. Hactenus ex ipsa Dei lege didicimus regem legibus
obtemperare debuisse; nec se præ cæteris efferre, qui etiam
fratres ejus sunt. Nunc an quid aliud Ecclesiastes moneat
videamus: Cap. 8. ver. 1. etc: *Mandatum regis observa; vel*
10 *propter juramentum Dei, ne perturbatè à facie ejus abito, ne*
persistito in re mala, nam quicquid volet faciet. Ubi verbum
regis, ibi dominatio, et quis dicat ei, quid facis? Satis constat
Ecclesiastem hoc in loco non synedrio magno, non senatui,
sed privato cuique præcepta dare. Jubet mandata regis ob-
15 servare, vel propter juramentum Dei; at quis jurat regi, nisi
rex vicissim in leges divinas atque patrias juratus sit? Sic Reu-
benitæ et Gaditæ obedientiam suam Jehosuæ pollicentur, Jos.
1: *Ut dicto audientes Mosi fuimus, ita erimus tibi, modò ut*
Deus tecum sit, quemadmodum fuit cum Mose. Conditionem
20 vides expressam; alioquin ipsum audi Ecclesiasten, cap. 9:
Verba sapientum submissa potiùs audienda esse, quàm clamo-
rem dominantis inter stolidos. Quid porrò monet? *Ne per-*
sistito in re mala, nam quicquid volet, faciet; in malos nimi-

law to punish the priests or even the least important magistrates, who might all, no matter what their guilt, with equal right and reason claim impunity because there is no positive law for their punishment; and yet none of them ever made
5 the claim, nor would it ever, I suppose, be allowed them on that ground.

Hitherto we have learned from the very law of God that a king ought to obey the laws, and not lift himself up above the rest, who also are his brethren. Let us now consider whether
10 the Preacher teaches any other doctrine, Chapter VIII. v. 1, etc. "I counsel thee to keep the king's commandment, and that in regard of the oath of God. Be not hasty to go out of his sight; stand not in an evil thing; for he doeth whatsoever pleaseth him. Where the word of a king is, there is power;
15 and who may say unto him, What doest thou?" It is well enough known that here the Preacher directs his precepts not to the Sanhedrim or to a parliament, but to private persons. He bids "keep the king's commandment, and that in regard of the oath of God"; but who makes oath to the king unless
20 the king for his part have made oath to the laws of God and his country? So the Reubenites and Gadites promise obedience to Joshua, Josh. I: "According as we hearkened unto Moses in all things, so will we hearken unto thee; so but God be with thee as he was with Moses." Here is an express
25 condition. Hear the Preacher else, Chapter IX: "The quiet words of wise men ought to be heard rather than the shouting of him that ruleth among fools." Next he cautions us, "Stand not in an evil thing; for he doeth whatsoever pleaseth

rum mala in re persistentes faciet, authoritate legum armatus;
nam leniter, aut severè agere, prout volet, potest. Nihil hìc
tyrannicum sonat, nihil quod vir bonus extimescat. *Ubi ver-*
bum regis, ibi dominatio; et quis dicat ei, quid facis? Et tamen legimus qui regi dixerit non solùm quid fecisti, sed etiam
stultè fecisti, 1 Sam. 13. At Samuel extraordinarius. Tuum
tibi regero, licèt infrà dictum pag. 49, *quid,* inquis, *extraordi-*
narium in Saule et Davide? itidem ego, quid, inquam, in
Samuele? Propheta fuit: sunt et illi hodie, qui ejus exemplo
faciunt; ex voluntate enim Dei vel *expressa* vel *insita* agunt:
quod etiam ipse infrà concedis, pag. 50. Prudenter igitur Ecclesiastes hoc in loco monet privatos, ne cum rege contendant:
nam etiam cum divite, cum potenti quovis, ut plurimùm
damnosa contentio est. Quid ergo? an optimates, an omnes
reliqui magistratus, an populus universus, quoties delirare libet
regi, ne hiscere quidem audebunt? an stolido, impio, furenti,
bonis omnibus perniciem machinanti non obstabunt, non
obviam ibunt, ne divina omnia atque humana pervertere occu-
pet, ne rapinis, ne incendiis, ne cædibus per omnes regni fines
grassetur, ita *legibus solutus, ut quod libet liceat?* O de Cap-
padocis eques catastis! quem omnis libera natio (si unquam

him." He does, certainly, to malefactors that persist in evil;
for he is armed with the law's authority, and may proceed
with mercy or severity as he will. Naught here sounds tyrannical; naught here that a good man need dread. "Where the
5 word of a king is, there is power; and who may say to him,
What doest thou?" And yet we read of one that did say to a
king not only "What hast thou done?" but "Thou hast done
foolishly." 1 Sam. 13. But Samuel, you may say, was an
extraordinary person. I answer you with your own words,
10 further on, from your forty-ninth page. "What was there
extraordinary," say you, "in Saul or David?" And so say I,
What was there in Samuel extraordinary? He was a prophet,
you will say. So are they today that follow his example, for
they act according to the will of God, either as "outspoken,"
15 or as "implanted in them"; which yourself grant farther on,
in your fiftieth page.

Prudently, then, does the Preacher in this passage advise
private persons not to contend with princes; for it is passing
dangerous to contend with any rich man even, or powerful
20 man soever. But what then? Shall the nobility, shall all the
other magistrates, shall the whole body of the people—when
a king chooses to rave, shall they not dare open their mouths?
Shall they not oppose a foolish, wicked, raging plotter of all
good men's ruin? Shall they not meet halfway his attempt to
25 overthrow all things divine and human—lest with plunderings and burnings and murders he riot through the realm—
being so "loosed from the law that what he listeth is lawful
to him"? O cavalier from Cappadocian slave-blocks! Whom

posthac in natione libera pedem ponere audebis) aut in ulti-
mas terras veluti portentum exportandum ejicere, aut servitutis candidatum dedere in pistrinum debebit, ea lege atque
omine, ut si te inde exemerit, ipsa sub aliquo tyranno, eóque
5 stultissimo, pro te molat. Quid enim poterit dici, aut ab aliis
dictum peti tam truculentum, aut ridiculum, quod in te non
cadat? Perge modò: *Israëlitæ regem à Deo petentes eodem
jure se ab eo gubernari velle dixerunt, quo omnes aliæ nationes, quæ hoc regimine uterentur. At Orientis reges summo*
10 *jure, et potestate non circumscriptâ regnabant, teste Virgilio.*

> — *Regem non sic Ægyptus et ingens*
> *Lydia, nec populi Parthorum, et Medus Hydaspes*
> *Observant.* —

Primùm quid nostrâ refert qualem sibi regem Israëlitæ volue-
15 rint, præsertim Deo irato, non solùm quòd regem vellent ad
exemplum gentium, et non suæ legis, sed planè quòd vellent
regem? Deinde regem injustum, aut legibus solutum peti-
visse credibile non est, qui Samuelis filios legibus obstrictos
ferre non potuerunt, et ab eorum tantùm avaritia ad regem
20 confugerunt. Postremò quod ex Virgilio recitas, non probat
reges Orientis *absoluta potestate* regnasse; Apes enim illæ
Virgilianæ, quæ vel Ægyptiis et Medis observantiores regum
sunt, teste tamen eodem Poëta,

> — *Magnis agitant sub legibus ævum.*

every free people, if hereafter you shall dare set foot among a
people that is free, ought to cast out and transport to the
world's end as a monstrosity of dire foreboding, or set aside
—fit candidate for slavery—to grind in the mill; solemnly
5 obliging themselves, if ever they let you go, to grind in your
stead under some tyrant—and him a fool. For what words
could be said or borrowed so expressive of cruelty or folly as
may not justly be applied to you?

But go on. "When the Israelites asked God for a king, they
10 said they would fain be governed by him under the same rule
as all the other nations which had a monarchy. But the kings
of the East had supreme rule and unlimited power, as Virgil
testifies:

    Not Egypt and huge Lydia, nor the hordes
15   Of Parthians, and Hydaspes, Median stream,
    Do so revere a king."

First, what is it to us, what sort of king the Israelites desired? Especially since God was angry with them not only
for desiring a king after the manner of the nations and not of
20 his own law, but for desiring a king at all. Nor is it credible
that they should have desired a king unjust or loosed from the
law, they who could not bear the government of Samuel's
sons, though bound by the law, and only from their covetousness sought refuge in a king. Lastly, what you quote out
25 of Virgil does not prove that the kings of the East reigned
"with absolute power"; for those bees in Virgil who more
revere their kings, he says, than do the Egyptians or Medes,
those bees, even by the witness of the same poet,

    Pass their lives under mighty laws—

Non ergo sub regibus omni lege solutis. At vide quàm tibi minimè velim malè; cùm plerique te nebulonem esse judicent, ostendam te personam tantùm nebulonis mutuam sumpsisse. In Apparatu ad primatum Papæ doctores quosdam Tridentinos exemplo Apium usos aïs, ut monarchiam Papæ probarent: ab his tu pari malitiâ hoc mutuum cepisti. Quod illis itaque respondisti cùm probus esses, jam factus nebulo tute respondebis tibi, tuáque tibi manu personam nebulonis detrahes. *Apium respub. est; atque ita Physici appellant: Regem habent, sed innocuum; ductor est potiùs quàm tyrannus, non verberat, non vellicat, non necat apes subditas.* Minimè igitur mirum, si ita observant. Istas mehercule apes malâ ave tibi tactio erat; Tridentinæ enim licèt sint, fucum te esse indicant. Aristoteles autem, rerum politicarum scriptor diligentissimus, monarchiæ genus Asiaticæ, quod et barbaricum vocat, κατὰ νόμον, id est, secundùm legem fuisse affirmat: Pol. 3. immo cùm monarchiæ quinque species enumeret, quatuor secundùm legem, et suffragante populo fuisse scribit, tyrannicas autem, quòd iis tanta potestas, volente licèt populo, data erat; regnum verò Laconicum maximè regnum videri, quòd non omnia penès regem erant. Quinta, quam is παμβασιλείαν vocat, et ad quam solam id refert, quod tu regum om-

—not, then, under kings that are loosed from all law. But now I will let you see how little ill-will I bear you. Though most people think you a knave, I will show that you have only put on the borrowed mask of a knave. In your *Appara-*
5 *tus ad Primatum Papae* you say that some divines of the Council of Trent made use of the example of the bees to prove the Pope's supremacy. This, with equal wickedness, you have borrowed from them. That very answer, therefore, which you gave them whilst you were an honest man, you shall yourself,
10 now you are grown a knave, give yourself, and with your own hand pull off the knave's mask. "The bees," say you, "have a commonwealth, and so do natural philosophers call it; they have a king, but a harmless one; he is a leader rather than a despot; he beats not, pulls not, kills not his subject bees." No
15 wonder therefore that they revere him so. Faith, 'twas under no lucky star of yours that you made contact with those *Tri-dentine* bees; three-toothed as they are, they show you up as a toothless drone.

Aristotle, a most exact writer on politics, affirms that the
20 Asiatic monarchy, which yet himself calls barbarous, was κατὰ νόμον, that is, according to law, *Pol.* 3. More: whereas he counts five sorts of monarchies, and four he calls governments according to laws, and with the people's approval, yet he calls them tyrannical, because, though with popular consent, so
25 much power had been lodged in them. But the kingdom of the Lacedemonians, he says, is most properly deemed a king-dom, because there not all power is lodged in the king. The fifth sort he calls παμβασιλείαν; to this alone he attributes what

nium jus esse scribis, ut ad libitum regnent, ubinam gentium,
aut quo tempore unquam obtinuerit non dicit: nec aliam ob
causam fecisse mentionem ejus videtur, quàm ut absurdam, injustam, et maximè tyrannicam esse demonstraret. Samuelem
5 aïs, cùm eos ab eligendo rege deterreret, *jus illis regium* exposuisse. Unde haustum, à lege Dei? at illa lex jus regium, ut
vidimus, longè aliud exhibuit: an ab ipso Deo per Samuelem
loquente? at improbavit, vituperavit, vitio dedit: non igitur
jus regium divinitùs datum, sed morem regnandi pravissi-
10 mum, superbiâ regum et dominandi libidine arreptum exposuit propheta; nec quid debebant reges, sed quid volebant
facere; rationem enim regis populo indicavit, sicut antea rationem sacerdotum Eliadarum eodem verbo (quod tu p. 33.
Hebraico etiam solœcismo מ·שׁפּת vocas) suprà indicaverat:
15 C. 2. *ratio sacerdotum istorum cum populo hæc erat, v.* 13.
impia videlicet, odiosa, et tyrannica: ratio itaque illa nequaquam jus erat, sed injuria. Sic etiam patres antiqui hunc locum exposuerunt; unus mihi erit multorum instar, Sulpitius
Severus, Hieronymi æqualis, eíque charus, et Augustini ju-
20 dicio vir doctrinâ et sapientiâ pollens. Is in historia sacra Samuelem aït dominationem regiam, et superba imperia populo
exponere. Sanè jus regium non est dominatio et superbia; sed

you call the right of all kings, the right to rule as they please;
but where in the world, or when in the whole course of time,
it ever obtained, he saith not. Nor seems he to have mentioned
it for any other purpose than to show that it is unjust, absurd,
5 and in the last degree tyrannical.

You say that when Samuel would deter the people from
choosing a king, he propounded "to them the right of kings."
But where did he get it—from the written law of God? Nay,
that law, as we have seen, has shown a very different right of
10 kings. Was it from God Himself speaking through Samuel?
But God disapproved it, blamed it, deemed it a fault; so that
the prophet expounded not any divinely appointed law for
kings, but a mode of government most corrupt, seized by the
pride of kings and lust to rule. He tells not what kings ought
15 to do, but what they were fain to do; for he showed the people
the manner of a king, as before he had shown the manner of
the priests, the sons of Eli—using the same word (which you
in your thirty-third page, by a solecism even in Hebrew, call
משׁפּט). Ch. 2. v. 13. "Those priests' manner with the people
20 was this"—surely an impious manner, and a hateful and
tyrannical. That manner then was nowise a right but a wrong.

The fathers too have explained this passage in the same
way: one will serve me as the measure of many—Sulpitius
Severus, a contemporary and friend of St. Jerome, and in
25 St. Augustine's opinion, a man of great wisdom and learning.
He tells us in his sacred history that Samuel is exhibiting to
the people the monarchical despotism and pride of power.
Now despotism and pride, to be sure, are not the right of

formulas legum sectatur, singulis penè literis immoratur, æquitatem non servat; aut scriptum jus callidè nimis et malitiosè interpretatur, ex quo illud proverbium Cicero ortum esse ait. Cùm autem jus omne de fonte justitiæ manare cer-
5 tum sit, impius sis necesse est, qui *regem injustum esse, iniquum, violentum, raptorem esse, et quales esse solebant* qui pessimi erant, jus regis esse dicas, idque *prophetam populo insinuâsse.* Quod enim jus summum aut remissum, scriptum aut non scriptum ad maleficia perpetranda esse potest? Id ne
10 tibi de aliis concedere, de rege pernegare in mentem veniat, habeo quem tibi opponam, et puto regem, qui istiusmodi jus regium et sibi et Deo invisum esse profitetur: Psal. 94; *an consociaretur tibi solium ærumnarum, formantis molestiam per statutum?* Noli igitur Deo hanc atrocissimam injuriam fa-
15 cere, quasi is regum pravitates et nefaria facinora jus esse regium docuerit, qui etiam hoc nomine societatem cum improbis regibus se detestari docet, quòd molestiam et ærumnas omnes populo juris regii titulo creare soleant. Noli Prophetam Dei falsò insimulare; quem tu dum juris regii isto loco
20 doctorem habere putas, non verum nobis affers Samuelem; sed, ut venefica illa, inanem umbram evocas; quamvis et illum ab inferis Samuelem non adeò mendacem fuisse credam, quin illud quod tu jus regium vocas, impotentiam potiùs tyranni-

legal right: when a man hunts after legal formulas, dwells almost upon the letters of the law, and regards not its justice; or too cunningly and maliciously interprets a statute; where-from, says Cicero, the proverb arose. But since it is certain

5 that all right flows from the fountain of justice, it follows inevitably that you are most wicked in affirming that "for a king to be unjust, rapacious, tyrannical, and such as they were who were worst," is the king's right, and that it was this "the prophet intimated to the people." For what right,

10 whether extreme or relaxed, whether written or unwritten, can there be to do wrong? Lest you take it into your head to admit this of other men, yet to keep on denying it of kings, I have one to object to you, a king methinks, who avows that your sort of right of kings is odious both to God and to him-

15 self: "Shall the throne of iniquity have fellowship with thee, that frameth mischief by law"? Psalm 94. Put not then so black an insult upon God as to ascribe to him the doctrine that the perversities and impious wickednesses of kings are the right of kings. Nay, God Himself tells us that he abhors all

20 fellowship with wicked princes for the very reason that under pretence of royal right they create misery and vexation for their subjects. Neither bring a false accusation against a prophet of God; for by supposing that in this passage he ex-pounds the right of kings, you bring not before us the right

25 Samuel, but call up an empty shade, as did the witch. Though for my part I verily believe that even that Samuel from Hell would not have been such a liar as not to call your right of kings rather the extravagance of tyranny.

cam dicturus fuisset. Jus datum sceleri legimus, túque *licen-*
tiæ jure concessæ reges minùs bonos uti consuevisse aïs. At jus
hoc ad perniciem humani generis abs te introductum, non esse
à Deo datum probavimus; restat, ut sit à Diabolo; quod in-
5 frà clariùs liquebit. *Hæc,* inquis, *licentia dat posse, si velis;*
et authorem hujus juris habere Ciceronem præ te fers. Nunquam ægrè facio ut testimonia tua recitem; tuis enim ipse testibus conficere te soles. Audi igitur verba Ciceronis in 4.
Philip. *Quæ causa justior est belli gerendi, quàm servitutis*
10 *depulsio? in qua etiamsi non sit molestus dominus, tamen est*
miserrimum posse si velit. posse vi scilicet; nam de jure si
loqueretur, repugnantia diceret, et ex justa belli causa injustam faceret. Non est igitur jus regium quod tu describis, sed
injuria, sed vis, et violentia regum. Transis ab regia licentia
15 ad privatam: *licet privato mentiri, licet ingrato esse.* Licet et
regibus; quid inde efficis? licebit ergo regibus impunè rapere,
occidere, stuprare? Quid interest ad injuriæ gravitatem rex
an latro, an aliunde hostis populum occidat, diripiat, in servitutem agat? eodem certè jure, et hunc et illum humanæ socie-
20 tatis inimicum et pestem propulsare, atque ulcisci debemus;
immo regem eò justiùs quòd is tot beneficiis et honoribus

We read of impiety countenanced by law, and you yourself say "it was the less good kings that were wont to make use of the right they got under leave granted." Now I have proved that this right, which you have introduced for the destruction of mankind, proceeds not from God; naught remains but that it comes from the Devil; as will appear more clearly hereafter. "This leave," say you, "grants the power if one will"; and for this you pretend to have Cicero's authority. I am never unwilling to mention your authorities, for it generally happens that you spoil your case by means of your own witnesses. Hear then what Cicero says in his Fourth Philippic: "What reason for war can be more just than the driving off a despotism? For under this, even though the master happen not to be irksome, yet 'tis a wretched thing that he can if he will." Can by force, that is; for if Cicero were speaking of a right, he would contradict himself, and of a just cause of war make an unjust cause. What you describe, then, is not the right of a king, but the wrongfulness of kings, their force and their fury.

From a king's leave and license you turn to a private man's. "A private man," say you, "may lie, may be ungrateful." And so may kings, but what then? Shall they therefore have leave to plunder, murder, ravish, with impunity? How does it affect the seriousness of the wrong done to a people whether it be the king, or a robber, or an enemy from some other quarter, that slays, plunders, and enslaves them? And questionless, being both alike enemies and plagues to human society, the one as well as the other ought by the same law to be driven off and punished—a king indeed with even more

nostris auctus commissam sibi sub juramento publicam salutem prodat. Concedis postremò, *leges dari à Mose secundùm quas rex ille quandoque eligendus imperare debebat, quamvis diversas ab illo jure quod Samuel proposuit*. Quod cum assertione tua dupliciter pugnat; cùm enim regem legibus omnino solutum posueris, nunc obstrictum dicis: dein jus juri contrarium ponis Mosis et Samuelis, quod est absurdum. At *servi*, inquit Propheta, *vos eritis regi*. Ut servos fuisse non abnuerim, non jure tamen regio servi fuerunt, sed regum fortasse plurimorum usurpatione et injustitia. Illam enim petitionem obstinatam non jure regio, sed suo merito in pœnam illis cessuram propheta præmonuit. At verò si regi legibus soluto quicquid libet licuerit, profectò rex longè plus quàm dominus erit, populus infra omnium servorum infimos plus quàm infimus. Servus enim vel alienigena legem Dei vindicem injuriosum in dominum habebat; populus universus, libera nimirum gens, vindicem in terris neminem, nullam legem habebit, quò læsus, afflictus et spoliatus confugiat: à servitute regum Ægyptiorum ideo liberatus, ut uni ex fratribus suis duriore si libuisset servitute opprimendus traderetur. Quod cùm neque divinæ legi, nec rationi consentaneum sit, dubium ne-

justice, because, though raised to that dignity by the honors that his people have conferred upon him, and though under his oath entrusted with the public safety, he yet betrays it.

At last you grant that "Moses prescribes laws according
5 to which the king sometime to be chosen ought to govern, though different from that right which Samuel promulgated" —a double contradiction to what you have said before. For whereas you had affirmed that a king is quite unbound by law, you here confess he is bound. And you set up two con-
10 trary systems of law or right, one according to Moses, the other according to Samuel; which is absurd.

"But," says the prophet, "ye shall be servants to the king." Suppose I did not deny that they were so; yet it was not by royal right, but maybe by the usurpation and injustice of most
15 of their kings. For the prophet had forewarned them that that importunate petition of theirs would turn to their punishment, not through a royal right, but through their own deserts. Indeed if a king, as unbound by the law, have leave to do what he list, he shall be far more than lord and master, and
20 his people sink down lower than the lowest of slaves. For even a slave foreign-born had the law of God to his defender against a cruel master; and shall a whole people, yea a free nation, find no protector upon earth, no law whither to betake themselves for refuge when hurt and stripped and stricken?
25 Were they set free from their bondage under the Egyptian kings only that they might be delivered to one of their own brethren to be crushed, should he choose, under a bondage yet sterner? All which being agreeable neither to the law of God

mini esse potest, quin propheta mores enarraverit, non jus
regum, neque mores prorsus regum omnium, sed plurimorum. Descendis ad rabbinos; duósque adducis eâdem, quâ
priùs, infelicitate: nam caput illud de rege in quo R. Joses jus
5 regium aiebat contineri, Deuteronomii esse, non Samuelis,
manifestum est. Samuelis enim ad terrorem duntaxat populo
injiciendum pertinere rectissimè quidem et contra te dixit R.
Judas. Perniciosum enim est id jus nominari atque doceri
quod injustitia planè est, nisi abusivè forsitan jus nominetur.
10 Quo etiam pertinet versus 18. *Et exclamabitis die illa propter
regem vestrum, sed non exaudiet vos Jehova;* obstinatos nimirum ista pœna manebat, qui regem nolente Deo dari sibi voluerunt. Quanquam ista verba non prohibent, quo minus et vota
et quidvis aliud tentare potuerint. Si enim clamare ad Deum
15 contra regem populo licebat, licebat proculdubio omnem etiam
aliam inire rationem honestam sese à tyrannide expediendi.
Quis enim quovis malo cum premitur, sic ad Deum clamat ut
cætera omnia quæ officii sunt sui negligat, ad otiosas tantùm
preces devolutus? Verum utcunque sit, quid hoc ad jus re-
20 gium, quid ad jus nostrum? qui regem nec invito Deo unquam petivimus, nec ipso dante accepimus; sed jure gentium
usi, nec jubente Deo nec vetante, nostris legibus constituimus.

nor to common sense, nobody can doubt that what the prophet declared to the people is not the right of kings, but their manner, nor yet the manner of all kings, but of most.

Then you come down to the rabbins, and quote two of
5 them, but with the same bad luck as you had before; inasmuch as that chapter about a king, which, as Rabbi Joses repeatedly said, contains the right of kings, clearly is the one in Deuteronomy, not the one in Samuel. For Rabbi Judah has declared very truly, and against you, that that discourse of
10 Samuel's was only to put fear into the people. It is most pernicious that a thing should be named a right, and so inculcated, which in itself is utter wrong — unless perhaps it be called a right ironically. Upon this argument verse 18 is in point: "And ye shall cry out in that day because of your king
15 which ye shall have chosen you; and the Lord will not hear you in that day." Yea, that punishment awaited them for obstinately persisting to desire a king against God's refusal.

Yet these words forbid them not to try prayers or anything else, for if the people might lawfully cry out to God against
20 the king, without doubt they might use all other honorable means to rid themselves of his tyranny. For who that is hard-pressed by misfortune merely cries out to God, and does naught but fall to his lazy prayers, so as to neglect all else his duty?
25   But be it how it will, what is all this to the rights of kings or of our English people? We neither asked a king against the will of God, nor had one at his hands, but — neither in obedience to nor against any command of God — exercised the right

Quæ cùm ita se habeant, non video quamobrem nobis laudi atque virtuti tribuendum non sit, regem abjecisse; quandoquidem Israëlitis crimini est datum regem petisse. Quod etiam res ipsa comprobavit; nos enim qui regem, cùm haberemus,

5 deprecati sumus, tandem exauditos Deus liberavit; illos, qui cùm non haberent, à Deo efflagitabant, servire jussit; donec Babylone redeuntes ad pristinum reipub. statum reversi sunt. Ludum Talmudicum deinde aperis; quin et hoc sinistro augurio tentatum. Dum enim regem non judicari cupis osten-

10 dere, ostendis ex Codice Sanhedrim *regem nec judicari nec judicare;* quod cum petitione istius populi pugnat, qui ideo regem petebant, ut judicaret: id frustra resarcire studes; intelligi nempe id de regibus Postbabylonicis debere. At ecce tibi Maimonides, qui *hanc inter reges Israëlitas et Judæos dif-*

15 *ferentiam ponit: Davidis enim posteros judicare et judicari;* Israëliticis neutrum concedit. Occurris tibi, tecum enim litigas, aut cum Rabbinis tuis; meam rem agis. Hoc *primis in regibus locum non habuisse,* quia dictum est v. 17. *vos eritis ei servi;* consuetudine scilicet, non jure; aut si jure, pœnas pe-

20 tendi regis, quamvis non sub hoc fortè vel sub illo, at sub ple-

of nations, and appointed a king by laws of our own. And this being the case, I see not why it should not redound to our virtue and our praise to have deposed our king, since it was reckoned a reproach to the Israelites to have asked for theirs. And this the event has confirmed; for we, when we had a king, prayed to God against him, and were heard, and at last delivered; but the Jews, who having no king kept importunately asking God for one, he bade be slaves, till, after their return from Babylon, they betook themselves to their former government again.

Next you throw open your Talmud School, but this too is an unlucky undertaking. In your desire to prove that kings are not to be judged, you quote from the treatise of the Sanhedrim "that the king neither judges nor is judged." But this runs counter to that people's own petition, who kept begging a king for the very purpose that he might judge them. Fain would you patch this up to fit your purpose (but in vain) by telling us that it is to be understood of those kings that reigned after the Babylonish captivity. For here against you is Maimonides, who "makes this difference betwixt the kings of Israel and those of Judah: that the kings of the posterity of David judge and are judged," but the kings of Israel do neither. You work against yourself; for you contradict yourself or your rabbins, and plead my cause. This, say you, "applied not to the first kings of Israel," for in the 17th verse it is said "Ye shall be his servants." To be sure—that is to say by his actual practice, not by any right; or if by right, then as a penalty for asking a king: a penalty which they kept on

risque luebant, quod nos non attingit. Tibi verò adversario
opus non est, adeò semper tibi adversaris. Narras enim pro
me, ut primò Aristobulus, pòst Jannæus cognomento Alexander, jus illud regium, non à synedrio juris custode, et inter-
5 prete acceperint, sed paulatim sibi assumpserint, et senatu re-
nitente usurpaverint: quorum in gratiam bella illa fabula de
primoribus synedrii *à Gabriele exanimatis* adinventa est, jusque hoc magnificum, quo niti maximè videris, *regem* scilicet
non judicari, ex illa fabula plusquam anili, utpote rabbinica,
10 conflatum esse fateris. Reges autem Hebræorum *judicari*
posse, atque etiam ad verbera damnari fusè docet Sichardus
ex libris Rabbinicis, cui tu hæc omnia debes, et tamen obstrepere non erubescis. Quinimmo legimus ipsum Saulem cum
filio Jonathane sortis judicium atque etiam capitale subiisse,
15 suóque ipsum edicto paruisse. Uzzias quoque à sacerdotibus
templo deturbatus, lepræ judicio, tanquam unus è populo, se
submisit, réxque esse desiit. Quid si templo excedere, quid si
magistratu abire et seorsim habitare noluisset, jus illud regium
legibus solutum sibi asseruisset, an passuros fuisse censes Ju-
20 dæos et sacerdotes templum contaminari, leges violari, popu-

paying under most of their kings, though not perhaps under this king or that. So your point has nothing to do with the case. But you need no antagonist, you are such a perpetual antagonist to yourself. For you tell, as if arguing on my side,

5 how first Aristobulus, and after him Jannaeus, surnamed Alexander, did not receive that kingly right of theirs from the Sanhedrim, guardian and interpreter of rights, but usurped it by degrees against the will of the Senate. To please these usurpers, you say, that pretty story of the principal men of the

10 Sanhedrim being "struck dead by Gabriel" was made up for the occasion. And thus you confess that this magnificent prerogative, upon which you seem mainly to rely, viz., "that a king is not to be judged," was forged out of this rabbinical fable, worse than an old wives' tale.

15   But that the Hebrew kings "were liable to be judged, and even to be punished with stripes," Sichardus shows at large out of the writings of the rabbins; to which author you are indebted for all this erudition, and yet you blush not to clamor against him. Nay, we read that even Saul thought himself

20 bound by a decree of his own making, and in obedience thereunto cast lots with his son Jonathan which of them two should die. Uzziah likewise, when the priests thrust him out of the temple as a leper, submitted as though he had been a subject, and ceased to be king. Suppose he had refused to go out from

25 the temple, to lay down the government, and to dwell in a several house, and had asserted that royal right unbound by law, think you the Jews and their priests would have suffered the temple to be defiled, the laws violated, and the whole

lum universum contagione periclitari? In leprosum ergo regem vigebunt leges, in tyrannum nihil poterunt? Ecquis tam
demens, aut stultus est, ut existimet, cùm rex morbosus ne
populum contagione lædat, cautum atque provisum legibus
5 sit, si rex impius, iniquus, crudelis populum diripiat, excru-
ciet, occidat, rempub. funditùs evertat, nullum his malis longè
gravioribus remedium legibus repertum esse? Verùm *exemplum ullius regis afferri non potest, qui judicium capitis sub-
ierit in jus vocatus.* Ad illud Sichardus haud absurdè respon-
10 det, perinde esse, ac si quis ad hunc modum dissereret. Cæsar
nunquam citatus est coram Electore; ergo si Palatinus diem
Cæsari dixerit, non tenetur Cæsar in judicio respondere. Cùm
tamen doceat Bulla aurea Carolum IV. se et successores suos
huic cognitioni subjecisse. Quid in corrupto populi statu re-
15 gibus adeò indultum fuisse miramur, ubi tot privati aut opibus
suis aut gratia impunitatem vel gravissimorum scelerum assequuntur? Illud autem ἀνυπεύθυνον, id est, *à nemine pendere,
nulli mortalium rationem reddere,* quod tu regiæ Majestatis
maximè proprium esse aïs, Aristoteles, Polit. 4. c. 10. maximè
20 tyrannicum, et in libera natione minimè ferendum esse affirmat. Tu verò Antonium tyrannum immanissimum, Romanæ
reipub. eversorem, idoneum sanè authorem producis, non esse

people endangered by infection? Shall laws then be of force against a leprous king, and avail naught against a tyrant? Can any man possibly be so mad and foolish as to fancy that while the law has carefully provided against a diseased king's
5 hurting his people, yet, should a wicked unjust cruel king tear and torture and slay them, and quite overturn the state, no legal relief had been devised against these far greater mischiefs?

"But," say you, "no precedent can be shown of any king
10 that has been arraigned in a court of justice, and condemned to die." Whereto Sichardus answers pat, that 'tis as if one should argue on this manner: The Emperor never has been summoned before an Elector; therefore, if the Elector Palatine should set a day for his appearance, the Emperor were not
15 bound to appear or plead; though from the Golden Bull it is clear that Charles IV submitted himself and his successors to that investigating jurisdiction.

No wonder if kings have been indulged so far when the people are depraved, and when so many private persons with
20 either money or interest escape the law, though guilty of crimes the most heinous. That ἀνυπεύθυνον, that is, "to be wholly independent upon any other, and accountable to none upon earth," which you say is peculiar to royal majesty, Aristotle in his *Politics,* Book 4, Chapter 10, calls most tyrannical,
25 and nowise to be endured by a free people. In proof that a king cannot rightfully be required to give an account of his actions, you cite as authority—proper authority forsooth!— that monstrous tyrant Mark Antony, destroyer of the Roman

justum reposci à Rege factorum suorum rationem: et tamen
Herodem cædis reum ad causam dicendam in Parthos proficiscens, accersivit ad se Antonius: et animadversurus etiam
in regem fuisse creditur, nisi rex eum auro corrupisset. Ita ab
5 eodem fonte profluxit regiæ potestatis Antoniana assertio, et
tua *regia defensio.* At non sine ratione, inquis; *nam reges ab
alio non habent quod regnant, sed soli Deo acceptum referunt.*
Dic sodes quinam? nam istiusmodi reges exstitisse unquam,
nego. Primus enim Saul, nisi populus, refragante etiam Deo,
10 regem voluisset, nunquam rex fuisset; et quamvis rex renun-
tiatus esset Mispæ, vixit tamen penè privatus, armentum patris secutus, donec Gilgale rex à populo secundùm creatus est.
Quid David, quamvis unctus à Deo, nonne iterum unctus est
ab Judæis Chebrone, deinde ab omnibus Hebræis, pacto ta-
15 men prius fœdere? 2 Sam. 5, 1 Chron. 11. fœdus autem obligat reges, et intra certos fines continet. Sedit Solomon, inquis,
super solium Domini, et cunctis placuit, 1 Par. 29. ergo et
placuisse populo aliquid erat. Constituit Jehoiadas regem Joa-
sum, fœdus tamen eodem tempore pepigit inter regem et popu-
20 lum, 2 Reg. 11. Hos reges, necnon et reliquos Davidis posteros
et à Deo et à populo constitutos fateor; cæteros omnes, ubicunque gentium, à populo tantùm constitutos esse affirmo; tu os-

commonwealth; yet Antony, when marching against the Parthians, summoned Herod before him to answer a charge of murder, and it is thought would have punished even a king, had not the king bribed him with gold. So that your *Royal*
5 *Defence* and Antony's assertion of the royal prerogative have flowed from one and the same spring.

Not without reason, say you, "for kings hold their authority from no other than God, but are indebted and obliged for it to Him alone." What kings, pray? For I deny that there
10 ever were any such kings. Saul, the first king of Israel, had never reigned but that the people desired a king even against the will of God, and though he was proclaimed king at Mizpah, yet he lived almost a private life, and came after the herd of his father, till he was created king a second time by
15 the people at Gilgal. And what of David? Though anointed by God, was he not anointed a second time in Hebron by the tribe of Judah, and then by all the Hebrews—yet even so only after a mutual covenant betwixt him and them? 2 Sam. 5; 1 Chron. 11. But a covenant binds kings and restrains them
20 within bounds. Solomon, you say, "sat on the throne of the Lord, and was acceptable to all men," 1 Chron. 29. So that it did use to be something to be well-pleasing in the eyes of the people! Jehoiadah, the priest, made Joash king, but first he made him and the people enter into a covenant to one
25 another, 2 Kings 11. I acknowledge that these kings and the rest of David's posterity were appointed both by God and by the people, but all other kings of what country soever were appointed, I affirm, by the people only. I challenge you to

tende constitutos esse à Deo; nisi eâ solum ratione quâ omnia
cùm maxima tum minima à Deo fieri et constitui dicuntur.
Solium itaque Davidis peculiari quodam jure solium Jehovæ
dicitur; solium aliorum regum non alio, atque cætera omnia,
5 Jehovæ sunt. Quod tu ex eodem capite didicisse debuisti, vers.
11, 12. *Tua sunt omnia in cœlo et in terra, tuum est, Jehova,
regnum, divitiæ et gloria à facie tua sunt, vis et potentia,* etc:
diciturque hoc toties, non ut intumescant reges, sed ut mone-
antur, quamvis deos se esse putent, Deum tamen supra se esse
10 cui debent omnia. Unde illa Essenorum et Poetarum doctrina,
reges *non sine deo, et ab Jove esse* facilè intelligitur; nam et
minores quoque magistratus, nempe judices ab eodem esse
Deo statuit rex ipse Solomon, Pro. 8. 15, 16. et ab eodem esse
Jove statuit Homerus Iliad. *α.*

15   —δικάσπολοι, οἵτε θέμιστας, *judices qui leges*
        Πρὸς Διὸς εἰρύαται—*ab Jove custodiunt.*

Et omnes certè homines à Deo itidem sumus, Deique genus.
Jus igitur hoc universum Dei, non tollit jus populi; quo minùs
omnes cæteri reges, non à Deo nominati, regnum suum soli
20 populo acceptum referant; cui propterea rationem reddere
tenentur. Quod, quanquam Vulgus assentari regibus solet,
ipsi tamen reges sive boni, ut Homericus ille Sarpedon, sive
mali, ut illi apud Lyricum tyranni, agnoscunt.

show that they were appointed by God, except in the sense
that all things, great and small, are said to be made and appointed by him. The throne of David, then, was in a peculiar
manner called "the throne of Jehovah," whereas the thrones
5 of other princes are Jehovah's no otherwise than are all things
else; which you should have learnt out of the same chapter,
verses 11, 12. "All that is in the heaven and in the earth is
thine; thine is the kingdom, O Lord. Both riches and honor
come of thee, and power and might." This is so often re-
10 peated, not that kings may be puffed up, but to warn them
that though they think themselves gods yet there is a God
above them to whom they owe all. Thus we easily understand what the poets and the Essenes mean when they tell
us that "it is by God that kings reign, and they are from
15 Jove"; for Solomon, himself a king, considers that even
lesser officers also, namely judges, are from the same God,
Prov. 8. 15, 16; and from the same Jove Homer, in the first
Iliad: ". . . judges who at Zeus's hand guard the dooms."
Surely all we are of God likewise, and God's offspring. There-
20 fore this universal right of God's takes not away the people's
right; so all other kings not named to their office by God are
indebted and obliged for their authority to the people only,
and consequently are accountable to them for it.

This, though the common people are apt to flatter their
25 kings, yet kings themselves acknowledge, whether good ones,
as Sarpedon in Homer, or bad ones, as those tyrants in the
Lyrist.

Γλαῦκε τίη δὴ νῶϊ τετιμήμεσθα μάλιστα, etc.
Glauce cur nos maximo honore afficimur
In Lycia, omnes autem nos tanquam Deos intuentur?

Ipse sibi respondet; *quia virtute cæteris prælucemus: quare*
5 *fortiter pugnemus,* inquit, *ne Lycii nobis ignaviam objiciant:*
quâ voce et honores regios à populo acceptos, et bellicæ administrationis rationem populo reddendam esse innuit. Mali
autem reges, ut metum populo incutiant, Deum imperii regii
authorem palàm prædicant: tacitis autem votis nullum nu-
10 men præter Fortunam venerantur. Juxta illud Horatii,

Te Dacus asper, te profugi Scythæ,
Regúmque matres barbarorum, et
Purpurei metuunt tyranni,
Injurioso ne pede proruas
15 Stantem columnam, neu populus frequens
Ad arma cessantes, ad arma
Concitet, imperiúmque frangat.

Si ergo reges hodie per Deum regnant, etiam populi per Deum
in libertatem se vindicant, quandoquidem omnia à Deo et per
20 Deum fiunt. Utrumque etiam æquè testatur Scriptura, et
reges per eum regnare, et per eum solio dejici; cùm tamen id
utrumque longè sæpius à populo fieri perspiciamus, quàm
à Deo. Jus itaque populi pariter ac regis, quicquid est, à Deo

Glaucus, wherefore have we twain the chiefest honor
In Lycia, and all men look on us as gods?

Himself answers himself: "Because we outshine the rest
in valor; wherefore let us fight manfully," says he, "lest the
5 Lycians tax us with cowardice." In which words he intimates
both that kings derive their royalty from the people, and that
for their conduct of war they are accountable to them. Bad
kings indeed, to strike terror into their people, declare publicly that God is the author of their royal power, yet in their
10 secret prayers reverence no other divinity but Fortune. The
well-known passage in Horace is in point:

Wild Dacians fear thee, thee nomad Scythians fear,
Barbarian tyrants' mothers dread thee,
Scarlet-enrobèd usurpers tremble,

15   Lest thou with foot irreverent tumble down
Their stately column, while the mob pouring in
To arms arouse the slow to arms and
Instantly shatter the tyrant's power.

If it is by God, therefore, that kings nowadays reign, it is
20 by God too that peoples assert their liberty, since all things
are of him and by him. Scripture bears like witness both that
by him kings reign and that by him they are cast down from
their thrones, though yet we perceive that the one and the
other are brought about far oftener by the people than by
25 God. The right of the people then is as much from God as is
the right of the king—whatever that is. And whenever any

est. Populus ubicunque sine Deo manifesto regem creavit,
potest eodem jure suo regem rejicere. Tyrannum sanè tollere
quàm constituere divinius est; plusque Dei cernitur in populo
quoties injustum abdicat regem, quàm in rege qui innocen-
5 tem opprimit populum. Immo reges noxios Deo authore judicat populus: hoc enim ipso honore dilectos suos decoravit
Deus, Psal. 149. ut Christum regem suum laudibus celebran-
tes, gentium reges, quales sub Evangelio sunt omnes tyranni,
vinculis coercerent, ínque eos jus scriptum exercerent, qui
10 jure omni scripto atque legibus solutos se esse gloriantur: ne
quis tam stolidè, ne quis tam impiè credat tanti esse apud
Deum reges, ferè mortalium ignavissimos, ut eorum nutu
orbis terrarum totus pendeat et gubernetur; eorum ut gratiâ,
præque illis, divinum, ut ita dicam, hominum genus eodem
15 quo bruta et vilissima quæque animalia loco atque numero
habendum sit. Age nunc, ne nihil enim agas, M. Aurelium,
quasi tyrannis faventem, in medium profers; at satius tibi fuit
Marcum Aurelium non attigisse. Ille an Deum de principibus
solùm judicare dixerit, nescio. Xiphilinus certè, quem citas,
20 de αὐταρχία, loquitur; περὶ αὐταρχίας ὁ Θεὸς μόνος κρίνειν
δύναται· αὐταρχίαν autem monarchiæ synonymum illic esse
non assentior; eóque minùs quo sæpiùs præcedentia lego; nam
qui cohæreat, aut quid sibi velit aliena illa sententia subitò in-

people, without some visible designation of God Himself, have appointed a king, they can by the same right put him down. To depose a tyrant certainly is a more godlike action than to set one up; and there appears much more of God in
5 the people whenever they depose an unjust king than in the king that oppresses an innocent people. Nay, the people have a warrant from God to judge wicked kings, for God has conferred this very honor upon his saints, Psalm 149, that while they celebrate the praises of Christ their own king, yet as for
10 the kings of the heathen, (and such, according to the Gospel, are all tyrants), "they shall bind them with chains . . . to execute upon them the judgment written"—even upon them that boast themselves unbound by any laws or judgment written! Let none then be so stupid and wicked as to think that
15 kings, commonly the worst of men, are so high in God's account that the whole world is to hang upon their nod and governance, and that for their sakes and on their account the human race divine, if I may so call it, should be reckoned and treated as abject brute beasts.

20   After all this, rather than say nothing, you publish your discovery that Marcus Aurelius countenanced tyranny; but you had better have let him alone. I cannot say whether he ever affirmed that God is the sole judge of princes. Xiphilinus, to be sure, whom you quote on an αὐταρχία, says: "Con-
25 cerning an αὐταρχία God alone has power to judge." But that an αὐταρχία is there synonymous with monarchy I cannot agree; and the less the oftener I read what goes before. Indeed any reader would wonder how that outlandish opinion, ab-

sititia, qui legerit miretur; præsertim cùm Marcus Aurelius
Imperatorum optimus, non aliter cum populo egerit, ut Capitolinus tradit, quàm est actum sub civitate libera; jus autem
populi quin supremum tunc fuerit nemo dubitat. Idem Thra-
5 seam, Helvidium, Catonem, Dionem, Brutum tyrannicidas
omnes, aut istam gloriam æmulantes coluisse, sibique reipublicæ formam proposuisse in qua æquis legibus, parique jure
omnia administrarentur, in primo libro de vita sua profitetur:
in quarto, non se, sed legem, dominum esse. Agnovit etiam
10 omnia Senatûs populique esse: nos, inquit, adeò nihil proprium habemus, ut in vestris ædibus habitemus. Hæc Xiphilinus. Tantum abfuit ut quicquam jure regio sibi arrogaret.
Moriens, filium suum regnaturum ea lege Romanis commen-
davit, si dignus esset: jus itaque illud regnandi absolutum
15 atque fictitium, tanquam a Deo per manus traditum, illam
denique αὐταρχίαν præ se non tulit. *Plena* tamen *omnia*
Græcorum et Latinorum monumenta esse aïs: at nusquam
visa: *plena Judæorum;* et tamen addis, *Judæos in plerisque*
regiæ potestati minùs æquos fuisse: immo Græcos et Latinos
20 multo minùs Tyrannis æquos et reperisti et reperies; multo
minus Judæos, si liber ille Samuelis in quo is, 1 Sam. 10, jus

ruptly engrafted upon the context, hangs together with it, or
what is its own meaning; especially since Marcus Aurelius, best
of emperors, conducted himself towards the people, Capitolinus tells us, just as if Rome had still been a free republic. And
5 we all know that when it was so, the supreme power was in
the people. The same emperor, in the first book of his auto-
biography, openly professes that he revered Thraseas, and
Helvidius, and Cato, and Dion, and Brutus, who were all
tyrant-slayers, or affected that reputation, and that he pro-
10 posed to himself a form of government under which all men
might equally enjoy the benefit of the law, and right and
justice be equally administered to all. And in his fourth book
he says the law is master, and not he. He acknowledged that
all power and property belong to the Senate and the people:
15 we are so far, says he, from having anything of our own, that
we live in your house. Thus Xiphilinus. So little did he arro-
gate aught to himself by virtue of a royal right. When he
was dying he offered the Romans his son for his successor, to
rule upon condition he should prove worthy. He exhibited
20 not, then, that absolute and imaginary right of sovereignty
supposed to be delivered by God's hand,—made, in short, no
pretence to that αὐταρχία of yours.

   Still you say that "the annals of Greece and Rome are full."
But nobody has seen them anywhere. "So are the annals of
25 the Jews." And yet, you add, "the Jews in most respects were
unfavorable to royal power." Nay, you have found and you
will find that both the Greeks and the Latins were exceedingly
unfavorable to tyrants; the Jews too—if that book that Sam-

regni descripserat, exstaret; quem librum Doctores Hebræorum à regibus discerptum aut combustum esse tradiderunt,
quo impuniùs tyrannidem in suos exercerent. Circumspice
jam, numquid captare possis: occurrit tibi rex David postre-
5 mò torquendus, Psal. 17; *á facie tua judicium meum prodeat:*
ergo, inquit Barnachmoni, *nullus judicat regem nisi Deus.*
Et tamen similius veri videtur, Davidem hæc scripsisse cùm à
Saule vexatus, ne Jonathanis quidem judicium, quamvis jam
tum unctus à Deo, detrectabat; *si est in me iniquitas, tu me*
10 *affice morte,* inquit, 1 Sam. 20. deinde ut quivis alius ab
hominibus falsò accusatus, ad judicium Dei provocat; id se-
quentia declarant, *tui oculi vident quæ recta sunt, cùm explo-*
raveris cor meum, etc. quid hoc ad judicium regium, aut fo-
rense? Sanè jus regium illi maximè labefactant atque destru-
15 unt, qui fundamentis tam fallacibus niti, atque exædificari
produnt. En tritum illud tandem, et aulicorum nostratium
argumentum palmarium, *Tibi soli peccavi,* Ps. 51. 6. quasi
verò rex David in mœrore et lacrymis pœnitentiam agens, sor-
didatus et squalidus in terra jacens, misericordiam à Deo sup-
20 pliciter petens, quicquam de jure regio cogitaverit hæc loqu-
utus; cùm se vix jure mancipii dignum esse arbitraretur. An
omnem Dei populum, fratres suos usque adeò præ se con-

uel wrote of "the manner of the kingdom," 1 Sam. 10., were
extant; which book, the Hebrew doctors tell us, the kings tore
in pieces or burnt that they might tyrannize over their subjects with the more impunity.

5   Now look about and see whether you can catch hold of
somewhat or other. Finally you come to wrest David's words
in Psalm 17: "Let my sentence come forth from thy presence": therefore, says Barnachmoni, "None but God judges
the king." And yet it seems rather likely that David penned
10 these words when he was persecuted by Saul, and when,
though already God's anointed, he did not decline being
judged even by Jonathan. "If there be iniquity in me, slay me
thyself," he says, 1 Sam. 20. Thereupon, like anyone else that
is falsely accused by men, he appeals to the judgment of God,
15 as appears in the sequel: "Thine eyes behold the thing that is
right, for thou has searched mine heart," etc. What has this
to do with a judgment passed by a king or a court of law?
Certainly they do most to shake and pull down the right of
kings who expose how it is built upon and rests upon so
20 treacherous a foundation.

Then you come with that threadbare argument, the prize
argument of our courtiers: "Against thee, thee only, have I
sinned," Ps. 51. 4. As if King David, when doing penance
with tears and grief, when in sackcloth and ashes he lay upon
25 the ground imploring God's mercy, said this with any thought
of a king's right, at a moment when he deemed himself scarce
worthy the right of a slave! And can we think that he despised
all God's people, his own brethren, to that degree, as to be-

tempsit, ut cædibus, adulteriis, rapinis peccare in eos non se
posse censeret? absit à rege tam sancto tanta superbia, támque
fœda ignoratio vel sui vel proximi. *Tibi* igitur *soli peccavi,*
proculdubio intelligendum est, tibi præcipuè. Utcunque sit,
5 profectò verba psallentis, et sententiæ affectibus plenæ haud-
quaquam sunt ad jus explicandum accommodatæ, aut eò tra-
hendæ. At *non est in jus vocatus, nec coram synedrio causam
capitis dixit.* Esto; quî enim potuit id resciri, quod adeò sine
arbitris, et secreto peractum fuit, ut per aliquot fortasse annos
10 (cujusmodi aulæ arcana sunt) vix unus aut alter conscius fuisse videatur, 2 Sam. 12, *Tu hoc clam fecisti.* Deinde quid si
in privatis etiam puniendis cessaret synedrium? numquis inde
puniendos non esse argumentabitur? Sed ratio obscura non
est; ipse se condemnaverat; v. 5, *reus capitis vir ille qui fecit
15 hoc;* cui statim subjicit propheta, *tu vir ille es;* prophetæ etiam
judicio capitis reus. Veruntamen Deus pro suo jure atque in
Davidem eximiâ clementiâ, et peccato absolvit regem, et
ipsâ mortis sententiâ, quam is in semetipsum pronuntiaverat,
v. 13, *non es moriturus.* Nunc in advocatum nescio quem
20 sanguinarium debaccharis, et in eo totus es ut perorationem

lieve that he might perpetrate upon them murder, and adultery, and robbery, and yet not be sinning against them? Far be it from so holy a king ever to have been guilty of such pride, or such abominable ignorance of himself and his

5 neighbor! Unquestionably, then, "against thee only have I sinned" means 'against thee chiefly.' But however this may be, the words and thoughts of the psalmist, rhapsodical and passionate, are nowise fitted to expound law, nor should be dragged into that use.

10   "But David was never summoned, or made to plead for his life before the Sanhedrim." Of course he was not. How could his sin have been found out, which was committed so secretly that perhaps for some years after (such are secrets at court) not above one or two seem to have been privy to it?

15 2 Sam. 12. "Thou didst it secretly." Moreover, if the Sanhedrim should neglect to punish private persons, would anyone allege this as proof that these are not punishable? But the reason why David was not proceeded against as a malefactor is not much in the dark. Though he had condemned

20 himself in the fifth verse, "The man that hath done this thing shall surely die," and though the prophet at once replies, "Thou art the man," so that in the prophet's judgment also he deserved death, yet God by his sovereignty and his singular mercy to David absolves him both from the guilt of his sin and

25 from the sentence of death as well which he had pronounced against himself: verse 13, "Thou shalt not die."

Next you rage against some "bloodthirsty" advocate or other, and go at it body and soul to refute his peroration. Let

ejus refellas: de qua ipse viderit; ego quod propositum mihi
est, id ago ut quàm paucissimis absolvam. Quædam tamen
præterire non possum; primùm, insignes repugnantias tuas:
qui p. 30 hæc habes: *Israëlitæ non deprecantur injustum re-*
5 *gem, violentum, raptorem, et quales esse solerent qui pessimi.*
At p. 42 Advocatum vellicas quòd Israëlitas tyrannum petîsse
arguerat. *An de fumo,* inquis, *in flammam ire præcipites ma-*
luerunt, id est, sævitiam pessimorum tyrannorum experiri po-
tiùs quàm judices malos pati quibus jam assueverant? Illic
10 Hebræos maluisse aïs tyrannos quàm judices, hic judices maluisse quàm tyrannos; et *nihil minùs quàm tyrannum volu-*
isse. De tuo igitur respondebit tibi advocatus; juxta enim te
omnis rex jure regio tyrannus est. Quod sequitur bene habet,
authoritatem in populo maximam tunc fuisse, quòd judices
15 *repudiârunt, regem optârunt.* Memineris, cùm hoc ego à te
reposcam. Negas *Deum iratum Israëlitis regem tanquam ty-*
rannum aut pœnam attribuisse, sed ut rem salutarem et bo-
nam. Quod tamen facilè refellitur. Cur enim exclamarent
propter regem illum quem elegerant, nisi quòd res mala erat
20 imperium regium; non quidem per se, sed quòd plerunque,
sicut Propheta hic monet, in superbiam et dominationem se
convertit. Si adhuc non satisfacio, agnosce jam tua, syngra-
pham agnosce tuam, et erubesce. Apparat. ad primatum, *Ira-*

him look to that; I will endeavor to be as short as I can in
what I have undertaken to perform. Yet some things I cannot
pass by,—first your extraordinary self-contradictions. On
your thirtieth page you say: "The Israelites are not begging
5 for an unjust, violent, rapacious king, such as kings are at
their worst." And yet, page 42, you rail at the advocate for
maintaining that the Israelites asked for a tyrant. "Would
they have chosen," say you, "to leap headlong out of the fry-
ing pan into the fire, and risk the cruelty of the worst tyrants,
10 rather than suffer the bad judges to whom they were by now
grown accustomed?" First you said the Hebrews preferred
tyrants to judges; here you say they preferred judges to tyrants, and "a tyrant was the thing they least desired." So
that the advocate will answer you out of your own book, for
15 according to your principle every king is by royal right a
tyrant.

What you say next is very true: "The supreme power was
then in the people, as appears by their rejecting judges and
choosing a king." Remember this when I shall ask you for
20 it again! It is not true, you say, that "God in his anger gave
the Israelites a king as a tyrant or a punishment, but as a thing
good and profitable." But that is easily refuted; for why
should they cry to God because of the king that they had
chosen, were it not that royal government was an evil—not in
25 itself, but because most commonly, even as the prophet here
warns, it does degenerate into pride and tyranny? If you are
not yet satisfied, acknowledge your own words, acknowledge
your own written bond, and blush. In your *Apparatus ad*

tus Deus regem illis dedit offensus eorum peccatis, quod Deum habere regem renuissent. Ita Ecclesia quasi in pœnam ejus delicti, quod à puro Dei cultu desciverat, in unius mortalis monarchæ plusquam regium dominatum data est. Tua igitur

5 similitudo si sibi constat, aut dedit Deus regem Israëlitis in pœnam, et tanquam rem malam, aut dedit Papam ecclesiæ in bonum, et tanquam rem bonam. Quid hoc homine levius, quid insanius? Quis huic in re minimâ fidem habeat, qui tantis in rebus quid asserat, et mox neget, nihil pensi habet. Af-

10 firmas p. 29, *regem legibus solutum esse apud omnes gentes; sic Oriens judicavit, sic Occidens:* At p. 43, *omnes reges Orientis* κατὰ νόμον *et legitimos fuisse; immo Ægypti reges in maximis minimisque rebus legibus obstrictos,* cùm initio capitis hoc te probaturum pollicitus sis, omnes reges *solutos*

15 *legibus esse, leges dare, non accipere.* Equidem non irascor tibi, aut enim insanis, aut stas à nobis. Hoc certè oppugnare est, non defendere, hoc regem est ludos facere. Sin minùs, Catullianum profectò illud in te aptissimè quadrat, sed inversum; nam quantò quis unquam optimus poeta fuit, tanto tu

20 pessimus omnium patronus. Certè nisi stupor ille quo advocatum esse *demersum* aïs, te potiùs obcæcavit, jam tute *obbrutuisse* te senties. Nunc *omnibus quoque gentium regibus*

Primatum, "God gave them a king in his anger," you say, "being offended at their sin in refusing to have God for their king. So the Church, as if in punishment for its crime of forsaking the pure worship of God, has been delivered up to the
5 more than kingly government of one mortal head." Therefore if your own comparison holds, either God gave the children of Israel a king to their loss and as an evil, or he gave the Church a Pope for its profit and as a good. Was there ever anything more lightheaded and mad than this man? Who
10 would trust him in the least thing, that in things of so great concern says and presently unsays without attaching the slightest weight to the matter? You tell us in your twentyninth page that "among all nations, kings are loosed from law; this was the judgment both of the Eastern and of the
15 Western world." And yet, page 43, you say "that all the kings of the East were legal and lawful, nay, that the very kings of Egypt in all matters great or small were tied to laws"; though in the beginning of this chaper you had undertaken to demonstrate "that kings are bound by no laws, that they give laws
20 but receive none." For my part I am not angry with you, for either you are mad or you are of our side. Surely this is attacking, not defending, the king; this is making game of him; or if you are in earnest, that phrase of Catullus's fits you squarely, but contrariwise, for by as much as anyone was ever the best
25 of poets, by so much are you the worst of all defenders. Unless that stupidity in which, you complain, the advocate you mention is "sunk," has blinded you instead, you shall now feel that you are yourself "become a very brute." For now

leges datas fuisse fateris; *non tamen ut iis tenerentur, judiciorum metu et pœnæ capitis.* Quod nequedum ex scriptura, neque ex ullo authore fide digno ostendisti. Tu igitur paucis accipe: leges civiles iis dare qui legibus non tenentur, stultum
5 et ridiculum est; omnes alios punire, uni duntaxat omnium scelerum impunitatem dare, cùm lex neminem excipiat, iniquissimum est. Quæ duo in sapientes legumlatores minimè cadunt, multò minùs in Deum. Ut omnes autem videant te nullo modo ex Hebræorum scriptis id probare, quod proban-
10 dum hoc capite susceperas, esse ex magistris tua sponte confiteris, *qui negant alium suis majoribus regem agnoscendum fuisse præter Deum, datum autem in pœnam fuisse.* Quorum ego in sententiam pedibus eo. Non decet enim, neque dignum est regem esse, nisi qui cæteris omnibus longè antecellit; ubi
15 multi sunt æquales, ut sunt in omni civitate plurimi, imperium ex æquo atque per vices dandum esse arbitror: æquali, aut plerumque deteriori, ac sæpissime stulto servire omnes, quis non indignissimum putet? Nec *ad commendationem regalis imperii* plus *facit,* quòd Christus à regibus originem
20 duxit, quàm facit ad pessimorum regum commendationem, Christum eos habuisse nepotem. *Rex est Messias:* agnoscimus, gaudemus, et quàm citissimè veniat oramus; dignus enim est, nec ei quisquam similis aut secundus: interim regia guberna-

you confess that "the kings of all nations too have laws prescribed to them, yet not so as to be held to them by fear of
judgment and captial punishment." Which yet you have
proved neither from Scripture nor from any authority worthy
5 of credit. Observe then in few: to prescribe civil laws to such
as are not bound by them is silly and ridiculous; to punish all
others, but leave some one man at liberty to commit all sorts
of wickedness without fear of punishment, is most unjust, for
law makes no exception. These two things simply do not
10 happen to wise lawgivers, much less to God. But for all to
see that you nowise prove out of the writings of the Hebrews
what you had undertook in this chapter to prove by them, you
confess of your own accord that there are some rabbins "who
affirm that a king other than God ought not to have been
15 acknowledged by their forefathers, yet was given them for
their punishment." With their opinion I agree.

He is not fit or worthy to be king that does not far excel
all the rest. But where many are equal, as in all governments
the majority are, they ought, I think, to have an equal inter-
20 est in the government, and hold it by turns. But that all men
should be slaves to one that is their equal, or, as generally
happens, their inferior, and most often a fool, who would
not think this a thing most unworthy? Nor does it "recommend royal government," that Christ had kings for ancestors,
25 any more than it recommends some very bad kings, that they
had Christ for a descendant. "The Messiah is a king." We
acknowledge him, we rejoice, and we pray that he will come
as soon as may be; for he is worthy, nor is there any that is like

tio commissa indignis et immerentibus, ut plerumque fieri
solet, plus mali quàm boni attulisse humano generi rectè existimatur. Nec continuò sequitur omnes reges tyrannos esse.
Verùm ita esto: do tibi hoc, ne me nimis tenacem putes; utere
5 tu jam dato. *Hæc duo sequuntur,* inquis, *Deus ipse rex fuerit
tyrannorum dicendus, et quidem tyrannus ipse maximus.*
Horum alterum si non sequitur, sequitur profectò illud quod
toto libro tuo semper ferè sequitur, te non scripturæ solùm,
sed tibimet perpetuò contradicere, ut qui proxima periodo
10 suprà dixeras, *unum Deum regem esse omnium rerum, quas
et ipse creavit.* Creavit autem et tyrannos et Dæmonas; eorum
itaque rex vel tuâ ipsius sententiâ. In alterum despuimus, et
blasphemum illud tibi os obturatum volumus, qui Deum
affirmes tyrannum esse maximum, si tyrannorum, quod ipse
15 sæpius dicis, rex et dominus dicatur. Sed nec rem regiam
multò plus adjuvas, dum ostendis, Mosen etiam cum *summa
potestate regem fuisse.* Nam fuerit sanè, vel quivis alius, dum-
modò is sit qui res nostras, quemadmodum Moses, *ad Deum
referre* possit, Exod. 18. 19. Verùm neque Mosi, quanquam
20 is Dei quasi sodalis fuit, licuit in Dei populo quicquid libuit
facere. Quid enim ille? *Venit ad me hic populus,* inquit, *ad
consulendum Deum;* non ergo ad mandata Mosis accipienda.
Tum suscipit Jethro, *esto tu pro hoc populo erga Deum, et*

unto him or that can follow him. Meanwhile the royal power, entrusted to unworthy and undeserving persons, as most commonly it is, may well be thought to have done mankind more harm than good. Nor does it follow for all this that all kings are tyrants. But suppose it did; I grant you this lest you think me obstinate; now make the best of it. "These two conclusions follow," you say; "God himself would properly be called king of tyrants, and indeed himself the greatest tyrant." If the first of these is a non-sequitur, at least there does follow the thing that almost always follows from your whole book, viz., that you perpetually contradict not only the Scriptures but your own self. For in the very next sentence above, you have affirmed that "there is one God, the king of all things, having himself created them." Now he created as well tyrants and devils, and consequently by your own reasoning is their king too. The second of your conclusions we detest, and wish that blasphemous mouth of yours stopped, with which you affirm God to be the worst of tyrants, if he is to be called, as you so often say he is, their king and lord.

Nor do you much advantage the royal cause by telling us that Moses "was a king, with supreme power." So mote he be indeed, or any other for that matter, who could, like Moses, "bring the causes unto God," Exod. 18. 19. But even Moses, though, so to speak, God's confidant, was not permitted to do whatever he pleased to God's people. For, what says he? "The people come unto me to inquire of God"—not, then, to receive Moses's own commands. Then Jethro takes up the point: "Be thou for the people to Godward, . . . and

commonefacias eos de legibus Dei. Et Moses, Deut. 4. 5. *do-*
cui vos statuta et judicia, quemadmodum præcepit mihi Deus.
Unde *fidelis* dicitur *in tota domo Dei,* Num. *12.* Rex itaque
Jehova tum populi fuit; Moses veluti interpres tantùm Je-
5 hovæ regis. Impium igitur et sacrilegum te esse oportet, qui
summam hanc potestatem à Deo ad hominem injussus ausis
transferre, quam ipse Moses non summam sed vicariam tantùm et intermediam sub præsenti numine obtinuit. Accedit
etiam cumulus ad improbitatem tuam, quòd Mosen hìc sum-
10 ma potestate regem fuisse dicis; cùm in Apparatu ad Primatum, p. 230, *Eum in commune cum* LXX *senioribus populum*
rexisse; et primum populi non dominum fuisse dixeris. Si
igitur rex fuit, ut erat certè, et regum optimus, idque, sicut ipse
aïs, cum *potestate planè summa et regia,* nec tamen dominus,
15 neque solus populum regebat, vel te authore, necessariò sequitur, reges, quamvis summa potestate præditos, jure tamen
regio atque summo non esse dominos, neque solos populum
regere debere; quanto minùs ad libitum suum? Jam verò quâ
impudentiâ Dei mandatum ementiris, *de rege statim atque*
20 *ingressi essent terram sanctam sibi constituendo,* Deut. *17.*
supprimis enim veteratoriè quod præcedit, *si dixeris, statuam*
super me regem: túque memento quid à te jam reposcam;

thou shalt teach them God's ordinances and laws." And
Moses again, Deut. 4. 5. "I have taught you statutes and judgments, even as the Lord my God commanded me." Hence it
is that he is said to have been "faithful in all God's house,"
5 Numb. 12. So that the people's king was then Jehovah, and
Moses as it were an interpreter only of Jehovah the king. Impious and sacrilegious you must needs be who without warrant have dared shift this supreme power from God to man—
a power which, as held by Moses himself, was not supreme,
10 but only deputed or intermediate under God's present deity.
To heap up your wickedness to its summit, you here say
Moses was a king with absolute power, yet in your *Apparatus
ad Primatum,* page 230, you say: "Together with the seventy
elders he ruled the people, and was their foremost, but not
15 their master." If Moses therefore was a king, as certainly he
was, and the best of kings, and had, as you say he had, "sovereign royal power," and yet, again as you say, was neither the
people's master nor their sole ruler, then it necessarily follows
that kings, though endued with the supreme power, yet
20 ought not by virtue of that sovereign royal right of theirs be
lords over the people, or sole rulers, much less rulers according to their own will and pleasure.

With what shamelessness you counterfeit a supposed command of God "to set up a king over them as soon as they
25 should be possessed of the Holy Land," Deut. 17! For you
craftily leave out the preceding words, *"When thou . . .
shalt say,* I will set a king over me." And pray call to mind
also what you said before, page 42, and what I shall now ask

cùm dixeris p. 42, *liberrima tunc potestate populus erat præ-
ditus.* Nunc iterum fanaticus an profanus esse velis, ipse
videris. *Deus,* inquis, *cùm tanto antè determinaverit regium
regimen instituendum tanquam optimum populi illius regendi statum, quomodo hæc conciliabuntur? Propheta re-
pugnavit, Deus sic egit cum propheta, ut quasi nollet.* Videt
se illaqueatum, videt se impeditum; Jam attendite quanta cum
malitia adversus Prophetam, impietate adversus Deum, expedire se quærat: *cogitandum in his est,* inquit, *Samuelem
esse cujus filii populum tunc judicabant, eos populus repudia-
bat ob corrupta judicia; Samuel igitur noluit filios suos à populo rejici; Deus ut gratificaretur prophetæ suo, innuit non
valde sibi placere, quod populus desideraret.* Dic uno verbo,
improbe, quod per ambages dicis; Samuel populo fucum fecit,
Samueli Deus. Non advocatus ergò, sed tu *ceritus* ille et *lym-
phaticus* es, qui modò ut regem honores, nil Deum revereris.
Isne tibi Samuel videtur, qui saluti aut charitati patriæ filio-
rum avaritiam et ambitionem præposuerit, qui populo recta
et salutaria petenti, tam callido consilio, tamque váfro illuserit,
falsa pro veris docuerit? Isne tibi Deus, qui in re tam turpi
cuivis gratificaretur, aut cum populo simulatè ageret? Aut

you to recite, viz. "The people were then possessed of quite unlimited power."

Now once more you shall decide whether you are sacrilegious or crazed. "God," you say, "having so long before appointed a kingly government as best and most proper for that people, what shall we say to the Prophet's opposing it, and God's own dealing with the Prophet as if himself were rather against it? How do these things agree?" He sees himself enmeshed, he sees himself entangled; observe now with how great malice against the Prophet, and impiety against God, he seeks to disentangle himself! "We must consider," says he, "that it was Samuel's own sons who then judged the people, and that the people rejected them because of their corruption; now Samuel was loth his sons should be laid aside, and God, to gratify his prophet, intimated that what the people desired did not much please him." Speak out, wretch, and never mince the matter: you mean, Samuel deceived the people, and God Samuel. It is not that advocate of yours, therefore, but yourself, that are the "frantic" and "raving" one; who, so you may but honor a king, cast off all reverence to God. Does Samuel seem to you one that would have preferred his sons' ambition and covetousness before his people's grace or safety; one that, when the people sought what was right and beneficial, would have imposed upon them with such sly crafty advice, and made them believe things that were not? Does God himself seem to you one that in so disgraceful an affair would stoop to oblige a friend? Would God act a part before the people? So, then, either what Samuel taught the people

ergò jus regium non erat quod Propheta populo exposuit, aut
jus illud, teste Deo et Propheta, malum, molestum, violentum, inutile, sumptuosum reipub. erat; aut denique, quod
nefas est dicere, et Deus et Propheta populo verba dare voluerunt. Passim enim testatur Deus valdè sibi displicuisse quòd
regem petîssent: ver. 7; *Non te, sed me spreverunt ne regnem
super ipsos, secundùm illa facta quibus dereliquerunt me et
coluerunt Deos alienos:* planè quasi species quædam idolo-
latriæ videretur regem petere, qui adorari se, et honores propè
divinos tribui sibi postulat. Sanè qui supra omnes leges terre-
num sibi dominum imponit, propè est ut sibi Deum statuat
alienum; Deum utique haud sæpe rationabilem, sed profligatâ
sæpiùs ratione brutum, et belluinum. Sic 1 Sam. 10. 19, *Vos
sprevistis Deum vestrum qui ipse servat vos ab omnibus malis
et angustiis vestris, cùm dixistis ei, Regem præpones nobis:*
et cap. 12. 12, Vos regem petistis, *cùm Jehova sit rex vester:*
et ver. 17, *Videte malum verum magnum esse coram Jehova,
petendo vobis regem.* Et contemptim Hosea de rege, c. 13.
10, 11; *Ubi rex tuus, ubinam est? servet te jam in civitatibus
tuis. Ubi vindices tui? quoniam dixisti, da mihi regem et proceres: dedi tibi regem in ira mea.* Hinc Gedeon ille Heros rege
major, *Non dominabor in vos, neque filius meus in vos do-*

was not the right of kings, or else that right, by the testimony of God and of the Prophet, was an evil thing, burdensome, injurious, unprofitable, and costly to the commonwealth; or lastly (which, as sacrilege, is inadmissible), both God and
5 the Prophet wished to deceive the people.

God frequently protests that he was extremely displeased with them for asking a king, verse 7: "They have not rejected thee, but they have rejected me, that I should not reign over them. According to all the works which they have
10 done . . . wherewith they have forsaken me, and served other gods." As if it were considered a kind of idolatry to ask for a king, who requires adoration and worship almost divine. Surely, whoever subjects himself to an earthly master that is above all law comes but little short of setting up a
15 strange god, a god that at least is seldom rational, but too often abjectly brutish and beastly. So 1 Sam. 10. 19.: "And ye have this day rejected your God, who himself saved you out of all your adversities and your tribulation, and ye have said unto him, Nay, but set a king over us"; and chapter 12,
20 verse 12: Ye asked for a king "when the Lord your God was your king"; and verse 17: "See that your wickedness is great, which ye have done in the sight of the Lord, in asking you a king." And Hosea speaks contemptuously of the king, chap. 13. 10–11: "Where is thy king? Let him now save thee in
25 thy cities. Where are thy judges? For that thou saidst, give me a king and princes, I gave thee a king in mine anger." Hence it is that heroic Gideon, greater than a king, "I will not rule over you," says he, "neither shall my son rule over

minabitur, sed dominabitur in vos Jehova, Jud. 8. planè ac si simul docuisset, non hominis esse dominari in homines, sed solius Dei. Hinc Hebræorum rempublicam, in qua Deus principatum solus tenuit, θεοκρατίαν vocat Josephus contra

5 Apionem Grammaticum Ægyptium et maledicum tuî simi-lem. Populus denique resipiscens apud Isaiam 26. 13, cala-mitosum hoc sibi fuisse queritur, quòd alios præter Deum dominos habuisset. Indicio sunt hæc omnia regem irato Deo Israëlitis fuisse datum. In historia tyranni Abimelechi quis

10 est cui non risum moveas? de quo dicitur, cùm is partim saxo à muliere, partim armigeri gladio interfectus fuit. *reddidit Deus malum Abimelechi. Hæc,* inquis, *historia potentissimè adstruit Deum solum regum judicem esse et vindicem:* immo tyrannorum, nebulonum, nothorum, si hoc valebit: quicun-

15 que per fas aut nefas tyrannidem occupaverit, is jus regium statim in populum adeptus erit, pœnas effugit, confestim arma magistratui de manibus fluent, mussare deinceps populus non audebit. Verùm quid si magnus aliquis latro hoc modo in bello periisset, an Deus ergo solus latronum vindex? Quid si

20 carnificis manu lege damnatus, an ideo minùs illi Deus ma-lum reddidisset? Ne judices quidem eorum unquam legisti

you; the Lord shall rule over you," Judges 8; intimating
thereby that it belongs not to a man, but to God only, to exercise dominion over men. And hence Josephus in his book
against Apion, an Egyptian grammarian and a foulmouthed
5 fellow like you, calls the commonwealth of the Hebrews, in
which God was sole ruler, a Theocracy. In Isaiah 26. 13 the
people, in their right minds at last, complain that it had been
mischievous to them to have had other rulers than God. All
which passages go to prove that the king was given the
10 Israelites in God's anger.

Who can forbear laughing at the use you make of the story
of the usurper Abimelech? Of whom it is said when he was
killed, partly by a woman that hurled a piece of millstone
upon him, and partly by the sword of his own armor-bearer,
15 that "God rendered the wickedness of Abimelech." "This
history," say you, "proves strongly that God alone is the judge
and punisher of kings." Yea, if this argument hold, he is the
only judge and punisher of tyrants, rascals, and bastard
usurpers. Whoever by hook or crook can seize a throne shall
20 have got a sovereign kingly right over the people, and is
out of all danger of punishment; instantly the weapons shall
fall from the magistrates' hands, and the people thenceforth
not dare to mutter. What if some strong thief had perished
in like manner by violence, would any man infer that God
25 alone is the judge and punisher of thieves? Or what if he had
been legally convicted, and had died by the executioner's hand
—would it have been any the less God that rendered his
wickedness? You have never read that the judges of the chil-

lege postulatos; tamen *in optimatum statu vel principem, si quid committat, posse ac debere judicari,* ultrò fateris *p.* 47. cur non item tyrannus in regno? quia Deus reddidit malum Abimelechi. At reddidit quoque mulier illa, reddidit etiam armiger, in quos ille ambos jus regium habere præ se tulit. Quid si reddidisset magistratus? an non is idcirco Dei gladium gerit, ut malum malis reddat? Ab hoc *potentissimo* de morte Abimelechi argumento ad verborum contumelias more suo se convertit; nil nisi *cœnum* et *lutum* ore funditat; cum eorum quæ promisit se probaturum, nihil vel ex sacris libris, vel ex rabbinicis probaverit. Nam neque regem legibus solutum esse, nec cur puniri, si delinquat, solus mortalium non debeat, quicquam ostendit. Immo suis ipse testibus se induit, et sententiam suæ contrariam esse veriorem suamet ipse opera demonstrat. Cúmque argumentis parùm proficiat, criminationibus atrocissimis omnium in nos odium excitare conatur, quasi rege optimo et innocentissimo crudeliter sublato. *An Solomon,* inquit, *melior rex Carolo I. fuit?* Sunt, ut verum fatear, qui patrem ejus Jacobum cum Solomone comparare non dubitaverint, et natalibus quidem anteferre. Solomon

dren of Israel were ever proceeded against according to law,
and yet you admit of your own accord (p. 47) that "in an
aristocracy even the prince may and ought to undergo judgment if he break the law." And in a kingdom why may not a
5 tyrant likewise undergo judgment? Because God rendered
the wickedness of Abimelech! So did the woman, and so did
his own armor-bearer, over both of whom he pretended to a
right of sovereignty. And what if a magistrate had rendered
his wickedness? Does not a magistrate bear God's sword for
10 that very purpose, to render the wicked their wickedness?

Having done with this "most powerful" argument from
the death of Abimelech, he betakes himself, as is his way, to
slanders and calumnies; his discourse does naught but sling
"mud and dirt"; but as for those things that he promised to
15 prove, he has proved not one, either from the Scriptures or
from the rabbinical writings. Nowise does he show that a
king is unbound by law, or why a king, alone of all mortal
men, if he commit a crime should not be punished. Nay, he
gets entangled in those very authorities that he makes use of,
20 and by his own discourse shows the opinion that he argues
against to be the truer. And perceiving that he is like to do but
little good with his arguments, he endeavors to bring odium
upon us by loading us with abominable accusations, as if we
had cruelly put to death the most virtuous innocent prince
25 that ever reigned. "Was Solomon," says he, "a better king
than Charles I?" I confess some have ventured to compare
his father King James with Solomon, nay, to prefer King
James for his illustrious descent. Solomon was David's son,

Davidis filius; is primò Saulis musicus erat: Jacobus, Darlii comitis filius, qui Davidem musicum, reginæ uxoris thalamos nocte ingressum, cum ostio pessulum obdidisse deprehendit, haud multò pòst interfecit, ut narrat Buchananus. Natalibus ergo illustrior Jacobus, et secundus Solomon sæpe dictus; quamvis Davidis musici filius an fuerit, divinandum lectoribus historia illa in medio reliquerit. At Carolum conferre cum Solomone, quî tibi in mentem venire potuerit non video. Quem enim tu Carolum tot laudibus tollis, ejus pervicaciam, avaritiam, crudelitatem, et sævum in omnes pios atque bonos dominatum, ejus bella, incendia, rapinas, et miserorum civium cædes innumeras, dum hæc scribo, Carolus ipse filius in illa publicæ pœnitentiæ sedecula apud Scotos coram populo confitetur atque deplorat: immò tuum illud regium jus ejurat. Verùm si Parallelis tantoperè delectaris, Carolum cum Solomone conferamus. Solomon à meritissimo *fratris* supplicio *regnum auspicatus est:* Carolus à patris funere; non dico à nece, quamvis indicia veneni omnia in corpore patris mortui conspecta sint; ita enim suspicio in Bucchinghamio constitit; quem tamen Carolus, et regis interfectorem et sui patris, non solùm in Summo regni concilio omni culpâ exemit, sed ne omninò res ea Senatûs cognitioni subjiceretur, conventum dissolvit. Solomon *gravissimis tributis*

and David used to be Saul's musician; but King James was the son of the Earl of Darnley, who, Buchanan tells us, caught David the musician in his wife the Queen's bedchamber at night with the door bolted, and killed him not long after. So that King James was of more distinguished origin, and was frequently called a second Solomon, though whether he was the son of David the musician the tale has left uncertain, for readers to guess. But how it could ever come into your head to make a comparison between Charles and Solomon, I cannot see. For that very Charles whom you praise thus to the sky, that very man's obstinacy, and covetousness, and cruelty, his hard mastership to all good and honest men, his wars, and arsons, and plunderings, and slaughters innumerable of his wretched subjects, all this, whilst I am a-writing, does his son Charles himself publicly confess and bewail on the stool of repentance in Scotland, nay, renounces there that kingly right of yours.

Still, if you take such pleasure in Parallels, let us compare King Charles and King Solomon. Solomon "began his reign" with the execution "of his brother," who had justly deserved it. Charles began his with his father's funeral—I do not say his father's *murder,* though all the evidences of poison appeared on the dead body, for that suspicion rested upon Buckingham; whom yet, though murderer of the king and Charles's father, Charles not only cleared of guilt in the highest Council of the realm, but dissolved Parliament to keep the affair by hook or crook from Parliamentary investigation. Solomon "oppressed the people with heavy taxes,"

populum pressit: at ille in templum Dei, et ædificia publica
impendit; Carolus in luxum. Solomon à plurimis uxoribus
ad Idolorum cultum pellectus est; hic ab una. Pellectus in fraudem Solomon, pellexisse alios non legitur; hic alios, non so-
5 lùm uberrimis corruptæ Ecclesiæ præmiis pellexit, sed etiam
edictis et canonibus ecclesiasticis coëgit, ut invisa reformatis
omnibus altaria statuerent, et pictos in pariete crucifixos alta-
ribus imminentes adorarent. At non est ideo *Solomon à populo capitis damnatus.* Nec inde, inquam, sequitur damnari
10 à populo non debuisse; multa enim incidere potuerunt, cur
id tum expedire populo non videretur. Populus certè quid
sui juris esset haud multo pòst et verbis et factis patefecit:
cùm Solomonis filium decem tribus expulerunt; et nisi ma-
turè se in fugam conjecisset, etiam lapidibus regem tantum-
15 modo minacem obruituros fuisse credibile est.

CAPUT III.

CUM satis jam disputatum atque conclusum sit, reges
Mosaïcos ex præscripto Dei omnibus obstrictos legibus pariter cum populo fuisse, nullas legum exceptiones perscriptas inveniri, ut reges *quod vellent, impunè*
20 *possent,* aut ut *à populo puniri ne possent, Deum* proinde *vindictam de his tribunali suo reservâsse* falsissimum esse, sine
authore, sine ratione dictum, videamus an id suadeat Evan-

but he spent that money upon the temple of God and other public buildings; King Charles spent his in extravagances. Solomon was enticed to idolatry by many wives, Charles by one. Though Solomon were himself seduced, we read not that he seduced others; but Charles, as well by the richest benefices of a corrupt Church seduced and enticed others, as by his edicts and ecclesiastical decrees he compelled them to set up altars, which all Protestants abhor, and to bow down to crucifixes painted over them on the wall. But yet not for all this "was Solomon by his people condemned to die." Nor does it follow because he was not, say I, that therefore he ought not to have been; for perhaps there were many circumstances that made it then inexpedient. But not long after, the people by both words and actions made clear what was their right, when ten tribes revolted from Solomon's son; and if he had not made speed to flee, very likely they would have stoned to death even a king who had but threatened them.

CHAPTER III.

IT HAS now been sufficiently argued and proved that the kings of the Jews were by God's ordinance bound to all the laws even as were the people, and that no exemptions from the law are found in Scripture; so that it is quite unauthorized, quite unreasonable, and quite untrue, to say that kings "may do what they list with impunity," or that "they may not be punished by the people," and accordingly that "God has reserved their punishment to his own tribunal."

gelium, quod dissuasit Lex, non imperavit: videamus an Evangelium, divinum illud libertatis præconium, nos in servitutem addicat regibus et tyrannis, quorum ab impotenti imperio etiam servitutis cujusdam magistra lex vetus populum Dei liberavit. Primum argumentum ducis à persona Christi, quem quis nescit non privati solùm, sed etiam servi personam ideò sumpsisse, ut nos liberi essemus. Neque hoc de interna tantùm libertate intelligendum est, non de civili: quàm enim aliena sunt ista quæ Maria, mater Christi, ejus in adventu cecinit, *superbos dissipavit cogitatione cordis ipsorum, detraxit dynastas è thronis, humiles evexit,* si adventus ejus tyrannos potiùs in solio stabilivit, Christianos omnes eorum sævissimo imperio subjecit? Ipse sub tyrannis nascendo, serviendo, patiendo omnem honestam libertatem nobis acquisivit: ut posse servitutem, si necesse est, æquo animo pati, sic posse ad libertatem honestè aspirare non abstulit Christus, sed majorem in modum dedit. Hinc Paulus 1 Cor. 7, non de evangelica solùm, sed de civili libertate sic statuit: *Servus vocatus es? ne sit tibi curæ; sin autem potes liber fieri, potiùs utere; pretio emti estis, ne estote servi hominum.* Frustrà igitur ab exemplo Christi ad servitutem nos hortaris, qui suæ servitutis pretio libertatem nobis etiam civilem confirmavit:

Let us now consider whether the Gospel recommend what
the Law not only did not command but discommended; let
us consider whether the Gospel, heavenly proclamation of
liberty, give us over in slavery to kings and tyrants, from
5 whose outrageous rule the old law, though it taught slavery
of some sort, did set God's people free.

Your first argument you take from the person of Christ.
But who does not know that he put himself into the condition
not only of a subject, but even of a servant, that we might be
10 free? Nor is this to be understood of inward liberty only, to
the exclusion of civil liberty. How out of place are the words
that Mary mother of Christ spake in prophecy of his coming
—"He hath scattered the proud in the imagination of their
hearts; he hath put down the mighty from their seats, and
15 exalted them of low degree"—if his coming rather established tyrants on their thrones, and cast all Christians down
beneath their cruel sway! He himself, by being born, and
serving, and dying, under tyrants, has purchased all rightful
liberty for us. As he has not withheld from us the resignation
20 to submit patiently, if we must, to slavery, so he has not forbidden us to strive nobly for our liberty—nay has granted
this in fuller measure. Hence it is that Paul, 1 Cor. 7. 21, has
resolved thus, not only of evangelical but also of civil liberty:
"Art thou called, being a servant? care not for it; but if thou
25 mayest be made free, use it rather. Ye are bought with a price;
be not ye the servants of men." Vainly then do you endeavor
to argue us into slavery by the example of Christ, who at the
price of servitude for himself established liberty for us, even

Et formam quidem servi nostra vice suscepit, animum verò
liberatoris nunquam non retinuit: unde jus regium quid sit,
longè aliter docuisse ostendam, atque tu doces; qui non regii,
sed tyrannici juris, idque in republica novus professor, si qua
5 gens tyrannum sive hæreditarium, sive adventitium, sive for-
tuitum sortita erit, eam non solùm necessitate, sed etiam religione servam esse statuis. Tuis autem, ut soleo, in te utar testimoniis. Interrogavit Petrum Christus, cùm ab eo coactores
quidam Galilæi didrachma exigebant, Mat. 17, à quibus acci-
10 perent reges terræ tributa, sive censum, à filiis suis, an ab
alienis? respondet ei Petrus, ab alienis. Ergo, inquit Christus,
liberi sunt filii; sed ne offendamus illos, da iis pro me et pro te.
Variè hic locus interpretes exercet, cuinam persolverentur hæc
didrachma, alii sacerdotibus in Sanctuarium, alii Cæsari: ego
15 quidem Herodi persoluta, interverso Sanctuarii reditu, sentio
fuisse. Varia enim ab Herode et filiis ejus exacta tributa, ab
Agrippa tandem remissa narrat Josephus. Hoc autem tribu-
tum per se exiguum, multis aliis adjunctum, grave erat: gra-
via autem fuerint oportet de quibus hic Christus loquitur;
20 alioqui, in republica etiam, pauperes capite censi fuerunt.

civil liberty. He took upon him indeed in our stead the shape
of a servant, but he never did off the soul and purpose of our
deliverer; whereby he taught, as I shall show, a quite other
notion of the right of kings than this you teach. For you
5 preach not the right of kings, but the right of tyrants (a novel
thing in a commonwealth!) and assert that whatever nation
has in fate's lottery drawn a tyrant, whether by inheritance or
by conquest or by chance, is enslaved not merely under compulsion, but under religious obligation.

10   Now, as usual, I will turn your own authorities against you.
When certain Galilean collectors of the tribute money demanded tribute of Peter, Christ asked him, Matt. 17, of
whom the kings of the earth took custom or tribute, of their
own children or of strangers. Peter answers him, Of strangers.
15 Jesus saith unto him: "Then are the children free. Notwithstanding, lest we should offend them, . . . give unto them
for me and thee." This passage troubles the commentators,
who disagree about whom the tribute was paid to. Some say
it was paid to the priests for the use of the sanctuary; others
20 that it was paid to the Emperor; I am of opinion that it was
paid to Herod, who converted to his own use the revenue of
the sanctuary; for Josephus mentions divers sorts of tribute
which Herod and his sons exacted, and which Agrippa finally
remitted. Now the tribute in question, though small in itself,
25 yet being accompanied with many more, was a heavy burden;
indeed that of which Christ speaks here must needs have been
oppressive; under other conditions, even during the commonwealth, poor persons were counted only, not taxed. Hence

Hinc itaque Christus Herodis injustitiam arguendi, cujus sub
ditione erat, occasionem cepit. Qui, cùm cæteri reges terræ
(siquidem patriæ parentes dici se cupiant) non filiis, id est,
civibus suis, sed alienis, bello nempe subactis graviora tributa
5 imperare soleant, hic contra non alienos, sed filios opprimeret.
Utcunque sit, sive filios hìc, cives regum proprios, sive filios
Dei, id est, fideles et in universum Christianos intelligi con-
cedas, ut intelligit Augustinus, certissimum est, si filius fuit
Petrus, et proinde liber, nos etiam authore Christo, liberos
10 esse: vel ut cives, vel ut Christianos: non esse ergo juris regii à
filiis et liberis tributa graviora exigere. Testatur enim Christus persolvisse se, non quod deberet, sed ne illos offendendo
qui exigebant, negotium sibi privatus exhiberet: cùm officium
ac munus longissimè diversum in illo vitæ suæ curriculo ex-
15 plendum sibi nosset. Dum igitur negat Christus jus regium
esse, graviora vectigalia liberis imponere, certè spoliare, diri-
pere, occidere, excruciare proprios cives, et præsertim Christianos, jus esse regium multo evidentiùs negat. Hunc in modum de jure regio cùm et aliàs disputâsse videatur, venire in
20 suspicionem quibusdam cœpit, non se tyrannorum licentiam
pro jure regio habere. Non enim de nihilo erat quòd Pharisæi interrogatione hujusmodi animum ejus tentarent, quòd

therefore Christ took occasion to censure the injustice of
Herod, under whose government he then was, in that,
whereas the rest of the kings of the earth, if indeed they desire
to be called fathers of their country, use not to impose exces-
5 sively heavy taxes upon their children, that is, their subjects,
but upon foreigners, especially when subdued in war; he,
quite contrary, oppressed not strangers but his children. However it be, whether you agree that children here is to be understood as the king's own subjects, or as the children of God,
10 that is, the faithful, and, in general, Christians, as Augustine
understands, this is certain, that if Peter was a child, and
therefore free, then we are so too on Christ's own authority,
either as citizens or as Christians, and that it therefore is not
the right of kings to exact excessive tribute from their own
15 children and freeborn subjects. Christ himself bears witness
that he paid this tribute not because he ought, but in order that
as an individual he might not bring trouble upon himself by
offending those that demanded it; for he knew in his own
mind that he had a far different duty and service to perform—
20 a far other race to run. In denying, then, that it is the right of
kings to burden their freeborn subjects with grievous exac-
tions, Christ yet more plainly denies that it is their right to
spoil and plunder, to massacre and torture their own citizens,
especially Christians. As he seems to have discoursed of the
25 right of kings to this same effect elsewhere too, he began to
fall under certain persons' suspicion that he did not consider
the license of tyrants to be the right of kings. It was not for
nothing that the Pharisees put such questions to him, tempt-

de jure regio percontaturi, eum neminem curare, non respi-
cere personam hominum dixerint; neque de nihilo, quòd is
proposita sibi istiusmodi quæstione irasceretur, Mat. 22. An
te quispiam si insidiosè aggredi, si loquentem captare vellet,
5 si elicere ex te quod fraudi futurum tibi esset, de jure regio sub
rege interrogaret? an tu cuipiam de istoc interroganti iras-
cerere? non opinor. Vel hinc ergo perspicias, non id eum de
jure regio sensisse quod regibus gratum erat. Idem ex responso ejus apertissimè colligitur, quo ille percontatores aman-
10 dare à se potiùs quàm docere videtur. Poscit numisma censûs;
Cujus, inquit, *imago ista est? Cæsaris. Reddite ergo Cæsari
quæ sunt Cæsaris, quæ Dei sunt Deo.* Immò quæ populi sunt
populo reddenda esse quis nescit? Reddite omnibus quod debetis, inquit Paulus, Rom. 13. non ergo Cæsari omnia. Li-
15 bertas nostra non Cæsaris, verùm ab ipso Deo natale nobis
donum est; eam Cæsari cuivis reddere, quam ab eo non accepimus, turpissimum esset, et humana origine indignissimum. Si enim os hominis et vultum aspiciens, interrogaret
quisquam, cujus ista imago esset, annon facilè quivis respon-
20 deret Dei esse? Cùm igitur Dei simus, id est verè liberi, ob
eamque causam soli Deo reddendi, profectò Cæsari nos, id

ing him, and that when they were about to press their in-
quiries concerning the right of kings they told him that he
cared not for any man and regarded not the person of men;
nor was it for nothing that he was angry when such an inquiry
5 was propounded to him, Matt. 22. What if someone should
endeavor slily to approach *you,* and entangle you in your
talk, and question you (this under a monarchy) upon your
own principles concerning the right of kings, in order to
draw from you somewhat to your hurt—would *you* be angry
10 at him? Oh, no! Hence then pray observe that *his* opinions
upon the right of kings were *not* agreeable to kings.

The same may be gathered very clearly from his answer,
by which he seems rather to send away his questioners than
to instruct them. He asks to be shown the tribute money.
15 "Whose image is that?" he says. "Caesar's," say they. "Render therefore unto Caesar," says he, "the things which are
Caesar's; and unto God the things that are God's." And is
there anyone who knows not as well that unto the people
should be rendered the things that are the people's? "Render
20 to all men their dues," says Paul, Rom. 13. So that not all
things are unto Caesar. Our liberty is not Caesar's, nay but
God's own birthday gift to us; and to render unto any Caesar
you like this which we got not from him were an action most
foul, most unworthy the origin of man. If one should look
25 upon the countenance of a man, and inquire whose image
was that, would not any one answer at once that it was God's?
Being then God's own, that is, free in very truth, and consequently to be rendered to none but God, surely we cannot

est, homini, et præsertim injusto, improbo, tyranno in servitutem tradere, sine piaculo et quidem maximo sacrilegio non
possumus. Interim quæ Cæsaris sint, quæ Dei, in medio re-
linquit. Quòd si idem erat hoc numisma quod didrachmum
5 illud Deo pendi solitum, ut certè postea sub Vespasiano fuit,
tum sanè controversiam non minuit Christus, sed implicavit:
cùm impossibile sit Deo et Cæsari idem simul reddere. At
enim ostendit quæ Cæsaris essent; numisma nempe illud Cæsaris imagine signatum. Quid igitur inde lucraris præter de-
10 narium vel Cæsari vel tibi? Aut enim Cæsari Christus præter
denarium illud nihil dedit, cætera omnia nobis asseruit, aut si
quicquid pecuniæ Cæsaris nomine inscriptum esset, id Cae-
sari dedit, contrarius jam sibi, nostra ferè omnia Cæsari dabit,
qui duo modò didrachma regibus non se ex debito persolvere,
15 et suo et Petri nomine professus est. Ratio denique infirma est
quâ niteris; non enim principis effigiem habet moneta ut principis esse, sed ut probam se esse moneat; útque se principis
effigie insignitam ne quis audeat adulterare. Sin autem ad jus
regium inscriptio tantum valeret, reges profectò nostras om-
20 nium facultates, uti essent suæ, sola nominis inscriptione statim perficerent; aut si nostra omnia jam sua sunt, quod tuum
dogma est, non idcirco Cæsari numisma illud reddendum erat,
quia Cæsaris nomen aut imaginem prætulit, sed quia Cæsaris
jam antea jure erat, nulla licèt imagine signatum. Ex quo

without sin and sacrilege the greatest deliver ourselves over
in slavery to Caesar, to a man, that is, and, what is more, to
an unjust man, a wicked man, a tyrant.

Christ leaves undecided, however, what things are God's,
5 and what Caesar's. If that piece of money was the same as the
didrachmum that was customarily paid to God, as it certainly
was later, under Vespasian, then Christ, instead of limiting
the controversy to its issue, has but entangled it; for it is impossible to give the same thing at the same time to God and
10 to Caesar. But, you say, he intimated to them what things
were Caesar's, to wit, that piece of money stamped with
Caesar's portrait. But does this profit either you or Caesar
more than a pennyworth? Either Christ gave Caesar nothing but that penny, and declared everything else ours, or
15 else, if he assigned to Caesar all money that has Caesar's
name upon it, he gives Caesar nearly all our property, and
contradicts himself; for when he was paying kings only two
didrachma of tribute, he protested that it was more than
either Peter or he was bound to do. The argument you rely on,
20 in fine, is weak, for coin bears the prince's portrait not as a
token of its being his property, but of its being good metal,
and that none may presume to counterfeit it. If indeed stamp-
ing or writing availed so much to establish royal right, kings
could instantly turn all our property over to themselves by
25 merely writing their names upon it. Or if all our possessions
be already theirs, which is your doctrine, then that piece of
money was to be rendered unto Caesar not because it bore his
name or image, but because of right it belonged to him before,

vester servus. Hæc tu nisi mente captus tecum facere credidisses? hisne te argumentis vincere, ut reges nostros rerum dominos existimemus? Tales in bello hostes nobis contingant, qui in castra hostium (quanquam et armatos vincere sat scimus) cæci atque inermes, utì tu soles, tanquam in suos incidant: ita semper quod tibi maximè adversatur, id demens veluti firmissimum causæ tuæ subsidium comparare consuevisti. Petebant Israëlitæ regem, *ut habebant omnes istæ gentes:* dissuasit Deus multis verbis, quæ Christus hìc summatim complexus est, *scitis principes gentium in eas dominari:* petentibus tamen iis dedit regem Deus, quamvis iratus: Christus, ne peteret omnino Christianus populus more gentium dominaturum, adhibita cautione antevertit; *inter vos non ita erit.* Quid hoc clarius dici potuit? non inter vos ista regum superba dominatio, tametsi specioso titulo Euergetæ et benefici vocentur; sed qui magnus inter vos fieri vult (quis autem principe major?) *esto vester minister:* et qui *primus* sive *princeps* (Luc. 22.) *esto vester servus.* Non erravit itaque Advocatus ille quem insectaris, sed authorem habuit Christum, si regem Christianum populi ministrum esse dixit, uti est certè omnis

and whosoever will be chief among you, let him be your servant." Unless you had been distracted, could you ever have
imagined that this passage makes for you, and that by such
reasonings you win us to regard our kings as masters over us
5 and ours? May enemies like you fall to our lot in war—
enemies who, though we know well enough we can beat them
even when they are armed, blunder blindly unarmed, as you
have a way of doing, into our hostile camp instead of their
own; for whatever makes most against you, that very thing
10 you usually are foolish enough to allege as the strongest support of your cause. The Israelites kept asking God for a king
"like as all the nations that are about" had; God dissuaded
them by many arguments, whereof Christ here gives an
epitome: "Ye know that the princes of the Gentiles exercise
15 dominion over them"; yet, because the Israelites persisted in
asking, God gave them one, though in his wrath. Christ,
lest a Christian people should anywise desire one who would
exercise dominion over them as did the kings of the Gentiles,
prevents them with the caution "but it shall not be so among
20 you." What could be said plainer than this? There shall not
be among you that haughty sway of kings, though by a plaus-
ible title they be called Euergetae and benefactors. But he that
will fain be great amongst you—and who is greater than the
prince?—"let him be your minister"; and he that will be
25 "foremost," or "prince" (Luke 22), "let him be your servant." So that the lawyer you inveigh against was not wrong,
but had Christ's authority if he said that a Christian king is
the people's servant, as every good magistrate certainly is.

bonus magistratus. Rex autem inter Christianos aut omnino
non erit, aut erit servus omnium: si planè vult esse dominus,
esse simul Christianus non potest. Quin et Moses, legis
quodammodò servilis institutor, non populo tamen superbè
5 dominabatur, sed onus ipse populi ferebat; ferebat in sinu
populum, ut nutricius lactentem: Num. 11. nutricius autem
servus est. Plato non dominos, sed servatores et adjutores populi appellandos esse magistratus docuit; Populum non servos,
sed altores magistratuum, ut qui alimenta et stipendia ma-
10 gistratibus etiam regibus præbeant. Eosdem Aristoteles custo-
des et ministros legum vocat, Plato et ministros et servos.
Ministros Dei Apostolus quidem appellat, quod tamen nequaquam obstat quò minùs sint et legum et populi; tam leges
enim quàm magistratus propter populum sunt. Et tamen
15 hanc tu *Fanaticorum Angliæ Molossorum opinionem* esse
clamitas. Molossos esse Anglos certè non putarem, nisi quòd
tu illos, hybrida, latratu tam degeneri oblatras; Lupi, si diis
placet, Sancti Dominus: Lupus nimirum sanctus queritur
Molossos esse fanaticos. Germanus olim, cujus ille Lupus
20 Trecassinus collega fuit, incesto apud nos regi Vortigerno authoritate sua regnum abrogavit. Sanctus itaque Lupus talem
te Lupi non sancti, sed famelici cujuspiam et latrunculi dominum, illo apud Martialem viperarum domino viliorem, asper-

Insomuch that a king either is no Christian at all, or is the people's servant: if he would be lord and master out and out, he cannot at the same time be Christian.

Moses himself, ordainer of a law that to a certain degree
5 legalized slavery, yet did not lord it haughtily over his people, but himself bore the burden of the people, and carried them in his bosom, as a nursing father does a sucking child, Numb. 11; moreover a nursing father is a servant. Plato would have the magistrates called not lords, but servants and helpers of
10 the people, nor the people called servants, but maintainers of their magistrates, because even when these are kings, the people give them food and wages. Aristotle called the magistrates the keepers and ministers of the laws; Plato, both ministers and servants. The Apostle, to be sure, calls them minis-
15 ters of God; but that does not prevent their being ministers of the laws and of the people; for the laws and the magistrates as well are for the people's sake.

Yet this, you keep howling, is merely "the opinion of the raving mastiffs of England." Of course I had not thought the
20 people of England mastiffs, did not you, mongrel, bark at them so currishly. The Lord and Seigneur de St. Loup, God 'ield you, yea the Holy Wolf himself, complains that the mastiffs rave! There was a time when St. Germain, whose colleague was that famous St. Loup of Troyes, deposed our
25 unchaste king Vortigern by his own authority. So St. Loup despise you, the master of no saintly wolf, but of some thievish starveling of a wolf, and more contemptible than that master of vipers of whom Martial makes mention. Yes, and

natur: qui et latrantem ipse domi Lyciscam habes, quæ tibi
lupi domino misere dominatur, titulisque tuis obstrepit, mag-
náque voce refragatur: unde mirum non est velle te regiam
dominationem aliis obtrudere, qui fœmineum ipse domi do-
5 minatum ferre tam serviliter assuevisti. Sis itaque Lupi Dominus, sit Lupa tuî domina, sis Lupus ipse, sis Lycanthropus,
molossis meherculè Anglicanis ludibrium debes. Verùm lu-
pos venari nunc non est otium; sylvis itaque egressi, in viam
regiam redeamus. Qui contra omnem in ecclesia primatum
10 nuper scripsisti, nunc *Petrum Apostolicæ coronæ principem
appellas.* Quis tibi authoritate tam fluxa homunculo fidem
habeat? Quid Petrus? *subjecti estote omni humanæ ordinationi propter Dominum; sive regi ut supereminenti, sive præsidibus, ut qui per eum mittantur, ad ultionem quidem facino-
15 rosorum, laudem verò benefacientium; quoniam ita est voluntas Dei.* Scripsit hæc Petrus non solùm privatis, sed etiam
advenis per minorem ferè Asiam dispersis atque dispalatis;
qui in iis ubi degebant locis nullius juris præterquam hospi-
talis capaces erant. An tu incolas, liberos, nobiles, indigena-
20 rum conventus, comitia, parlamenta idem in sua patria, quod
sparsos et peregrinos in aliena decere putas? an idem privatos

at home you even have a barking Lycisca too, and, though
you be Lord of the Wolf, this She-wolf lords it pitifully over
you, and loudly rails at your Seigneurie, and unlords your
lordship. No wonder, then, that you endeavor to obtrude
5 absolute regal government upon others, who are yourself
grown accustomed to bear female rule so slavishly at home.
Go on then, be Master of the Wolf; a She-wolf be your mistress; be a Wolf yourself, be a Werewolf: be what you will,
you are bound to be the English mastiffs' plaything. But I
10 have no time now to hunt wolves; so having got out of the
woods, let us go back to the King's highway.

You that but of late writ against all primacy in the church,
now call "Peter prince of the Apostolic fellowship." Who can
trust you, little man, when your own principles are so un-
15 stable? What says Peter? "Submit yourselves to every ordinance of man for the Lord's sake: whether it be to the king,
as supreme; or unto governors, as unto them that are sent by
him for the punishment of evildoers and for the praise of
them that do well: for so is the will of God." This epistle
20 Peter wrote to persons who were not only private individuals,
but actually strangers scattered astray throughout most of
Asia Minor, and who in those places where they sojourned
had no other right than what the laws of hospitality entitled
them to. Do you think that what befits scattered strangers
25 in a strange land befits likewise inhabitants freeborn and
noble, or meetings, assemblies, and parliaments of native
citizens in their own country? or that, in their own land,
what befits private persons equally befits members of Parlia-

hoc est, Nero an Claudius tunc temporis rerum potiretur, et
illi qui subjecti esse jubentur, advenæ, dispersi, privati, non
consules, non prætores, non Senatus Romanus erant. Nunc
Paulum adeamus, (quoniam tu quod nobis de regibus licere
5 non vis, id tibi de Apostolis licere autumas, ut principatum
Petro modò des, modò eripias) Paulus hæc ad Romanos: c. 13,
omnis anima potestatibus supereminentibus subjecta esto; non
est enim potestas nisi à Deo; quæ autem sunt potestates à Deo
sunt ordinatæ: Romanis hæc scribit, non, ut Petrus, advenis,
10 dispersis, sed privatis tamen potissimùm et plebeiis; ita etiam
scribit, ut totam reipub. administrandæ rationem, originem,
finem luculentissimè doceat. Quo magis obedientiæ quoque
nostræ vera ac distincta ratio, ab omni servitute disjuncta elu-
ceret. *Omnis anima,* hoc est, quisque homo *subjectus esto.*
15 Quid sibi Apostolus proponat hoc capite satis explanavit
Chrysostomus, ποιεῖ τοῦτο δεικνὺς, &c. *facit hoc,* inquit, *ut*
ostendat Christum leges suas non ad hoc induxisse, ut commu-
nem politiam everteret, sed ut in melius statueret. Non ergo
ut Neronem, aut tyrannum quemvis alium supra omnem
20 legem et pœnam constituendo, crudelissimum unius imperium in omnes mortales constabiliret. *Utque simul doceret*
superflua et inutilia bella non esse suscipienda; non ergo bella
damnat contra tyrannum, hostem patriæ intestinum, atque
adeò periculosissimum suscepta. *Pervulgatus tunc erat homi-*

whether it was Nero or Claudius that then held sway; moreover they that are bidden to submit were scattered foreign
private persons, not consuls or high officers of the law, not
the Roman Senate.

5   Now let us come to Paul (for with the Apostles you allow
yourself liberties that you will not allow us to take with
princes; now you give Peter the primacy, now you snatch it
away). Paul, Romans 13, says: "Let every soul be subject
unto the higher powers. For there is no power but of God:
10 the powers that be are ordained of God." This he writes to
the Romans, not to strangers dispersed, as Peter did, but rather to private persons and those of the meaner rank; writes it,
too, so as to set forth brilliantly the whole reason, origin, and
end of government. Whereby also it is clear as day that the
15 true and proper ground of our obedience has no connection
whatsoever with slavery. "Let every soul," says he, that is,
every man, "be subject." What the Apostle purposes in this
chapter Chrysostom has sufficiently explained. "St. Paul
writes thus," says he, "to make it plain that Christ introduced
20 his principles with no intent to overthrow civil government,
but rather to establish it upon truer foundations." He never
intended, then, by placing Nero or any other tyrant beyond
all laws and penalties, to set up cruelest despotism over all
mankind. "He intended too," says the same author, "to dis-
25 suade from unnecessary and fruitless wars." He does not,
therefore, condemn a war taken up against a tyrant, a bosom
enemy of his own country, and consequently the most dangerous enemy possible. "It was a common slander in those

num sermo traducens apostolos tanquam seditiosos, et nova-
tores, quasi omnia ad evertendum leges communes et face-
runt et dicerent; his nunc ora obstruit. Non ergo tyrannorum
defensiones conscripserunt Apostoli, quod tu facis, sed ea
5 fecerunt, ea docuerunt, quæ suspecta omnibus tyrannis defensione apud illos potiùs, et interpretatione quadam egebant.
Propositum Apostolo quid fuerit, ex Chrysostomo vidimus;
nunc verba scrutemur: *Omnis anima potestatibus supere-*
minentibus subjecta esto; quæ tamen istæ sint non statuit: non
10 enim jura atque instituta omnium nationum abolere, unius
libidini omnia permittere in animo erat. Certè optimus quisque imperator authoritatem legum et Senatûs authoritate sua
longè superiorem semper agnovit. Idem apud omnes natiqnes
non barbaras jus semper sanctissimum fuit. Unde Pindarus
15 apud Herodotum νόμον πάντων βασιλέα legem omnium regem esse dixit; Orpheus in hymnis non mortalium solùm, sed
immortalium etiam regem appellat: Ἀθανάτων καλέω καὶ θνητῶν
ἁγνὸν ἄνακτα Οὐράνιον νόμον. Reddit rationem: Αὐτὸς γὰρ μοῦ-
νος ζώων οἴηκα κρατύνει; *Lex enim sola viventium gubernacu-*
20 *lum tenet.* Plato in legibus τὸ κρατοῦν ἐν τῇ πόλει, id quod in
civitate plurimum debet posse, legem esse aït. In epistolis eam
maximè rempub. laudat, ubi lex, et domina et rex hominum,
non homines tyranni legum sunt. Eadem Aristotelis sententia
in Politicis, eadem Ciceronis in legibus, ita leges præesse magi-

days that the Apostles were seditious revolutionists who did and said everything to overturn the general laws. The Apostle in this chapter stops the mouths of such traducers." So that the Apostles did not write defences of tyrants as you do, but
5 did such things and preached such things as made them suspected of all tyrants—things that in the eyes of such needed to be defended and interpreted.

What the Apostle's design was we have just seen in Chrysostom; let us now examine the words: "Let every soul be
10 subject to the higher powers." These, however, he defined not, for he never intended to do away with the laws and constitutions of all nations, and turn all things over to one man's will and pleasure. Certainly every good emperor acknowledged his authority to be far below that of the laws and the
15 Senate; so among all but barbarous nations it is the law that has been holy above all else. Therefore it is that Pindar, as cited by Herodotus, declared the law king over all. Orpheus in his hymns calls it king not of mortals only but even of immortals:

$$\text{'}A\theta\alpha\nu\acute{\alpha}\tau\omega\nu \; \varkappa\alpha\lambda\acute{\epsilon}\omega \; \varkappa\alpha\grave{\iota} \; \theta\nu\eta\tau\tilde{\omega}\nu \; \grave{\alpha}\gamma\nu\grave{\delta}\nu \; \check{\alpha}\nu\alpha\varkappa\tau\alpha$$
20 $$O\grave{\upsilon}\rho\acute{\alpha}\nu\iota\nu\nu \; \nu\acute{\delta}\mu\nu\nu.$$

He gives the reason: for that the law controls single-handed the helm of living things. Plato in *The Laws* says the law is that which ought to have the greatest power in the state. In
25 his epistles he commends that form of government in which the law is ruler and king over men, and not men tyrants over the law. Aristotle is of the same opinion in his *Politics,* and so is Cicero in his *Laws,* that the laws govern the magistrates

stratibus, ut magistratus præsunt populo. Cùm itaque sapientissimorum virorum judicio, prudentissimarum civitatum
institutis lex semper potestas summa atque suprema habita
sit, nec evangelii doctrina cum ratione aut cum jure gentium
5 pugnet, is utique potestatibus supereminentibus verissimè subjectus erit, qui legibus et magistratibus juxta leges Rempub.
gubernantibus ex animo paret. Non ergo solùm populo sub-
jectionem hanc, sed regibus etiam præcipit; qui supra leges nequaquam sunt. *Non est enim potestas nisi à Deo;* id est nulla
10 reipub. forma, nulla homines regendi legitima ratio. Antiquis-
simæ etiam leges ad authorem Deum olim referebantur; est
enim lex, ut Cicero in Phil. 12, *nihil aliud nisi recta et à numine deorum tracta ratio, imperans honesta, prohibens contraria.* A Deo igitur est magistratum institutio, ut eorum ad-
15 ministratione gens humana sub legibus viveret: hanc autem
vel illam administrationis formam, hos vel illos magistratus
eligendi optio proculdubio penes liberas hominum nationes
semper fuit. Hinc Petrus et regem et præsides ἀνθρωπίνην
κτίσιν humanam creationem vocat; et Hosea c. 8, *constituunt*
20 *reges, at non ex me; præficiunt principes, quos non agnosco.*
In ista enim sola Hebræorum repub. ubi Deum variis modis
consulere poterant, de regis nominatione ad Deum referri ex
lege oportebat: cæteræ gentes mandatum à Deo nullum istius-

as the magistrates govern the people. Therefore, since by the judgment of the wisest men and by the constitutions of the best-ordered states the law has always been accounted the highest power on earth, and since the teachings of the gospel

5 clash not with reason or with the law of nations, then certainly that man is most truly subject to the higher powers, who heartily obeys the law, and the magistrates so far as they govern according to the law.

St. Paul, then, charges this subjection not only upon the

10 people, but upon kings themselves, who are nowise above the laws. "For there is no power but of God," that is, no way of constituting a state, no lawful ground for rule over men. Nay, the most ancient laws that are known to us were formerly ascribed to God as their author; the law, as Cicero says

15 in his twelfth *Philippic,* "is no other than right reason, derived from the command of the gods, enjoining whatever is virtuous, and forbidding the contrary." So that the establishment of magistrates is from God, and its purpose is that by their governance mankind may live under law. But the lib-

20 erty to choose whether this form of government or that, and these officers or those, indubitably always belonged to the free nations of men. Hence St. Peter calls kings and governors a human institution or ordinance; and Hosea 8, "They have set up kings, but not by me; they have made princes, and

25 I knew it not." For in the commonwealth of the Hebrews (and there only) where in divers ways they could consult with God, the appointment of a king must by law be referred to him; all we other nations have received no such command.

modi accepimus. Nonnunquam aut ipsa regiminis forma, si
vitiosa sit, aut illi qui potestatem obtinent, et ab hominibus,
et à diabolo sunt. Luc. 4; *Tibi dabo potestatem hanc omnem;*
nam mihi tradita est, et cui volo do illam. Hinc princeps
5 hujus mundi dicitur; et Apocalyp. 13, dedit Bestiæ Draco potentiam suam, et thronum suum, et potestatem magnam.
Quapropter necesse est hìc intelligi non potestates quascunque, sed legitimas cujusmodi etiam infra describuntur; necesse est intelligi potestates ipsas, non semper eos qui impe-
10 rium obtinent. Hinc dilucidè Chrysostomus, *Quid ais?* inquit, *omnis ergo princeps à Deo constitutus est? non dico: non*
enim de quovis principe, sed de ipsa re loquitur Apostolus;
non dicit, non princeps nisi à Deo, sed non est potestas. Hæc
Chrysost. *Quæ autem potestates sunt, à Deo sunt ordinatæ.*
15 Legitimas ergo vult hìc intelligi Apostolus; malum enim et
vitium, cùm ataxia sit, non est ut possit ordinari, et esse simul
vitiosum. Hoc enim duo simul contraria ponit, taxin et
ataxian. *Quæ autem sunt,* ita interpretaris ac si diceretur, *quæ*
nunc sunt; quo faciliùs probare possis etiam Neroni, qui, ut
20 opinaris, tunc *imperavit,* Romanos obtemperare debuisse;
nostrâ sanè bonâ veniâ: quàm enim voles de Anglicana repub.
malè sentias, in ea tamen Anglos acquiescere debere, quoniam *nunc est,* et à *Deo ordinatur,* ut Neronis olim imperium,
necesse habebis concedere. Neque enim Nero minùs quàm

Sometimes either the very form of government, if it be faulty, or those persons that have the power in their hands, are not of God, but of men, yes and of the devil too, Luke 4: "All this power will I give thee, . . . for that is delivered 5 unto me; and to whomsoever I will I give it." Hence he is called the prince of this world; and in Revelations 13. the Dragon gave to the Beast his power, and his seat, and great authority. Therefore St. Paul must be understood to mean, not all sorts of powers, but lawful ones, of the sort described 10 in what follows; and to mean the powers themselves, not the men, always, in whose hands they are lodged. Upon this passage Chrysostom speaks plainly. "What!" says he, "is every prince then appointed by God? No such thing. The Apostle speaks not of the person of the prince, but of the 15 thing. He does not say, there is no *prince* but of God; he says there is no *power* but of God." Thus far Chrysostom. The Apostle, then, when he says "The powers that be are ordained, or *ordered,* of God," would have it understood of lawful powers, for 'tis impossible that a thing evil and faulty, 20 being disordered, can be ordered: to say so asserts two contraries at once—order and disorder.

The words "that be" you interpret as "that *now* be," the easier to prove that the Romans ought to obey Nero, who you suppose was then emperor. Content! For then, think as ill 25 as you like of our English Commonwealth, you must needs grant that Englishmen ought to yield obedience to it, for "it now is," and is "ordained of God," like Nero's power of old. And lest you should answer that Nero had got *his* by lawful

Tiberius *artibus matris imperium nihil ad se pertinens* occupaverat, ne legitimè partum fuisse respondeas. Quò sceleratior et doctrinæ retractator ipse tuæ, Romanos potestati quæ tunc fuit subjectos esse vis, Anglos potestati quæ nunc est, sub-
5 jectos esse non vis. Verùm nullæ in hoc orbe terrarum res duæ magis è regione adversæ sibi sunt, quàm tu nequissimus nequissimo semper ferè adversus es tibi. Quid autem facies miser? acumine hoc tuo regem adolescentem planè perdidisti; ab ipsa enim tua sententia extorquebo ut fatearis,
10 hanc potestatem in Anglia, quæ nunc est, à Deo ordinatam esse; atque omnes proinde Anglos intra ejusdem reipublicæ fines eidem potestati subjectos esse debere. Attendite igitur Critici, et manus abstinete, Salmasii nova hæc emendatio est, in epistola ad Romanos; non quæ sunt potestates, *sed quæ*
15 *nunc existunt,* reddi debere adinvenit; ut Neroni tyranno tunc scilicet imperanti subjectos esse omnes oportuisse demonstraret. At ô bone, ληκύθιον ἀπώλεσας· ut regem modò, ita nunc interpretamentum hoc tam bellum perdidisti. Quam tu epistolam sub Nerone scriptam esse aïs, sub Claudio scripta
20 est principe simplici, et non malo: hoc viri docti certissimis argumentis compertum habent; quinquennium etiam Neronis laudatissimum fuit, unde argumentum hoc toties incul-

succession, I say that he no less than Tiberius had seized "by
means of his mother's intrigues a power which nowise belonged to him." So that you are all the more unprincipled,
and retract your own assertions, in affirming that the Romans
5 owed subjection to the power that then was, and yet denying
that Englishmen owe subjection to the power that now is.
But, you worthless thing, there are no two things in this
world more directly opposite to one another than you nearly
always are to your worthless self. What then will become of
10 you, wretch? With this keen wit of yours you have quite
ruined the young king, for upon your own theory I will rack
you to confess that the power that now is in England is ordained of God, and that all Englishmen within the confines
of that Commonwealth are bound to submit to it. Therefore
15 give ear ye critics all! Hands off from this the new emendation of Salmasius upon the Epistle to the Romans! He has discovered for the occasion that the words ought to be rendered
not "the powers that be," but "the powers that *now* be"; and
all to prove that everybody owed submission to the tyrant
20 Nero, then emperor to wit!

But, my good man, your pitcher is gone once too often to
the well. As you ruined the king but a moment ago, even
thus you now ruin this so pretty emendation. The Epistle
which you say was writ in Nero's time was writ in Claudius's,
25 a guileless ruler and no villain: scholars hold this for a certainty upon surest evidence. Besides, there were five years
even of Nero's reign that were excellent. So that this oft-
obtruded argument, which many have at their tongues' ends,

catum, quod multis in ore est, multis imposuit, tyranno paren-
dum esse, eò quòd Paulus hortatus est Romanos ut Neroni essent subjecti, callidum indocti cujuspiam commentum esse
reperitur. *Qui obsistit potestati,* scilicet legitimæ, *Dei ordi-*
5 *nationi obsistit.* Astringit etiam reges præceptum hoc, qui
legibus et Senatui obsistunt. At verò qui potestati vitiosæ, aut
potestatis non vitiosæ corruptori et eversori obsistit, num is
Dei ordinationi obsistit? sanus, credo, non dixeris. Tollit
omnem dubitationem sequens versiculus, de legitima tantùm
10 potestate Apostolum hic loqui. Definiendo enim explicat,
nequis errare, et opiniones hinc stolidas aucupari possit, qui
sint magistratus potestatis hujus ministri, et quam ob causam
subjectos esse nos hortetur: *Magistratus non sunt timori bonis*
operibus, sed malis; boni à potestate hac laudem adipiscentur;
15 *Magistratus minister est Dei nostro bono datus; non frustra*
gladium gerit, vindex ad iram ei qui malum facit. Quis negat,
quis recusat, nisi improbus, quin hujusmodi potestati aut potestatis administro libens se subjiciat? non solùm ad vitandam
iram et offensionem, aut pœnæ metu, sed etiam *propter con-*
20 *scientiam.* Sine magistratibus enim, et civili gubernatione,
nulla respublica, nulla societas humana, nulla vita esse potest.
Quæ autem potestas, qui magistratus contraria his facit, neque
illa, neque hic à Deo propriè ordinatus est. Unde neque tali

and which has cheated many, to wit, that a tyrant is to be obeyed because Paul urged the Romans to submit to Nero, is found to be the sly invention of some dunce.

"Whosover . . . resisteth the power," the lawful power,
5 that is, "resisteth the ordinance of God." This principle makes kings liable when they resist the laws and the Senate. But he that resists an unlawful power, or resists a person who goes about to overthrow and destroy a lawful one—does he resist the ordinance of God? In your right wits you would not say
10 so, I trow. The next verse removes any uncertainty that the Apostle speaks here of a lawful power only; for lest anyone mistake, and thence go chasing stupid notions, it explains, by defining bounds and limitations, who are the officers that are the ministers of this power, and why he urges us to submit.
15 "Rulers," says he, "are not a terror to good works, but to evil. . . . Do that which is good, and thou shalt have praise of the same: For he is the minister of God to thee for good . . . He beareth not the sword in vain: for he is . . . a revenger to execute wrath upon him that doth evil." Who
20 but the wicked denies, who but the wicked refuses, willingly to submit to such a power or its minister? And that not only to avoid "the wrath" and the stumbling block, and for fear of punishment, but even "for conscience sake."

Without magistrates and civil government there can be no
25 commonwealth, no human society, no living in the world. But whatever power or whatever magistrate acts contrary to these precepts—neither the one nor the other is in any proper sense ordained of God. Neither to such a power nor to such

vel potestati, vel magistratui subjectio debetur aut præcipitur, neque nos prudenter obsistere prohibemur: non enim potestati, non magistratui obsistemus, qui hic optimè depingitur, sed prædoni, sed tyranno, sed hosti; qui si magistratus tamen

5 dicendus erit, eò duntaxat quòd habet potestatem, quòd ad pœnam nostram ordinari à Deo videri potest, etiam diabolus hoc modo magistratus erit. Sanè unius rei una vera definitio est: si ergo Paulus hic magistratum definit, quod quidem accuratè facit, eadem definitione, iisdem verbis tyrannum, rem

10 maximè contrariam, definire non potuit. Unde quem ipse magistratum definivit atque descripsit, ei duntaxat subjectos nos esse voluisse, non ejus contrario tyranno certissimè colligitur. *Propter hoc tributa solvitis;* rationem adjungit ad præceptum; unde Chrysostomus, *Cur,* inquit, *vectigalia regi da-*

15 *mus? Annon tanquam nobis prospicienti, curæ ac tuitionis mercedem solventes? atqui nihil illi solvissemus, nisi ab initio utilem nobis talem esse præfecturam cognovissemus.* Quapropter illud repetam quod suprà dixi; quandoquidem subjectio hæc non simpliciter, sed cum adjuncta ratione à nobis

20 requiritur, illa profectò ratio quæ adjungitur, subjectionis nostræ vera norma erit: Cum ista ratione non subjecti, rebelles; sine ista ratione subjecti, servi erimus et socordes. *At Angli,* inquis, *nihil minùs quàm liberi, quia mali, quia flagi-*

a magistrate, therefore, is submission owed or commanded,
nor are we forbidden to resist them with discretion, for we
shall be resisting not the power or the magistrate here excellently described, but a robber, a tyrant, a public enemy.
5 If he is notwithstanding to be called a magistrate just because
he holds power, just because he may appear to be ordained by
God for our punishment—in this sense the devil too shall be
a magistrate!

Certain it is that there can be but one true definition of one
10 and the same thing. So that if Paul here defines a magistrate,
which he certainly does, and with careful precision, he could
not possibly in the very words of this definition define a
tyrant, the exact opposite. Hence the sure consequence: that
he would have us submit to such a magistrate only as he him-
15 self has writ down and by definition limited, and not to a
tyrant, that magistrate's opposite. "For this cause pay ye tribute also": he adds a reason to his command. Hence Chrysostom: "Why pay we revenue to the king? Is it not as we pay
hire for protection and care to one who watches out for us? We
20 should have paid him nothing had we not originally come to
know that such supervision was good for us." Wherefore I
shall repeat what I have said already, that since this subjection
is demanded not absolutely but upon an express reason added,
that reason will be the true rule of our subjection. Where that
25 reason holds, we are rebels if we submit not; where it holds
not, we are cowards and slaves if we submit.

"But," say you, "the English are far from being free men,
for they are infamous villains." For my part I will not re-

tiosi. Nolo ego Gallorum vitia commemorare, quamvis sub regibus sint; neque Anglorum nimis excusare; dico tamen illa esse flagitia, quæ sub regibus tanquam in Ægypto didicerunt; neque dum in deserto, licèt Dei sub imperio, dediscere statim potuerunt. Spes est tamen de plerisque bona; ut ne sanctissimos hic optimosque viros et veritatis studiosissimos collaudare incipiam; quorum apud nos non minorem credo esse numerum, quàm ubi tu maximum esse existimas. At *jugum Anglis durum imponitur.* Quid si illis, qui jugum cæteris civibus imponere studebant? Quid si suo deinde merito subactis? nam cæteri puto non molestè ferunt, exhausto civilibus bellis ærario, sumptibus propriis suam se tolerare libertatem. Relabitur jam ad Rabbinos nugivendos. Regem legibus adstrictum esse negat, ex iis tamen probat *læsæ majestatis reum esse posse, si jus suum patiatur imminui:* astrictus itaque et non astrictus, reus et non reus rex erit: adeò frequenter enim solet repugnare sibi, ut ipsa Repugnantia huic homini germana atque gemella esse videatur. Atqui Deus, inquis, multa regna Nebuchadnezzari in servitutem dedit. Fateor ad certum tempus dedisse, Jer. 27. 7. Anglos in servitu-

count the vices of the French, though they live under a monarchy; neither will I too much excuse those of the English; yet this I say, that the acts which disgrace them are those they learnt under their Pharaohs in Egypt, as it were; nor have
5 they been able to unlearn them at once while yet in the wilderness, though under God's immediate government. But there is good hope of many amongst us—not now to begin an eulogy of those most excellent saintly men and lovers of the truth; whose number among us I think not less than where
10 you think there are most such. But "a heavy yoke is laid upon the English nation." What if it be laid upon those that endeavored to lay the yoke upon all their fellow-citizens? What if it be laid upon those that were deservedly subdued? As for the rest, I question not but they are very well content,
15 now the public treasury is exhausted by the civil wars, to bear the burden of maintaining their own liberty at their own expense.

Now he betakes himself again to his piddling rabbins. He asserts that a king is bound by no laws, and yet on their au-
20 thority proves that "a king may be guilty of lese-majesty if he suffer the rights of his crown to be diminished." So kings are bound by laws, and not bound by laws; they may be criminals and yet not criminals. The man contradicts himself so perpetually that Contradiction herself seems his twin-born
25 sister.

You say that God gave many kingdoms over in slavery to Nebuchadnezzar. I confess he did so for a time, Jer. 27. 7; but do you make appear if you can that he gave the English

tem Carolo Stuarto ad semihorulam dedisse ostende; permisisse
non negaverim, dedisse nunquam audivi. Aut si Deus in servitutem dat populum, quoties tyrannus plus populo potest, cur
non idem liberare dicendus erit, quoties plus potest populus
5 tyranno? an is Deo tyrannidem suam, nos Deo libertatem
nostram acceptam non feremus? Non est malum in civitate
quod Deus non immittat, Amos 3. famem, pestilentiam, seditionem, hostem; ecquod nam horum civitas ab se non totis
viribus amolietur? faciet profectò, si possit, quamvis ab ipso
10 Deo immissa hæc esse sciat; nisi è cœlo ipse secùs jusserit. Cur
non tyrannos pariter amovebit, si plus polleat? an ejus unius
impotentiam ad commune malum esse magis à Deo crede-
mus, quàm potentiam totius civitatis ad commune bonum?
Absit à civitatibus, absit ob omni cœtu hominum ingenuo-
15 rum doctrinæ tam stupidæ, támque pestiferæ labes, quæ vitam
omnem civilem funditus delet, gentem humanam universam
propter unum atque alterum tyrannum, ad quadrupedum
propè conditionem detrudit: cùm illi supra omnem legem excelsi par in utrunque genus et pecudum et hominum jus atque
20 imperium obtinebunt. Mitto jam stulta illa dilemmata, in quibus ut te jactes, nescio quem fingis, *potestatem illam supere-
minentem de populo velle intelligere;* tametsi affirmare non

nation over for a single minute in slavery to Charles Stuart. That God allowed them I would not deny, but I have never heard that he gave them. Or if God be said to give a people into slavery whenever a tyrant prevails over the people, why
5 ought he not as well be said to set them free whenever the people prevail over a tyrant? Shall the tyrant credit and owe his tyranny to God, and not we our liberty? There is no evil in the state that the Lord hath not let in, Amos 3. Famine, plague, sedition, a public enemy—is there a single one of
10 these that the state will not strive with all its might to shake off? Shake them off it surely will if it can, though it know them to be sent by God, unless himself from heaven should command the contrary.

Upon the same reasoning why may not the state rid itself
15 of a tyrant if it be stronger than he? Why should we suppose the uncontrolled passions of this one man to be appointed by God for the common ill, rather than the self-controlled power of the whole state for the common weal? Far be it from all states and all societies of freeborn men to maintain principles
20 so senseless, plague-spots of such ignominy, which wipe out the whole life of the state, and, to gratify a tyrant or two, thrust mankind down to the level of four-footed brutes; for tyrants, once lifted up above all law, will wield the same law and sway over men as over cattle.

25 I pass by those foolish dilemmas of yours, to indulge in which you invent someone's authority for the assertion that "that sovereign power means the people's power"; though for my part I hesitate not to assert that such is the source

dubito omnem magistratûs authoritatem à populo proficisci.
Hinc Cicero pro Flacco; *Illi nostri sapientissimi, et sanctissimi*
majores, quæ scisceret plebs, quæ populus juberet, juberi ve-
tarique voluerunt. Hinc Lucius Crassus Orator eximius, et
5 Senatûs eo tempore princeps, cujus tum causam agebat ad
populum. *Nolite,* inquit, *sinere nos cuiquam servire, nisi*
vobis universis, quibus et possumus et debemus. Quamvis
enim Senatus Populum regeret, Populus tamen illam mode-
randi et regendi sui potestatem senatui tradiderat. Unde ma-
10 jestatem, populo Romano frequentiùs quàm regibus olim
attributam legimus. Idem Marcus Tullius pro Plancio;
Est enim conditio liberorum populorum, præcipuéque hujus
principis populi et omnium gentium domini, posse suffragiis
vel dare vel detrahere quod velit cuique; nostrum est ferre
15 *modicè populi voluntates: honores si magni non putemus,*
non servire populo; sin eos expetamus, non defatigari suppli-
cando. Egóne ut regem populi servum dicere metuam, cùm
Senatus Romanus tot regum dominus servum se populi professus sit? Vera sunt hæc, inquies, in populari statu; nondum
20 enim lex regia potestatem populi in Augustum, et successores
ejus transtulerat. Hem tibi ergo Tiberium illum quem tu
tyrannum, plus vice simplici, fuisse aïs, ut revera fuit, is tamen dominus, etiam post legem illam regiam, appellatus à

of all the power that any magistrate has. Hence Cicero in his
Oration for Flaccus says: "Our wise and reverend ancestors
appointed those things to be bidden and forbidden which
the multitude resolved and the sovereign people ordained."
5 Hence too Lucius Crassus, a distinguished orator, and then
president of the Senate, whose cause he was pleading with the
people, says: "I beseech you, suffer not us to be subject to any
but your own entire body, to whom we can and must submit."
For though the Senate governed the People, yet it was the
10 People that had given over that very power to regulate and
govern themselves unto the Senate. Hence, in our reading we
find majesty in those days more frequently ascribed to the
Roman people than to kings. Marcus Tullius again in his
Oration for Plancius: "It is the condition of free peoples, and
15 especially of this people, chief and lord of all nations, by vote
to give or take away, to or from any, what it will. It is for us
patiently to submit to the people's wishes. Those that care not
much for office have the less obligation upon them to court
the people; those that seek office must not grow weary of
20 entreating them." Should I scruple to call a king the servant
of his people, when I hear the Roman Senate, which was the
master of so many kings, profess itself to be but the people's
servant? You will object perhaps that all this is very true
under democratic conditions, for that the Lex Regia had not
25 yet transferred the people's power unto Augustus and his
successors. But pray look at Tiberius, "a tyrant several times
over," you say, as he certainly was—who yet, Suetonius says,
when someone called him Lord or Master, though after the

quodam, ut tradit Suetonius, denuntiavit ne se ampliùs contumeliæ causâ nominaret. Audisne? tyrannus iste dominus dici contumeliæ sibi duxit. Idem in Senatu; *Dixi et nunc, et sæpe aliàs, patres Conscripti, bonum et salutarem principem, quem* 5 *vos tanta et tam libera potestate instruxistis, Senatui servire debere, et universis civibus sæpe, et plerumque etiam singulis; neque id dixisse me pœnitet; et bonos et æquos et faventes vos habui Dominos, et adhuc habeo.* Nec simulata hæc ab eo si dixeris, ut erat simulandi callidissimus, quicquam proficies; 10 quis enim id videri se cupit, quod esse non debet? Hinc ille mos non Neroni solùm, quod scribit Tacitus, sed cæteris etiam imperatoribus fuit, populum in Circo adorandi. De quo Claudianus, VI. *Cons. Honorii:*

> *O quantum populo secreti numinis addit*
> 15   *Imperii præsens species, quantámque rependit*
> *Majestas alterna vicem, cùm regia Circi*
> *Connexum gradibus veneratur purpura vulgus,*
> *Consensúque cavæ sublatus in æthera vallis*
> *Plebis adoratæ reboat fragor.* ——

enacting of that Lex Regia, gave notice that this person must name him so no more, for that it was an insult. Do you hear? That tyrant deemed it an insult to be called Lord. The same emperor addressing the Senate, "I have said," says he, "fre-
5 quently heretofore, and now I say again, that a good prince and serviceable, whom you have invested with so great and unrestricted power, ought to submit to the Senate, often to the body of the people, and sometimes even to particular persons; nor do I repent of having said so: I confess that you have
10 been both good and just masters to me, as well as indulgent ones, and that you are yet so." It will not help you to say that, proficient in the art of hypocrisy as he was, he feigned all this; for does any man desire to *seem* other than he *ought* to be? Hence it was the custom not only for Nero, as Tacitus tells
15 us, but for the rest of the emperors, to do homage to the people at the Circus. Claudian, in his Panegyric upon the Sixth Consulate of Honorius, says of this:

> Authority divine, mysterious,
> Here present visibly unto the people—
> 20 Lo, how it graces them! And they in turn—
> How grand their answering majesty's requital!
> To throngs upon the Circus seats assembled
> The royal purple makes obeïsance,
> And with one crash the adorèd multitude
> 25 Rebellows from the theatre's hollow vale
> Its uproar to the skies.

Qua adoratione quid aliud Imperatores Romani, nisi universam plebem, etiam post legem regiam, suos esse dominos fatebantur? Atque illud est quod initio statim suspicatus sum, te glossariis pervolutandis, et tricis quibusdam laboriosis magnificè divulgandis operam potiùs dedisse, quàm bonis authoribus attentè et studiosè perlegendis; qui veterum scriptorum sapientiâ ne leviter quidem imbutus, rem præstantissimorum opinionibus Philosophorum, et prudentissimorum in republica principum dictis celebratissimam, novam esse prorsus et Enthusiastarum tantummodo deliriis somniatam censes. I nunc, Martinum illum sutorem, et Gulielmum Pellionem quos adeò despicis, ignorantiæ collegas et mystagogos tibi sume: quanquam erudire te poterunt illi, et illos tibi gryphos dissolvere stolidissimos, An in Democratia serviat Populus, cùm serviat rex in Monarchia; utrùm totus an pars ejus. Ita illi, cum tibi Oedipi vice fuerint, tu illis Sphinx in malam rem præceps abeas licebit; alioquin fatuitatum tuarum et ænigmatum finem nullum fore video. Rogas, Cùm reges Apostolus nominat, an de populo eos intelligemus? Pro regibus quidem orandum esse Paulus docet, 1 Tim. 2. 2. at priùs pro populo orandum esse docuerat, v. 1. Sunt tamen et de regibus, et de populo nonnulli, pro quibus orare etiam vetamur.

By this adoration could the emperors of Rome possibly mean anything else than to acknowledge that even after the enacting of the Lex Regia the whole body of the people were their masters?

5   I find, as I suspected at first, that you have spent more time and pains in turning over glossaries and pompously publishing laborious trifles than in the careful and diligent reading of sound authors. 'Tis because you have not the slightest tincture of the wisdom of the ancients that you account as new, and as 10 the dream of mere "enthusiasts' delirium," a matter which has been perfectly well known through the opinions of the most eminent philosophers and the words of the most far-sighted statesmen. Your Martin Cobbler and William Tanner, whom you so despise, you had better take unto yourself 15 as your partners and guides in ignorance; though indeed they will be able to instruct you, and to solve those stupid riddles of yours, as thus: "Since in a Monarchy the king is supposed to be a servant, is the People supposed to be a servant in a Democracy?—All the People, or a part?" And when they 20 have played Oedipus to you, you have my permission to be Sphinx to them, and go headlong to the devil; else I see no end to your conundrums and follies.

You ask, "When the Apostle says *kings,* does he mean the *people*?" St. Paul does indeed tell us to pray for kings, 25 1 Tim. 2. 2, but he had already told us, verse 1, to pray for the people. Yet there are some for all that, both among kings and common people, that we are forbidden to pray for; and if a man may not so much as be prayed for, may he not be law-

Pro quo non orem, eúmne ex lege non puniam? quid vetat?
Atqui *cùm hæc scriberet Paulus, imperabant vel pessimi:* hoc
etiam falsum est; scriptam enim sub Claudio et hanc Epistolam fuisse certissimis argumentis evincit Ludovicus Capellus.

5 De Nerone cùm mentionem facit Paulus, non regem, sed
Leonem, id est belluam immanem vocat, cujus ex ore ereptum
se gaudet, 2 Tim. 4. Pro regibus itaque, non pro belluis,
orandum, ut vitam tranquillam et quietam transigamus, cum
pietate tamen *omni et honestate.* Vides non tam regum hìc

10 quàm tranquillitatis, pietatis, honestatis etiam rationem esse
habendam. Quis autem populus non se suósque liberos tuendo
(contra tyrannum an contra hostem nil interest) vitam *sollici-*
tam, inquietam, bellicosam, honestam mallet agere, quàm
sub hoste vel tyranno, non solùm æque sollicitam et inquie-

15 tam, sed turpem etiam, servilem et inhonestam? Audi apud
Livium Samnites utrumque statum expertos: rebellâsse se,
quòd pax servientibus gravior, quàm bellum liberis esset.
Immo teipsum audi; te enim ipsum sæpenumero jam testem
adhibeo; non quo tanti sis, sed ut perspiciant omnes quàm sis

20 duplex, et discors tibi, et mancipium regis mercenarium. *Quis,*
inquis, *non perferre mallet repub. Aristocratica ex optimatum*
æmulatione dissensiones oriri solitas, quàm ex uno monarcha,
tyrannico more imperare consueto certam miseriam ac per-

fully punished? What is to hinder? But, you say, "When Paul wrote this epistle, the rulers were the most profligate persons in the world." That is false too, for Ludovicus Capellus proves by the most trustworthy evidence that this epistle likewise was writ in Claudius's time. When St. Paul has occasion to speak of Nero, he calls him not a king but a lion,—that is, a savage beast, out of whose mouth he is glad he was delivered, 2. Tim. 4. So that it is for kings, not for beasts, we are to pray, that under them "we may live a quiet and peaceable life," but, observe, "in all godliness and honesty." What we are here to take account of, clearly, is not so much kings as peace and quiet, godliness and honesty. Yet what nation would not choose, in defense of themselves and their children,—against tyrant or enemy is all one,—to live a life "perturbed and restless," warlike and honorable, rather than under the power of tyrant or enemy to lead a life just as perturbed and restless, but vile into the bargain, in slavery and ignominy? Listen while the Samnites, who had tried both conditions, testify, according to Livy, that they had gone to war again because war, with freedom, was less intolerable than peace with slavery. Nay, listen to your own words; for I often put you on the witness-stand, not to do you honor, but that all men may observe how double-tongued you are, and self-contradictory, and a king's hireling slave. "Who would not rather," say you, "bear with the dissensions that through the rivalries of great men often occur under an Aristocracy, than with the misery and ruin that are sure to come of a monarch accustomed to absolute rule? The people

niciem? Populus Romanus prætulit statum illum Reipub.
quantumlibet discordiis agitatæ jugo Cæsarum intolerabili.
Populus qui vitandæ seditionis causâ monarchicum statum
præoptavit, ubi expertus est levius esse malum quod vitare
5 *voluit, ad priora sæpe redire expetit.* Hæc et plura tua verba
sunt in illa de episcopis dissertatione, sub Walonis Messalini
adscititio nomine editâ, p. 412; contra Petavium Loiolitam,
cùm ipse magis Loiolita sis, et eo de grege pessimus. Quid
hac de re Scriptura sacra statuerit, et vidimus, et omni dili-
10 gentia investigasse non pœnitet: unde quid senserint Patres
antiqui per tot ingentia volumina exquirere pretium fortasse
operæ non erit. Si quid enim afferunt, quod Scriptura non
exhibuit, eorum authoritatem, quantacunque sit, meritò re-
pudiamus. Quod autem ex Irenæo profers, *reges Dei jussu*
15 *constitui aptos his qui in illo tempore ab iis reguntur,* cum
Scriptura pugnat evidentissimè. Cùm enim judices ad regen-
dum populum suum aptiores regibus esse palàm signifi-
câsset Deus, id tamen totum voluntati atque arbitrio populi
permisit, ut aptiorem sibi sub optimatibus formam reipub.
20 deteriore sub regibus, si vellent, permutarent. Legimus etiam
sæpe regem malum bono populo datum, et contra, regem bonum populo malo. Virorum itaque sapientissimorum est per-
spicere quid populo aptissimum et utilissimum sit: constat

of Rome preferred that condition of their Republic, no matter
how much vexed with civil broils, to the unbearable yoke of
the Caesars. When a people which to avoid sedition has preferred a monarchy finds by experience that what it wished to
5 avoid is the lesser evil, often it desires to return to its former
government." These are your own words, and more you have
to this purpose, at page 412 of that discourse concerning bishops, which under the fictitious name of Walo Messalinus you
wrote against Petavius the Jesuit—though yourself are more
10 a Jesuit, nay the worst of that crew.

We have already heard the sense of Holy Scripture upon
this subject, and are not sorry to have searched it out with all
possible care. Therefore perhaps it will not be worth our
while to seek after the judgment of the Fathers through all
15 their huge volumes. For if they assert anything which has not
been allowed by Scripture, we rightly reject their authority,
great though it be. That passage which you cite from Irenaeus,
that "Kings are by God's command appointed suitable to
the people they then govern" is clear against Scripture. For
20 though God himself declared openly that for the government
of his own people judges were more suitable than kings, yet
he left it wholly to the people's will and decision to exchange,
if they would, their government by nobles, which was suitable
to them, for one by kings, which was less suitable. And we
25 read that frequently a bad king was given to a good people,
and contrariwise, a good king to a bad people. What is most
suitable and profitable to a people, then, is something for the
wisest men to ascertain; for certain it is that the same form of

enim neque omni populo, neque eidem semper eundem reipub. statum convenire, sed vel hunc vel illum, prout civium
virtus et industria nunc augescit, nunc minuitur. Qui tamen
potestatem adimit populo eligendi sibi quam velit reipub.
5 formam, adimit profectò id in quo civilis libertas tota ferè consistit. Citas deinde Justinum Martyrem Antoninis imperatorum optimis obsequium deferentem; quis iis tam egregiis
et moderatis non detulisset? *At quantò,* inquis, *nos hodie pejores Christiani? tulerunt illi principem diversæ religionis.*
10 Privati scilicet, et viribus longè inferiores. *Nunc sanè ponti-
ficii regem non ferrent reformatum,* nec *reformati Pontifi-
cium.* Facis tu quidem prudenter, ut ostendas te nec ponti-
ficium esse, nec reformatum; facis etiam liberaliter; ultro
enim largiris quod nunc non petivimus, omnes hodie Chris-
15 tianos in hoc planè consentire, quod tu solus insigni audaciâ
atque scelere oppugnas, Patrum etiam quos laudas dissimilli-
mus; illi enim pro Christianis, ad profanos reges, defensiones
conscribebant, tu pro rege pontificio atque deterrimo contra
Christianos et Reformatos. Multa deinde ex Athenagora,
20 multa ex Tertulliano futiliter depromis, quæ ab ipsis Apostolis
multo clariùs et explanatiùs dicta jam sunt. Tertullianus autem longissimè à te dissentit, qui regem vis esse dominum:

government is not equally fitting for all nations, or for the
same nation at all times; but sometimes one, sometimes another, may be more proper, according as the diligence and
valor of the people wax or wane. Yet whoso takes from a
5 people their power to choose what government they wish
takes that indeed in which all civil liberty is rooted.

Then you tell us of Justin Martyr's humble and submissive
behavior to the Antonines, those best of emperors; as if anybody would not pay deference to princes so excellent, princes
10 so measured in the exercise of their power! "How much worse
Christians," you say, "are we in these days than they were!
They submitted to a prince of a different religion." Of course
they did, being private persons, and far inferior in strength.
"But now Papists will not endure a Protestant king," or
15 "Protestants a Papist." As for you, you show yourself to be
neither Papist nor Protestant: how discreet of you, and generous too; for you concede of your own accord what we have
not now asked of you, that all Christians today agree in that
very thing that you alone with so much impudence and wick-
20 edness oppose, in a manner too, most unlike those Fathers
that you praise. They unto pagan kings kept writing defences
for Christians; you write your Defence for a wicked Popish
king against Christians and Protestants.

Next you fetch out of Athenagoras and Tertullian—quite
25 ineffectually—quantities of things that had already been
said much more plainly and intelligibly by the Apostles themselves. Tertullian, moreover, is far from agreeing with you
that a king is lord and master; as you either knew not, or

quod tu aut nescivisti, aut nequiter dissimulâsti. Is enim Christianus ad Imperatorem Ethnicum in Apologetico ausus est scribere, non oportere Imperatorem appellari Dominum. *Augustus,* inquit, *imperii formator ne dominum quidem dici se* 5 *volebat, hoc enim Dei est cognomen: dicam planè imperatorem dominum, sed quando non cogor ut dominum Dei vice dicam: cæterùm liber sum illi, Dominus meus Deus unus est, etc.* et ibidem, *qui pater patriæ est, quomodo Dominus est?* Gratulare nunc tibi de Tertulliano, quem sanè præstabat missum 10 fecisse. *At parricidas appellat qui Domitianum interfecerunt.* Rectè appellat; uxoris enim et famulorum insidiis, à Parthenio, et Stephano interceptarum pecuniarum reo est interfectus. Quod si Senatus Populúsque Romanus hostem judicatum, ut Neronem antea judicabant, et ad supplicium quære- 15 bant, more majorum punivissent, eos parricidas appellaturum fuisse censes? immo si appellâsset, dignus ipse supplicio fuisset; uti tu furcâ jam dignus es. Origeni responsum idem quadrabit quod Irenæo. Athanasius reges terræ ad humana tribunalia vocare nefarium esse dicit. Quis hoc dixit Athanasio? 20 verbum enim Dei nullum hìc audio. Credam itaque ego imperatoribus potiùs et regibus de se falsum hoc esse fatentibus, quàm Athanasio. Adfers deinde Ambrosium ex proconsule et

wickedly pretended you knew not. For he, a Christian, dared
in his *Apologeticum* to write to a heathen Emperor that an
Emperor ought not to be called Lord. "Augustus himself,"
says he, "that formed the empire, would not be called 'Lord,'
5 for this is God's title. I will, of course, call the Emperor
'Lord,' but only when I am not forced to call him so in God's
place. For the rest, as regards the Emperor I am a free man;
my Lord is God alone, etc." And in the same discourse: "He
who is Father of his Country, how should he be its Master?"
10 Now take joy to yourself of Tertullian, whom you had better
have let alone. But, you say, "the slayers of Domitian he
calls parricides." And rightly so, for it was through a conspiracy of Domitian's wife and servants that he was killed, by
Parthenius and by Stephanus, a person accused of stealing
15 moneys. If the Senate and the people of Rome had adjudged
him a public enemy as erewhile they adjudged Nero, whom
then they searched out and put to death,—had they, I say,
thus punished Domitian according to the custom of their ancestors, think you Tertullian would have called them parri-
20 cides? If he had, he would have deserved to be hanged, as
you do now.

Unto Origen the same answer will fit as did fit unto Irenaeus.

Athanasius says that it is an abomination to summon the
25 kings of the earth before human tribunals. Who told him
so? For in this I hear none of God's Word. And rather than
Athanasius I will believe kings and emperors who admit that
they have no such exemption. Then you bring in Ambrose,

catechumeno episcopum, verba illa Davidis, *tibi soli peccavi,*
imperitè, ne dicam assentatoriè interpretantem. Volebat
is omnes alios imperatori subjectos esse, ut imperatorem
ipse subjiceret sibi. Quàm enim superbè, et fastu plusquam
5 pontificio Theodosium imperatorem Mediolani tractaverit,
cædis Thessalonicensis reum ipse judicaverit, ingressu ecclesiæ prohibuerit, quàm se deinde novitium et rudem evangelicæ doctrinæ ostenderit, omnibus notum est. Imperatorem ad
pedes ejus provolutum excedere salutatorio jussit; sacris tan-
10 dem restitutum, et postquam obtulisset, altari adstantem his
vocibus extra cancellos exegit. *O imperator, interiora loca*
tantùm sacerdotibus sunt attributa, quæ cæteris contingere
non licet. Doctórne hic Evangelii, an Judaïcorum pontifex
rituum fuit? Hic tamen (quæ omnium ferè ecclesiasticorum
15 artes sunt) imperatorem cæteris dominum imposuit, ut imperatoris ipse dominus esset. His itaque verbis Theodosium tanquam sibi subjectum repulit; *Coæqualium hominum es im-*
perator et conservorum; unus enim omnium dominus rex et
Creator. Bellè profectò; quam veritatem calliditas et assen-
20 tatio episcoporum obscuravit, eam iracundia unius, et ut mol-
liùs dicam, zelus ineruditus protulit in lucem. Ambrosii im-

who after he had been a proconsul and then a catechumen at
last commenced bishop; you cite, I say, his interpretation of
those words of David, "Against thee only I have sinned,"—
an interpretation which is ignorant, not to say adulatory.
5 Ambrose was willing all others should be enthralled to the
emperor, that he might enthrall the emperor to himself.
Everybody knows with what a more than high-priestly popish
pride and arrogance he treated the emperor Theodosius at
Milan, how he took upon himself to declare him guilty of
10 the massacre at Thessalonica, and forbade him to enter the
church; and what a raw beginner in Gospel lore he next
showed himself to be. When the emperor fell down at his
feet, he commanded him to get him out of the church porch;
at length when he was received again into the communion of
15 the church, and had made offering, and remained standing at
the altar, Ambrose with these words ordered him outside the
rails: "Emperor, these inner places are for priests only; it is
not lawful for others to come within them." Was this a
preacher of the Gospel, or was it a pontifical high priest of the
20 Jewish rite? Yet this man put the emperor to lord it over
everyone else, that he himself might lord it over the emperor—
quite an usual trick of churchmen. With words to this purpose he put Theodosius back as inferior to himself: "You are
ruler over men that are your like and fellow-servants with
25 yourself, for there is one only lord and king and Creator over
all." Excellent indeed! This truth, which the craft and flattery of bishops kept hid, was then brought to light by the
irascibility, or to speak more mildly, by the ignorant zeal of
one of them.

peritiæ tuam subjungis ignorantiam aut hæresin, qui disertè
negas *sub veteri fœdere remissionem peccatorum per sanguinem Christi locum tunc habuisse, cùm David Deo confiteba-
tur ei soli se peccavisse;* p. 68. Orthodoxi, non nisi per san-
5 guinem agni mactati ab initio mundi, peccata unquam remissa fuisse credunt; te novum hæreticum cujusnam discipulus sis nescio; certè summi Theologi discipulus ille quem
exagitas, à vero non aberravit, cum dixit potuisse quemvis
è populo pari jure cum Davide Deum his verbis inclamâsse,
10 *tibi soli peccavi.* Augustinum deinde ostentas, Clericos Hip-
ponenses nescio quos producis; nam Augustini quæ sunt
abs te allata nobis non obsunt. Quidni enim fateamur
cum propheta Daniële, Deum tempora mutare, regna dare,
et regna auferre, per homines tamen. Si regnum Deus solus
15 Carolo dedit, idem Carolo abstulit, optimatibus et Populo
dedit. Si ea de causa præstandam Carolo obedientiam fuisse
dicis, eandem nunc magistratibus nostris præstandam esse
dicas necesse est. Nam Deum et nostris etiam magistratibus
eandem dedisse potestatem quam dat malis regibus *ad casti-
20 ganda populi peccata* ipse concedis; nostros itaque à Deo pariter constitutos removere à magistratu nemo vel tuo judicio nisi
Deus potest. Atque ita, uti soles, tuum tibi ipse mucronem in

To Ambrose's incompetence you now join your own ignorance or heresy in denying point blank (p. 68) that "under
the old covenant there was forgiveness of sins through the
blood of Christ at the time when David confessed to God that
he had sinned against him only." It is the orthodox belief that
any remission of sins there ever was, was but by the blood of
the lamb that was offered up from the beginning of the world.
I know not whose disciple you are that set up for a broacher
of new heresies, but certain I am that that great Divine's disciple whom you so censure was not in error when he said that
anyone of David's subjects might have cried upon God,
"Against thee only have I sinned," with as much right as
David himself.

Then you show off Austin, and trot out an obscure company of Hipponensian divines. What you bring in from
Austin makes not at all against us; why should we not acknowledge with the prophet Daniel that God changeth times,
sets up one kingdom, and pulls down another? Certainly,—
yet it is by means of men. If 'twas God alone gave a kingdom
to King Charles, God alone took it away, and gave it to the
Lords and Commons. If you say it was for that reason our
allegiance was due to King Charles, then you must needs say
that for the same reason it is due to our present rulers. For
you yourself grant that God has given even our rulers such
power as he gives wicked kings "to punish the people's sins";
so that, according to your own opinion, our present rulers,
being likewise appointed by God, cannot lawfully be removed
from office but by God. Thus, as usual, you turn your point

temet vertis, tuus tibi ipse sicarius es; neque injuriâ, cùm eò
improbitatis et impudentiæ processeris, eò stuporis et insaniæ,
ut quos digito violandos non esse tot argumentis probas, eosdem omnium suorum bello persequendos esse idem affirmes.
5 Ismaëlem Godoliæ Præfecti interfectorem ab Hieronymo parricidam esse nominatum ais, et meritò; præsidem enim Judææ,
virum bonum, sine ulla causa interemit. Idem Hieronymus
in Ecclesiasten, præceptum illud Solomonis, *Os regis observa,*
cum præcepto Pauli concordare dixit; et laudandus quidem,
10 quod locum istum cæteris sui temporis moderatiùs exposuit.
Ad inferiora tempora post Augustinum non descendes, ut
doctorum sententiam exquiras. Ut omnes tamen intelligant
faciliùs mentiri te posse quàm tacere, si quos adhuc haberes
tuæ sententiæ fautores, post unam statim periodum non tem-
15 peras tibi quò minùs ad Hispalensem Isidorum, Gregorium
Turonensem, Ottonem Frinsingensem etiam in mediam barbariam descendas. Quorum authoritas quàm nullius apud nos
pretii sit si modò scivisses, non huc eorum obscurum testimonium per mendacium adduxisses. Vultis scire cur ad hæc
20 tempora descendere non audet, cur abdit se, cur subitò evane-

against yourself, and are your own assassin. Serves you right too; for you have reached such a pitch of wickedness and shamelessness, of stupidity and madness, that those very persons whom, as you prove with so many arguments, we ought
5 not to lift a finger against, you yourself assert should be hunted down in war by all their subjects.

You tell us that St. Jerome calls Ishmael, who slew Gedaliah the Deputy-Governor, a parricide; and rightly, for it was without cause that Ishmael slew that ruler over Judea, who
10 was a good man. Jerome also in his comment upon Ecclesiastes says that Solomon's counsel "Keep the king's commandment" agrees with St. Paul's doctrine upon the same subject; and he deserves commendation for having made a more moderate construction of that text than did the rest of his con-
15 temporaries.

You say you will not "come down to times later than Austin to search out the opinions of the doctors." Yet, for all men (supposing you still had any adherents) to learn that you can more easily lie than say nothing, you do not refrain, after
20 but one sentence more, from coming down at once to Isidore of Seville, Gregory of Tours, and Otto of Freising—even into the midst of mediaeval barbarism. Had you but known how worthless we consider their authority, you had not told a lie to quote their unintelligible evidence.

25 Readers, would ye know why he dare not come down to the present time, why he hides away and on a sudden disappears? I will tell you: 'tis because he knows full well that he shall encounter as many keen adversaries as there are eminent

scit? dicam: quot sunt Ecclesiæ reformatæ præstantissimi doctores, tot videt acerrimos sibi adversarios fore. Faciat modò
periculum, sentiet quàm facilè reluctantem, omnes in unum
vires conferentem, Lutheris, Zwingliis, Calvinis, Buceris,
5 Martyribus, Paræis in aciem eductis fundam atque obruam.
Leidenses etiam tuos tibi opponam, quorum Academia, quorum respub. florentissima, libertatis olim domicilium, isti denique literarum humaniorum fontes atque rivi, servilem illam
æruginem tuam et innatam barbariem eluere non potuerunt.
10 Qui cùm Theologum orthodoxum habeas neminem tibi faventem, quem tuo commodo nominare possis, omnium præsidio reformatorum nudatus confugere ad Sorbonam non
erubescis: quod tu Collegium doctrinæ pontificiæ addictissimum, nullius apud orthodoxos authoritatis esse non ignoras.
15 Sorbonæ igitur absorbendum tam sceleratum tyrannidis propugnatorem tradimus; tam vile mancipium nostrum esse no-
lumus; qui *populum universum regi ignavissimo parem*
esse negat. Frustra id in papam deonerare atque transferre
contendis, quod omnes liberæ nationes, omnis religio, omnes
20 Orthodoxi sibi sumunt, in se suscipiunt. Papa quidem cum
episcopis suis, dum tenuis, et nullarum virium erat, tuæ hujus
fœdissimæ doctrinæ author primus extitit: iis demùm artibus
magnas opes, magnámque potentiam paulatim adeptus, tyrannorum ipse maximus evasit. Quos tamen omnes sibi fir-
25 missimè devinxit, cùm populis, quorum animos jamdiu superstitione oppressos tenuerat, suaderet, non posse regibus

divines of the Protestant Church. Let him but put it to the test, and though he strive with all his might, he shall find how easily I will rout and overwhelm him, once I get the Luthers, Zwinglis, Calvins, Bucers, Peter Martyrs, and
5 Pareuses, marshaled out in battle array. I will set against you even your Leyden colleagues, whose University, whose flourishing commonwealth, where freedom dwelt of old—yea not even those fountains and streams of polite learning—could wash away that slavish rust and native barbarism of yours.
10 With not one orthodox divine to take your part (name any you please), stripped, I say, of all Protestant support, you blush not to take refuge in the Sorbonne, a College you know to be utterly given over to the teachings of popery, and of no authority among the orthodox. We surrender so wicked a
15 champion of tyranny: Sorbonne, absorb him!

We will not own a slave so despicable as to maintain that "the whole body of a nation is not the equal of a king the most slothful and cowardly." You labor in vain to unload and lay upon the Pope a doctrine which all free nations and religions
20 and all the Orthodox take unto themselves for their very own. True, the Pope, when he and his bishops were low and of but small account in the world, was the first author of this foul doctrine of yours; 'twas precisely by preaching such doctrine that little by little he got great riches and power into his own
25 hands, and himself turned out to be the worst of tyrants. Yet these tyrants he bound to himself by the closest tie, for he persuaded the nations, whose minds he had long held crushed beneath their superstitions, that it was unlawful to depose a

quamlibet pessimis, nisi se fidelitatis sacramentum solvente, imperium abrogari. Verùm tu scriptores Orthodoxos devitas, et quæ communis et notissima ipsorum sententia est, eam à Papa introductam esse causatus, veritatem in invidiam rapere conaris. Quod nisi astutè faceres, appareret te neque Papanum esse neque reformatum, sed nescio quem semibarbarum Edomæum Herodianum, qui tyrannum quemque immanissimum tanquam Messiam cœlo demissum colas atque adores. *Demonstrâsse te* hoc dicis *ex doctrina patrum, primorum quatuor sæculorum, quæ sola evangelica et Christiana censeri debet.* Periit huic homini pudor; quàm multa sunt ab illis dicta atque scripta, quæ Christus et Apostoli neque docuerint neque approbarint? quàm multa in quibus reformati omnes à patribus dissentiant? Quid autem ex patribus demonstravisti? *reges etiam malos à Deo constitui.* Fac esse constitutos, ut omnia etiam mala quodammodo à Deo constituuntur: *eos proinde Deum solum habere judicem, supra leges esse, nulla lege scripta, non scripta, naturali, neque divina posse reos fieri à subditis, neque apud subditos suos.* Quare? certè nulla lex vetat, nulla reges excipit: ratio, et jus, et fas omne animadverti in omnes qui peccant indiscriminatim jubet. Neque tu legem ullam scriptam, non scriptam, naturalem aut divinam protulisti quæ vetaret. Cur ergo non in reges quoque animadvertendum? *quia sunt etiam mali à Deo constituti.* Ne-

king, though never so bad, unless the Pope absolved them
from their oath of allegiance. But you avoid Orthodox writers,
and endeavor to bring odium upon the truth by making out
the Pope to be the originator of what is a known and common
5 received opinion amongst them. If you did not do it cunningly you would bewray yourself for what you are, neither
Papist nor Protestant, but some sort of half-barbarous Edom-
ite Herodian, who worship and adore a monstrous tyrant as
if he were a Messiah sent down from heaven.

10   Your opinions you say you "have proved by the teaching of
the fathers that flourished in the first four centuries—teaching which alone should be deemed evangelical and Christian."
This man is past all shame. How many things did they say
and write which Christ and his Apostles would neither have
15 taught nor have approved? How many things in which all
Protestants disagree with them? But what have you proved
out of the fathers? Why, "that even evil kings are appointed
by God." Allow that they, like all other evils, are, in some
sense, by God appointed. What then? why, "therefore they
20 have no judge but God alone; they are above the laws; by no
law written or unwritten, law of nature or law of God, can
they be indicted by or before their own subjects." But why?
Certainly no law forbids it; no law excepts kings; and all
reason and right both human and divine requires that all of-
25 fenders be punished without distinction. Nor have you produced any law whatever, written or unwritten, of God or of
nature, which forbids. Then why may not kings be proceeded
against? "Because they, even the bad ones, are appointed by

bulonem te magis an bardum et caudicem esse dicam? nequissimus sis oportet qui doctrinam perniciosissimam in vulgus
disseminare audeas, stupidissimus qui ratione tam stolida
maximè nitaris. Dixit Deus Isaiæ 54, *Ego creavi interfecto-*
5 *rem ad perdendum;* ergo interfector supra leges est; excute
hæc, et pervolve quantum voles, parem utrobique consequen-
tiam invenies. Nam et Papa etiam eodem modo quo tyrannus à Deo est constitutus, et ecclesiæ in pœnam datus, quod
supra ex scriptis etiam tuis ostendimus; tamen *quia in fasti-*
10 *gium potestatis non ferendum tyrannidi non absimilis prima-*
tum suum evexit, cùm eum, tum episcopos meliori jure tol-
lendos esse affirmas *quàm fuere constituti:* Wal. Mes. p. 412.
Papam et episcopos quamvis ab irato Deo constitutos ex ecclesia tollendos esse aïs, quia sunt tyranni; tyrannos ex repub.
15 tollendos esse negas quia sunt ab irato Deo constituti. Ineptè
prorsus et absurdè: cum enim Papa ipsam conscientiam, quæ
sola regnum ejus est, invito quoquam lædere non possit, eum
qui revera tyrannus esse non potest, quasi tyrannum gravissimum tollendum esse clamas; tyrannum autem verum qui
20 vitam et facultates nostras omnes in potestate sua habet, et sine
quo papa in ecclesia tyrannus esse nequit, eum in repub. omnino ferendum esse contendis. Hæc tua sibi invicem collata

God." Had I best call you knave, or fool and blockhead?
A vile wretch you must be to dare propagate a doctrine so
destructive and pernicious, and a dunce to lean upon such silly
arguments. God says, Is. 54, "I have created the slayer to
5 destroy." Then a slayer is above the laws. Weigh and turn
it round as much as you will, you shall find this conclusion
to be as valid as yours.

For the Pope too is appointed by God just as much as tyrants are, and set up for the punishment of the church, as I
10 have already demonstrated out of your own writings. And
yet you say, *Wal. Mes.,* page 412: "Because he has raised his
primacy to an insufferable pinnacle of power, so that it is
nowise different from a tyranny, both he and his bishops may
be more lawfully removed than they were appointed." You
15 tell us that the Pope and the bishops, *though* God in his wrath
appointed them, ought to be removed from the church because they are *tyrants*; and yet you deny that *tyrants* ought to
be removed from the commonwealth, *because* God in his
wrath appointed *them!* How utterly irrelevant and self-con-
20 tradictory! On the one hand, though the Pope cannot without
a man's consent harm even the conscience, which alone is his
realm, yet you cry out that he—who in point of fact has not
the power to tyrannize—should be removed as a tyrant intolerable; on the other hand you urge that a tyrant indeed, a
25 tyrant that holds all our lives and estates in his grip, and
without whose support the Pope himself cannot lord it in the
church, must in the commonwealth by all means be borne
withal. These assertions compared with one another bewray

tam imperitum te támque puerilem sive falsi sive veri argu-
tatorem produnt, ut levitas tua, inscitia, temeritas, incogitan-
tia neminem posthac latere queat. At ratio subest altera, *re-*
rum vices inversæ viderentur, quippe in melius; actum enim
5 esset de rebus humanis, si quæ res pessimo loco sunt, in eodem
semper starent: in melius inquam; authoritas enim regia ad
populum rediret, ab cujus voluntate atque suffragiis profecta
primò, atque in unum ex suo numero derivata erat: potestas
ab eo qui injuriam intulit, ad eum qui injuriam est passus,
10 æquissima lege transiret; cùm tertius nemo inter homines idoneus esse possit; alienigenam enim judicare quis ferret? omnes æquè homines legibus tenerentur, quo nihil justius esse
potest: Deus mortalis nemo esset. Quem qui inter homines
constituit, non minùs in rempub. scelestus est, quàm in Eccle-
15 siam. Tuis iterum in te armis utar. *Maximam hæresin esse*
aïs, quâ creditur unum hominem in loco Christi sedere: duæ
hæ notæ Antichristum signant, infallibilitas in spiritualibus,
et omnipotentia in temporalibus, Apparat. ad Primat. pag.
171. An Reges infallibiles? Cur ergo omnipotentes? aut si
20 hoc sunt, cur minùs exitiales rebus civilibus quàm Papa spiritualibus? An verò Deus res civiles prorsus non curat? si non

you as so ignorant and childish a chatterer—whether the
thing you say is true or false—that your fickleness and ignorance, your rashness and heedlessness, can be hidden no
longer from anybody.

5   But you allege another reason: "Human affairs would
seem turned upside down." They would, and for the better.
It would be all over with human affairs if being once at their
worst they must be always so. I say they would be changed
for the better, for the king's power would revert to the
10 people, by whose will and vote it first proceeded and was conferred upon one of themselves. And most rightfully would
the power be transferred from the doer of the wrong to the
sufferer; since among all mankind there can be no third party
qualified to wield it; for who would submit to the jurisdiction
15 of a foreigner? All men would equally be subject to the laws;
—and than such a condition nothing can be more just. There
would be then no God of flesh and blood; whoever sets up
such among men is an offender no less heinous against the
State than against the Church.

20   Now I mean to turn your own weapons upon you again.
To believe that one man sits in Christ's seat, "this," you say,
"is the greatest heresy. These two signs mark Antichrist, infallibility in spirituals, and omnipotence in temporals." *Appa-*
rat. ad Prim., page 171. Are kings infallible? Why then
25 should they be omnipotent? And if they are, why are they
not as destructive to temporalities as is the Pope to spirituali-
ties? Does God really concern himself nowise with civil affairs? If he does not, surely he does not forbid us to take care

curat, certè nos curare non prohibet; si curat, eandem in republica reformationem atque in ecclesia vult fieri; præsertim
si infallibilitatem et omnipotentiam attributam homini easdem malorum omnium utrinque causas esse exploratum sit.
5 Non enim in negotiis civilibus eam patientiam præcepit, ut
sævissimum quemlibet tyrannum respublica ferret, ecclesia
non ferret; immo contrarium potiùs præcepit: et ecclesiæ quidem nulla arma præter patientiam, innocentiam, preces, et
disciplinam evangelicam reliquit; reipublicæ et magistratibus
10 simul omnibus non patientiam, sed leges et gladium, injuriarum et violentiæ vindicem in manus tradidit. Unde hujus
hominis perversum et præposterum ingenium aut mirari subit
aut ridere; qui in ecclesia, Helvidius est et Thraseas et planè
tyrannicida; in republica, commune omnium tyrannorum
15 mancipium et satelles. Cujus sententia si locum habeat, non
nos solùm rebellavimus, qui regem, sed reformati etiam
omnes qui Papam dominum invitis regibus rejecerunt. Jam
diu autem est quòd suis ipse telis concisus jacet. Sic enim homo
est, modò manus adversarii ne desit, ipse in se tela abunde
20 suppeditat: nec quisquam ad refutandum se, aut irridendum
commodiores ansas ministrat. Defessus etiam cædendo citiùs
quis abscedat, quàm hic terga præbendo.

of them. If he does, he would have the same reformation made
in the commonwealth as in the church, especially if it has
been put to the proof that the assigning of infallibility and
omnipotency to man is the identical cause of all the evils in
5 both. In civil affairs God has not enjoined such patience that
the state must submit to the cruelties of tyrants, but not the
church; nay, rather has he enjoined the contrary; indeed he
has left unto the church no arms but patience and innocence,
prayer and the teaching of the gospel; but into the hands of
10 the state and its officers altogether he has entrusted not patience, but the sword of the law, avenger of wrong and violence. So this man's upside-down back-foremost mind ex-
poses itself to either astonishment or laughter: in the church
he is Helvidius and Thraseas, tyrant-queller out and out; in
15 the state the common slave and lackey of tyrants all. If his
doctrine hold, not we only that have cast off our king, but
Protestants in general, who against the wishes of their kings
have cast off the Pope's supremacy, are rebels all alike.

But long it is ere now that he lies felled by his own shafts.
20 For, let but his enemy's hand not fail, and Salmasius, such is
his nature, himself furnishes an overplus of weapons against
himself. Nor does any man offer you a handle more easy to
refute and ridicule himself withal. You will sooner give over
in actual weariness of flogging him, than he of offering his
25 back to the lash.

CAPUT IV.

MAGNAM à regibus iniisse te gratiam, omnes principes et terrarum dominos demeruisse defensione hac regia te fortè putas, Salmasi, cùm illi, si bona sua, rémque suam ex veritate potiùs quàm ex adulationibus tuis
5 vellent æstimare, neminem te pejùs odisse, neminem à se longius propellere atque arcere debeant. Dum enim regiam potestatem supra leges in immensum extollis, admones eâdem operâ omnes ferè populos servitutis suæ nec opinatæ; eóque vehementiùs impellis ut veternum illum, quo se esse liberos inani-
10 ter somniabant, repente excutiant; moniti abs te quod non putabant, servos se esse regum. Eóque minùs tolerandum sibi esse regium imperium existimabunt, quò magis tu iis persuasum reddideris tam infinitam potestatem non suâ patientiâ crevisse, sed ab initio talem atque tantam ipso jure regio natam
15 fuisse. Ita te tuámque hanc defensionem, sive populo persuaseris, sive non persuaseris, omnibus posthac regibus funestam, exitialem, et execrabilem fore necesse erit. Si enim populo persuaseris, jus regium omnipotens esse, regnum amplius non feret; si non persuaseris, non feret reges, dominationem
20 tam injustam pro jure usurpantes. Me si audiant, quibus in-

CHAPTER IV.

PERHAPS you think, Salmasius, that by this Royal Defence you have much ingratiated yourself with kings, and deserved well of all princes and lords of the earth; but if they would reckon their interest and advantage accord-
5 ing to truth, not according to your flatteries, they ought to hate nobody worse than you, and banish and keep away nobody farther from their presence. For in the very act of exalting the power of kings above law and beyond measure, you remind most nations that they are under a slavery they
10 had not guessed before, and the more violently drive them to shake off upon a sudden that lethargy in which they kept vainly dreaming they were freemen; for you admonish them what before they recked not, that they are slaves to their kings. And they will count royal government all the less endurable
15 the more you persuade them that it is not by their sufferance and submission that this exorbitant power swelled up, but that from the beginning, even such and so great as it is, it sprang full-grown from the royal right itself. So that whether you convince the nations or not, you and this Defence of yours
20 must needs be to all kings hereafter calamitous and ruinous and accursed. For if you shall persuade a nation that royal right is power without limit, they will no longer endure a monarchy; if you persuade them not, then they will not endure kings who assume so unlawful a power as if it were
25 lawfully theirs.

If kings who are yet uncommitted as to this will heed me,

tegrum hoc est, séque circumscribi legibus patiantur, pro
incerto, imbecillo, violento imperio quod nunc habent, cura-
rum atque formidinum pleno, firmissimum, pacatissimum
ac diuturnum sibi conservabunt. Consilium hoc sibi, suisque
5 regnis adeò salutiferum si propter authorem contempserint,
sciant non tam esse meum, quàm regis olim sapientissimi:
Lycurgus enim Spartanorum rex, antiqua regum stirpe oriun-
dus, cùm propinquos videret suos Argis et Messenæ rerum
potitos, regnum quemque suum in tyrannidem convertisse,
10 sibique pariter suisque civitatibus exitio fuisse, ut patriæ simul
saluti consuleret, et dignitatem in familia sua regiam quàm
diutissimè conservaret, consortem imperii senatum, et Ephororum potestatem in ipsum regem quasi censoriam, firma-
mentum regno suo induxit. Quo facto regnum suis nepotibus
15 firmissimum in multa secula transmisit. Sive, ut alii volunt,
Theopompi, qui centum ampliùs annis post Lycurgum Lace-
dæmone regnabat, ea moderatio fuit, ut popularem Ephororum potestatem superiorem quàm suam constitueret, eóque
facto gloriatus est, stabilivisse se regnum, multóque majus ac
20 diuturnius filiis reliquisse, exemplum profectò haud ignobile
hodierni reges ad imitandum habuerint, eundem etiam consilii tutissimi authorem egregium. Majorem enim legibus dominum ut perferrent homines hominem omnes unum, nulla
lex unquam sanxit; ne potuit quidem sancire. Quæ enim lex

and will suffer themselves to be limited by the laws, then instead of the uncertain, weak, and violent government, full of
cares and fears, which now they have, they will secure unto
themselves a government perfectly steadfast, peaceable, and
5 lasting. If they slight this counsel, so wholesome to them and
their kingdoms, because of its author, then let them know
that it belongs less to me than to a very wise king of old. Lycurgus king of the Spartans, who was sprung of an ancient
royal stock, observed that his kinsmen in power at Argos and
10 Messene had each turned his rule into a tyranny, and had
been the ruin of themselves and their states; thereupon, that
he might at once benefit his country and secure the kingly
office to his own family as long as possible, he made the senate
a partner in his power, and subjected himself, even the king,
15 to the almost censorial office of the Ephors—all this to prop
his throne. By this means he handed down the royal power
unshaken to his posterity for many generations. Others think
it was Theopompus, who ruled over Lacedaemon more than
a hundred years after Lycurgus, that adopted this polity, so
20 self-restrained as to set up the popular power of the Ephors
above his own, and who thereupon boasted that he had settled the royal power on a sure foundation, and had left it to
his posterity much augmented and much more lasting. However this may be, surely the kings of today would have here
25 no base pattern to copy, and distinguished authority too, for a
counsel thoroughly safe.

That all men should submit to any one man as superior to
law, no law ever did enact, or ever could, for whatever law

leges omnes evertit, ipsa lex esse non potest. Cùm itaque eversorem te, et parricidam legum omnium rejiciant ab se leges,
exemplis redintegrare certamen, hoc capite, conaris. Faciamus itaque periculum in exemplis: sæpe enim, quod leges
5 tacent, et tacendo tantùm innuunt; id exempla evidentiùs
docent. Ab Judæis auspicabimur voluntatis divinæ consultis-
simis; *postea ad Christianos* tecum *descendemus.* Initium
autem altiùs petitum ab eo tempore facimus, quo Israëlitæ
regibus quocunque modo subjecti, jugum illud servile cervici-
10 bus dejecerunt. Rex Moabitarum Eglon Israëlitas bello sube-
gerat; sedem imperii inter ipsos Jerichunte posuerat: numinis
contemptor non erat, facta enim Dei mentione, è solio sur-
rexit: servierant Israëlitæ Egloni annos duodeviginti; non ut
hosti, sed ut suo regi munus miserant. Hunc tamen dum pub-
15 licè munerantur ut regem suum, interficiunt per insidias ut
hostem. Verùm Ehudes qui interfecit, Dei monitu id fecisse
creditur. Quid factum hujusmodi commendare magis potuit?
Ad honesta enim quæque et laudabilia hortari solet Deus,
non ad injusta, infida, truculenta. Expressum autem Dei
20 mandatum habuisse nusquam legimus. *Clamârunt filii Isra-*
ëlis ad Jehovam; clamavimus et nos; excitavit iis Jehova ser-
vatorem; excitavit et nobis. Ille ex vicino domesticus, ex hoste

overthrows all law cannot itself be law. Now, seeing that law spurns you off as an underminer and murderer of law, you try in this chapter to renew the fight by means of examples. Let us make trial, then, of examples, for often they make plain
5 what the laws are silent in, yet hint at.

We will begin with the Jews, whom we suppose to have known most of the will of God, and then, according to your own method, we will "come down to the Christians." But we will make an earlier start, at the time when the Israelites,
10 however they had been subjected to kings, cast that slavish yoke from off their necks. Eglon the king of Moab had made a conquest of them, and had set up his throne at Jericho in the midst of them; he was no contemner of the true God, for at mention of His name he rose from his seat: the Israelites had
15 served him eighteen years, and had sent a present to him, not as to an enemy, but as to their own king. Yet in the very act of publicly making a present to him as their king, they kill him by stratagem as an enemy to their country. To be sure, Ehud, who slew him, is believed to have had a warrant from
20 God for so doing. What greater argument of its being a warrantable and praiseworthy action? God uses not to put men upon deeds that are unjust, treacherous, and cruel, but upon deeds honorable and praiseworthy. But we read nowhere that he had express command from God. "The children of Israel
25 cried unto the Lord"; so did we. The Lord raised them up a saviour; so did he for us. Eglon from their neighbor became their inmate, and from their enemy their king. Our gentleman from our king became our enemy, and so no king, for

rex factus erat: Noster ex rege hostis; non ergo rex erat; nam neque civis ullo modo esse potest, qui reipublicæ est hostis; neque Consul habebatur Antonius, neque Nero imperator, ex quo uterque hostis à Senatu est judicatus. Quod Cicero quartâ

5 Philippicâ de Antonio clarissimè docet: *Si consul Antonius, Brutus hostis; si conservator Reipublicæ Brutus, hostis Antonius. Quis illum consulem nisi latrones putant?* Pari ego jure, quis tyrannum, inquam, regem nisi hostes patriæ putant? Fuerit itaque Eglon externus, fuerit Noster domesticus

10 nécne, quandoquidem uterque hostis et tyrannus, parùm refert. Si illum Ehudes jure trucidavit, nos nostrum supplicio jure affecimus. Quin et heros ille Sampson, incusantibus etiam popularibus suis, Jud. 15. *An nesciebas Phelisthæos dominium habere in nos?* suis tamen dominis bellum solus

15 intulit, neque unum sed multos simul patriæ suæ tyrannos, sive Dei, sive propriæ virtutis instinctu occidit; conceptis priùs ad Deum precibus ut auxilio sibi esset. Non impium ergo sed pium Sampsoni visum est, dominos, patriæ tyrannos occidere; cùm tamen pars major civium servitutem

20 non detrectaret. At David, rex et propheta, noluit Saulem interimere *unctum Dei.* Non quicquid noluit David, continuò nos obligat ut nolimus; noluit David privatus; id statim nolle synedrium, Parlamentum, totum populum necesse erit? noluit inimicum dolo occidere, nolet ergo Magistratus noxium

no man can anywise be at once a member of the state and an
enemy to it. Antony was never held a consul, Nero an emperor, after the Senate had voted them both enemies. This
Cicero tells us unmistakably in his fourth *Philippic:* "If
5 Antony be a consul, Brutus is an enemy; if Brutus is a saviour
and preserver of the commonwealth, Antony is an enemy.
Who but robbers count him a consul?" By the same reason,
say I, who but enemies to their country count a tyrant a king?
So that whether or not Eglon was a foreigner, and Charles a
10 countryman of ours, makes no difference, since each was an
enemy and a tyrant. If Ehud killed him justly, we too have
done justly in putting Charles to death.

Samson, that renowned champion, though his countrymen
blamed him (Judg. 15, "Knowest thou not that the Philis-
15 tines are rulers over us?"), yet made war singlehanded against
his rulers; and whether instigated by God or by his own valor
only, slew not one, but many at once of his country's tyrants.
And as he had first duly prayed to God to be his help, it
follows that he counted it no wickedness, but a duty, to
20 kill his masters, his country's tyrants, even though the greater
part of his countrymen refused not slavery. Yet, you urge,
David, who was both a king and a prophet, refused to take
away Saul's life, because he was "the Lord's anointed."
David's refusal to do a thing doth not necessarily bind us
25 to the same refusal. It was as a private person that David
refused; is that a precedent binding at once upon a Council
of State, upon a Parliament, upon a whole nation? David
would not kill his private enemy by stealth; shall a public

lege punire? noluit regem occidere, timebit ergo Senatus tyrannum plectere? religio erat illi unctum Dei interficere, an ergo religio erit populo unctum suum capitis damnare? præsertim qui unctionem illam vel sacram vel civilem totus

5 cruore civium delibutus tam longa hostilitate aboleverat? Equidem reges, vel quos Deus per prophetas unxit, vel quos ad certum opus, sicuti olim Cyrum, nominatim destinavit, Isa. 44, unctos Domini agnosco; cæteros vel populi, vel militum, vel factionis tantummodò suæ unctos esse arbitror. Ve-

10 rùm ut concedam tibi omnes reges esse unctos Domini; esse tamen idcirco supra leges, non esse ob scelera quæcunque puniendos, nunquam evinces. Quid enim? et sibi et privatis quibusdam interdixit David, ne extenderent manus suas in unctum Domini. At regibus interdixit ipse Dominus, Psal.

15 105, ne attingerent unctos suos, id est, populum suum. Unctionem sui populi prætulit unctioni, siqua erat, regum. An ergò fideles punire, si quid contra leges commiserint, non licebit? Unctum Domini sacerdotem Abiatharem prope erat ut rex Solomon morte multaret; neque illi, quòd unctus Domini

20 esset, pepercit, sed quòd patris fuerat amicus. Si ergo summum sacerdotem, summum eundem in plerisque magistratum, unctio illa Domini et sacra et civilis eximere supplicio

officer therefore not punish a criminal according to law? He
would not kill a king; will a Senate therefore be afraid to
strike a tyrant? He scrupled to kill the Lord's anointed; must
the people therefore scruple to condemn to death their own
5 anointed?—especially one who by so long acting the public
enemy was all besmeared with his own subjects' blood, and
thus had done away his royal unction, whether sacred or civil.
Those kings indeed whom God by his prophets anointed, or
by name appointed to some special service, as of old he did
10 Cyrus, Isa. 44, I acknowledge as the Lord's anointed; the rest
are in my opinion the people's anointed, or the army's, or
the anointed of their own faction only. But that all kings are
the Lord's anointed, yet that therefore they are above all laws,
and not to be punished no matter what villainies they perpe-
15 trate—this you will never force me to grant you. What if
David forbade himself and some private persons to stretch
forth their hands against the Lord's anointed? God himself
forbade kings to touch his anointed—that is his people, Psal.
105. He preferred the anointing wherewith his people were
20 anointed, before that of kings, if any such there were. Yet
shall it not be lawful to punish even God's own believers if
they have transgressed against the laws? King Solomon was
about to put to death Abiathar the priest, though he were the
Lord's anointed too; and did not spare him because he was
25 the Lord's anointed, but because he had been his father's
friend. If therefore the Lord's sacred and civil unction could
not exempt from death the high priest, the same being in
many cases the highest officer of state, how comes a merely

non potuit, cur unctio tantùm civilis tyrannum eximeret? At *Saul quoque tyrannus erat, et morte dignus;* esto: non inde enim sequetur, dignum, aut idoneum fuisse Davidem qui sine populi authoritate, aut magistratuum jussu Saulem regem
5 quocunque in loco interficeret. Itáne verò Saul tyrannus erat? Utinam diceres; quinimmo dicis; cùm tamen suprà dixeris, *cap. 2. pag. 32, Tyrannum non fuisse, sed bonum et electum.* Ecquid causæ est nunc cur in foro quadruplator aut falsarius quispiam stigmate notetur, tu eâdem careas ignominiæ notâ?
10 cùm meliore profectò fide sycophantari soleant illi, quàm tu scribere, et res vel maximi momenti tractare. Saul igitur, si id ex usu est tuo, bonus erat rex; sin id minùs tibi expedit, repentè non rex bonus, sed tyrannus erit; quod certè mirum non est; dum enim potentiæ tyrannicæ tam impudenter lenoci-
15 naris, quid aliud facis quàm ex bonis regibus tyrannos omnes. At verò David quamvis regem socerum multis de causis, quæ ad nos nihil attinent, interimere nollet, sui tamen tuendi causâ copias comparare, Saulis urbes vel occupare vel insidere non dubitavit; et Cheilam oppidum contra Saulem etiam præsidio
20 tenuisset, nisi oppidanos erga se malè animatos cognovisset. Quid si Saul urbe obsessa, scalis muro admotis, primus ascendere voluisset, an censes Davidem arma protinus abjecturum, suos omnes uncto hosti proditurum fuisse? non existimo. Quidni enim fecisset quod nos fecimus, qui rationum suarum

civil unction to exempt a tyrant? But you say, "Saul too was
a tyrant, and deserved death." What then? It does not thence
follow that David, wherever he happened to be, was qualified
or empowered to kill King Saul without the people's author-
5 ity, or the command of the magistracy. But really and truly
was Saul a tyrant? I wish you would say so; indeed you do
say so, though you had said before in your second chapter,
page 32, that "he was no tyrant, but a good king, and chosen
of God." Now is there any reason why base informers and
10 perjurers should be publicly branded, and you escape without
the same mark of ignominy? For they are wont to practice
their falsifications with less treachery and deceit than you are
wont to write and to treat even matters of the greatest moment.
So Saul was a good king, if that serves your turn; if it suits you
15 not, he shall be, of a sudden, no good king but a tyrant. No
wonder; for in so shamelessly pandering to tyrannic power,
what do you else than turn good kings into tyrants all? But
David, though he would not put to death the king his father-
in-law for a number of reasons that we have nothing to do
20 withal, yet in his own defence hesitated not to raise an army,
and to take or besiege Saul's cities, and would have defended
the town of Keilah against the king's forces, had he not understood that the citizens were ill disposed toward him. Suppose
Saul had besieged the city, and set up ladders against the walls,
25 and himself resolved to be the first to scale them; do you think
David would straightway have thrown down his arms, and
have betrayed all his followers to his anointed enemy? I trow
not! Why should he not have done what we did? When his

necessitate coactus, Philistæis patriæ hostibus operam prolixè
suam pollicitus, id fecit contra Saulem quod nos in nostrum
tyrannum credo nunquam fecissemus. Pudet me, et jam diu
pertæsum est mendaciorum tuorum; *Inimicis potiùs parcen-*
5 *dum quàm amicis,* Anglorum esse dogma fingis; *séque regi*
suo parcere non debuisse, quia amicus erat. Quis unquam hoc
priùs audivit, quàm à te confictum esset, hominum mendacissime? Verùm ignoscimus: deerat nempe huic capiti præ-
stantissimum illud et tritissimum orationis tuæ pigmentum,
10 jam quintò, et ante finem libri decies ex loculis tuis et myro-
theciis expromendum, *molossis suis ferociores.* Non tam
Angli suis molossis ferociores sunt, quàm tu cane quovis ra-
bido jejunior, qui ad illam, quam toties evomuisti, cramben
duris ilibus identidem redire sustines. *David* denique *Ama-*
15 *lechitam* interfici jussit, Saulis, ut simulavit ipse, interfectorem; nulla hic neque facti neque personarum similitudo.
Quòd nisi David ad Philistæos defecisse, et pars eorum exercitûs fuisse visus, eò diligentiùs omnem à se suspicionem ma-
turandæ regi necis amovere studuit, non erat, meo quidem
20 judicio, cur virum illum tam malè exciperet, qui moribun-
dum jam regem et ægrè morientem opportuno vulnere se
confecisse nuntiavit. Quod idem factum in Domitiano, qui

interests so required, he freely proffered aid to the Philistines, the enemies of his country, thus doing against Saul what I am sure we should never have done against our tyrant.

I am ashamed, and have long been weary, of your lies. Falsely you declare it to be a principle of the English "That enemies are rather to be spared than friends, and that because their king was their friend they ought not to spare him." You impudent liar, what mortal ever heard this whimsy before you invented it? Yet we overlook it, for this chapter did not as yet present that most egregious worn-out rhetorical cosmetic of yours, which you now for the fifth time fetch out from the cabinets of pour perfumery-shop, and which before the end of your book is to be fetched thence ten times—that stuff about the English being "fiercer than their mastiffs!" The English are not so much fiercer than their own mastiffs as you are hungrier than any mad dog whatsoever, who with your tough guts can bear to return again and again to the cabbage you have so often vomited.

Then you tell us that David commanded the Amalekite to be put to death, who pretended to have killed Saul. But here is no likeness either in the deed or in the persons. There was, in my opinion at least, no motive for David's severe treatment of that man—who professed to have given the king a *coup de grâce* when the king was already at the point of death, and dying in anguish—unless David, because to all appearance he had gone over to the Philistines and joined their army, did the more zealously endeavor to clear himself from all suspicion of plotting the king's murder. The same action all men

Epaphroditum similiter capite damnavit, eò quòd Neronem in adipiscenda morte adjuvisset, ab omnibus reprehenditur. Novâ deinde audaciâ quem tyrannum modò dixeras, et *malo spiritu agitatum,* hunc non jam satis habes unctum Domini, 5 sed *Christum Domini* vocare; adeò tibi vile Christi nomen videtur, ut illo tam sancto nomine vel Dæmoniacum tyrannum impertire non metuas. Venio nunc ad exemplum illud, in quo qui jus populi jure regis antiquius esse non videt, cæcus sit oportet. Mortuo Solomone, populus de constituendo ejus 10 filio Sechemi comitia habebat; profectus est eò Roboamus candidatus, ne regnum tanquam hæreditatem adire, ne populum liberum tanquam paternos boves possidere videretur: proponit populus conditiones regni futuri; ad deliberandum rex triduum sibi dari postulat; consulit seniores; nihil illi de jure 15 regio, sed ut populum obsequio et pollicitationibus conciliet sibi, suadent, penès quem erat, vel illum creare regem vel præterire. Consulit deinde æquales suos, secum à pueris educatos; illi Salmasiano quodam œstro perciti, nil præter jus regium intonare, scuticas et scorpiones ut minitetur hortari. Horum 20 ex consilio respondit Roboamus populo. Videns itaque totus Israel regem *non auscultâsse sibi,* suam protinus libertatem et populare jus liberis palàm vocibus testatur: *Quæ nobis portio cum Davide? ad tentoria tua Israel; jam ipse videris de domo*

blame in Domitian, who put to death Epaphroditus likewise for helping Nero to kill himself. Next—another instance of your impudence—you call him not only the "anointed of the Lord," but "the Lord's Christ," whom you had just called a
5 tyrant, and one "driven and actuated by an evil spirit." Such base thoughts you have of the name of Christ that you fear not to give that so holy name to a tyrant possessed of a devil.

Now I come to that instance in which whoever sees not that the right of the people is superior to that of kings must indeed
10 be blind. When Solomon was dead, the people assembled at Sichem to make his son Rehoboam king. Thither himself went Rehoboam, as one that stood for the office, that he might not seem to claim the kingdom for his inheritance, or to hold a freeborn people as if they were his father's sheep and
15 oxen. The people propose conditions upon which his royal power shall rest. He desires three days time to advise; he consults with the old men; they advise him nothing about a royal right, but to comply with the people, and speak them fair, it being in their power to make him king or pass him by.
20 Then he consults with the young men that were grown up with him; they, as if stung mad by Salmasius's gadfly, keep dinning in his ears naught but royal right, and urging him to threaten whips and scorpions. Rehoboam answered the people as these advised him. So when all Israel saw that the
25 king "hearkened not unto them," at once with bold words they openly protest their own liberty and the right of the people. "What portion have we in David? To your tents, O Israel! now see to thine own house, David." When the king

tua David. Missum deinde à rege Adoramum lapidibus ob-
ruerunt; exemplum fortasse aliquod etiam in regem edituri,
nisi maxima celeritate se in fugam contulisset. Parat ingentem exercitum, quo in suam ditionem Israëlitas redigeret:
5 prohibet Deus; *ne ascendite,* inquit, *ne pugnate contra fratres
vestros, filios Israelis, nam à me facta est res ista.* Adverte jam
animum; populus antea regem volebat, displicuit id Deo;
eorum tamen juri noluit intercedere: nunc Populus Roboa-
mum non vult regem; id Deus non solùm penès populum esse
10 sinit, sed regem eo nomine bella moventem vetat ac reprimit:
nec ideo rebelles, sed nihilo minùs fratres eos qui desciverant
appellandos esse docet. Collige te nunc jam; sunt omnes, inquis, reges à Deo; ergo populus vel tyrannis resistere non
debet. Vicissim ego, sunt, inquam, populi conventus, comitia,
15 studia, suffragia, plebiscita pariter à Deo, teste hîc ipso; ergò
et rex itidem resistere non debet populo, authore etiam eodem
Deo. Quàm enim certum est, esse hodie reges à Deo, quámque hoc valet ad imperandam populo obedientiam, tam est
certum esse à Deo etiam hodie libera populi concilia, támque
20 hoc valet vel ad cogendos in ordinem reges, vel ad rejiciendos;
neque magis propterea bellum populo inferre debebunt,
quàm debuit Roboamus. Quæris cur ergò non defecerint Isra-

sent Adoram to them, they stoned him with stones, and perhaps were ready to make an example of the king himself had
he not made speed to flee. He raises a great army to reduce the
Israelites to their allegiance. God forbids: "Ye shall not go
5 up," says he, "nor fight against your brethren the children of
Israel; for this thing is from me." Now consider: heretofore
the people had desired a king; God was displeased with them
for it, but yet would not interpose against their right. Presently
the people reject Rehoboam from ruling them; and God not
10 only leaves the matter in their hands, but forbids Rehoboam
to make war against them for it, and stops him; and teaches
him withal, that those that had revolted from him were not
on that account to be called rebels, but none the less brethren.
Now look to your defences! You say that all kings are of God,
15 and that therefore the people ought not to resist even tyrants.
I answer you that the meetings and assemblies of the people,
their votes, their acts, endeavors, and decrees, are likewise of
God, by the testimony of God himself in this place; and consequently, by the authority of God himself, a king likewise,
20 according to your argument, ought not to resist the people.
For as certain as it is that at present kings are of God, and
whatever argument thence follows to enforce a people's obedience, so certain is it, that at present free assemblies of the
people are also of God, and this affords the same argument
25 for their right of keeping their kings in order, or for casting
them off; nor will kings on this account be any more justified
than was Rehoboam in making war on their subjects.

Why, then, you ask, did the Israelites not revolt from Sol-

elitæ à Solomone? quis præter te tàm stulta interrogaret, cùm
defecisse constet impunè à tyranno? In vitia quædam lapsus
est Solomon; non idcirco statim tyrannus: sua vitia magnis
virtutibus, magnis de repub. meritis compensabat: fac tyran-
5 num fuisse; sæpe est ut populus nolit tyrannum tollere, sæpe
est ut non possit: satis est sustulisse cùm potuerit. At *factum
Jeroboami semper improbatum fuit, et Apostasia ejus dete-
stata, successores ejus pro rebellibus semper habiti.* Apostasiam
ejus non à Roboamo, sed à vero cultu Dei reprehensam sæpiùs
10 lego; et successores quidem ejus sæpe reprobos, rebelles nusquam dictos memini. *Si quid fiat,* inquis, *juri et legibus contrarium, ex eo jus fieri non potest.* Quid quæso tum fiet juri
regio? Sic tuus ipse perpetuò refutator es. *Quotidie,* inquis,
adulteria, homicidia, furta impunè committuntur. An nescis
15 nunc te tibi respondere quærenti cur toties tyrannis impunè
fuerit? *Rebelles fuerunt isti reges, prophetæ tamen populum
ab eorum subjectione non abducebant.* Cur ergò, sceleste, et
pseudopropheta, populum Anglicanum à suis magistratibus,
tuo sint licèt judicio rebelles, abducere conaris? *Allegat,* in-
20 quis, *Anglicani latrocinii factio, se ad id scelus, quod tam nefariè suscepit, nescio qua voce cœlitùs missâ impulsos fuisse.*

omon? Who but you would ask a question so impertinent in view of the certainty that they did revolt from a tyrant, and with impunity? It is true, Solomon fell into some vices, but he was not therefore a tyrant; he made amends for his vices 5 by many excellent virtues and by deserving greatly of the commonwealth. But admit that he had been a tyrant; yet circumstances are often such that the people will not, and often such that they cannot, depose a tyrant: enough that they did it when it was in their power. "But," say you, "Jeroboam's 10 act was ever had in detestation, and his defection abominated; his successors were ever accounted rebels." Rather I find plenty of passages that blame his defection not from Rehoboam but from the true worship of God; and I remember that his successors are frequently called wicked, certainly, but 15 nowhere rebels.

"From an act that is contrary to law and right," say you, "no right can arise." Pray what then becomes of your right of kings? Thus do you perpetually confute yourself. You say, "Adulteries, murders, thefts are daily committed with im- 20 punity." Are you not aware that here you answer your own question how tyrants so often escape unpunished? You say: "Those kings were rebels, and yet the prophets made no attempts to seduce the people from their allegiance." And why do you, you rascally false prophet, endeavor to seduce the 25 people of England from their present magistrates, even supposing these to be rebels as you think? "This English faction of robbers," say you, "allege that they were put upon their wicked impious undertaking by some immediate voice from

Anglos hoc unquam allegâsse, de innumeris mendaciis et fig-
mentis tuis est unum. Sed pergo exemplis tecum agere; *Libna*
Urbs validissima ab Joramo rege defecit, quia is dereliquerat
Deum; defecit ergo rex, non urbs illa, neque defectione ista
5 notatur; sed si adjectam rationem spectes, approbari potiùs
videtur. *In Exemplum trahi non debent hujusmodi defec-
tiones.* Cur ergo tantâ vaniloquentiâ pollicitus es, exemplis
te nobiscum toto hoc capite decertaturum, cùm exempla ipse
nulla præter meras negationes, quarum nulla vis est ad pro-
10 bandum, afferre possis: nos quæ certa et solida attulimus, negas in exemplum trahi debere? Quis te hoc modo disputan-
tem non explodat? Provocâsti nos exemplis; exempla protu-
limus; quid tu ad hæc? tergiversaris, et diverticula quæris;
progredior itaque. Jehu regem à Propheta jussus occidit,
15 etiam Achaziam suum regem legitimum occidendum curavit.
Si noluisset Deus tyrannum interimi à cive, si impium hoc, si
mali exempli fuisset, cur jussit fieri? si jussit, certè licitum,
laudabile, præclarum fuit. Non tamen tyrannum perimi,
quia Deus jussit, idcirco bonum erat et licitum, sed quia bo-
20 num et licitum erat, idcirco Deus jussit. Jam septem annos

Heaven." That the English pretend to any such warrant as a justification of their actions is one of those many lies and fictions of yours.

But I proceed to treat you with examples. Libnah, a power-
5 ful city, revolted from King Joram, because he had forsaken God: it was the king therefore that revolted, not the city, nor is the city blamed for that revolt, but rather, if the added reason be considered, seems to be approved. "Revolts of this sort are not to be taken as examples," say you. But why did
10 you then so vauntingly promise that throughout this chapter you would contend with me by examples, whereas you can produce no examples but mere denials, which have no valid-ity as proofs, and when we have produced examples that are sure and substantial, you say they are no precedents? For
15 arguing like this who would not hiss you from the platform? You challenged us at precedents; we produced them; and what do you do? you turn your back, and look for byways of escape.

I proceed: Jehu, at the command of the prophet, slew a
20 king; nay, he ordered the death of Ahaziah, his own liege prince. If God would not have tyrants put to death by their own subjects, if it were a wicked thing, a thing of bad ex-ample, why did God himself command it? If he commanded it, it was lawful, commendable, and glorious. It was not
25 because God commanded it that it was right and lawful to kill a tyrant, but it was because it was right and lawful that God commanded it. Again, Jehoiada the high priest did not scruple to depose Athaliah, and kill her, though she had been

regnantem Athaliam Jehoiada sacerdos regno pellere et tru-
cidare non est veritus. *At regnum,* inquis, *non sibi debitum
sumpserat.* Annon Tiberius multo postea *imperium ad se nihil
pertinens?* illi tamen, et id genus tyrannis aliis, ex doctrina
5 Christi obediendum esse suprà affirmabas: ridiculum planè
esset, si potestatem regiam non ritè adeptum interficere liceret, pessimè gerentem non liceret. At per leges regnare non
potuit, utpote fœmina; *constitues autem super te regem,* non
reginam. Hoc si sic abibit, constitues, inquam, super te regem,
10 non tyrannum: discrepat enim longius rex à tyranno quàm
mas à fœmina. Amaziam regem ignavum et Idololatram non
conjurati quidam, sed principes et populus, quod verisimilius
est, morte affecerunt: nam fugientem Hierosolymis, et adju-
tum à nemine, Lachisum usque persecuti sunt. Hoc consilium
15 iniisse dicuntur *ex quo is Deum* deseruerat, neque ullam ab
Azaria filio de morte patris quæstionem habitam fuisse legimus. Multùm rursus nugaris ex Rabbinis, ut Regem Judaïcum
supra synedrium constituas; ipsa regis verba Zedechiæ non
attendis. Jer. 38. *Non is est rex qui possit contra vos quic-*
20 *quam.* Sic principes alloquitur; fassus se planè suo senatu

seven years in actual possession of the crown. "But," you say, "she had taken the government when she had no right to it." And did not Tiberius long after assume, as you say, "a sovereignty nowise belonging to him"? And yet you then kept affirming that, according to Christ's teaching, he and other such tyrants ought to be obeyed. It were a most ridiculous thing to imagine, that a king who gets in by usurpation may lawfully be deposed, but one that rules tyrannically may not. But, say you, according to the law, she could not possibly reign, being a woman. "Thou shalt set over thee a king," not a queen. If this comes off, I put it thus: "Thou shalt set over thee a king," not a tyrant. For there is a far greater unlikeness between a king and a tyrant than between a male and a female.

Amaziah a cowardly idolatrous king was put to death, not by a few conspirators, but rather, it should seem, by the nobility and the people. For he fled from Jerusalem, and had none to stand by him, and they pursued him even to Lachish. This counsel against him, says the history, they took "after the time that Amaziah did turn away from following the Lord"; and we do not find that Azariah as a son made any public investigation into his father's death.

And now once more you quote much silly stuff out of the rabbins, to prove that the king of the Jews was superior to the Sanhedrim, but you do not consider king Zedekiah's own words, Jer. 38: "The king is not he that can do anything against you." This is how he addresses the princes, clearly confessing himself inferior to the great council of the realm.

inferiorem. *Fortasse,* inquis, *nihil negare illis ausus metu seditionis.* At tuum illud *fortasse* quanti quæso est, cujus asseveratio firmissima non est pili? quid enim te levius, quid inconstantius; quid instabilius? quoties te varium et versico-
5 lorem, quoties tibimet discordem, dissidentem à temetipso, et discrepantem offendimus? Rursus comparationes instituis Caroli cum bonis Judææ regibus. Davidem imprimis quasi contemnendum aliquem nominas; *Sume tibi Davidem,* inquis, *adulterii simul et homicidii reum; nihil tale in Carolo.*
10 *Solomon ejus filius qui sapiens audiit vulgo.* Quis non indignetur maximorum et sanctissimorum virorum etiam regum nomina ab impurissimo nebulone et vappa hunc in modum jactari? Túne Carolum cum Davide, superstitiosum et Christianæ doctrinæ vix initiatum cum rege et propheta
15 religiosissimo, stolidum cum sapientissimo, imbellem cum fortissimo, iniquissimum cum justissimo conferre sustinuisti? castimoniam tu ejus et continentiam laudes, quem cum Duce Bucchingamio flagitiis omnibus coopertum novimus? secretiora ejus et recessus perscrutari quid attinet, qui in Theatro
20 medias mulieres petulanter amplecti, et suaviari, qui virginum et matronarum papillas, ne cætera dicam, attrectare in propatulo consueverat? Te porro moneo Pseudoplutarche, ut istiusmodi Parallelis ineptissimis dehinc supersedeas, ne ego

"Perhaps," say you, "he durst not deny them anything for fear of sedition." But what does your "perhaps" signify, when your most positive assertion is not worth even the estimation of a hair? For what can be more fickle and shifty and
5 inconsistent than you? How often have I caught you changing sides and colors, disagreeing with yourself, unsaying with one breath what you have said with another?

You make comparisons again betwixt king Charles and some of the good kings of Judah. First you mention David as
10 one to be despised. "Take David," you say, "guilty at once of adultery and murder; no such thing in Charles. Solomon his son, commonly called the wise," etc. Who would not grow indignant at this filthy rascally fool's bandying about the names of worthies, nay of kings, eminent in greatness and
15 piety? Dare you compare King David with King Charles; a most religious king and prophet with a superstitious prince and a mere novice in the Christian religion; a most prudent wise prince with a stupid one; a valiant prince with a cowardly; a most just prince with a most unjust? Can you com-
20 mend the chastity and self-control of one whom together with the Duke of Buckingham we know to be covered with every kind of infamy? It were to no purpose to inquire into the private actions of his life, who in public at the theatre would wantonly embrace and kiss women, and handle virgins'
25 and matrons' breasts, not to mention the rest. I advise you in your turn, you counterfeit Plutarch, henceforth to abstain from such absurd Parallels, lest I be forced to publish con-

quæ tacerem alioqui libens de Carolo, necesse habeam enun-
tiare. Contra tyrannos quid tentatum à Populo aut peractum
fuerit, et quo jure, per ea tempora quibus ipse Deus Hebræorum rempub. suo nutu ac verbo quasi præsens regebat, hacte-
5 nus liquet. Quæ sequuntur ætates non nos sua authoritate
ducunt, sed ad majorum suorum normam et rationem omnia
dirigentes, imitatione sua nostram tantummodò confirmant.
Cùm itaque Deus post captivitatem Babylonicam nullum iis
de repub. mandatum dedisset novum, quamvis regia soboles
10 extincta non esset, ad antiquam et Mosaïcam reipub. formam
reverterunt. Antiocho Syriæ regi, cui erant vectigales, ejusque
præsidibus, quòd is vetita imperaret, per Maccabæos pontifices
restiterunt; séque armis in libertatem vindicârunt; dignissimo
deinde cuique principatum dederunt: donec Hyrcanus Simo-
15 nis Judæ Maccabæi fratris filius, expilato Davidis sepulcro,
militem externum alere, et regiam quandam potestatem ad-
jicere sacerdotio cœpit; unde filius ejus Aristobulus diadema
sibi primus imposuit. Nihil in eum populus quamvis tyrannum movit aut molitus est; neque mirum, annum tantum-
20 modo regnantem. Ipse etiam morbo gravissimo correptus, et
suorum facinorum pœnitentiâ ductus, mortem sibi optare non
destitit, donec inter ea vota expiravit. Ejus frater Alexander
proximus regnabat. *Contra hunc* äis *neminem insurrexisse,*

cerning king Charles what otherwise I would fain pass over in silence.

So far it is clear what the People acted or attempted against tyrants, and by what right, in those times when God himself did immediately, as it were, by his word of command govern the Hebrew commonwealth. The ages that succeed do not guide us by their own authority, but, in governing all according to the rule and reason of their forefathers, they only confirm us in our opinion. For after the Babylonish captivity, when God gave no new command concerning the state, though the royal line was not extinct, the people returned to the old mosaical form of government. They were one while tributaries to Antiochus, king of Syria; yet when he enjoined them things that were unlawful, it was under the conduct of their high priests, the Maccabees, that they resisted him and his governors, and by force regained their former liberty. After that, whoever was accounted most worthy of it had the principality conferred upon him, till at last Hyrcanus the son of Simon, the brother of Judas Maccabaeus, plundered David's sepulchre, and began to keep foreign soldiers, and to invest the priesthood with a kind of regal power; whereupon his son Aristobulus was the first that assumed the crown. Though he was a tyrant, the people stirred not against him, which is no great wonder, for he reigned but one year. And he himself being overtaken with a grievous disease, and repenting of his crimes, ceased not to wish for death, till amid his wishes he breathed his last. His brother Alexander succeeded him; "and nobody rose against him," you say,

tyrannus cùm esset. O te securè mendacem si periisset Josephus, restaret tantùm *Josippus* tuus, ex quo Pharisæorum quædam nullius usus apophthegmata depromis. Res itaque sic se
habet: Alexander, cùm et domi et militiæ rempub. malè ad-
5 ministraret, quamvis magna Pisidarum et Cilicum manu con-
ductitiâ se tutaretur, populum tamen cohibere non potuit,
quin ipsum etiam sacrificantem, utpote indignum eo munere,
thyrsis palmeis et citreis penè obrueret; exinde per sexennium
gentis ferè totius gravi bello petitus est; in quo Judæorum
10 multa millia cùm occidisset, et pacis tandem cupidus interrogaret eos quid vellent à se fieri, responderunt uno ore omnes,
ut moreretur; vix etiam mortuo se veniam daturos. Hanc
historiam tibi incommodissimam, quoquo modo avertere ut
posses, fraudi tuæ turpissimæ pharisaïcas quasdam sententio-
15 las obtendisti; cùm exemplum hoc aut omnino prætermisisse,
aut rem, sicuti gesta erat, fideliter narrâsse debuisses, nisi vete-
rator et lucifugus mendaciis longè plus quàm causæ con-
fideres. Quinetiam Pharisæi illi octingenti, quos in crucem
tolli jussit, ex eorum numero erant, qui contra ipsum arma
20 ceperant: quique omnes cùm cæteris una voce testati sunt,
se regem morte affecturos fuisse, si bello victus in suam
potestatem venisset. Post maritum Alexandrum Alexandra
regnum capessit; ut olim Athalia, non legitimè, nam regnare

tyrant though he were. Ah, you might have lied quite fear-
less of discovery had but Josephus been lost, and only your
"Josippus" left extant, from whom you fetch out some in-
effectual utterances of the Pharisees. The facts are these: Al-
5 exander governed ill, both in war and in peace; and though
he kept a great troop of Pisidian and Cilician mercenaries for
a bodyguard, yet could he not restrain the people; but even
whilst he was sacrificing they fell upon him as unworthy
of that function, and had almost smothered him with boughs
10 of palm trees and citron trees. Afterward, for six years,
almost the whole nation made war upon him; and when
he had slain many thousands of the Jews in this war, and at
length desired peace, and asked what they would have him
do, they answered with one voice that he should die, nay,
15 that they should hardly pardon him after his death. To get
rid by hook or crook of this history, so inconvenient to
you, you hid it behind a few trifling sententious Pharisaical
speeches—to your own deep disgrace and damage; for you
ought either to have let this example quite alone, or to have
20 told the facts;—were it not that, like the old daylight-shun-
ning trickster that you are, you give far more weight to your
lies than to your cause. Even those eight hundred Pharisees
whom he commanded to be crucified, were of their number
that had taken up arms against him; and they and the rest of
25 the people had unanimously protested that they would put
him to death if they could defeat him and lay hands upon
him. After the death of Alexander, his wife Alexandra seized
the crown, like Athaliah of old, not according to law, for (as

fœminam leges non sinebant, quod ipse modò fassus es, sed
partim vi, (extraneorum enim exercitum ducebat;) partim
gratiâ, nam Pharisæos, qui apud vulgus plurimum poterant,
sibi conciliaverat hac lege, ut nomen imperii penès illam, im-
5 perium ipsum penès illos foret. Haud aliter atque apud nos
nuper Scoti Presbyteri nomen Regis Carolo concesserunt, ea
mercede ut regnum sibi reservare possent. Post Alexandræ
obitum Hyrcanus et Aristobulus ejus filii de regno conten-
dunt; hic viribus et industria potior fratrem natu majorem
10 regno pellit. Pompeio deinde in Syriam à Mithridatico bello
divertente, Judæi nactos se jam æquissimum libertatis suæ arbitrum Pompeium rati, legationem pro se mittunt; fratribus
utrisque regibus renuntiant; ad servitutem se ab iis adductos
queruntur; Pompeius Aristobulum regno privavit; Hyrcano
15 pontificatum reliquit et principatum more patrio legitimum;
exinde Pontifex et Ethnarcha dictus est. Iterum sub Archelao
Herodis filio Judæi, missis ad Augustum Cæsarem quinquaginta legatis, et Herodem mortuum et Archelaum graviter
accusârunt; regnum huic pro sua virili parte abrogârunt, Cæ-
20 sarem orant ut Populum Judaïcum sine regibus esse permitteret. Quorum Cæsar precibus aliquantum permotus, non
regem eum, sed Ethnarcham duntaxat constituit. Ejus anno

you have just remarked) the laws of the Jews admitted not a
woman to the throne, but partly by force, for she maintained
an army of foreigners, and partly by favor, for she had got
the support of the Pharisees, who had the greatest influence
5 over the people, upon the understanding that she was to have
the royal name, but they the power. Just so in my country the
Scotch Presbyterians lately granted Charles the name of king,
but for a consideration—namely that they might keep the
royal authority in their own hands. After the death of Alex-
10 andra, Hyrcanus and Aristobulus her sons were at strife for
the sovereignty: Aristobulus, who was more active, and had
stronger support, forced his elder brother out of the kingdom.
A while after, when Pompey turned aside into Syria from the
Mithridatic war, the Jews, thinking that in him they had now
15 found a wholly disinterested arbiter of their liberty, dispatch
an embassy to him in their own name; they renounce the rule
of both the brothers, and complain that they had been enslaved by them. Pompey deposed Aristobulus, and left to
Hyrcanus the priesthood and the royal rank to which ances-
20 tral law entitled him: thenceforward he was called High
Priest and Ethnarch. Once more, in the reign of Archelaus
the son of Herod, the Jews sent fifty ambassadors to Augustus
Caesar; made serious charges against Herod that was dead,
and Archelaus; deposed the latter as much as in them lay, and
25 petitioned the emperor to let the people of the Jews be without a king. Caesar, somewhat moved at their entreaty, made
the appointee not a king but only an Ethnarch. Yet again, in
the tenth year of this governorship, the People by their am-

decimo rursus eum Populus per legatos ad Cæsarem tyrannidis accusat; quibus Cæsar benignè auditis Romam accer-
situm, et judicio damnatum Viennam in exilium misit. Jam
mihi velim respondeas; qui suos reges accusatos, qui damna-
5 tos, qui punitos volebant, annon ipsi, si potestas facta, si optio
data sibi esset, annon ipsi, inquam, judicio damnâssent, ipsi
supplicio affecissent? Jam in Romanos præsides avarè et crudeliter provinciam administrantes, populum et primores etiam
sæpiùs arma sumpsisse non negas; causas more tuo stultissimas
10 affingis, *nondum jugo erant assueti;* sub Alexandro scilicet,
Herode, ejúsque filiis. At C. Cæsari et Petronio *bellum inferre*
noluerunt. Prudenter illi quidem, non poterant. Vis ipsorum
audire verba? πολεμεῖν μὲν οὐ βουλόμενοι διὰ τὸ μηδ᾽ ἂν δύνασθαι.
Quod ipsi fatentur imbecillitatis esse suæ, hoc tu hypocrita
15 ad religionem refers? Magno dein molimine prorsus nihil
agis, dum ex patribus probas, quod et antea tamen pari osci-
tatione feceras, pro regibus orandum esse. Nam pro bonis
quis negat? pro malis quoad spes est; pro latronibus etiam et
pro hostibus; non ut agros depopulentur, aut nos occisione
20 occidant, sed ut resipiscant. Oramus pro utrisque; illos tamen
legibus, hos armis vindicare quis vetat? *Liturgias Ægyptiacas*

bassadors to Caesar accused the Ethnarch of tyranny. Caesar heard them graciously, sent for him, and upon his conviction banished him to Vienne. Answer me now: a people that accused their kings, that desired their condemnation, that desired their punishment, would not they themselves rather, if it had been in their power, and that they might have had their choice, would not they themselves, I say, have convicted them, and put them to death? You do not deny that the people and the nobles often took up arms against Roman governors who ruled provinces avariciously or cruelly; but you give a ridiculous reason for this, as usual: "They were not yet accustomed to the yoke." Very likely, under Alexander, Herod, and his son! But, say you, they would not "make war against" Gaius Caesar and Petronius. And very wise of them, too, for they were not able. Will you hear their own words? "Not wishing to make war because we cannot." What they themselves acknowledge to be due to weakness, do you, you hypocrite, attribute to religion?

Next with much ado you do nothing; for you endeavor to prove out of the fathers what you had proved as superficially before, that kings are to be prayed for. That good kings are to be prayed for, no man denies; nay, and bad ones too, as long as there is any hope of them: nay and highwaymen, and our enemies. But how? not that they may lay waste our territory, or slay us with slaughter, but that they may come to their right minds. We pray for both thieves and enemies, and yet who would forbid us to punish the one by law and the other by arms? I value not your "Egyptian liturgies"; but that priest

nîl moror; sacerdos autem ille qui orabat, uti aïs, ut *Commo-dus patri succederet,* meo quidem judicio non orabat, sed Romano imperio pessima imprecatus est. *Fidem,* aïs, *fregisse nos, de authoritate et majestate regis conservanda solenni* 5 *conventione non semel interpositam.* Expecto te fusiùs ista de re infrà, illic te rursus conveniam. Redis ad patrum commen-tationes, de quibus hoc summatim accipe: Quicquid illi dixe-rint, neque ex libris sacris, aut ratione aliqua satis idonea con-firmaverint, perinde mihi esse, ac si quis alius è vulgo dixisset. 10 Primum adfers Tertullianum, scriptorem haud orthodoxum, multis erroribus notatum, ut si tecum sentiret, pro nihilo ta-men hoc esset. Quid autem ille? damnat tumultus, damnat rebelliones; damnamus et nos, neque hinc statim de jure omni populorum, de privilegiis, et Senatusconsultis, de pote-15 state magistratuum omnium cæterorum præterquam unius regis, præjudicatum esse volumus: loquuntur isti de sedi-tionibus temerè conflatis, et multitudinis insania, non de ma-gistratibus, non de Senatu, aut Parlamento ad legitima arma populum contra tyrannos convocante. Unde Ambrosius quem 20 citas, *Non repugnare, flere, gemere, hæc sunt munimenta Sacerdotis, et quis est qui potest vel unus vel inter paucos dicere Imperatori, Lex tua mihi non probatur? non permit-*

who prayed, you say, "that Commodus might succeed his father," was not praying at all, in my opinion, but did imprecate all the mischiefs imaginable upon the Roman state.

You say "that we have broken our word, which we pledged more than once in solemn assemblies, to preserve the authority and majesty of the king." I wait for you further on, where you speak more fully upon this subject, and shall meet you there again.

You return then to the comments of the fathers; concerning whom take this in short. Whatever they say which is not warranted by the authority of the scriptures, or by good and sufficient reason, shall be of no more regard with me, than if any other and ordinary man had said it. The first that you quote is Tertullian, who is no orthodox writer, and is notorious for many errors; so that his authority, if he were of your opinion, would yet stand you in no stead. But what says he? He condemns riots and rebellions. So do we. But in saying so, we would not have a premature decision rendered upon all the people's rights and privileges, all the acts and resolutions of senates, and the power of all magistrates, the king alone excepted. The fathers are condemning seditions rashly kindled by the heat of a mad multitude; they speak not of magistrates, of senates, of Parliaments, summoning the people to lawful arms against their tyrants. Hence Ambrose, whom you quote: "Not to resist," says he, "but to weep and groan, these are the Priest's protection and defence. Who is there that, whether alone or among a little number, dare say to the Emperor, 'I do not like your laws'? This is

titur hoc dicere Sacerdotibus, permittetur Laicis? Vides jam
planè de quibus hic loquatur; de Sacerdotibus, de Laïcis privatis, non de Magistratibus: vides quàm infirma tamen et
præpostera ratione usus, dissensioni inter Laïcos et Sacerdotes,
5 de legibus etiam civilibus postmodùm futuræ facem prætulerit. Sed quoniam primorum Christianorum exemplis ur-
geri nos maximè, et redargui putas, quòd illi omnibus modis
vexati *bellum in Cæsares non moverent,* ostendam primò non
potuisse, deinde quoties poterant movisse; postremò etiamsi,
10 cùm possent, non movissent, non esse tamen cæteroqui dignos
quorum ex vita et moribus, tantis in rebus, exempla sumamus.
Primùm ignorare hoc nemo potest, ex quo Romana respublica nulla fuit, omnes imperii vires rerúmque summam ad
unum Cæsarem rediisse; omnes legiones sub uno Cæsare sti-
15 pendia meruisse: adeò ut Senatus ad unum omnis, totus ordo
Equester, plebs universa, si novis rebus studuisset, poterant se
quidem internecioni objecisse, ad libertatem tamen recupe-
randam nihil prorsus effecissent; nam imperatorem si forte
sustulissent, imperium tamen mansisset. Jam verò Christiani,
20 innumeri licet, at sparsi, inermes, plebeii et plerunque infimi,
quid potuerunt? quantam eorum multitudinem una legio in

not allowed the priests, and shall laymen pretend to it?" It is evident of whom he speaks, viz., of priests, and of private laymen, not of the magistrates; you see nevertheless by how weak and perverse an argument he carried his torch in the
5   van of the dissensions that were afterwards to arise betwixt the laity and the clergy concerning even civil laws.

But because you think you confute us and press hardest upon us with the examples of the primitive Christians, who, though they were harassed every way, yet "never took up
10 arms against the emperor," I will show in the first place that for the most part they could not; secondly, that whenever they could, they did; and thirdly, that even if they did not when they could, yet in other respects they deserve not that in so many matters we should take pattern after their lives
15 and conduct.

First, as everybody knows, when the republic of Rome ceased, the whole and sovereign power in the empire was settled in the Emperor alone; all the soldiers were under the pay of the Emperor alone; insomuch that if the whole body
20 of the senate, the equestrian order, and all the common people had endeavored a revolution, they might indeed have exposed themselves to massacre, but could accomplish absolutely nothing towards retrieving their lost liberty; for though they might perhaps have killed the emperor, the empire
25 would still have continued. This being so, what could the Christians do? It is true there were a great many of them, but they were scattered and unarmed, and were of the common people, generally of the lowest class. How many of

officio facilè continuisset? Quod magni sæpe duces cum in-
teritu suo et veteranorum exercituum deletione incassum
tentârunt, isti è plebecula ferè homuli posse se ad exitum per-
ducere sperarent? cùm annis à Christo nato prope trecentis,
5 ante Constantinum plùs minùs viginti, imperante Diocletiano,
sola Thebæa legio Christiana esset; eóque ipso nomine à re-
liquo exercitu in Gallia ad Octodurum oppidum cæsa est.
Cum Cassio, cum Albino, cum Nigro non conjurârunt: idne
illis gratiæ vult apponi Tertullianus, quòd sanguinem pro in-
10 fidelibus non profuderunt? Constat igitur Christianos ab
imperatorum imperio liberare se non potuisse: cum aliis conjurare non Christianis nequaquam sibi expedivisse, quamdiu
imperatores Ethnici regnabant. Bellum autem tyrannis postea intulisse Christianos, aut armis se defendisse, aut tyran-
15 norum facta nefaria sæpe ultos esse nunc ostendam. Primus
omnium Constantinus jam Christianus consortem imperii
Licinium Orientalibus Christianis gravem bello sustulit; quo
facto illud simul declaravit, posse à magistratu in magistratum animadverti; cùm is Licinium pari jure secum regnan-
20 tem subditorum ejus causâ supplicio affecerit, nec Deo soli
pœnam reliquerit: poterat enim Licinius Constantinum, si
Constantinus populum sibi attributum iis modis oppressisset,
eodem supplicio affecisse. Postquam igitur à Deo ad homines

them might not one legion easily have kept in subjection? That which many great generals, at the price of their own deaths and the wiping out of armies of tried and seasoned troops attempted in vain, could those rabble manikins expect to accomplish? About A.D. 300, more or less twenty years before Constantine, when Diocletian was emperor, only the Theban legion was Christian; and for no other reason it was slain by the rest of the army at Octodurum in Gaul.

The Christians, say you, conspired not "with Cassius, with Albinus, with Niger"; and does not Tertullian count it creditable to them that they poured not out their blood for infidels? It is evident therefore that the Christians could not free themselves from the sway of the Emperors; and it could be no ways advantageous to their interest to conspire with infidels as long as heathen emperors reigned.

That afterwards, however, the Christians did make war upon tyrants, and defend themselves by force of arms, and many times punish tyrants' abominations, I shall now make plain. First of them all, Constantine, after his conversion to Christianity, made war upon Licinius his co-emperor, who oppressed the Eastern Christians, and destroyed him. By this act of his he made it clear that one magistrate might punish another, for he for his subjects' sake put to death Licinius, who was as absolute in the empire as himself, and did not leave the vengeance to God alone; and Licinius might likewise have put to death Constantine if Constantine had likewise crushed the people committed to his government. So then, since the matter is referred by God to men, why did

redacta res est, quod Licinio Constantinus erat, cur non idem
Carolo Senatus? Constantinum enim milites, Senatum jura
constituerunt regibus parem, imo superiorem. Constantio
imperatori Arriano Byzantini, quoad poterant, armis restite-
5 runt; missum cum militibus Hermogenem, ad pellendum
ecclesiâ Paulum orthodoxum episcopum, facto impetu repu-
lerunt, et incensis ædibus, quò se receperat, semiustum et
laniatum interfecerunt. Constans fratri Constantio bellum
minatur, ni Paulo et Athanasio episcopis sedes suas restituat;
10 vidésne ut istos sanctissimos patres, de episcopatu cùm agitur,
bellum fraternum in regem suum concitare non puduerit?
Haud multò pòst Christiani milites, qui tunc temporis quos
volebant imperatores creabant, Constantem Constantini filium dissolutè et superbè regnantem interfecerunt, translato ad
15 Magnentium imperio. Quid? qui Julianum nondum apostatam, sed pium et strenuum, invito Constantio imperatore suo
imperatorem salutârunt, annon ex illis Christianis fuerunt,
quos tu exemplo nobis proponis? Quod factum Constantius
cum suis literis ad populum recitatis acriter prohiberet, cla-
20 mârunt omnes, fecisse se ut Provincialis, et miles, et reipublicæ authoritas decreverat. Iidem bellum Constantio indixe-

not Parliament stand to King Charles as Constantine to
Licinius? The soldiers made Constantine what he was; but
our laws have made our Parliament equal, nay, superior to
our kings.

5   The inhabitants of Constantinople resisted Constantius, an
Arian emperor, by force of arms, as long as they were able,
and when he sent Hermogenes with troops to depose Paul
the orthodox bishop, they charged him and repulsed him,
fired the house whither he had betaken himself, mangled
10 and half-burned him, and at last killed him outright. Constans threatened to make war upon his brother Constantius
unless he would restore Paul and Athanasius to their bishoprics. You see how those holy fathers, when their bishoprics
were at stake, were not ashamed to stir up their king's own
15 brother to make war upon him. Not long after, the Christian soldiers, who then made whom they would emperors,
put to death Constans the son of Constantine because he behaved himself dissolutely and proudly in the government,
and turned the empire over to Magnentius. When Julian was
20 not yet apostate, but virtuous and valiant, certain persons
saluted him as Emperor, against the will of Constantius their
actual emperor. How now? Are they not amongst the number of those primitive Christians whom you place as a pattern
for us? When Constantius, by letter openly read to the people,
25 sharply forbade this action of theirs, they all cried out that
they had but done what their Provincial and the army and
the authority of the commonwealth had decided. The same

runt, et quantum in se erat, imperio ac vita spoliârunt. Quid Antiocheni, homines apprimè Christiani? orârunt credo pro Juliano jam Apostata, quem palàm adire, et convitiis proscindere solebant, cujus barbam illudentes promissam, funes 5 ex ea conficere jubebant. Cujus morte audita supplicationes, epulas, et lætitiam publicè indixerunt, ejus pro vita et incolumitate preces fudisse censes? Quid? quòd eundem etiam à Christiano commilitone interfectum esse ferunt. Sozomenus certè scriptor ecclesiasticus non negat; immo, siquis ita fecis 10 set, laudat: οὐ γὰρ ἀπεικός τινα τῶν τότε στρατευομένων, &c. *Non est mirum,* inquit, *aliquem ex militibus hoc secum cogitâsse; non Græcos solùm, sed omnes homines ad hanc usque ætatem tyrannicidas laudare solitos esse, qui pro omnium libertate mortem oppetere non dubitant; nec temere quis hunc* 15 *militem reprehendat, Dei et religionis causâ tam strenuum.* Hæc Sozomenus ejusdem ætatis scriptor, vir bonus et sanctus; ex quo quid reliqui ea tempestate viri boni hac de re senserint, facilè perspicimus. Ipse Ambrosius ab imperatore Valentiniano minore jussus urbe Mediolano excedere, parere noluit, sed 20 circumseptus armato populo se atque basilicam suam contra regios præfectos armis defendit; et summæ potestati resistere, contra quàm docuit ipse, est ausus. Constantinopoli haud

persons declared war against Constantius, and, as much as in them lay, deprived him of his empire and his life.

What of the inhabitants of Antioch, who were Christians exceedingly? After Julian apostatized, I suppose they prayed for him, when they used to brave him to his face, and defame and revile, and scoff at his long beard and bid him make ropes of it! Think you they used to pray for the health and long life of one upon the news of whose death they offered thanksgivings, made feasts, and gave public demonstrations of joy? Nay, is it not reported that he was killed by a Christian soldier in his own army? Sozomen, a writer of ecclesiastical history, does not deny it, but commends him that did it, if the fact were so: "For it is no wonder," says he, "that some one of his own soldiers might think within himself that not only the Greeks but all mankind hitherto had been wont to praise tyrant-killers, who go unhesitating to death to procure the liberty of all: so that that soldier ought not rashly to be condemned who in the cause of God and of religion was so zealous and valiant." These are the words of Sozomen, a contemporary author, and a good and religious man; by which we may easily apprehend what the general opinion of good men in those days was upon this point. Ambrose himself being commanded by the emperor Valentinian the younger to depart from Milan, refused to obey him, but, hedged about by his people in arms, defended himself and his basilica against the emperor's officers, and, contrary to his own doctrine, dared resist the higher powers. At Constantinople more than once there was great insurrection

semel propter exilium Chrysostomi contra Arcadium imperatorem seditio maxima commota est. In tyrannos igitur quid
antiqui Christiani fecerint, non milites solùm, sed populus,
sed ipsi patres, vel resistendo, vel gerendo bellum, vel conci-
5 tando, usque ad Augustini tempora, quoniam tibi ulteriùs
progredi non libet, breviter exposui. Valentinianum enim
Placidiæ filium interfectum à Maximo patricio, ob stuprum
uxori ejus illatum, taceo: Avitum etiam imperatorem dimissis
militibus suis luxuriâ diffluentem à Senatu Romano confes-
10 tim exutum imperio non commemoro: quia annos aliquot
post Augustini obitum ista acciderunt. Verùm dono tibi hoc
omne, tu nihil horum exposuisse me finge, paruerint per omnia suis regibus veteres Christiani, quicquam contra tyrannos
ne fecerint, aut fecisse voluerint, non esse tamen eos quorum
15 authoritate niti debeamus, aut à quibus exempla petere salutariter possimus, quod superest, nunc docebo. Jam diu ante
Constantinum populus Christianus multum de primæva illa
sanctimonia et sinceritate cùm doctrinæ tum morum deperdi-
derat. Postquam immensis opibus ditata ab eo ecclesia, ho-
20 nores, dominatum, et potentiam civilem adamare cœpit,
statim omnia in præceps ruere. Primò luxus et segnities, errorum deinde omnium et vitiorum caterva, veluti solutis aliunde
carceribus, in ecclesiam immigravit; hinc invidentia, odium,
discordia passim redundabat; tandem haud mitius inter se

against the emperor Arcadius, by reason of Chrysostom's
exile. I have now briefly shown how the primitive Christians
behaved themselves towards tyrants; how not soldiers only,
but the people, yea the very fathers of the church, resisted
5 them, and made or incited war upon them, till Austin's time:
for it suits you yourself to go no lower. Therefore I make no
mention of Valentinian the son of Placidia, who was slain by
Maximus a nobleman, for committing adultery with his wife:
nor do I mention Avitus the emperor, whom, because he dis-
10 banded the soldiers, and gave himself wholly to his lusts, the
Roman senate immediately deposed; because these things
came to pass some years after Austin's death.

But I will make you a present of all this; pretend that I have
not set forth any of it; suppose it conceded that the primitive
15 Christians obeyed their kings through thick and thin, and
never took or wished to take any action against tyrants; yet
as I will now show, they were not such that we ought to rely
upon their authority, or can safely follow their example. Long
before Constantine's time the generality of Christians had lost
20 much of the primitive sanctity and integrity both of their religion and of their conduct. Afterwards, the church, which
he had vastly enriched, began to fall in love with offices, absolute rule, and secular power, and then the Christian religion
went to wrack. First luxury and sloth, and then a crew of all
25 the heresies and vices, as if their dungeons had been set open
from behind, trooped over into the church; thereupon envy,
hatred, and discord overflowed everywhere, and at last they
that were linked together into one brotherhood by that dear

charissimo religionis vinculo fratres quàm hostes acerrimi dis-
sidebant; nullus pudor, nulla officii ratio restabat; milites, et
copiarum præfecti quoties ipsis visum erat, nunc imperatores
novos creabant, nunc bonos pariter ac malos necabant. Quid
5 Vetranniones et Maximos, quid Eugenios à militibus ad imperium subitò evectos, quid Gratianum optimum principem,
quid Valentinianum minorem non pessimum, occisos ab iis
commemorem? Militum hæc quidem facinora et castren-
sium, sed tamen Christianorum illius ætatis, quam tu maximè
10 evangelicam et imitandam esse aïs. Jam ergo de ecclesiasticis
pauca accipe: Pastores et Episcopi, et nonnunquam illi, quos
admiramur, Patres, sui quisque gregis ductores, de episcopatu
non secus quàm de tyrannide certabant: nunc per urbem, nunc
in ipsa ecclesia, ad ipsum altare sacerdotes, et Laïci promiscuè
15 digladiabantur; cædes faciebant, strages utrinque magnas
nonnunquam ediderunt. Damasi et Ursicini, qui cum Ambro-
sio floruerunt, potes meminisse. Longum esset Byzantinos,
Antiochenos, et Alexandrinos illos tumultus, sub Cyrillo præsertim, quem tu laudas obedientiæ prædicatorem, duce ac
20 patre; occiso penè à monachis in illo urbico prælio, Oreste
Theodosii præfecto. Jam tua quis vel impudentia vel supini-
tate non obstupescat? *Usque ad Augustinum,* inquis, *et infra
ejus ætatem, nulla cujusquam privati aut præfecti, aut plurium conjuratorum extat in historiis mentio, qui regem suum*

and gracious bond of religion were as much at variance and
strife as the bitterest enemies. No reverence, no consideration of their duty was left: the soldiers and commanders of
the army, as oft as they pleased themselves, now created new
5 emperors, now killed good ones and bad ones alike. I need
not mention such as Vetrannio, Maximus, Eugenius, whom
the soldiers all of a sudden lifted up to the imperial throne, or
Gratian, an excellent prince, or Valentinian the younger, none
of the worst, whom they put to death. True, these were the
10 deeds of soldiers and camp-followers,—but yet of Christians
of that age which you call most evangelical and most to be
imitated! Therefore you shall now hear a few words about
the clergy. Pastors and Bishops, and sometimes those Fathers
whom we admire, each a leader of his flock—those very men,
15 I say, would fight for a bishopric as if for a tyrant's throne;
priests and laymen promiscuous would clash swords now
throughout the city, now in the very church at the very altar,
and keep up their carnage sometimes with great slaughter on
both sides. You may remember Damasus and Urcisinus, who
20 were Ambrose's contemporaries. Long it were to relate the
notorious insurrections of the inhabitants of Constantinople,
Antioch, and Alexandria, especially those instigated and conducted by Cyril, whom you extol as a preacher of obedience;
when the monks in that city battle had almost slain Orestes,
25 Theodosius's deputy. Now who would not be stunned at your
impudence or your negligence? "Till Austin," you say, "and
later than his time, there is no mention extant in history, of
any private person, of any commander, or of any number of

necaverint, aut contra eum armis pugnârint: nominavi ego
ex historiis notissimis et privatos, et proceres, qui non malos
tantùm, sed vel optimos reges suâ manu trucidaverint; totos
Christianorum exercitus, multos cum iis episcopos, qui contra
5 suos imperatores pugnaverint. Adfers patres, obedientiam
erga regem, multis verbis aut suadentes aut ostentantes; ad-
fero ego partim eosdem, partim alios patres haud paucioribus
factis obedientiam, etiam licitis in rebus detrectantes, armis se
contra imperatorem defendentes, alios præsidibus ejus vim
10 et vulnera inferentes, alios, episcopatûs competitores, civilibus præliis inter se dimicantes; scilicet de episcopatu Christianos cum Christianis, cives cum civibus confligere fas erat, de
libertate, de liberis et conjugibus, de vita, cum tyranno, nefas.
Quem non pœniteat hujusmodi patrum? Augustinum indu-
15 cis *de potestate domini in servos, et regis in subditos* idem pro-
nuntiantem; respondeo, si ita pronuntiavit Augustinus, ea
dixisse quæ neque Christus neque ejus Apostoli unquam dixerunt; cùm eorum tamen sola authoritate rem alioqui apertissimè falsam commendare videatur: deinde ut ita pronun-
20 tiet, nostræ tamen causæ non nocere: cùm enim de potestate
domini in servos ita dixerit, lib. 19. cap. 14 de Civitate Dei;
In domo justi viventis ex fide, etiam qui imperant, serviunt

conspirators, that have put their king to death, or taken up arms against him." Out of well-known histories I have named to you both private persons and officials that with their own hands slew not only bad but very good kings: whole armies
5 of Christians, many bishops among them, that fought against their own emperors. You produce some of the fathers who with a great multitude of words persuade or boast of obedience to kings, and I on the other side produce both these same fathers and others besides, that by no less multitude of
10 actions refused obedience, even in lawful matters, and defended themselves in arms against the emperor, others that opposed forcibly and wounded his deputies, and others that, being competitors for bishoprics, maintained civil wars against one another. So of course it was lawful for Christians to wage
15 war with Christians, and citizens with citizens, for a bishopric, but unlawful to fight against a tyrant, for our liberty, our wives and children, and our lives! Who would not be out of all patience with such fathers?

You bring in Austin, who, you say, asserts that "the power
20 of a master over his slaves, and of a king over his subjects," is one and the same. But I answer: if Austin has asserted any such thing, he has said what neither Christ nor his Apostles ever said. However, since he apparently recommends upon their authority alone something otherwise manifestly untrue,
25 then even though he say so, yet it hurts not my cause. For concerning a master's power over his slaves he has said, *de Civitate Dei,* Book 19, Chapter 14: "In the house of a righteous man who liveth by the faith, even they who command

iis quibus videntur imperare; si dixit idem *de potestate regis in subditos,* ut tu aïs, nec sibi contradixit, pronuntiavit etiam reges, præsertim bonos, quibus imperare videntur, revera servire: interim de potestate mali regis in subditos et latronis in obvios quosque idem certè pronuntiavit, lib. 4. cap. 4 de Civit. Dei; *Remota justitia, quid sunt regna,* nisi *magna latrocinia; quia et ipsa latrocinia quid sunt, nisi parva regna?* Vides quò deduxeris ex Augustino tuum istud jus magnificum, jus regium quidlibet audendi; non ut pictorum aut poetarum, sed ut latronum æqualis atque eadem potestas sit. Quæ supersunt hujus capitis tres vel quatuor paginæ, aut mera esse mendacia, aut oscitationes identidem repetitas, ex iis quæ à nobis responsa jam sunt, per se quisque deprehendet. Nam ad Papam quod attinet, in quem multa gratis peroras, facilè te patior ad ravim usque declamitare. Quod tamen ad captandos rerum imperitos tam prolixè adstruis, *regibus sive justis sive tyrannis subjectum fuisse omnem Christianum, donec potestas papæ regali major agnosci cœpta est, et subjectos sacramento fidelitatis liberavit,* id esse falsissimum plurimis exemplis *et usque ad Augustinum, et infra ejus ætatem*

serve them whom they seem to command." So that if he said the very thing you quote him as saying about "the power of a king over his subjects," and did not contradict himself, then he asserted that even kings, good kings especially, do
5 actually serve whom they seem to command. Meanwhile he has assuredly asserted that the power of an ill king over his subjects, and the power of a highway robber over everyone he meets, is one and the same (*de Civitate Dei,* Bk. 4, Ch. 4): "If righteousness be put away, what are kingdoms but great
10 robbers' dens—for what are robbers' dens themselves but little kingdoms?"—You see how far you have succeeded in deriving out of Austin that grand and glorious right of yours, that royal right to dare do anything they please: so far indeed that the power of kings is found equal and identical not with
15 that of painters or poets, but with that of highway robbers!

That the three or four remaining pages of this fourth chapter are either mere lies or sleepy negligences oft repeated, everyone will perceive for himself from my previous refutations. For what concerns the Pope, against whom you declaim
20 so much without occasion, I am content you should bawl at him till you are hoarse. But as for your attempt to catch the ignorant with the long additional argument that "every Christian yielded entire obedience to kings, whether good or bad, till the papal power began to be acknowledged superior
25 to the royal, and absolved subjects from their oath of allegiance," I have sufficiently proved by many examples "both before and since the age of Austin," that nothing can be more false.

prolatis demonstravimus. Sed neque illud quod postremò dicis, *Zachariam pontificem Gallos juramento fidelitatis absolvisse,* multo verius esse videtur. Negat Franciscus Hotomanus, et Gallus, et jurisconsultus, et vir dictissimus in Francogallia sua, *cap.* 13. abdicatum authoritate Papæ Chilpericum, aut regnum Pipino delatum; sed in magno gentis concilio pro sua pristina authoritate transactum fuisse id omne negotium, ex annalibus Francorum vetustissimis probat. Solvi deinde illo sacramento Gallos omnino opus fuisse, negant ipsa Gallorum monumenta, negat ipse papa Zacharias. Monumentis enim Francorum traditur, teste non solùm Hotomano, sed Girardo historiarum illius gentis notissimo scriptore, veteres Francos ut eligendi, sic abdicandi, si videretur, suos reges jus sibi omne antiquitus reservâsse; neque aliud sacramentum regibus, quos creabant, dicere consuevisse, quàm se illis hoc pacto fidem et officium præstituros, si vicissim illi quod eodem tempore jurati etiam spondent, præstiterint. Si ergò Reges rempublicam sibi commissam malè gerendo, fidem jurisjurandi fregerint priores, nil opus est Papa, ipsi suâ perfidiâ populum sacramento solverunt. Papa denique Zacharias, quam tu authoritatem sibi aïs arrogâsse, eam in epistola illa ad Francos ab te citata ipse sibi derogavit, po-

Neither does that seem to have much more truth in it, which you say in the last place; viz., that "Pope Zachary absolved the Frenchmen from their oath of allegiance to their king." For Francis Hotman, both a Frenchman and a lawyer and a very learned man, in the 13th chapter of his *Francogallia,* says that it was not by the Pope's authority that Chilperic was deposed, or the kingdom translated to Pepin; and he proves out of very ancient chronicles of the Franks that the whole affair was transacted in the great national council pursuant to its original authority. That thereafter there was any necessity of absolving the French from their allegiance is contradicted by the French historical documents, and by Pope Zachary himself. The records of the Franks relate, according not only to Hotman, but to Gerard, a very eminent historian of that nation, that the ancient Franks had reserved to themselves from of old an unimpaired right both to choose their kings, and to depose them if they thought fit; and that by custom they swore to the king whom they were putting in office no other oath than that they would perform their word and duty upon condition that the kings for their part would perform what they too, by oath at the same time sworn, did pledge and promise. So that if kings, by misgoverning the state entrusted to their charge, have first broke their own oath, there needs no Pope; the kings themselves by their own breach of faith have absolved their subjects. Finally Pope Zachary himself, in that very letter of his to the Franks, which you yourself quote, disclaimed for himself and ascribed to the people the authority which you say he assumed to himself.

pulo attribuit. Nam *si princeps populo, cujus beneficio reg-*
num possidet, obnoxius est, si plebs regem constituit, et desti-
tuere potest, quæ ipsius verba sunt Papæ, verisimile non est
voluisse Francos de antiquo jure suo, ullo postmodùm jure-
5 jurando, præjudicium facere; aut unquam ita sese obstrinx-
isse, quin semper sibi liceret quod majoribus licuit, reges bonos
quidem colere, malos amovere; nec eam præstare fidem tyrannis, quam bonis regibus sese dare arbitrati sunt. Tali obstrictum juramento populum, vel tyrannus ex rege factus, vel
10 ignavia corruptus, suo ipse perjurio solvit, solvit ipsa justitia,
solvit naturæ lex ipsa: unde pontifex quod solveret, etiam
ipsius pontificis judicio nihil prorsus erat.

CAPUT V.

QUANQUAM in ea sum opinione, Salmasi, sem-
pérque fui, legem Dei cum lege naturæ optimè
15   consentire, adeóque, si satis ostendi quid divina
lege sit de regibus statutum, quid à populo Dei factum et
Judaico et Christiano, ostendisse me eodem tempore eadém-
que opera quid legi naturali maximè consentaneum sit, tamen
quia *confutari nos lege naturæ validissimè nunc posse* arbi-
20 traris, quod supervacuum esse modò existimabam, id nunc
ultrò necessarium fatebor; ut contra te hoc capite planum
faciam, nihil congruentius naturæ etiam legibus esse, quàm

For "if a king be liable to punishment by the people through whose favor he holds his royalty; if the people have set up the king and have power to put him down" (the words of that very Pope), it is not likely that the Franks would afterwards

5 by any oath impair that ancient right, or ever tie their own hands so as not to have the same right that their ancestors always had to depose bad kings, as well as to honour and obey good ones; nor would they yield to tyrants that obedience which they thought they were yielding only to good

10 kings. When people are bound by such an oath, a king turned tyrant or rotted with cowardice releases them by breaking his oath; justice herself releases them; the very law of nature releases them; wherefore even by the Pope's own opinion there simply was nothing for the Pope to release.

CHAPTER V

15 I AM of opinion, Salmasius, and always have been, that the law of God does exactly agree with the law of nature, and that therefore, if I have shown what by God's law is established with respect to kings, and what has been the practice of the people of God, both Jews and Christians, I

20 have at the same time and by the same attempt shown what is most agreeable to the law of nature. Yet because you think that we "can now be most effectually confuted by the law of nature," I will be content to admit to be necessary, what before I had thought superfluous; so as in this chapter I

25 shall prove against you that nothing is more suitable to the law of nature than that tyrants be punished. Which if I do

tyrannos plecti. Id nisi evincam, non recuso quin Dei quoque legibus puniri non posse, è vestigio tibi concedam. Non est consilium de natura jam, déque origine civilis vitæ longam orationem contexere; istud enim argumentum viri disertissimi cùm Græci, tum Latini copiosè pertractârunt; ipse et brevitati, quantùm licet, studeo, et huic rei do operam, ut non tam ego, qui labori huic parsissem libens, quàm tute te redarguas, têque subvertas. Ab eo igitur quod ipse ponis, incipiam, et disputationis hujus futuræ fundamenta jaciam. *Lex,* inquis, *naturæ est ratio omnium hominum mentibus insita, bonum respiciens universorum populorum, quatenus homines inter se societate gaudent. Bonum illud commune non potest procurare, nisi etiam, ut sunt quos regi necesse est, disponat quoque qui regere debeant.* Ne scilicet ut quisque fortior est, debiliorem opprimat; atque ita quos mutua salus ac defensio unum in locum congregaverat, vis atque injuria distrahat, et ad vitam agrestem redire cogat. Estne hoc quod volebas, etsi verbosiùs? *Ex ipsorum* itaque *numero qui in unum convenere, deligi* äis *oportuisse quosdam sapientia aut fortitudine cæteris præstantes, qui vel vi vel persuadendo malè morigeros in officio continerent, sæpe unum id præstare potuisse, cujus excellens sit Virtus et Prudentia; interdum plures, qui mutuis*

not demonstrate, I will then not decline to grant you on the spot, that likewise by the law of God they are exempt. I do not purpose to frame a long discourse of nature, and the beginnings of man's political life; that subject has been handled at large by many learned men, both Greek and Latin. But I shall endeavor to be as short as may be; and my design is not so much that I, who would willingly have spared this pains, may confute you, as that you shall confute yourself and destroy your own position.

I will begin therefore with what you yourself lay down, and shall make it the basis of the following discussion. "The law of nature," you say, "is a principle implanted in all men's minds, to regard the good of all mankind in so far as men are united together in societies. But it cannot procure that common good unless, as there are people that must be governed, it also ascertain who shall govern them." To wit, lest the stronger oppress the weaker, and thus those whom their mutual safety and protection had brought together be disunited and divided by injury and violence, and reduced to a savage life again. This I suppose is what you intended, though you take more words to say it. "Out of the number of those that united into one body," you say, "there must needs have been some chosen, superior to the rest in wisdom or courage, who either by force or by persuasion were to hold to their duty those that were refractory. Often it would so fall out that one single person whose Valour and Discretion was extraordinary might be able to do this, and sometimes several, who would accomplish it together by interchange of advice

consiliis id faciant. Cæterùm cum unus omnia providere et administrare non possit, necesse est ut consilia cum pluribus participet, et in societatem regiminis alios admittat. Ita sive ad unum revocetur imperium, sive ad universum redeat po-
5 *pulum, quia nec omnes simul rempub. gubernare possunt, nec unus omnia, ideo revera penès plures semper regimen consistit.* Et infra. *Ipsa autem regendi ratio sive per plures, sive per pauciores, sive per unum dispensetur, æquè naturalis est, cùm ex naturæ ejusdem principiis descendat, quæ non patitur*
10 *ita unius singularitatem gubernare, ut non alios socios imperandi habeat.* Hæc cùm ex Aristotelis tertio Politicorum decerpsisse potuissem, malui abs te decerpta transcribere, quæ tu Aristoteli, ut ignem Jovi Prometheus, ad eversionem monarcharum, et perniciem ipsius tuam surripuisti. Jam enim
15 prolatam à temetipso naturæ legem excute quantum voles; nullum juri regio, prout tu jus illud explicas, in natura locum, nullum ejus vestigium prorsus invenies. *Lex,* inquis, *naturæ cùm disponeret qui regere alios deberent, universorum populorum bonum respexit.* Non igitur unius, non monarchæ.
20 Est itaque rex propter populum: populus ergo rege potior et superior; superior cùm sit et potior populus; nullum jus regis existere potest, quo populum is affligat, aut in servitute habeat, inferior superiorem. Jus malè faciendi cùm sit regi nullum,

and counsel. Indeed since any one man cannot order and manage all things himself, he must consult with more, and let others into the governing company. So that whether the supreme power be confined to one person or reside in the body of the people, in either case, since it is impossible that all should administer the affairs of the commonwealth, or that one man should do all, therefore the government does always actually lie upon the shoulders of many." And afterwards you say: "The form of government itself, whether placed in the hands of many, or few, or a single person, is equally natural, for it is derived from the grounds of nature itself, which suffers not one man's single self so to rule that he have no sharers in the government."

Though I might have gathered all this out of the third book of Aristotle's *Politics,* I chose rather to transcribe it out of your own book, for you stole it from him, as Prometheus did fire from Jupiter, to the overthrow of monarchs and destruction of yourself. For search all you will into the law of nature, as just now exhibited by you, you will not find a place in nature for the royal right as you expound it—no, not so much as a trace of it. "The law of nature," you say, "in ordering who should govern others, regarded the good of all mankind." Not then of any one person—of a monarch. Hence the king exists for the people, and consequently the people are above him and to be preferred to him; which being allowed, there can be no right of the king whereby he, the inferior, may oppress or enslave the people, the superior. Since the king has no right to do wrong, the right of the people remains

manet jus populi naturâ supremum; ut quo jure homines consilia et vires mutuæ defensionis gratia, ante reges creatos, primò consociavere, quo jure ad communem omnium salutem, pacem, libertatem conservandam unum vel plures cæteris præfecerunt, eodem jure quos propter virtutem et prudentiam cæteris præposuerant, possent eosdem aut quoscunque alios rempub. malè gerentes, propter ignaviam, stultitiam, improbitatem; perfidiam vel coërcere vel abdicare: cùm natura non unius vel paucorum imperium, sed universorum salutem respexerit semper et respiciat; quicquid de imperio vel unius vel paucorum fiat. Jam verò populus quosnam delegit? *sapientia* inquis *aut fortitudine cæteris præstantes,* nempe qui naturâ maximè regno idonei visi sunt, *cujus excellens virtus, et prudentia præstare id* muneris *potuit.* Jus igitur successionis naturâ nullum, nullus naturâ rex, nisi qui sapientia et fortitudine cæteris omnibus præcellit; cæteri vel vi, vel factione contra naturam reges sunt, cum servi potiùs esse deberent. Dat enim natura sapientissimo cuique in minùs sapientes imperium, non viro malo in bonos, non stolido in sapientes: his igitur imperium qui abrogant, omnino convenienter naturæ faciunt. Cui fini sapientissimum quemque natura constituat regem ex temetipso audi; ut vel naturæ vel legibus *malè morigeros in officio contineat.* Continere autem in officio potestne is alios, officium qui negligit, aut nescit,

by nature supreme; and therefore, by that right whereby, before kings were instituted, men first united their strength and
counsels for their mutual defence, by that right whereby, for
the preservation of all men's liberty, peace, and safety, they
5 appointed one or more to govern the rest, by the same right
they may punish or depose, for cowardice or folly or dishon-
esty or treachery, those very persons whom for their valour
or wisdom they had advanced to the government, or any
others that rule disorderly; since nature hath regarded and
10 doth regard the good not of one, or of a few, but of all in
general, whatever become of one man's or of a few men's
power.

Now as to the sort of persons whom the people chose. You
say they were "superior to the rest in wisdom or courage,"
15 to wit, such as by nature seemed fittest for government,
"whose extraordinary valour and discretion was adequate"
to such an office. Hence there is no right of succession by the
law of nature, no king by the law of nature except him who
excels all the rest in wisdom and courage; and all kings else
20 are such by force or faction, contrary to nature, being fit rather
to be slaves. For unto the wisest man nature gives command
over men less wise, not unto a wicked man over good men, a
fool over wise men: and consequently they that take the government out of such men's hands, act quite according to the
25 law of nature. To what end nature appoints the wisest man
king, you shall hear in your own words; viz., "that he may
hold to their duty those that are refractory" against either
nature or the laws. But how should he hold others to their

aut pervertit ipse suum? Cedò jam quodvis naturæ præceptum quo jubeamur instituta naturæ sapientissima in rebus publicis et civilibus non observare, non curare, pro nihilo habere, cùm ipsa in rebus naturalibus et inanimatis ne suo fine 5 frustretur, sæpissimè res magnas atque miras efficere soleat. Ostende ullam vel naturæ vel naturalis justitiæ regulam, quâ oporteat reos minores puniri, reges et malorum omnium principes impunitos esse, immò inter maxima flagitia coli, adorari, et Deo proximos haberi. Concedis *ipsam regendi ratio-* 10 *nem, sive per plures, sive per pauciores, sive per unum dispensetur, æquè naturalem esse.* Non est ergo rex vel optimatibus vel populi magistratibus naturà sanctior, quos cùm puniri posse ac debere, si peccant, supra sis largitus, idem de regibus, eidem fini ac bono constitutis fateare necesse est. *Non* enim 15 *patitur natura,* inquis, *ita unius singularitatem gubernare, ut non alios socios imperandi habeat.* Minimè ergo patitur monarcham, minimè unum ita imperare, ut cæteros omnes sui unius imperii servos habeat. Socios autem imperandi qui tribuis regi, *penès quos semper regimen consistat,* das eidem col- 20 legas et æquales; addis qui punire, addis qui abdicare possint. Ita, uti semper facis, dum potestatem regiam, non jam ex-

duty, that neglects, or knows not, or turns against his own?

Allege now, if you can, any dictate of nature by which we are enjoined to disregard and neglect and hold of no account in matters of human state and polity the wise institutions of
5 the law of nature, when nature herself, rather than lose her end, continually produces great and admirable results in her own province of matters inanimate and non-human. Produce any rule of nature or natural justice by which inferior criminals ought to be punished, but kings and princes to go un-
10 punished for all their evil deeds—nay but, amid their monstrous crimes, be worshiped and revered and held in honor next to God. You grant that "the form of government itself, whether placed in the hands of many, or few, or a single person, is equally natural." So that a king is not by the law of
15 nature more sacred than nobles, or than magistrates chosen from amongst the common people, and as you have granted heretofore that those may be punished, and ought to be if they offend, consequently you must admit the same of kings, who are appointed to rule for the very same end and purpose. For,
20 say you, "Nature suffers not one man's single self so to rule that he have no sharers in the government." It does not therefore suffer a monarch; it does not suffer one single person so to rule as to hold all others in slavery to his single power. In giving the king such partners in his power "that the govern-
25 ment does always lie upon their shoulders," you give him colleagues and equals; more, you give them the power to punish, you give them the power to depose him.

So while you go about, not indeed to magnify royal power,

auges, sed tantummodò natura constituis, aboles: adeò ut
nihil putem inauspicatius accidere regibus potuisse, quàm te
defensorem. O infelicem ac miserum, quæ te mentis caligo
in hanc impulit fraudem, ut latentem antehac diu, et quasi
5 personatam improbitatem atque inscitiam tuam nunc tanto
conatu insciens nudares ipse, et omnibus patefaceres: tuoque-
met opprobrio operam ipse tuam locares, tuo ipse ludibrio tam
gnaviter inservires? Quæ te ira numinis quâsve pœnas luen-
tem, in lucem et ora hominum evocavit, ut tanto apparatu
10 causam teterrimam impudentissimè simul et stolidissimè de-
fenderes, atque ita defendendo invitus pérque inscitiam pro-
deres? Quis te pejùs perditum vellet, quis miseriorem, cui
jam sola imprudentia, sola væcordia saluti esse potest, ne sis
miserrimus, si tyrannos quorum causam suscepisti, imperita
15 ac stulta defensione tantò magis invisos ac detestabiles omnibus, contrà quàm sperabas, reddideris, quanto iis majorem
malefaciendi et impunè dominandi licentiam de industria at-
tribueris; eóque plures eorundem hostes inconsultò excitaveris? Sed redeo ad tua tecum dissidia. Cùm tantum in te scelus
20 admiseris, ut tyrannidem naturâ fundare studeas, præ cæteris
gubernandi rationibus monarchiam primò laudandam tibi

but just merely to establish it in nature, you destroy it, as you always do. No greater misfortune, consequently I think, could befall sovereign princes, than to have you to defend them. Poor unhappy wretch! what fog in your wits hath
5 driven you to such a pass of self-deception that you should unwittingly take all these pains to lay bare and open to all men your knavery and ignorance, which until now was long concealed and almost masked; that you should set your labor to hire at the price of your own ignominy, and devote your-
10 self so assiduously to making yourself a laughing-stock? What offence does the wrath of heaven punish you for, in making you appear in public, and with such parade undertake the defence of a hateful cause in the height of impudence and stupidity at once, and, by thus defending it, against your in-
15 tent and through your ignorance betray it? Who could wish you more forlorn and wretched than you are, when you can be saved from the depth of misery only by an act of short-sighted folly? Since by your unskilful and fatuous defence you have rendered the tyrants whose cause you undertook
20 just so much more odious and detestable (the opposite of what you were expecting) and have unintentionally roused up just so many more enemies against them,—as you have intentionally ascribed to them the greater liberty of doing mischief and tyrannizing with impunity.
25 But I return to your self-contradictions. Having resolved to be so wicked as to endeavor to found tyranny in nature, you saw yourself compelled to begin by extolling monarchy above other forms of government; which, as is your way, you can-

esse vidisti; id, uti soles, incœptare sine repugnantia nequis.
Cùm enim modò dixisses, *ipsam regendi rationem, sive per*
plures, sive per pauciores, sive per unum, æque naturalem esse,
statim *eam quæ per unum exercetur, ex his tribus, magis na-*
5 *turalem esse* aïs; immo qui etiam recèns dixeras, *non patitur*
natura unius singularitatem gubernantis. Jam tyrannorum
necem objice cui voles, qui et monarchas omnes, et monarchiam ipsam tua fatuitate jugulâsti. Verùm quæ sit melior
administrandi rempub. ratio, per unum an per plures, non est
10 nunc disserendi locus. Et monarchiam quidem multi cele-
bres viri laudârunt, si tamen is qui solus regnat, vir omnium
optimus, et regno dignissimus sit; id nisi contingat, nihil monarchia procliviùs in eam tyrannidem, quæ pessima est, labi-
tur. Jam quòd ad unius *exemplar Dei expressam esse* dicis,
15 quis potentiam divinæ similem in terris obtinere dignus est,
nisi qui cæterorum omnium longè præstantissimus, etiam bo-
nitate ac sapientia est Deo simillimus; is autem solus, meâ
quidem sententiâ, expectatus ille Dei filius est. Quòd regnum
in familiam rursus contrudis, ut patrifamilias regem assimi-
20 les, pater certè suæ familiæ regnum meretur, quam omnem
vel generavit, vel alit: in rege nihil est hujusmodi, sed planè
contrà sunt omnia. Animalia deinde nobis gregalia, imprimis
aves, et in iis *apes,* siquidem te Physiologo aves istæ sunt, imi-

not go about without contradicting yourself. For having said but a little before, "that the form of government itself, whether by more, or by fewer, or by a single person, is equally natural," now you tell us that "of these three, that which is
5 wielded by one person is most natural": nay, though you had said in express terms but lately: "Nature suffers not one man's single self to govern." Now upbraid whom you will with the putting of tyrants to death; since you yourself by your own folly have cut the throats of all monarchs, nay even of mon-
10 archy itself. But this is not the place to dispute which form of government is best, by one single person or by many. Many eminent men have indeed extolled monarchy, yet only if the monarch be very excellent and best deserve to reign; without such supposition, no other form of government so easily slips
15 into the worst sort of tyranny.

As for your saying that "it is modeled upon the pattern of the One God"—I ask you who is worthy to hold on earth a power that shall resemble the divine power, save one who, as he far excels other men, is even in wisdom and goodness
20 likest unto God? and such a person, in my opinion, none can be but the Son of God we wait for. As for your forcing a *kingdom* once more into the genus *family,* that you may liken a king to a paterfamilias: a father of course deserves to exercise dominion over his household, all of which he either
25 begot or supports; nothing of the sort with a king, but obviously quite the opposite. Next you set before us for our imitation those animals that live in communities, first birds, and among them bees, since these are birds, on your authority as

tandas proponis. *Apes regem habent.* Tridentinæ scilicet, annon meministi? cæterarum, te teste, *respub. est.* Verum tu
desine de apibus fatuari, musarum sunt, oderunt te scara-
bæum, et ut vides, redarguunt. *Coturnices sub Ortygometra.*
5 Istos onocrotalis tuis tende laqueos; nos tam stolido aucupio
non capimur. Atqui jam tua res agitur, non nostra; *Gallus
gallinaceus,* inquis, *tam maribus quàm fœminis imperitat.*
Quî potest hoc fieri? Cùm tu ipse Gallus, et, ut ferunt, vel
nimiùm gallinaceus, non tuæ gallinæ, sed illa tibi imperitet,
10 et in te regnum exerceat: si gallinaceus ergo plurium fœmi-
narum rex est, tu gallinæ mancipium tuæ, non gallinaceum
te, sed stercorarium quendam esse Gallum oportet. Pro libris
certè nemo te majora edit sterquilinia, et gallicinio tuo sterco-
reo omnes obtundis; hoc unicum galli gallinacei habes. Jam
15 ego multa hordei grana daturum me tibi promitto, si totum
hoc vertendo sterquilinium tuum, vel unam mihi gemmam
ostenderis. Sed quid ego tibi hordeum? qui non hordeum, ut
Æsopicus ille, simplex et frugi gallus, sed aurum, ut Plautinus ille nequam, scalpturiendo quæsisti; quamvis exitu ad-
20 huc dispari; tu enim centum Jacobæos aureos inde reperisti,
cùm Euclionis fuste potiùs, quo misellus ille Plautinus, ob-
truncari dignior sis. Sed pergendum est. *Eadem utilitatis et*

Physiologus! "The bees have a king." The bees of Trent, that is—do not you remember? All other bees, on your own admission, "have republics." But leave off playing the fool with bees; they belong to the Muses, and hate, and, you see,

5 confute such a beetle as you are. "The quails are under a 'Quail mother'." Lay such snares for your own bitterns; we are not caught by so foolish a fowler.

The next point, however, is not our affair, but yours. *"Gallus gallinaceus,* the cock," you say, "wields imperial power

10 over both males and females." How can that be, since you yourself that are Gallic, and (they say) but too cocky, wield not imperial power over your hen, but she over you? So that if the gallinaceous cock be king over many females, you that are slave to your hen must needs be not Gallus gallinaceus,

15 but some sort of Gallus stercorarius, or dunghill-cock. For the matter of books, in fact, nobody publishes huger dung-hills, and you deafen us all with your crowing over them; that is the only point in which you resemble a true cock. I promise to give you many barley-corns if in ransacking this whole

20 dunghill-book of yours you can show me but one jewel. But why should I give barley to you, who, quite unlike the honest plain cock in Aesop, scratched not for barley, but like the good-for-nothing cock in Plautus, scratched eagerly for gold? The outcome, to be sure, was different to this extent, that by

25 scratching you found a hundred gold Jacobuses, though you more deserved to be struck dead with Euclio's club, like that wretched bird in Plautus.

But let us go on: "That same motive—the advantage and

*tiones, dissensiones, discordias optimatium et populi, longè
levius esse malum,* affirmabas, *quàm sub uno monarcha tyranno certam miseriam ac perniciem.* Et vera tu quidem affirmabas; nondum enim insaniebas, nondum Carolinis Jaco-
5 bæis deauratus, in hanc auriginem seu morbum regium inci-
deras. Dicerem fortasse, nisi is esses qui es, pudeat te tandem
prævaricationis tuæ turpissimæ; tibi verò dirumpi facilius est
quàm erubescere; qui ut rem faceres, pudorem jam diu ami-
sisti. Annon ipse memineras Romanos florentissimam et glo-
10 riosissimam Rempub. post exactos reges habuisse? potuit fieri
ut Batavorum obliviscerere? quorum respub. Hispaniarum
rege pulso post bella diutina, feliciter tamen gesta, libertatem
fortiter et gloriose consequuta est, téque grammaticastrum
Equitem stipendio alit suo, non ut juventus Batavica te præ-
15 varicatore et sophistâ tam nihil sapere discat, ut ad servitutem
Hispanicam redire mallet, quàm paternæ libertatis ac gloriæ
hæres esse; istam doctrinæ pestem ad Riphæos ultimos, et gla-
cialem oceanum, quò te in malam rem abire par est, tecum
auferas licebit: Exemplo denique sunt Angli, qui Carolum
20 tyrannum bello captum, et insanabilem obtruncârunt. At *in-
sulam beatam sub regibus, et luxu affluentem discordiis de-
formârunt.* Immo luxu penè perditam, quò tolerantior servitutis esset, extinctis deinde legibus, et mancipata religione,

and discords of the nobles and commons are a much lighter
mischief than sure misery and destruction under the government of one monarch that plays the tyrant." And you said
very true, for you were not yet going mad, and being ungilt
5 with Charles his Jacobuses, had not yet got this gold-itch or
king's evil. I should tell you perhaps, if you were not who you
are, that you ought at length to be ashamed of your disgraceful
double-dealing. But you can sooner burst than blush, who
long ago cast off shame for profit.

10   Did you not remember that the Romans had a most flourishing and glorious commonwealth after they had banished
their kings? Could you possibly forget the Dutch, whose Republic, when it had shook off the king of Spain after long but
successful wars, bravely and gloriously got its freedom, and
15 keeps you in its pay, knight grammaticaster!—yet with no
design that the Dutch youth may learn from you, sophist and
double-dealer, such unwisdom as to choose rather to return to
the bondage of Spain than inherit their fathers' glorious liberty. Go take along with you your plaguy teaching to utmost
20 Siberia and the Arctic Ocean, and there, while you are about
it, you may just as well go to the devil!

Your last example is the English, who put to death their
tyrant Charles after he had been taken a prisoner of war, and
found incurable. "With their quarrels they defaced and dis-
25 honored an island which under its kings was happy and
swam in luxury." Yea, when its moral ruin through luxury
was almost accomplished that it might the more indifferently
bear with enslavement—when its laws were abolished, and

servientem liberârunt. En autem Epicteti cum Simplicio editorem, Stoïcum gravissimum, cui *luxu affluens insula* beata esse videtur! Ex porticu Zenonis nunquam tale, sat scio, documentum prodiit. Quid refert? an te doctore quicquid libet
5 regibus licebit, tibi ipsi non licebit Lupi domino ex Lupanari tuo, tanquam ex novo quodam lycéo quamcunque libet emittere philosophiam? sed resume nunc quam suscepisti personam. *Nunquam sub ullo rege tantum cruoris haustum est, tot familiæ desolatæ:* Hoc totum Carolo imputandum est, non
10 Anglis; qui exercitum Hibernicorum priùs in nos paraverat, omnes Hibernos conjurare contra Anglos suo ipse diplomate jusserat; per illos ducena circiter millia Anglorum unà in provincia Ultonia occiderat; de reliquis nihil dico: binos exercitus in exitium Parlamenti Anglicani urbisque Londini sollicita
15 verat; multa alia hostiliter fecerat, priusquam à populo aut magistratibus tuendæ Reipub. causâ vel unus miles conscriptus esset. Quæ doctrina, quæ lex, quæ unquam religio sic homines instituit, ut otio consulendum, ut pecuniæ, ut sanguini, ut vitæ potiùs parcendum esse ducerent, quàm hosti obviam
20 eundum? nam externo an intestino, quid interest? cùm interitus reipub. sive ab hoc, sive ab illo funestus æquè, et acerbus impendeat. Vidit totus Israël non posse se sine multo sanguine Levitæ uxorem stupro enectam ulcisci; num igitur quiescen-

its religion bought and sold—then they delivered it from slavery. Behold now a Stoic of the severest, editor of Epictetus with Simplicius's commentary, who considers "an island swimming in luxury" to be happy! I am sure no such
5 doctrine ever came from Zeno's porch. What of that? Shall kings, according to your teaching, have leave to do as they please, and shall not you yourself, Sire du Loup, have leave to send forth whatever philosophy you please from your wolf-bitch's den, as from some strange new Lyceum?

10 Now begin again to act your part. "Never in any king's reign was so much blood spilt, so many families ruined." All this is to be imputed not to the English nation but to Charles, who had first raised an army of Irishmen against us, had by his own warrant bidden the Irish nation unite in arms against
15 the English, and had by their means slain near two hundred thousand Englishmen in the single province of Ulster; to say nothing of his other crimes—of how he had incited two armies to destroy the Parliament of England and the City of London, and had committed many other acts of war, before the Parlia-
20 ment or the people had enlisted a single soldier to protect the realm.

What principles, what law, what religion ever taught men to consult their ease, to save their money, their blood, nay their very lives, rather than oppose the public enemy—
25 whether foreign or domestic what matter, since both alike threaten bitter calamity and ruin to the nation? All Israel saw that without great bloodshed they could not punish the outrage that had been done upon the Levite's wife; did they

dum sibi esse duxit, num bello civili, quamvis truculentissimo, supersedendum, num unam igitur mulierculam mori inultam est passus? Certè si natura nos docet quamvis pessimi regis dominatum potiùs pati, quàm in recuperanda libertate, plu-
5 rimorum civium salutem in discrimen adducere, doceret eadem non regem solùm perferre, quem tamen solum perferendum esse contendis, sed optimatium, sed paucorum quoque potentiam; latronum etiam nonnunquam et servorum rebellantium multitudinem. Non Fulvius aut Rupilius bel-
10 lum servile post cæsos exercitus prætorios, non Crassus in Spartacum post deleta consularium castra, non Pompeius ad piraticum bellum exiisset. Romani vel servis, vel piratis, ne tot civium sanguis effunderetur, hortante scilicet natura, succubuissent. *Hunc* itaque *sensum,* aut hujusmodi ullum *gen-*
15 *tibus impressisse naturam* nusquam ostendis: et tamen non desinis malè ominari, et vindictam divinam, quam in te augurem tuique similes avertat Deus, nobis denuntiare; qui nomine tantùm regem, re hostem acerbissimum debito supplicio ulti sumus; et innumerabilem bonorum civium cædem
20 authoris pœnâ expiavimus. Nunc magis naturalem esse monarchiam ex eo probari aïs, quod *plures nationes et nunc et*

therefore think they must be still, or refrain from civil war,
though of the cruelest? Did they on that account suffer one
poor humble *petite femme* to die unavenged? Certainly if
nature teaches us to endure the despotism of a king, no mat-
5 ter how bad, rather than endanger the safety of a great many
men in the recovery of our liberty, she must teach us likewise
to endure not only a kingly government, which yet is the
only one that you argue ought to be submitted to, but even an
aristocracy and an oligarchy too—nay, and sometimes a gang
10 of robbers and mutinous slaves! Fulvius and Rupilius must
then not have engaged in the Servile War after the Praetorian
armies were slain; Crassus must not have marched against
Spartacus, after the camp of the ex-consuls was destroyed; nor
must Pompey have gone to war against the pirates. Romans,
15 at nature's behest, forsooth, Romans, lest the blood of so many
citizens should be shed, must have knuckled down to slaves
or to pirates! Nowhere do you show that "nature has imprinted this feeling upon the nations"—or any feeling of the
sort; and yet you cannot forbear boding us ill, and denounc-
20 ing God's vengeance upon us—which may heaven divert
upon yourself and all such prognosticators as you!—denounc-
ing it, I say, upon us, though we have done no more than
inflict the death that was his due upon him that was our king
only in name, but in fact our implacable enemy, and atone for
25 the countless deaths of our good countrymen by punishing the
author and cause of them.

Then you tell us that a kingly government appears to be
more according to the laws of nature because "more nations,

olim regium statum receperint, quam optimatem et popu-
larem. Respondeo primùm neque Deo neque natura suadente
id factum esse; Deus nisi invitus, populum suum sub regio
imperio esse noluit; natura quid suadeat et recta ratio, non ex
5 pluribus, sed ex prudentissimis nationibus optimè perspicitur.
Græci, Romani, Itali, Carthaginienses, multique alii suopte
ingenio vel optimatium vel populi imperium regio prætule-
runt; atque hæ quidem nationes cæterarum omnium instar
sunt. Hinc Sulpitius Severus, *regium nomen cunctis ferè*
10 *liberis gentibus semper invisum* fuisse tradit. Verùm ista non
jam huc pertinent, nec quæ sequuntur multa, inani futilitate
à te sæpiùs repetita: ad illud festino, ut quod rationibus fir-
mavi, id exemplis nunc ostendam, esse vel maximè secundùm
naturam, tyrannos quoquo modo puniri; id omnes gen-
15 tes, magistrâ ipsâ naturâ, sæpiùs fecisse; ex quo impudentia
tua prædicanda, et turpissima mentiendi licentia omnibus
innotescere dehinc poterit. Primos omnium inducis Ægyptios; et certè quis te per omnia Ægyptizare non videat?
Apud hos inquis, *nusquam mentio extat ullius regis à po-*
20 *pulo per seditiones occisi, nullum bellum illatum, aut quic-*
quam factum à populo quo è solio dejiceretur. Quid ergo
Osiris rex Ægyptiorum fortasse primus? annon à fratre Ty-
phone, et viginti quinque aliis conjuratis interemptus est?

both in our days and of old, have adopted monarchy than aristocracy and democracy." I answer first that this was not done at the behest of either God or nature. It was only unwillingly that God allowed his own people to be under a king; and what
5 nature and right reason dictates, is best ascertained from the practice not of most nations, but of the wisest. The Grecians, the Romans, the Italians, the Carthaginians, and many others, have in accordance with their own natural temper preferred a government by their aristocracy or by their people rather than
10 by a king; and these nations are proper examples to stand for the rest. Hence Sulpitius Severus reports that "the name of king has always been hateful to nearly all free nations."

But these things concern not our present purpose, nor do the many that come after, which in your empty folly you re-
15 peat again and again. I hasten to make plain by examples what I have established already by reason; viz., that it is in the highest degree agreeable to the law of nature, that tyrants should be punished anyhow; and that all nations, taught by nature herself, have punished them; which will expose
20 your impudence, and make it evident to all men that you take a shameful liberty to publish lies. You begin with the Egyptians; and indeed who does not see that you play the gipsy throughout? "In their history," say you, "there is no mention of any king that was ever slain by the people in a
25 popular insurrection, no war made upon any of their kings by their subjects, no attempt made to depose any of them." What think you then of Osiris, perhaps the first king of the Egyptians? Was not he slain by his brother Typhon and five-and-

quos et magna pars populi secuta magnum cum Iside et Oro,
regis conjuge, et filio prælium commisit? prætereo Sesostrin
à fratre per insidias penè oppressum; Chemmin etiam et Ce-
phrenem, quibus populus meritò infensus, quos vivos non po-
5 terat, mortuos se discerpturum minatus est. Qui reges optimos obtruncare sunt ausi, eósne putas naturæ lumine, aut religione aliqua retentos, à pessimis regibus manus abstinuisse?
qui reges mortuos, et tum demùm innocuos, sepulcro erui-
turos se minitabantur, ubi etiam pauperculi cujusque corpus
10 inviolatum esse solet, vivósne illi et nocentissimos propter naturæ legem punire, si modò viribus valerent, vererentur? Af-
firmares hæc, scio, quamlibet absurda; verùm ego ne affirmare audeas elinguem te reddam. Scito igitur multis ante Ce-
phrenem seculis regnâsse apud Ægyptios Ammosin; et ty-
15 rannum, ut qui maximè, fuisse; eum Ægyptii æquo animo
pertulerunt. Triumphas; hoc enim est quod vis. At reliqua
audi vir optime et veracissime, Diodori enim verba sunt quæ
recito; μέχρι μέν τινος ἐκαρτέρουν οὐ δυνάμενοι, etc. *tolera-*
bant aliquandiu oppressi, quia resistere potentioribus nullo
20 *modo poterant.* Quamprimùm verò Actisanes Æthiopum rex
bellum gerere cum eo cœpit, nacti occasionem plerique defecerunt, eóque facilè subacto, Ægyptus regno Æthiopum ac-

twenty other conspirators? And did not a great part of the
body of the people side with them, and fight a great battle
with Isis and Orus, the king's wife and son? I pass by Sesos-
tris, whom his brother had well-nigh put to death by treach-
5 ery, and Chemmis and Chephren, against whom the people
were deservedly enraged, and threatened to tear them in
pieces after they were dead, being unable to do it while they
were alive. Do you think that a people that durst cut off their
best kings were restrained either by the light of nature or
10 by any religious scruple from laying hands upon their worst
ones? A people that repeatedly threatened to tear their
kings, though dead and now at last beyond the power to
do harm, from the tomb, where the body of any the meanest pauper is wont to be inviolable — would they, if they
15 had the power, stand back in awe, and fear to punish according to the law of nature kings alive and noxious? I
know you would not stick to answer me in the affirmative,
how absurd soever it be; but that you may not dare, I will
silence you. Know then that many centuries before Cheph-
20 ren's time Ammosis was king of Egypt, and was as great a
tyrant as any the greatest; him the people patiently bore with.
You exult: this is what you like. But hear what follows, my
honest Telltruth. I quote Diodorus: "Weighed down, they
bore with him for some while, for they were nowise able to
25 resist them that were more powerful." But as soon as Actisanes king of Ethiopia began to make war upon him, most
of them took the opportunity to revolt, and when he was
easily subdued, Egypt was added to the kingdom of Ethiopia.

cessit. Vides hìc Ægyptios, quamprimùm poterant, arma
contra tyrannum tulisse, copias cum externo rege conjunxisse,
ut regem suum ejúsque posteros regno privarent, bonum et
moderatum regem, qualis erat Actisanes, maluisse externum,
5 quàm tyrannum domesticum. Iidem Ægyptii consensu omnium maximo Aprien tyrannum suum, conductitiis copiis
præsidentem, duce Amasi prælio victum strangulârunt;
Amasi viro nobili regnum dederunt. Hoc etiam adverte;
Amasis captum regem ad tempus in ipsa regia honestè asser-
10 vabat: incusante demùm populo, injustè eum facere qui suum
et ipsorum hostem aleret, tradidit populo regem; qui eum
prædicto supplicio affecit. Hæc Herodotus et Diodorus. Quid
amplius tibi quæris? ecquem tyrannum censes non maluisse
vitam securi quàm laqueo finire? Postea sub Persarum impe-
15 rium *redacti* Ægyptii, *fideles,* inquis, *exstitere:* Quod falsissimum est; in fide enim Persarum nunquam permansere; sed
quarto post anno quàm subacti à Cambyse fuerant, rebellârunt. Domiti deinde à Xerxe, haud multò pòst ab ejus filio
Artaxerxe defecerunt, regem Inarum quendam sibi adscive-
20 runt. Cùm eo victi iterum desciscunt, et constituto rege Tacho
Artaxerxi Mnemoni bellum indicunt. Sed neque suo regi fide-
liores, ablatum patri regnum filio Nectanebo tradunt: donec

You see here that the Egyptians, as soon as they could, took up
arms against a tyrant, joined forces with a foreign prince to
depose their own king and disinherit his posterity, and preferred a moderate and good king, as Actisanes was, though a
5 foreigner, to a tyrant of their own. These same Egyptians by
the hearty consent of them all took up arms against Apries
their tyrant, who relied upon his mercenary troops. Under
the command of Amasis they conquered and afterwards
strangled him, and gave the kingdom to Amasis, who was a
10 noble gentleman. And note this too: Amasis kept the captive
king a good while in the palace, and treated him well; at last,
when the people complained that he did wrong in maintaining his enemy and theirs, he delivered him over to the people,
who put him to death in the manner I have mentioned. These
15 things are related by Herodotus and Diodorus. What more
do you want? Do you think that any tyrant would not choose
the axe rather than the noose?

Afterwards, you say, when the Egyptians were "brought
into subjection" by the Persians, they "continued loyal to
20 them"; which is utterly false, for they never remained loyal
to the Persians, but in the fourth year after Cambyses had
subdued them, they rebelled. Afterwards, when Xerxes had
tamed them, within a short time they revolted from his son
Artaxerxes, and set up one Inarus to be their king. With him
25 they were conquered, but rebelled again, and created Tachus
king, and made war upon Artaxerxes Mnemon. Neither were
they better subjects to their own king, for they deposed
Tachus, and conferred the government upon his son Nec-

tandem ab Artaxerxe Ocho rursus in ditionem Persarum re-
diguntur. Sub Macedonum etiam imperio, quantum in se erat,
tyrannos coërcendos esse factis indicârunt; statuas et imagines
Ptolemæi Physconis dejecerunt, ipsum mercenario exercitu
5 præpollentem interficere nequiverunt. Alexander ejus filius
ob cædem matris concursu populi in exilium agitur: filium
item ejus Alexandrum insolentiùs dominantem Alexandrinus
populus vi abreptum ex regia in gymnasio publico interfecit:
Ptolemæum denique Auleten ob multa flagitia regno expulit.
10 Hæc tam nota cùm non possit nescire vir doctus, non debuerit
qui hæc docere profiteatur, qui fidem tantis in rebus haberi
sibi postulet, quis non pudendum et indignissimum esse dicat,
hunc, vel tam rudem et indoctum tanta cum infamia bona-
rum literarum pro doctissimo circumferre se tumidum, et
15 stipendia regum et civitatum ambire, vel tam improbum et
mendacem, non insigni aliquâ ignominiâ notatum, ex omnium communitate et consortio tum doctorum tum bonorum
exterminari. Postquam Ægyptum lustravimus, ad Æthiopes
jam proximos visamus. Regem à Deo electum, ut credunt,
20 quasi Deum quendam adorant: quoties tamen eum Sacerdotes damnant, ipse mortem sibi consciscit. Sic enim, Dio-

tanebus, till at last Artaxerxes Ochus brought them again under subjection to the Persian empire. Even under the Macedonian empire they declared by their actions, as far as in them lay, that tyrants ought to be punished: they threw down the statues and images of Ptolemy Physco, but were unable to kill him, for his mercenary army was too strong. His son Alexander was forced by a popular uprising to leave his country because he had killed his mother. *His* son Alexander likewise, when he lorded it too insolently, the people of Alexandria dragged out of the palace, and killed in the public gymnasium. The same people, finally, deposed Ptolemy Auletes for his many crimes. Now since a learned man cannot be ignorant of such notorious facts, and a man whose profession it is to teach them, and who asks to be believed in matters of such moment, is in duty bound not to be ignorant of them; who would not pronounce it a shame and a disgrace that this person, if so ignorant and illiterate, should to the scandal of true scholarship puff himself about as a great scholar, and solicit pay from kings and commonwealths, or, if such a knave and liar, should not be branded with some special mark of infamy, and banished out of the company and fellowship of all scholars and gentlemen?

Having examined the Egyptians for examples, let us now look at the Ethiopians their neighbors. Their king, chosen, as they think, by God, they worship as a sort of God, and yet whenever the priests condemn him, he kills himself; and on that manner, says Diodorus, they punish all their other crim-

doro teste, omnes alios maleficos puniunt; non ipsi morte affi-
ciunt, sed ipsos reos lictore misso mori jubent. Ad Assyrios
deinde et Medos et Persas regum observantissimos accedis:
Jus illic regium summa cum licentia quidlibet faciendi con-
5 *junctum fuisse* contra omnium Historicorum fidem affirmas.
Narrat imprimis Daniel ut regem Nebuchadnezzarem plus
nimio superbientem homines à se depulerint, et ad bestias able-
gaverint. Jus eorum non regium, sed Medorum et Persarum,
id est populi jus appellatur; quod cùm irrevocabile esset, reges
10 etiam obligavit. Darius itaque Medus eripere manibus satra-
parum Danielem, quanquam id maximè agebat, non potuit.
Populi, inquis, *nefas esse tum credebant regem repudiare
quòd illo jure abuteretur.* Inter ipsa tamen hæc verba adeò
miserè obtorpes, ut dum istorum populorum obedientiam et
15 modestiam laudas, ereptum Sardanapalo regnum ab Arbace
tua sponte commemores. Eripuit autem is non solus, sed partim à Sacerdotibus juris peritissimis, partim à populo adjutus,
atque hoc præsertim nomine eripuit, quòd is jure regio, non
ad crudelitatem, sed ad luxuriam tantummodo et mollitiem
20 abuteretur. Percurre Herodotum, Ctesiam, Diodorum, intel-
liges omnino contrà esse quàm dicis, *à Subditis ut plurimùm
ea regna destructa fuisse, non ab externis:* Assyrios reges à

inals: they put them not to death, but send an officer of justice to bid the guilty die.

Next you come to the Assyrians, the Medes, and the Persians, who most revere their kings; and you affirm, contrary
5 to the authority of all historians, that "the royal power there
had an unbounded liberty annexed to it of doing what the
king listed." In the first place, the prophet Daniel tells us
how, when Nebuchadnezzar grew proud beyond excess, they
drove him from men, and sent him away to the beasts. The
10 law of those countries was not entitled royal law, but the law
of the Medes and Persians, that is, of the people; which law,
being irrevocable, bound the kings themselves; insomuch that
Darius the Mede, though he earnestly labored to deliver
Daniel from the hands of the presidents and princes, yet could
15 not effect it. "Nations in those days," say you, "thought it an
impiety to reject a king because he abused that royal right."
But in the very writing of these words you are so abjectly
stupid that while you are commending the obedience and submissiveness of those nations, you go out of your way to men-
20 tion that Arbaces deprived Sardanapalus of the crown. Not
single-handed, however, for he was helped partly by the priests,
who were very well versed in the law, and partly by the people;
and he deposed him chiefly upon the ground that he abused
his royal right, by way not of cruelty, but only of lust and
25 effeminacy. Run over the histories of Herodotus, Ctesias,
Diodorus, and you will find, clean contrary to your assertion,
the fact to be "that those kingdoms were destroyed for the
most part by *subjects,* and *not* by *foreigners*"; you will find

Medis, Medos à Persis, utrisque tum *Subditis,* sublatos fuisse. *Cyrum* ipse *rebellâsse,* et *arreptas tyrannides in diversis imperii locis* fateris. Hoccine est jus regium apud Medos et Persas, et observantiam eorum in reges, quod instituisti, asserere?

5 Quæ te Anticyra tam delirum sanare potest? *Persarum reges quali jure regnârint ex Herodoto,* inquis, *liquet. Cambyses,* cùm sororem in matrimonio habere cuperet, judices regios consulit, delectos *ex populo viros,* legum interpretes, ad quos omnia referri solebant. Quid illi? negant se invenire legem

10 quæ jubeat fratrem secum in matrimonium sororem jungere; aliam tamen invenisse, quâ liceat Persarum regi facere quæ libeat. Primùm si rex omnia pro suo jure poterat, quid alio legum interprete quàm ipso rege opus erat? supervacanei isti judices ubivis potiùs quàm in regia mansissent. Deinde si Regi

15 Persarum quidvis licuit, incredibile est id adeò nescivisse Cambysem dominationis cupidissimum, ut quid licitum esset, judices illos percontaretur. Quid ergo? vel *gratificari* volentes *regi,* ut fateris ipse, vel à tyranno sibi metuentes, ut aït Herodotus, facilem quandam se reperisse legem simulant, palpum

20 regi obtrudentes: quod in judicibus et legum peritis hac etiam ætate novum non est. At verò *Artabanus Persa dixit ad The-*

that the Assyrians were deposed by the Medes their subjects, and the Medes by the Persians likewise their subjects. You yourself admit that "Cyrus rebelled, and that in divers parts of the empire despotic governments were seized." Is this how you vindicate the royal right among the Medes and Persians, and their reverence for their kings, which you have set up? What Anticyra can medicine thee thus raving?

You say: "With what power the Persian kings ruled is apparent from Herodotus." Cambyses being desirous to marry his sister, consulted the royal judges, "eminent men chosen from among the people," interpreters of the laws, to whom all difficulties were submitted. What answer had he from them? They told him that they found no law which bids a brother marry his sister, but that they did find another law whereby the king of Persia may do as he likes. Now to this I answer, if the king of Persia were really so absolute, what need was there of any other interpreter of the laws than the king himself? Those superfluous unnecessary judges would have remained anywhere you will but in the palace! Again, if the king of Persia might do whatever he would, it is not credible that Cambyses, eager for power as he was, should be so ignorant as to interrogate those judges concerning his liberties. What was the matter then? Either they designed "to humor the king," as you admit, or they were afraid of what the tyrant might do to them, as Herodotus says, and feigned that they had found a law that would do, and fooled him, which even nowadays is no new thing with judges and gentlemen learned in the law. "But," say you, "Artabanus a Persian told The-

mistoclem, nullam legem apud Persas esse meliorem illâ quâ
sancitum fuerat; regem esse honorandum et adorandum.
Præclaram tu quidem legem de adoratione regum introducis
etiam à patribus antiquis damnatam; præclarum etiam legis
5 commendatorem Artabanum, qui ipse haud multò pòst sua
manu Xerxem regem suum trucidavit. Probos regum defen-
sores regicidas nobis adfers: suspicor te regibus insidias quasdam moliri. Claudianum citas poëtam, Persarum obedientiæ
testem. At ego te ad res eorum gestas et annales revoco, de-
10 fectionibus Perfarum, Medorum, Bactrianorum, Babylonio-
rum, etiam cædibus regum refertissimos. Proximus tibi author est Otanes Persa, ipse etiam Smerdis interfector sui regis,
qui cum odio potestatis regiæ, injurias et facinora regum exponat, violationes legum, cædes indemnatorum, stupra, adul-
15 teria, hoc tu jus regium vis appellari, et Samuelis iterum ca-
lumniandi in mentem tibi venit. De Homero qui reges esse ab
Jove cecinit, suprà respondi: Philippo regi jus regium inter-
pretanti tam credam quàm Carolo. Ex Diotogenis deinde
Pythagoréi fragmento quædam producis, at quali is de rege
20 dicat taces. Accipe igitur quo ille usus est exordio; ad quod
referri quæ sequuntur cuncta debent. Βασιλεὺς κ᾽ εἴη ὁ δικαι-
ότατος, etc. *Rex ille fuerit, qui justissimus est; justissimus*

mistocles there was no better law in Persia than the one which enacted that kings were to be honored and worshiped." An admirable law for you to cite—a law enjoining king-worship! —a law long ago condemned by even the early Fathers! And
5 an admirable person to recommend this law too—Artabanus, who himself a little while after with his own hand slew Xerxes his king! Right king-defenders these you cite—these king-killers! I suspect you have some secret design upon kings!

In the next place, you quote the poet Claudian to prove how
10 obedient the Persians were. But I refer you to their histories and annals, which are stuffed full of the revolts of the Persians, the Medes, the Bactrians, and the Babylonians, and with the murders of their kings. Your next authority is Otanes the Persian, who likewise killed Smerdis his king. While he, out
15 of his hatred of royal government, sets forth the impieties and injurious actions of kings, their violation of the laws, their putting men to death without legal conviction, their rapes and adulteries, you will have all this called the right of kings, and slander Samuel again. You quote Homer, who says that
20 kings derive their authority from Jupiter; to which I have already given an answer. For king Philip of Macedon as an expounder of the right of kings, I had as lief take his interpretation as King Charles's!

Then you quote some sentences from a fragment of Di-
25 otogenes the Pythagorean, but you do not tell us what sort of king he speaks of. Observe therefore how he begins, for whatever follows must be understood to have relation to it: "Let him be king," says he, "that of all is most just, and most

autem, qui maximè legitimus; nam sine justitia nullus *rex esse poterit, neque justitia sine lege.* Hæc cum jure tuo regio è regione pugnant. Eadem abs te recitatus Ecphantas philosophatur. δεῖ δὲ καὶ τὸν εἰς αὐτὰν καταστάντα, etc. *oportet*

5 *qui regnum suscipit purissimum et lucidissimum naturâ esse:* et infra, ὁ κατ' ἀρετὰν ἐξάρχων, etc. *ille qui imperat secundùm virtutem, nominatur rex, et est.* Quem tu igitur regem vocas, Pythagoreorum judicio rex non est. Jam tu vicissim Platonem audi in Epistola octava, Ἀρχὴ γιγνέσθω

10 ὑπεύθυνος βασιλική, etc. *Sit regia potestas reddendæ rationi obnoxia; leges dominentur et aliis civibus et ipsis etiam regibus, si quid præter leges fecerint.* Addo Aristotelem Polit. 3. ἐν μέν τοι ὁμοίοις καὶ ἴσοις οὔτε συμφέρον ἐστίν, etc. *inter similes et æquales neque utile est neque justum, esse unum*

15 *omnium dominum, neque ubi leges non sunt, neque ut ipse lex sit, neque ubi sunt leges; neque bonum bonorum, neque non bonum non bonorum dominum esse.* Et lib. quinto, *Quem populus non vult, statim is non rex, sed tyrannus est,* c. 10. Hem tibi etiam Xenophontem in Hierone ἀντὶ τοῦ τιμωρεῖν

20 αἱ πόλεις αὐτοῖς, etc. *tantum abest ut tyrannorum necem civitates ulciscantur, ut magnis honoribus afficiant eum, qui tyrannum interfecerit, imagines etiam tyrannicidarum in templis statuant.* Testem oculatum adjiciam Marcum Tullium pro Milone. *Græci homines deorum honores tribuunt iis*

25 *viris qui tyrannos necaverunt: quæ ego vidi Athenis, quæ aliis in urbibus Græciæ, quas res divinas talibus institutas viris,*

just is he that acts most according to law"; for without justice
no man "can be king, and without law there can be no justice." This is directly opposite to that royal right of yours.
And Ecphantas, whom you likewise quote, reasons to the
5 same effect: "Whosoever takes upon him to be king, ought
to be naturally most pure and clear from all imputation." And
a little after: "He that governs according to virtue is called,
and is, a king." He whom you call a king is therefore, in the
judgment of the Pythagoreans, no king at all. Hear now, in
10 your turn, what Plato says in his Eighth Epistle: "Let the
royal power be liable to be called to account. Let the laws
control not only the people but kings themselves, if they do
anything not warranted by law." I will mention what Aristotle says in the Third Book of his *Politics*: "Among likes and
15 equals it is neither profitable nor just that any one should be
lord and master over all the rest, or should himself be the law,
either where there are no laws, or where there are laws; or
that a good man should be lord over other good men, or a bad
man over other bad men." And in the Fifth Book, says he,
20 "That king whom the people do not wish, is no longer a king
but a tyrant." Hear what Xenophon says in Hiero: "Cities
are so far from punishing the killing of tyrants, that they
confer great honor upon him that kills one, and erect statues
of tyrannicides in their temples." Of this I can produce an
25 eye-witness, Marcus Tullius, in his oration *Pro Milone*: "The
Greeks," says he, "ascribe divine worship to men who have
killed tyrants. What have I myself seen at Athens and in
other cities of Greece—what religious observances instituted

quos cantus, quæ carmina? prope ad immortalitatem, et re-
ligionem, et memoriam consecrantur. Polybius denique author gravissimus, Historiarum sexto, τότε δὲ ταῖς ἐπιθυμίαις
ἑπόμενοι, etc. *cùm principes,* inquit, *cupiditatibus obsequi cœ-*
5 *perunt, tum de regno facta est tyrannis, et conspiratio in caput*
dominantium inibatur; cujus quidem authores erant non de-
terrimi civium, sed generosissimi quique et maximi animi.
Longè plura cùm mihi suppeterent, hæc pauca delibavi: ob-
ruor enim copiâ. A philosophis ad poetas jam provocas, eò te
10 libentissimè sequimur. *Potestatem nullis legibus, nullis ju-*
diciis obnoxiam in Græcia reges obtinuisse vel unus, inquis,
Æschylus potest docere; qui in tragœdia, Supplices, Regem
Argivorum ἄκριτον πρύτανιν *vocat, non judicabilem rectorem.*
Verum tu scito, (præcipitem enim te et nullius judicii esse,
15 quocunque te vertis, eò magis perspicio) scito, inquam, non
quid poëta, sed quis apud poëtam quidque dicat, spectan-
dum esse: variæ enim personæ inducuntur, nunc bonæ, nunc
malæ, nunc sapientes, nunc simplices, non semper quid
poëtæ videatur, sed quid cuique personæ maximè conveniat
20 loquentes. Danai filiæ quinquaginta ex Ægypto profugæ ad
Argivorum regem supplices se contulerant; orant uti se contra

in their honor — what poems, songs, and hymns in their praise! They are almost consecrated to immortality in adoration and remembrance." And lastly, Polybius, a weighty authority, in the Sixth Book of his History, says thus: "When
5 princes began to indulge their own lusts and avarice, then royal government turned into tyranny, and conspiracies against the lives of the despots were entered into; nor were the instigators the dregs of the citizenry, but the most noble and magnanimous." These few passages I have picked out to
10 taste, for I have store far greater, and am overwhelmed with plenty.

   From the philosophers you now appeal to the poets, and I am very willing to follow you. "Aeschylus by himself is enough to inform us," you say, "that kings in Greece held a
15 power not liable to any laws or any judicature; for in the tragedy of *The Suppliants* he calls the king of the Argives 'a ruler not subject to judgment'." Know you (for the greater the variety of your arguments, the more I discern how recklessly uncritical you are), know then, I say, that we must not
20 regard the poet's words as his own, but consider who it is that speaks in the play, and what that person says; for different persons are introduced, sometimes good, sometimes bad, sometimes wise men, sometimes fools, and they speak not always the poet's own opinion, but what is most fitting to
25 each character. The fifty daughters of Danaus, being banished out of Egypt, betook themselves to the king of the Argives as suppliants, and begged him to protect them against the violence of the Egyptians, who were pursuing them with a fleet

vim Ægyptiorum classe insequentium defendat; respondet
rex non posse se, nisi rem priùs cum populo communicet.

> Ἐγὼ δ'ἂν οὐ κραίνοιμ' ὑπόσχεσιν πάρος
> Ἀστῶν δὲ πᾶσι τοῖσδε κοινώσας πέρι.

5 Mulieres peregrinæ et supplices incerta populi suffragia veri-
tæ, regem denuò blandiùs compellant.

> Σύ τοι πόλις, σὺ δὲ τὸ δήμιον,
> Πρύτανις ἄκριτος ὤν.
> *Tu instar urbis es et populi,*
> *Prætor injudicatus.*

10 Rursus rex,

> Εἶπον δὲ καὶ πρὶν, οὐκ ἄνευ δήμου τάδε
> Πράξαιμ' ἂν οὐδέπερ κρατῶν——
> *Dixi antea, non sine populo hæc facerem,*
> *Ne si possem quidem.*

15

De re itaque tota ad populum refert,

> Ἐγὼ δὲ λάους συνκαλῶν ἐγχωρίους
> Πείσω τὸ κοινόν.

Populus itaque decernit opem Danai filiabus ferendam; unde
20 illa senis Danai lætantis,

> Θαρσεῖτε παῖδες, εὖ τὰ τῶν ἐγχωρίων
> Δήμου δέδοκται παντελῆ ψηφίσματα.

of ships. The king told them he could not without first imparting the matter to the people.

> Ἐγὼ δ' ἂν οὐ κραίνοιμ' ὑπόσχεσιν πάρος
> Ἀστῶν δὲ πᾶσι τοῖσδε κοινώσας πέρι.

5 The women, being strangers and suppliants, and fearing the uncertain suffrages of the people, urge him anew, this time with more flattery:

> Σύ τοι πόλις, σὺ δὲ τὸ δήμιον,
> Πρύτανις ἄκριτος ὤν.

10 "Thou standest for city and people, a ruler not to be judged." The king answers:

> Εἶπον δὲ καὶ πρὶν, οὐκ ἄνευ δήμου τάδε
> Πράξαιμ' ἂν οὐδέπερ κρατῶν —

"I told you before that I could not do it without the people's 15 consent; nay, and though I could, I would not." So he brings the whole matter before the people.

> Ἐγὼ δὲ λάους συγκαλῶν ἐγχωρίους
> Πείσω τὸ κοινόν.

The people decrees therefore that aid is to be given the daugh-20 ters of Danaus; whence these words of Danaus in his joy:

> Θαρσεῖτε παῖδες, εὖ τὰ τῶν ἐγχωρίων
> Δήμου δέδοκται παντελῆ ψηφίσματα.

Bono estote animo filiæ, benè decreverunt
Indigenarum, in conventu populari, perfectissima
    suffragia.

Hæc nisi protulissem, quàm temere statuisset sciolus iste de
5 jure regio apud Græcos ex ore mulierum, et peregrinarum, et
supplicum; cùm et ipse rex, et ipsa res gesta longè aliud nos
doceat. Idem etiam docet Euripidis Orestes, qui, mortuo
patre, Argivorum ipse rex, ob cædem matris à populo in judicium vocatus, ipse causam dixit, et suffragiis populi capite
10 damnatus est. Athenis regiam potestatem legibus obnoxiam
fuisse testatur idem Euripides etiam in Supplicibus, ubi hæc
Theseus Athenarum Rex

——— *οὐ γὰρ ἄρχεται*
῾*Ενὸς πρὸς ἀνδρὸς, ἀλλ᾽ ἐλευθέρα πόλις,*
15 *Δῆμος δ᾽ ἀνάσσει* ———
    non regitur
Ab uno viro, sed est libera hæc civitas,
Populus autem regnat ———

Sic ejus filius Demophoon Rex item Atheniensium apud eun-
20 dem poëtam in Heraclidis.

Οὐ γὰρ τυραννίδ᾽ ὥστε βαρβάρων ἔχω,
᾽*Αλλ᾽ ἦν δίκαια δρῶ, δίκαια πείσομαι.*
Non enim iis tyrannicè tanquam barbaris impero,
Sed si facio justa quæ sunt, justa mihi redduntur.

25 Non aliud Thebis jus regium antiquitùs fuisse testatur Sophocles in Oedipo tyranno, unde et Tiresias et Creon Oedipo ferociter responsant, ille,

"Be of good cheer, daughters, for the all-accomplished votes of the people of the country in popular assembly have decided well." Had I not related the whole thing, how rashly would this smatterer have laid down the law concerning the right of
5 kings among the Grecians, out of the mouths of women that were both strangers and suppliants, though both the king himself and the very action of the drama lead us to a far different conclusion!

The same conclusion appears from the story of Euripides'
10 Orestes, who being after his father's death himself king of the Argives, was yet brought to trial by the people for the slaying of his mother, pleaded his own cause, and by the people's vote was condemned to die. That at Athens the kingly power was subject to the laws, the same Euripides bears witness in his
15 play likewise called *The Suppliants,* where Theseus, king of Athens, says: "Not ruled by one man, but free, is the city; yet the people reigns." In the same poet's *Heraclidae,* Theseus' son Demophoon, likewise king of the Athenians, says: "For I do not exercise tyrannical power over them, as if they
20 were Barbarians: but if I do right, right is done me." Sophocles in his *Oedipus Tyrannus* shows that anciently in Thebes the right of kings was even so. Hence both Tiresias and Creon answer back courageously to Oedipus. The former says, "I am not your slave"; the latter, "I have some right in this city
25 as well as you." And in the *Antigone,* Haemon tells Creon: "That is no city which belongs to one man."

All men know that the kings of Lacedaemon have been brought to trial, and sometimes put to death judicially. And

Οὐ γάρ τι σοὶ ζῶ δοῦλος

Non servus tibi sum.

Hic,

Κἀμοὶ πόλεως μέτεστι τῆς δ᾽ οὐ σοὶ μόνῳ.

5   *Est et mihi jus in hac civitate non tibi soli.*

Et Æmon Creonti in Antigone:

Πόλις γὰρ οὐκ ἔσθ᾽, ἥτις ἀνδρὸς ἔσθ᾽ ἑνός.

Non est civitas, quæ unius est viri.

Jam verò Lacedæmoniorum reges in judicium sæpe adductos,
10 et interdum morte multatos nemo ignorat: nec mirum; quando ipse Lycurgus, qui eorum scripsit leges, non alio fuisse
jure heroicis etiam temporibus reges, ab Homero, quem stu-
diose perlegerat, didicisse potuit. Apud eum Achilles Aga-
memnonem, postquam eum ipsum esse pestem populi pesti-
15 lentia tum laborantis comperisset, non dubitavit, in concione
frequentissima Græcorum, rex ipse regem suo populo judicandum his verbis subjicere:

Δημοβόρος βασιλεὺς, ἐπεὶ οὐτιδανοῖσιν ἀνάσσεις.

῾Η γὰρ ἂν ᾽Ατρείδη νῦν ὕστατα λωβήσαιο. Iliad. *α.*

20   *Populi vorator rex, quoniam hominibus nihili imperas.*

   Alioqui enim Atrida, nunc postremùm injuriam faceres.

Sensisse idem quod heroes de jure regio etiam omnium ordinum homines, testis esse potest Lyricorum princeps Alcæus;
cujus carmina, tametsi per se gratissima, eo tamen acceptiora
25 populo fuisse refert Horatius, quòd eorum continerent laudes
qui tyrannos ex civitatibus ejecerant:

no wonder, when Lycurgus himself, their lawgiver, might have learned from Homer, whom he had read attentively from beginning to end, that even in the heroic times kings were subject to the very same laws. Homer's Achilles, having found 5 that Agamemnon was himself a pestilence unto his people, who were then suffering under a pestilence, did not, though himself a king, hesitate, in an assemblage of the Greeks frequent and full, to submit a king to his own subjects for judgment. These are his words (*Iliad* I.):

10   King, devourer of the people, since thou rulest over men
       of naught,
    For else, Atrides, hadst thou now committed outrage for
       the last time.

That men of all ranks felt as the heroes did about the royal 15 right, Alcaeus may witness, chief of lyric poets; whose poems, most delightful in themselves, were all the more popular, says Horace, in that they sang the praises of those who had cast out tyrants from their cities:

"The shades look on in wonder while the one and the 20 other sing things that deserve to be listened to in reverent silence; but the populace, crowded shoulder to shoulder, drink in yet more with eager ear tales of battles and of tyrants driven out." *Odes* 2.13.29.

To these, in support of the same opinion, let me join 25 Theognis, who was in his prime not so long before the Persian Wars, at a time when there flourished in every part of Greece many worthies distinguished for their wisdom. The teach-

Utrumque sacro digna silentio
Mirantur umbræ dicere: sed magis
Pugnas et exactos tyrannos
    Densum humeris bibit aure vulgus: Od. 2. 13. 29.

5 Addam his in eandem sententiam Theognidem; qui nec ita
multo ante adventum in Græciam Medorum floruit, quo tempore per omnem Græciam multi sapientia insignes viri floruerunt, et ipse quæ versibus præcepta tradidit, à sapientibus
accepisse se profitetur:

10   Δημοφάγον δὲ τύραννον ὅπως ἐθέλεις καταχλῖναι.
    Ὀυ νέμεσις πρὸς θεῶν γίγνεται οὐδεμία.
    Populi voratorem regem ut libet dejice.
    Ira à diis inde existit nulla.

Atque hæc quidem antiquum in Græcia jus regium quale
15 fuerit satis declarant. Ad Romanos veniamus. Tu ad illud
imprimis recurris non Sallustianum, sed C. Memmii apud
Sallustium, *impunè quidvis facere:* cui suprà responsum est.
Sallustius ipse disertis verbis author est, *Romanos imperium*
legitimum, nomen imperii regium habuisse; quod cum *se in*
20 *dominationem convertit,* ut nôsti, expulerunt. Sic M. Tullius
in Pisonem, ego Consulem esse putem, qui Senatum esse in
repub. non putavit? et sine eo consilio consulem numerem,
sine quo Romæ ne reges quidem esse potuerunt? Audin' regem Romæ sine Senatu nihil fuisse? *At Romulus, ut libitum,*
25 *Romanis imperitaverat, ut ait Tacitus.* Nondum enim fun-
data legibus colluvies potiùs convenarum quàm respub. erat:
omnes olim mortales sine legibus vivebant, cùm respublicæ

ings which he handed down in his verses he himself avows that he had got from the Wise Men.

> Cast down how thou wilt a king that devours his people:
> For this the gods have no resentment—none.

5 These instances make clear enough what was the royal right in Greece. Let us consider now the Romans.

First you return to that phrase not of Sallust but of C. Memmius quoted in Sallust, "to do with impunity what you list." This I have answered already. Sallust himself says ex-
10 pressly that "the government of Rome was a government by law, though its name was regal," and when "it grew into a tyranny," you know they thrust it out. Cicero likewise in his oration against Piso, "Shall I," says he, "reckon as consul one who reckoned not upon the Senate's existence in the common-
15 wealth? Shall I count as consul him who consults not that without which there could not even be kings at Rome?" Do you hear? At Rome the very king was naught without the Senate. "But," you say, "Romulus, according to Tacitus, had governed the Romans exactly as he pleased." Yes, for, having
20 as yet no foundation of laws, they were a rabble concourse of strangers rather than a state. Of old, before states came into being, all men lived lawless. But, as Livy informs us, when Romulus was dead, though all the people desired a king, not having yet tasted the sweets of liberty, "Yet the sovereign
25 power was allowed to remain in the hands of the people; so that they gave not up more right than they kept." The same author tells us: "That right was afterwards extorted from

nondum essent. Post Romulum autem, authore Livio, etsi
regem omnes volebant, libertatis dulcedine nondum expertâ,
Populo tamen summa potestas permissa est, ut non plus
darent juris quam detinerent; jus illud à Cæsaribus *vi ademp-*
5 *tum fuisse* idem aït. Servius Tullius dolo primùm quasi Tar-
quinii Prisci vicarius regnabat; postea verò ad populum ipse
retulit, *vellent juberentne se regnare;* tandem, ut aït Tacitus,
sanctor legum fuit queis etiam reges obtemperarent. Fecis-
sétne hanc sibi et posteris injuriam, si supra leges antea fuisse
10 jus regium censuisset? Ultimus illorum regum Tarquinius
superbus *morem de omnibus Senatum consulendi primus sol-*
vit; ob hæc et alia flagitia populus L. Tarquinio regi imperium abrogavit; exulémque esse cum conjuge ac liberis jussit.
Hæc ferè ex Livio et Cicerone; quibus alios juris regii apud
15 Romanos haud tu interpretes attuleris meliores. Ad dictatu-
ram quod attinet, temporaria tantùm fuit, nunquam adhibita
nisi difficillimis reipub. temporibus, et intra sex menses depo-
nenda. Jus autem imperatorum quod vocas, non jus illud, sed
vis planè erat; imperium nullo jure præterquam armis par-
20 tum. At *Tacitus,* inquis, *qui sub imperio unius floruit,* ita
scripsit. *Principi summum rerum arbitrium dii dederunt,*
subditis obsequii gloria relicta est. Nec dicis quo loco; tibi
conscius nimirum insigniter lectoribus imposuisse; quod mihi
quidem statim suboluit, etsi locum illum non statim reperi.

them" by the Caesars. Servius Tullius at first reigned by indirection, and as it were a deputy of Tarquinius Priscus; but afterwards he referred it to the people "whether they would have him and bid him reign." At last, says Tacitus, "he be-
5 came the author of laws such as even the kings obeyed." Do you think he would have done such an injury to himself and his posterity, if he had deemed that the right of kings before he did so had been above all laws? Their last king, Tarquinius Superbus, "was the first that put an end to the custom of
10 consulting the Senate about everything"; and for this and other enormities the people annihilated the power of king Lucius Tarquinius, and banished him with his wife and children. To this effect speak Livy and Cicero, than whom you will hardly produce any better expositors of the right of kings
15 among the Romans. As for the dictatorship, that was but temporary, was never applied but in the state's extremities, and was to be laid down within six months.

What you call the right of the Roman emperors was no right, however, but downright force, a power gained through
20 no law but that of arms. "But Tacitus," say you, "that lived under the government of a single person," writes thus: "'The gods have given the sovereign power in human affairs to princes; what has been left to subjects is the honor of submitting.'"
But you tell us not where Tacitus has these words, doubtless
25 because you were conscious that you had egregiously put upon your readers; which I smelt out at once, though I could not at once find the place. For those words are not Tacitus's own, who is an approved writer, and the greatest possible enemy to

Non enim Taciti hæc verba sunt, scriptoris boni, et tyrannis adversissimi, sed apud Tacitum M. Terentii cujusdam equitis Romani, qui capitis reus, inter alia, quæ metu mortis ab eo dicta sunt, sic Tiberium adulatur, annalium 6º. *Tibi sum-* 5 *mum rerum judicium dii dederunt, nobis obsequii gloria re-licta est.* Hanc tu quasi Taciti sententiam profers, qui senten-tias tibi commodas non ex pistrina solùm, aut tonstrina, sed ex ipsa carnificina oblatas non respueres: ita omnia vel osten-tationis causâ, vel imbecillitatis conscientiâ undecunque cor-10 radis. Tacitum ipsum si legere maluisses, quàm alicubi de-cerptum negligentiùs transcribere, docuisset te is, jus illud imperatorum unde ortum sit. *Post Actiacam victoriam, verso civitatis statu, nihil usquam prisci aut integri moris; omnes exuta æqualitate jussa principis aspectare;* docuisset idem an-15 nalium tertio, unde tuum omne jus regium: *Postquam exui æqualitas, et pro modestia ac pudore ambitio et vis incedebat, provenere dominationes, multósque apud populos æternum mansere.* Idem ex Dione poteras didicisse, si innata levitas et inconstantia tua quicquam te altiùs percipere pateretur. Nar-20 rat enim is l. 53. abs te citato, ut partim armis, partim dolo et

tyrants, but are quoted by Tacitus as the words of M. Teren-
tius, a gentleman of Rome, who being charged with capital
crime, amongst other things that he said in fear of death,
flattered Tiberius in this manner, *Annals* VI: "The gods have
5 entrusted you with the ultimate judgment in all things; what
has been left to us is the honor of submitting." And this you
cite as if it were Tacitus's opinion! Whatever your motive—
whether you would show off, or are conscious of your weakness—so indiscriminately do you scrape together everything
10 from everywhere, that you would not reject opinions to suit
your argument though they were the sweepings of a baker's
shop or a barbershop—yes, or of the very gallows! Had you
chosen to read Tacitus himself rather than copy too carelessly
an extract you found somewhere, he would have taught you
15 whence that imperial right had its origin. "After the victory
of Actium," says he, "the whole state of our affairs was turned
upside down; nothing of our ancient or uncorrupted manners
anywhere; all men put off political equality and began to
attend to the orders of the chief of state." This you might have
20 learned out of the third Book of his *Annals,* whence you have
all your regal right. "When equality was laid aside, and instead of moderation and self-restraint factiousness and violence stepped in, tyrannical forms of government started up,
and fixed themselves in many countries." The same thing
25 you might have learned out of Dio, if your natural levity and
unsettledness of judgment would have suffered you to apprehend anything above you. He tells us in his fifty-third Book,
from which you have quoted, that partly by the violence and

simulatione Octaviani Cæsaris, effectum sit, ut imperatores legibus soluti essent; dum enim pro concione pollicetur se principatu abiturum, legibus et imperiis etiam aliorum obtemperaturum, per causam belli in provinciis suis gerendi, 5 retentis apud se semper legionibus, dum simulatè renuit imperium, sensim invasit. Non est hoc legibus ritè solutum esse, sed legum vincula, quod gladiator ille Spartacus potuit, vi solvere; nomen deinde principis aut imperatoris et αὐτοκράτορος sibi arrogare, quasi Deus aut naturæ lex omnes et homines et 10 leges illi subjecisset. Vis altiùs paulò juris Cæsarei originem cognoscere? Marcus Antonius, jussu Cæsaris, qui armis in rempublicam nefariè sumptis tum plurimum poterat, Consul factus, cùm Lupercalia Romæ celebrarentur, ex composito, ut videbatur, diadema capiti Cæsaris cum gemitu et plangore 15 populi imposuit: ascribi deinde jussit in fastis ad Lupercalia, C. Cæsari Antonium Consulem, jussu populi, regnum detulisse. Qua de re Cicero in secunda Philippica; *Ideone L. Tarquinius exactus, Spurius Cassius, Sp. Melius, M. Manlius necati, ut multis post seculis à M. Antonio, quod fas non est,* 20 *rex Romæ constitueretur?* Tu verò omni malo cruciatu atque

partly by the fraud and hypocrisy of Octavianus Caesar, things were brought to that pass that the emperors were loosed from the laws. For though Octavianus promised before the popular assembly that he would lay down the principate, and obey 5 the laws, and even the commands of others, yet under pretence of making war in his provinces he still kept the legions at hand, and so, while in appearance he declined power, he gradually entered upon the possession of it. This was not being duly released from the laws, but breaking forcibly 10 through their bonds, as Spartacus the gladiator might have done; and then assuming to himself the style of *princeps* or *imperator* and αὐτοκράτωρ, as if God or the law of nature had put all men and all laws into subjection under him.

Would you inquire a little further back into the origin of 15 the right of the Caesars? Mark Antony had been made consul at the bidding of Caesar, who by impiously taking up arms against the commonwealth had got all the power into his hands. Now at the celebration of the Lupercalia at Rome, Antony, by previous arrangement it seems, set a crown upon 20 Caesar's head, amid the people's groans and lamentations. Thereupon he caused it to be entered upon the Calendar as a record of the events at the Lupercalia that Marcus Antonius had offered Caesar royal power at the people's instance! Of which action Cicero in his second *Philippic* says: "Was it for 25 this that Lucius Tarquinius was expelled, and Spurius Cassius, Spurius Melius, and Marcus Manlius put to death—that after many generations Mark Antony against the law should make a king in Rome?" Truly you deserve every form of

infamia sempiterna etiam ipso Antonio dignior, quanquam
noli hinc superbire, non enim te hominem despicatissimum,
ulla re alia quàm scelere cum Antonio confero, qui in hisce
tuis Lupercalibus nefandis non uni tantùm, sed omnibus ty-
5 rannis diadema cunctis legibus solutum, nulla solvendum
Lupercus dissolutissimus imponere studuisti. Certè si ipsorum
Cæsarum oraculo credendum est, sic enim appellant Christiani imperatores Theodosius et Valens edictum suum cod. l. 1.
tit. 14. de authoritate juris imperatorum pendet authoritas.
10 Majestas ergo regnantis, vel ipsorum Cæsarum sive judicio
sive oraculo, submittenda legibus est, de quibus pendet. Hinc
adulta jam potestate imperatoria ad Trajanum Plinius in
Panegyrico; *Diversa sunt naturâ, dominatio, et principatus.*
Trajanus regnum ipsum arcet ac summovet, sedemque obti-
15 *net principis, ne sit domino locus.* Et infrà, *Omnia quæ de*
aliis principibus à me dicta sunt, eò pertinent ut ostendam,
quàm longa consuetudine corruptos, depravatósque mores
principatûs parens noster reformet, et corrigat. Quod depra-
vatos principatûs mores Plinius, id téne pudet jus regium per-
20 petuò vocitare? Verùm hactenus de jure regio apud Romanos
breviter. Quid illi in tyrannos suos, sive reges, sive Imperatores fecerint, vulgò notum est. Tarquinium expulerunt; et

torture and everlasting disgrace even more than Antony himself. Yet be not therefore puffed up, for I compare you not,
most contemptible of men, with Antony in aught but wickedness: you that in these unspeakable Lupercalia of yours, most
5 loose-lived Lupercus, or Scare-Wolf, have taken pains to bind
about the head not of one tyrant only, but of all tyrants, a
diadem loosed from all laws, but never to be loosened by any!

Indeed if we must believe the "oracle" of the emperors
themselves—for so the Christian emperors Theodosius and
10 Valens call their edict, Cod. lib. 1. tit. 14—the authority of
the emperors depends upon that of the law. So that the majesty of the person that reigns, even by the judgment or the
oracle of the emperors themselves, must submit to the laws on
which it depends. Hence Pliny tells Trajan in his Panegyric,
15 when the power of the emperors was grown to its height: "A
principate and a despotism are quite different in their nature.
Trajan restrains and puts far from him power that is actually
royal, and holds the throne as a prince, that there may be no
room for a despot." And afterwards: "Whatever I have said
20 of other princes, I said that I might show how our prince
moulds anew and straightens the way of principates, which
by long custom have been corrupted and perverted." What
Pliny calls the corrupt and depraved customs of principates,
are you not ashamed still to keep on calling the right of kings?
25 So much, then, briefly, concerning the right of kings among
the Romans.

How they dealt with their tyrants, whether kings or emperors, is generally known. They expelled Tarquin, yes and

more quidem majorum: aut enim expulsi civitate Agyllina Mezentii tyranni antiquissimum exemplum Hetruria vicina præbuit, aut eâ fabulâ summus artifex decori Virgilius, quo jure apud cunctas gentes, idque ab omni vetustate, fuissent
5 reges, regnanti etiam tunc Romæ Octaviano Cæsari voluit ostendere, Æneid. l. 8.

> *At fessi tandem cives infanda furentem*
> *Armati circumsistunt, ipsúmque, domúmque:*
> *Obtruncant socios; ignem ad fastigia jactant.*
> 10 *Ille inter cædes, Rutulorum elapsus in agros*
> *Confugere, et Turni defendier hospitis armis.*
> *Ergo omnis furiis surrexit Etruria justis:*
> *Regem ad supplicium præsenti Marte reposcunt.*

Vides hic justâ irâ inflammatos cives tyrannum non solùm ad
15 necem repentino impetu quæsisse, non regno tantùm expulisse, sed profugum et exulem ad judicium, immò ad supplicium, bello suscepto, repetisse. *Sed quomodo,* inquis, *Tarquinium expulerunt? an in jus vocârunt? nequaquam; Portas venienti clauserunt.* Ridiculum caput, quid ni clauderent ad-
20 volanti cum parte copiarum? quid refert exulare jussus fuerit an mori, si modò pœnas dedisse constat? C. Cæsarem tyrannum excellentissimi illius ætatis viri in Senatu interfecerunt;

by ancestral custom even then; for either their neighbor Etruria offered a very ancient precedent in the expulsion of the tyrant Mezentius from the city of Agylla, or Virgil, past master of the fitting and beautiful, meant by that tale in the eighth Aeneid to show even Caesar Octavianus, who then ruled in Rome, what rights kings had among all nations—and this from the utmost antiquity.

"But while the madman yet meditates crimes unspeakable, the citizens, wearied out at last, in armed bands press round both him and his house, and slay his train, and hurl fire upon his rooftree. Slipping away from amid the slaughter, he betakes him to the territory of the Rutuli for refuge, and is defended by the arms of Turnus a stranger. 'Twas for this that all Etruria rose up in righteous rage: in open war they claim the king for execution."

Here you see that subjects, fired with righteous wrath, not only sought their tyrant upon a sudden violent impulse to murder him, not only drove him from his kingdom, but when he was a fugitive and an exile made war to get him back again for trial, yea for capital punishment.

"But," say you, "*how* did the Romans expel Tarquin? Did they bring him to trial? No such matter: when he would have come into the city, they shut the gates against him." Ridiculous fool! what could they do but shut the gates, when he was hurrying thither with part of the army? Banished or put to death—what odds, so long as he surely was punished?

Gaius Caesar the tyrant was killed in the senate by the choice and master spirits of that age. This action Marcus Tul-

id factum M. Tullius et ipse vir optimus, et pater patriæ pub-licè dictus, miris laudibus, cùm alibi passim, tum in secunda Philippica celebravit. Pauca recitabo. *Omnes boni, quantum in ipsis fuit, Cæsarem occiderunt; aliis consilium, aliis animus,* 5 *aliis occasio defuit, voluntas nemini.* Et infra, *Quæ enim res unquam, proh sancte Jupiter, non modò in hac urbe, sed in omnibus terris est gesta major, quæ gloriosior, quæ commen-datior hominum memoriæ sempiternæ? in hujus me consilii societatem, tanquam in equum Trojanum, includi cum prin-* 10 *cipibus non recuso.* Illud Senecæ tragici et ad Græcos referri potest, et ad Romanos:

> *— Victima haud ulla amplior*
> *Potest, magisque opima mactari Jovi*
> *Quàm rex iniquus —*

15 Nam si ad Herculem spectes, cujus hæc sententia inducitur, quid senserint illa ætate Græcorum summi viri ostendit: Si ad poëtam, qui sub Nerone floruit (et sensum ferè suum poëtæ personis optimis affingere solent) significabat et quid ipse, et quid omnes viri boni, ætate etiam Neronis, faciendum tyranno 20 censuerint; quámque pium, quamque diis gratum esse duxe-rint tyrannicidium. Sic optimi quique Romanorum, quantum in se erat, Domitianum occiderunt. Palàm hoc profitetur Plinius secundus in illo ad Trajanum imperatorem Panegy-

lius, himself an excellent man, and publicly entitled the father
of his country, extols wonderfully in many passages of his
works, particularly in his second *Philippic*. I will repeat some
of his words: "All good men killed Caesar as far as in them
5 lay. Some lacked the plan, others the courage, others the opportunity; none the wish." And afterwards: "What action
ever was performed, oh venerable Jove! not in this city only
but in all the world, that was greater, more glorious, and more
to be commended to the everlasting remembrance of man-
10 kind? Not loath am I to be included in the fellowship that
planned it, as with the band of chieftains in the Trojan horse."

That familiar passage of Seneca the tragedian may relate
both to the Romans and to the Greeks:

There can be slain
15 No sacrifice to God more acceptable
Than an unjust and wicked king.

For if this be taken as the sentiment of Hercules, who speaks
the words, it shows what was the opinion of the most eminent
Greeks in that age; if it be taken as the sentiment of the poet,
20 who flourished under Nero (and poets generally put something like their own opinions into the mouths of their best
characters), then this passage betokened what both Seneca
himself and all good men, even in Nero's time, thought
should be done to a tyrant, and how virtuous an action, how
25 acceptable to the gods, they thought it to kill one. So every
good man of Rome, as far as in him lay, killed Domitian.
Pliny the Younger owns it openly in that Panegyric to the

rico: *Juvabat illidere solo superbissimos vultus, instare ferro,*
sævire securibus, ut singulos ictus sanguis dolorque sequere-
tur: Nemo tam temperans gaudii, quin instar ultionis videtur
cernere laceros artus, truncata membra, postremò truces hor-
5 *rendásque imagines abjectas excoctásque flammis.* Et deinde,
non satis amant bonos principes, qui malos satis non oderint.
Tum inter flagitia Domitiani ponit, quòd is Epaphroditum
Neronis utcunque interfectorem trucidaverit, *An excidit do-*
lori nostro modò vindicatus Nero, permitteret credo fa-
10 *mam vitámque ejus carpi, qui mortem ulciscebatur?* Planè
quasi sceleri proximum esse judicaret, non interfecisse Neronem, scelus gravissimum vindicâsse interfectum. Ex his manifestum est, Romanorum præstantissimos quosque viros non
solum tyrannos quoquo modo, quoties poterant, occidisse, sed
15 factum illud, ut Græci olim, in maxima laude posuisse: Vi-
vum enim tyrannum quoties judicare non poterant viribus
inferiores, mortuum et judicabant, et lege Valeriâ damna-
bant. Valerius enim Publicola Junii Bruti collega cum videret
non posse stipatos suis militibus tyrannos ad judicium per-
20 duci, legem tulit, quâ indemnatum quovis modo occidere
liceret; deinde facti rationem reddere. Hinc C. Caligulam,

emperor Trajan: "There was pleasure in dashing those overweening looks against the ground, in piercing him with
swords, in mangling him with axes, as if he bled and felt
pain at every stroke. No man could so moderate his joy, but
5 that he counted it as good as revenge to behold his mangled
limbs, his members torn asunder, and at last his grim and
horrid statues thrown down and melted in the fire." And
afterwards: "They cannot love good princes enough, that
cannot enough hate bad ones." Then amongst the enormities
10 of Domitian he reckons this, that he put to death Epaphroditus, who in a way had killed Nero: "Have we ceased to grieve
at the vengeance taken but just now for Nero's death? Is it
likely that one who was avenging Nero's death would let his
life and reputation be ill spoken of?" Pliny actually seems to
15 have thought it almost a crime not to kill Nero, and a very
grievous crime to punish his murder.

By what has been said, it is evident that the most excellent
of the Romans did not only kill tyrants however and whenever they could, but like the Greeks before them thought the
20 deed most praiseworthy. For whenever they could not proceed judicially against a tyrant in his lifetime, being less
powerful than he, yet after his death they would both judge
him and by the Valerian Law condemn him; and Valerius
Publicola, Junius Brutus his colleague, perceiving that as
25 tyrants were guarded by soldiers they could not be brought
to trial, proposed a bill making it lawful to kill them uncondemned any how, and give an account afterwards. Hence,
when Cassius had killed Gaius Caligula with a sword, and

quem Cassius ferro, omnes votis interfecerunt, Valerius Asiaticus, vir consularis, cùm non adesset, ad milites tamen ob
necem ejus tumultuantes exclamat, *utinam ego interfecissem;*
Senatus eodem tempore abolendam Cæsarum memoriam, ac
5 diruenda templa censuit; tantum abfuit ut Cassio irasceretur;
Claudium à militibus imperatorem mox salutatum vetant per
tribunum plebis principatum capessere; vis autem militum
vicit. Neronem Senatus hostem judicavit, et ut puniretur
more majorum, quærebat; id genus pœnæ erat, ut nudi cervix
10 insereretur furcæ, corpus virgis ad necem cæderetur. Vide
quantò mitiùs et moderatiùs Angli cum tyranno egerint suo,
qui multorum judicio plus ipso Nerone sanguinis fundendi
author fuerat. Sic Domitianum mortuum Senatus damnavit;
quod potuit, imagines ejus coràm detrahi, et solo affligi jussit.
15 Commodus à suis interfectus, non vindicatus à Senatu aut
Populo, sed hostis judicatus est, qui etiam cadaver ejus ad
supplicium quærebant. Ea de re Senatusconsultum extat apud
Lampridium; *Hosti patriæ honores detrahantur, Parricida*
trahatur, in spoliario lanietur, hostis deorum, carnifex Sena-
20 *tûs unco trahatur,* &c. Iidem Didium Julianum imperatorem

everybody else had done it with prayers and desires, Valerius
Asiaticus, a governor of consular rank, then absent, cried out
to the soldiers that began to mutiny because of the Emperor's
death, "Would I had been the one to kill him!" The Senate
5 at the same time were so far from being displeased with Cassius that they resolved to extirpate the memory of the emperors, and to raze their temples. When Claudius soon after
was saluted Emperor by the soldiers, the Senate forbade him
by the tribune of the people to take the government upon him;
10 but the power of the soldiers prevailed. The Senate declared
Nero a public enemy, and searched him out to have him punished after the way of their ancestors, which required that he
should be stripped naked, his neck thrust beneath the fork,
and with rods be whipped to death. Consider now how much
15 more mildly and moderately the English dealt with their
tyrant, though many are of opinion that he caused more
bloodshed than Nero himself. So the Senate condemned
Domitian after his death; they commanded his statues to be
publicly pulled down and dashed to pieces, which was all they
20 could do. Commodus, slain by his own officers, was not
avenged, but adjudged a public enemy, by both the Senate and
the people, who sought out even his dead corpse for mutila-
tion. The Senate's resolution upon this matter is extant in
Lampridius: "Let the enemy of his country be deprived of
25 all his titles; let the parricide be drawn, let him be torn in
pieces in the gladiators' stripping-place; let the enemy of the
gods, the executioner of the senate, be dragged with a hook,"
etc. The same persons in a very full session of the Senate con-

frequentissimo Senatu capitis damnârunt; et misso Tribuno,
occidi in Palatio jusserunt. Idem Maximino imperium abrogârunt, hostémque judicârunt. Juvat ipsum Senatusconsultum ex Capitolino recitare. *Consul retulit; Patres Conscripti,*
5 *de Maximinis quid placet?* responsum est, *hostes, hostes, qui*
eos occiderit, præmium merebitur. Vis scire populus Romanus
et provinciæ Maximino imperatori an Senatui paruerint? audi
eundem Capitolinum. *Literas mittit Senatus* ad omnes provincias, ut communi saluti, libertatique subveniant; quæ auditæ
10 sunt ab omnibus. Ubique amici, administratores, duces, tribuni,
milites Maximini interfecti sunt: Paucæ civitates fidem hosti
publico servaverunt. Eadem tradit Herodianus. Quid plura
de Romanis? Jam apud finitimas nationes quale jus regum
illa ætate fuerit videamus. Apud Gallos rex eorum Ambiorix
15 *sua ejusmodi esse imperia* fatetur, *ut non minus haberet in se*
juris multitudo, quàm ipse in multitudinem. Judicabatur ergo
non minùs quam judicabat. Rex item Vercingetorix proditionis insimulatus est à suis; tradit hæc Cæsar bellum Galli-
cum scribens. Nec *Germanorum regibus infinita aut libera*
20 *potestas* erat, *de minoribus rebus principes consultant, de ma-*
joribus omnes. Rex aut princeps auditur authoritate suadendi

demned the emperor Didius Julianus to death, and sent a
tribune to slay him in the palace. The same Senate deposed
Maximin, and declared him a public enemy. It will be well
to read from Capitolinus the Senate's resolution concerning
5 him: "The consul put the question: 'Conscript Fathers, what
is your pleasure concerning the Maximins?' They answered:
'They are enemies, they are enemies; whoever kills them shall
be rewarded.'" Would you know whether the Roman people
and the provinces obeyed the Senate, or obeyed Maximin the
10 emperor? Hear what the same author says: "The Senate sent
letters" to all the provinces, requesting them to come to the
rescue of the common safety and liberty; the letters were publicly read. Everywhere the friends, the deputies, the generals, the tribunes, the soldiers of Maximin, were slain. Very
15 few cities kept their allegiance to the public enemy. Herodian
relates the same thing. What need of more instances from
Roman history?

Let us now see what manner of thing the right of kings
was in those days among the neighboring nations. Ambiorix
20 king of the Gauls confesses "the nature of his dominion to be
such that the people had as much right over him as he over
them." Consequently he was always subject to judgment as
much as he exercised judgment. Vercingetorix, king likewise,
was accused of treason by his own people. These things Caesar
25 relates in his history of the Gallic wars. Nor was "the power
of the German kings absolute and unbounded: lesser matters are ordered and disposed by the chiefs, greater matters by
all the people. The king or prince is heeded more through the

*magis quàm jubendi potestate; si displicuit sententia, fremitu
aspernantur.* Hæc Tacitus. Tu vero quod inauditum prorsus
esse modò exclamabas, nunc sæpiùs factum concedis, *quinquaginta* nimirum *Scotorum reges aut expulsos aut incarcera-*
5 *tos, aut necatos, quosdam etiam in publico capitali supplicio
affectos.* Quod in ipsa Britannia factitatum est, cur tu, tyrannorum vespillo, infandum, inauditum esse tanta ejulatione
vociferaris? Pergis Judæorum et Christianorum erga tyrannos
suos religionem extollere, et mendacia ex mendaciis serere,
10 quæ jam toties refutavimus. Modò Assyriorum et Persarum
obedientiam latè prædicabas, nunc eorum rebelliones enume-
ras; et quos nunquam rebellâsse paulò antè dixeras, nunc cur
iidem toties rebellaverint multas causas affers. Ad narrationem deinde sumpti de rege supplicii tandiu intermissam re-
15 vertis, ut, si tunc fortè satis sedulò ineptus et ridiculus non
eras, nunc esses. *Per aulæ suæ membra ductum* narras. Quid
per aulæ membra intelligas scire gestio. Romanorum calami-
tates ex regno in rempub. verso recenses, in quo te tibimet
turpissimè mentiri suprà ostendimus. Qui ad Loiolitam, *sedi-*

influence of his persuasions than through his power to command. If his opinion has not pleased them, they reject it with a murmur." So says Tacitus. Indeed you yourself now confess that what but of late you exclaimed against as absolutely
5 unheard of has been often done, to wit, that "no less than fifty Scottish kings have been either banished or imprisoned or put to death, nay, and some of them publicly executed." Which having been done over and over again in Britain itself, why do you, who spirit your tyrants away like paupers, hug-
10 ger-mugger, for burial at dusk to conceal their violent deaths, how can you, I say, cry out upon it with so lamentable a voice as a thing unheard of?

You proceed to commend the Jews and Christians for their reverent obedience to tyrants, and with lies to sow a harvest
15 of more lies, which I have so often confuted. A while ago you were praising far and wide the obedience of the Assyrians and Persians, and now you reckon up their rebellions; a little while ago you said they never rebelled at all, and now you give us a great many reasons why they rebelled so often! Then
20 you resume your long-suspended narrative of our king's execution, in order that if perhaps you had not taken care enough to be a ridiculous fool then, you may do it now. You say, "He was led through the members of his court." What you mean by the members of the court, I yearn to know. You enumerate
25 the disasters that the Romans underwent through changing their kingdom into a commonwealth; in which I have shown above how grossly you give yourself the lie. You, who when you wrote against the Loyolite, used to point out that "in an

*tiones tantùm sub optimatibus et populo, certam sub tyranno
perniciem esse* demonstrabas, nunc, hominum vanissime et
corruptissime, *ob reges olim ejectos seditionum illa mala tanquam supplicia illos hausisse* audes dicere? scilicet quia cen-
5 tum Jacobæis donavit te postea rex Carolus, idcirco reges expulsos luerunt Romani. At malè cessit Julii Cæsaris interfectoribus. Sanè si cui unquam tyranno, huic parcitum vellem:
quamvis enim regnum in repub. violentiùs invadebat, erat tamen regno fortasse dignissimus: nec ideo quenquam magis
10 putem interfecti Cæsaris pœnas pependisse, quàm deleti
Catilinæ Cajum Antonium Ciceronis collegam: quo postea
de aliis criminibus damnato, ut inquit Cicero pro Flacco,
sepulchrum Catilinæ floribus ornatum est. Fautores enim
Catilinæ exultabant, *justa Catilinæ tum facta esse dictitabant,*
15 ad invidiam cæteris conflandam, qui Catilinam sustulerant.
Hæ sunt improborum artes, quibus viros præstantissimos à
supplicio tyrannorum, et puniendis etiam sæpè facinorosissi-
mis deterreant. Dicerem ego contrà, quod facile esset, quoties
bene cessit, et prosperè tyrannorum interfectoribus, si quid
20 certi de eventu rerum inde statuere quis posset. Objectas,
quòd *regem hæreditarium Angli non illo affecerint supplicio,*

aristocracy or a democracy there could be seditions and tumults only, whereas under a tyrant destruction was sure,"
dare you now say, you empty-headed and thoroughly corrupt
mortal, that "they drank the cup of the ills that arose from
5 their seditions as punishments for banishing their kings aforetime"? To wit, because King Charles afterwards made you a
present of a hundred Jacobuses: that is the reason why the
Romans expiated the banishing of their kings!

You say it went ill with the murderers of Julius Caesar.
10 Indeed, if I would have had any tyrant spared, it should have
been he. He did, to be sure, though a citizen of a republic,
forcibly enter upon the exercise of royal power; yet he perhaps
more than anyone else deserved it. Nor do I for this reason
suppose anyone to have been punished for killing Caesar, any
15 more than Gaius Antonius, Cicero's colleague, was punished
for destroying Catiline. Afterward, when he was condemned
for other crimes, says Cicero in his oration *pro Flacco,* "Catiline's tomb was decked with flowers," for they that favored
Catiline then rejoiced, and "gave out then that Catiline's
20 deeds were righteous," to kindle hatred against those that had
cut him off. These are the artifices of wicked men to deter
most excellent men from cutting off tyrants, and often from
punishing even the most atrocious criminals. I might easily
tell against you how often it hath gone well and prosperously
25 with them that have killed tyrants, if from such cases any
certain inference might be drawn concerning the outcome of
human affairs.

You object further, "that the English put their hereditary

quo tyranni solent mactari, sed eo, quo latrones et proditionis rei. Primùm hæreditas ad maleficiorum impunitatem quid conferat nescio: conferre quicquam ut credat sapiens fieri vix potest. Quod tu deinde ad *immanitatem* refers, in eo lenitas

5 potiùs Anglorum, et moderatio prædicanda erat; qui, cùm tyrannum esse, omnes in patriam impietates, latrocinia, proditiones, perduelliones in se complectatur, satis habebant supplicium haud gravius de tyranno sumere, quàm de simplici latrone quovis, aut proditore vulgari sumere solebant. Speras

10 *exorituros esse aliquos Harmodios et Thrasybulos, qui, nostrorum cæde, tyranni manibus parentent.* At tu citiùs animum despondebis, et vitam te dignam, omnibus bonis execrandus, antè suspendio finieris, quàm Harmodios Harmodiorum sanguine litantes tyranno videas. Tibi enim illud accidere

15 verisimillimum est, déque te tam scelerato quis augurari rectiùs possit: alterum est impossibile. Tyrannorum triginta mentionem facis qui sub Gallieno rebellârunt. Quid si tyrannus tyrannum oppugnat, an omnes ergo qui oppugnant tyrannum, aut tollunt, tyranni erunt ipsi? haud tu id persua-

20 seris, mancipium equestre; neque is qui author tibi est, Trebellius Pollio, historicorum propè ignobilissimus. *Si qui ho-*

king to death not as tyrants use to be sacrificed, but as robbers and traitors are executed." In the first place I do not know
what heredity should contribute to impunity for crimes; that
it contributes anything is scarcely possible for a wise man to
5 believe. Next, in the conduct which you ascribe to "savage
cruelty" there commendably appeared rather our English
clemency and moderation; for, though to be a tyrant comprises within itself all sorts of enormities, robberies, treacheries, and treasons, against the whole nation, yet they were
10 content to inflict no greater punishment upon a tyrant than
they used of course to do upon any plain highwayman or.
common traitor!

You hope "that some Harmodius and Thrasybulus will rise
up and make expiation" to the tyrant's manes by the slaughter
15 of my fellow-countrymen. But sooner will you run mad with
despair, and, as you deserve all good men's curses, will first
put an end to a life worthy of yourself by hanging yourself,
ere you see Harmodiuses offer the blood of Harmodiuses in
atonement to a tyrant! That you will come to such an end is
20 most probable (for who could foretell a more suitable fortune
for such a rascal?) but the other thing is an utter impossibility.
You mention thirty tyrants that rebelled in Gallienus's time.
And what if one tyrant opposes another, must therefore all
they that resist or destroy a tyrant be accounted such them-
25 selves? You cannot persuade men into such a belief, you
slave-knight, nor can your authority Trebellius Pollio, well-
nigh the most inconsiderable of historians. "If any of the
emperors were declared enemies by the Senate," you say, "it

stes, inquis, *à Senatu judicati sunt, factio id fecit, non jus.*
Nobis in memoriam revocas quid fecit Imperatores; factio
nempe, et vis, et ut planiùs dicam, furor Antonii, non jus fecit,
ut contra Senatum populúmque Romanum ipsi priùs rebella-
rent. *Dedit,* inquis, *pœnas Galba, qui contra Neronem insur-*
rexit. Dic etiam quas pœnas dedit Vespasianus, qui contra
Vitellium. *Tantum,* inquis, *abfuit Carolus à Nerone, quan-*
tum isti laniones Anglicani à Senatoribus illius temporis Ro-
manis. Trifurcifer! à quo laudari vituperatio est, vituperari
laus magna: Paucis modò periodis interpositis hac ipsa de re
scribens, *Senatum sub imperatoribus togatorum mancipio-*
rum consessum fuisse aïebas, nunc eundem *Senatum* aïs *con-*
sessum regum fuisse: hoc si ita est, quid obstat quin reges, te
authore, togata mancipia sint? Beatos hoc laudatore reges!
quo inter homines nihil nequius, inter quadrupedes nihil
amentius: nisi si hoc illi peculiare dicam esse, quòd nemo lite-
ratiùs rudit. Senatum Angliæ Neroni vis esse similiorem
quàm Senatui Romano: Cogit me cacoëthes hoc tuum inep-
tissimas conglutinandi similitudines, ut corrigam te; et quàm
similis Neroni fuerit Carolus, ostendam. *Nero,* inquis, *ma-*
trem suam ferro *necavit.* Carolus et patrem et regem veneno;
nam ut alia omittam indicia, qui Ducem veneficii reum legi-

was done by faction, not law." You put us in mind what it was that first made emperors: it was faction and violence, and to speak plainer, the madness of Antony, and not any law or right, that originally made the emperors themselves take
5 the start in rebelling against the Senate and the people of Rome. "Galba," you say, "was punished for taking up arms against Nero." Tell us likewise how Vespasian was punished for taking up arms against Vitellius! "There was as much difference," you say, "betwixt Charles and Nero, as betwixt
10 those English butchers and the Roman Senators of that age." Gallows-bird! by whom it is scandalous to be commended, and a praise to be evil spoken of: but a few sentences before, discoursing of this very thing, you said: "The Senate under the emperors was in effect but an assembly of toga'd slaves";
15 and now you say: "the Senate was an assembly of kings." If this be so, why should not kings, according to your own opinion, be considered to be toga'd slaves? Blessed are kings in such a praiser! than whom no man is more a rascal, nor four-footed beast more void of sense, unless this may be said
20 to be his singular property, that none brays more learnedly.

You make out that the Parliament of England is more like to Nero than to the Roman Senate. This itch of yours to paste together utterly inappropriate comparisons forces me to set you right: and I will let you see how like King Charles was to
25 Nero. "Nero," you say, "slew his own mother" with a sword. But Charles murdered with poison one that was both his father and his king. For to omit other evidences: he that snatched from the law the Duke that was charged with the poisoning

bus eripuit, fieri non potuit quin ipse reus quoque fuerit. Nero
multa millia Christianorum occidit, Carolus multo plura.
Non defuerunt, teste Suetonio, qui Neronem mortuum lau-
darent, qui desiderarent, qui per longum tempus, *vernis æsti-*
5 *visque floribus tumulum ejus ejus ornarent,* ejus inimicis omnia mala ominarentur: non desunt qui Carolum eâdem insaniâ desiderent, et summis laudibus extollant, quorum tu,
patibularis eques, chorum ducis. *Milites Angli molossis suis*
ferociores novum et inauditum tribunal instituerunt. En acu-
10 tissimum Salmasii sive symbolum sive adagium, jam sexies
inculcatum, *Molossis suis ferociores;* adeste rhetores, vósque
ludimagistri, delibate, si sapitis, flosculum hunc elegantissi-
mum, qui tam Salmasio in deliciis est; codicillis vestris et capsulis mandate copiosissimi hominis pigmentum, ne intereat.
15 Adeóne etiam verba tua consumpsit rabies, ut cuculi in modum eadem identidem occinere cogaris? Quid hoc monstri
esse dicam? Rabies, ut fabulantur, vertit Hecubam in canem;
te Sancti Lupi dominum vertit in cuculum. Jam novas exordiris repugnantias: supra *p.* 113. affirmaveras *Principem*
20 *legibus solutum esse, non cogentibus* solùm, sed *dirigentibus,*
nullas esse omninò quibus teneatur; nunc dicturum te aïs
infrà de regum differentia quatenus potestate alii minore alii

cannot but have shared the guilt. Nero slew many thousands
of Christians, but Charles slew many more. There were those,
says Suetonius, that praised Nero after he was dead, that
longed to have had him again, that for a long time "used to
5 deck his tomb with spring and summer flowers," and that
boded all evils to his enemies. And some there are that with
the like frenzy wish for king Charles again, and exalt him
with the highest praise; you, Knight of the Halter, lead their
troop.

10 "The English soldiers, more savage than their own mastiffs, erected a new and unheard-of court of justice." Observe
this ingenious symbol or adage of Salmasius, now obtruded
six times over: "more savage than their own mastiffs." Come
all ye orators and schoolmasters; pluck, if you are wise, this
15 elegant flower, which Salmasius is so very fond of; commit
to your tablets and cabinets this rhetorical cosmetic of this
most eloquent man, lest it perish. Has your madness so destroyed your words that, cuckoo-fashion, you must needs
sing the same ill-omened song over and over again? What
20 sort of monstrosity shall I call this? Madness, says the tale,
turned Hecuba into a dog; you, Seigneur of St. Wolf, it has
turned into a cuckoo.

Now you come out with fresh inconsistencies. You had
said before, page 113, that "the prince was loosed from the
25 laws,—not from laws coercive" only, but as well "from laws
directory; that there are none at all by which he is held." Now
you say that "you will discourse further on of the difference
betwixt some kings and others, in so far as some have had

majore in regnando fuerunt. Vis probare, *reges non potuisse judicari, nec damnari à subjectis suis argumento,* ut ipse aïs, *firmissimo,* revera stolidissimo; *nihil,* inquis, *aliud inter judices et reges discrimen fuit: atqui Judæi judicum tædio* 5 *odióque adducti reges postulabant.* An quia judices illos magistratum malè gerentes judicare et damnare poterant, ideóne putas tædio odióque eorum adductos postulâsse reges quos jura omnia violantes punire, aut in ordinem cogere non possent? quis, excepto te uno, tam fatuè argumentari solet? 10 Aliud igitur quiddam erat cur regem peterent, quàm ut haberent dominum legibus superiorem; de quo nunc divinare nihil attinet: quicquid erat, haud prudenti consilio factum et Deus et Propheta ejus testatus est. Iterum Rabbinis tuis, ex quibus probâsse te suprà asserebas regem Judæorum non ju- 15 dicari, nunc litem acerrimam intendis, quòd regem et judicari et verberari posse tradiderint: quod idem planè est acsi fatere ementitum te tunc esse, quod ex Rabbinis probâsse dixeras. Eo demùm descendis ut de numero equilium Solomonis, quot *is equorum præsepia habuerit,* oblitus regiæ defensionis, 20 controversias putidulas concites. Tandem ab agasone ad equitem redis aretalogum et tautologum, vel potiùs ad id monstri

more power, some less." By what you call "a most solid argument" you would prove "that kings cannot be judged or condemned by their own subjects"; but it is a very stupid one.
You say: "There was no other difference betwixt judges and
5 kings; and yet the reason why the Jews kept asking for a king
was that they were weary of the judges, and hated them."
Do you think that because they *could* judge and condemn
judges for malfeasance in office they were therefore led by
hatred and weariness of them to ask for kings, whom they
10 could *not* punish or restrain though they should break
through all laws? Who but you ever argued so idiotically?
They desired a king, then, for some other reason than that
they might have a master whose power should be superior
to that of the law; to guess what it was is not to our present
15 purpose. Whatever it was, both God and his Prophet have
witnessed that it was ill-advised in the people to desire a king.
Once more you fall foul of your rabbins, out of whose writings
you said before you had proved that a king of the Jews could
not be judged, for saying that a king might be not only
20 judged, but condemned as well to undergo stripes;—which
is tantamount to confessing that you had made up out of the
whole cloth what you said you had proved out of their writings. Nay, you come at last to forgetting the king's defence,
and raising wretched quibbles about the number of Solomon's
25 stables, and how many "mangers he had for his horses."

Finally from a horse-boy you become once more the Knight
of the Virtuous Preachments and Identical Repetitions, or
rather the sort of monster you were before, a raving distracted

quod priùs eras, cuculum rabiosum. Quereris enim *postremis hisce seculis disciplinæ vigorem laxatum, regulam corruptam;* quòd uni scilicet tyranno cunctis legibus soluto disciplinam omnem laxare, mores omnium corrumpere impunè non liceat.

5 Hanc doctrinam *Brunistas inter reformatos* introduxisse aïs. Ita Lutherus, Calvinus, Zuinglius, Bucerus et Orthodoxorum quotquot celeberrimi Theologi fuere, tuo judicio Brunistæ sunt. Quo æquiore animo tua maledicta perferunt Angli, cùm in ecclesiæ doctores præstantissimos, totámque adeò ecclesiam

10 reformatam, iisdem propè contumeliis debacchari te audiant.

CAPUT VI.

POST legem Dei et naturæ agitatam abs te frustrà, et pessimè tractatam, unde nihil præter ignorantiæ simul et improbitatis ignominiam retulisti, quid deinde, in hac causa regiâ, præter nugas agere possis, non video. Cùm

15 autem omnibus et bonis et doctis viris, huic etiam causæ nobilissimæ abunde me satisfecisse sperem, etiamsi hoc loco finem respondendi facerem, tamen ne interea videar aliis varietatem potius et acumen tuum, quàm immodicam loquacitatem defugisse, quò voles usque progrediar: ea tamen bre-

20 vitate, ut facilè appareat, me iis omnibus perfunctum, si minus quæ dignitas, at saltem quæ necessitas causæ requirebat, nunc

cuckoo. You complain that in these "latter ages, the force of order has been slackened, and its rule destroyed"; because forsooth one tyrant loosed from every law is not allowed with impunity to slacken all order, and destroy all men's morals! 5 This doctrine, you say, was introduced by "the Brownists amongst those of the reformed religion"; so that Luther, Calvin, Zwingli, Bucer, and all the most celebrated orthodox divines, are Brownists in your opinion. The English bear your reproaches the more calmly because they hear you rave 10 with nearly the same slanders against the most eminent doctors of the Church, and in effect against the whole Reformed Church itself.

CHAPTER VI.

AFTER your fruitless and futile mishandling of the law of God and nature, from which you have brought 15 off nothing but the reproach of ignorance and knavery combined, I do not see what you can farther allege in your royal cause but mere trifles. Though I for my part hope that even should I end my answer here, I have done enough to satisfy fully all men that are neither ignorant nor knavish,— 20 yes, done enough for this noble cause itself,—yet lest others should think that I am retreating from what they suppose your manysidedness and keenness, rather than your immeasurable talkativeness, I will go on as far as you like, but with such brevity as shall make it appear that after having per- 25 formed all that if not the dignity, yet the urgency of the cause

hominum quorumvis expectationi, vel etiam curiositati morem gerere. *Hinc alius,* inquis, *et major argumentorum mihi surget ordo.* An major eo argumentorum ordine quem lex Dei et Naturæ suppeditabat? Fer opem, Lucina, parturit
5 Mons Salmasius; non de nihilo nupsit uxori; fœtum aliquem ingentem exspectate mortales. *Si is qui rex est ac dicitur, postulari posset apud aliam potestatem, eam omnino regiâ majorem esse oporteret; quæ autem major statuetur, hanc verè regium dici et esse necesse esset. Sic enim definienda*
10 *potestas regia: Quæ summa est in repub. et singularis; et supra quam nulla alia agnoscitur.* O murem verè montanum, et ridiculum! Succurrite grammatici grammatico laboranti; actum est non de lege Dei, aut naturæ, sed de glossario. Quid si sic responderem tibi? cedant nomina rebus; non est nostrum
15 nomini cavere, qui rem sustulimus; curent id alii quibus cordi sunt reges; nos nostrâ utimur libertate; responsum sanè haud iniquum auferres. Verùm ut me per omnia ex æquo et bono tecum agere intelligas, non ex mea solùm, sed ex optimorum olim et prudentissimorum virorum sententiâ respondebo, qui
20 et nomen et potestatem regiam cum potestate legum et populi majore, posse optimè consistere judicârunt. Lycurgus imprimis, vir sapientiâ clarissimus, cùm vellet maximè potestati regiæ consulere, ut author est Plato, nullam aliam ejus con-

demanded, I now do but comply with some people's expectation or, perhaps, curiosity.

"From now on," say you, "there rises before me another and a grander order of arguments." What! grander arguments than what the law of God and nature afforded? Help, Lucina! Mount Salmasius is in labor! It is not for nothing that he was married by a he-wife. Mortals, expect some huge and monstrous birth. "If he that is and is called king might be impeached before another power, this must of necessity be greater than the royal power. But the power that is constituted the greater must be called and be indeed the royal power, for royal power is to be thus defined: the power which is supreme in the state, and unique, and above which no other is acknowledged." A mountainous mouse, and a ridiculous! Help, grammarians! help this grammarian in travail! the law of God and nature is safe; but 'tis all up with the dictionary!

What if I should answer you thus? Let names give way to things; to be cautious about the name is not our affair, who have got rid of the thing; let others, who are in love with kings, look to that; we are content with the enjoyment of our liberty. Such would be no unfair answer. But to let you see that I deal fairly and justly with you throughout, I will give you an answer based not upon my own opinion alone, but upon that of the best and wisest men of old, who have thought that both the name and the power of a king are entirely consistent with a greater power in the people and the law. In the first place, Lycurgus, a man very eminent for wisdom, designing, as Plato says, to provide in the highest degree for the in-

servandæ rationem invenire potuit, quàm ut Senatûs et Ephororum, id est, populi potestatem regiâ majorem in sua patria constitueret. Idem sensit Theseus Euripidéus, qui cùm Athenarum rex esset, populo tamen Atheniensi in libertatem cum
5 magna sua gloria vindicato, et potestatem popularem extulit supra regiam, et regnum nihilo secius in illa civitate suis posteris reliquit. Unde Euripides in Supplicibus ita loquentem inducit.

Δῆμον κατέστησ' αὐτὸν εἰς μοναρχίαν

10 *'Ελευθερώσας τήνδ' ἰσόψηφον πόλιν.*

Populum constitui ipsum in monarchiam,
Liberans hanc Urbem æquale jus suffragii habentem.

Et rursus ad præconem Thebanum.

Πρῶτον μὲν ἤρξω τοῦ λόγου ψευδῶς ξένε

15 *Ζητῶν τύραννον ἐνθάδ', οὐ γὰρ ἄρχεται*

'Ενὸς πρὸς ἀνδρὸς, ἀλλ' ἐλευθέρα πόλις,

Δῆμος δ' ἀνάσσει———

Primùm incœpisti orationem falsò hospes,
Quærens tyrannum hic; non enim regitur
20 *Ab uno viro, sed est libera hæc civitas,*
Populus autem regnat———

Hæc ille; cùm tamen rex in illa civitate et esset et dictus esset. Testis est etiam divinus Plato in epistola octava. *Induxit Lycurgus senatum et Ephororum potestatem,* τῆς βασιλικῆς ἀρ-
25 χῆς σωτήριον *potestati regiæ maxime salutarem, quæ hac ratione per tot sæcula magna cum laude conservata est; postquam lex domina, rex facta est hominum.* Lex autem rex esse non potest, nisi sit qui in regem quoque, si usus venerit, lege

terests of kingly government, could find no other expedient
to preserve it than by making the power of the senate and of
the Ephors, that is, of the people, superior to it in his own
country. Theseus in Euripides was of the same opinion; for
5 he, though king of Athens, yet to his great honor restored the
Athenian people to liberty, and advanced the power of the
people above that of the king, and left the regal power in that
city none the less to his posterity. Whence Euripides, in *The
Suppliants,* introduces him speaking on this manner: "I have
10 established the people themselves in sovereignty, having freed
this city, which hath an equal right of suffrage." And in
another place, to the herald of Thebes: "In the first place you
begin your speech, stranger, with a thing that is not true, in
asking for the monarch here; for this city is not governed by
15 a single person, but is free; the people is its lord." These were
his words, though in that city he yet both was, and was called,
king. Another authority on the same point is the divine Plato
in his eighth epistle: "Lycurgus introduced the power of the
senate and of the Ephors, τῆς βασιλικῆς ἀρχῆς σωτήριον, a
20 thing very preservative of kingly government, which by this
means has been kept in great honor for so many ages, because mistress law was made king." Now the law cannot be
king, unless there be somebody who, if there should be occasion, may enforce it against the king too. A kingly govern-
25 ment so modified and limited, he himself commends to the
Sicilians: "Let there be liberty together with royal power;
let royal power be ὑπεύθυνος, liable to give account; let law
prevail even against kings, if they shall act contrary to law."

possit agere. Sic temperatam potestatem regiam Sicilensibus
commendat, ἐλευθερία γιγνέσθω μετὰ βασιλικῆς ἀρχῆς, etc.
sit libertas cum regia potestate; sit regia potestas ὑπεύθυνος
reddendæ rationi obnoxia; dominetur lex etiam regibus si-
5 *quid præter legem fecerint.* Aristoteles denique politicorum
tertio, *In repub. Spartanorum videtur,* inquit, *regnum esse*
maximè, eorum regnorum quæ sunt secundùm legem: omnes
autem regni species secundum legem fuisse aït, præter unam
quam vocat παμβασιλείαν, neque talem usquam extitisse
10 meminit. Tale itaque regnum maximè omnium propriè et
dici et esse regnum sensit Aristoteles, quale apud Spartanos
fuit; talem proinde regem non minùs propriè et dici et esse
regem, ubi tamen populus supra regem erat, negare non
potuit. Cùm tot tantique authores et nomen et rem regiam
15 suâ fide salvam regi præstiterint, etiam ubi populus penès se
summam potestatem, tametsi exercere non solet, tamen, quoties opus est, obtinet, noli tam angusto animo summæ rerum
Grammaticalium, hoc est vocabulorum, sic timere, ut potiùs
quàm glossarii tui ratio turbetur, aut detrimenti quid capiat,
20 prodere libertatem omnium, et rempub. velis. Scito etiam
dehinc, nomina rebus servire, non res nominibus; ita plus
sapies, nec *in infinitum,* quod metuis, *ibis. Frustrà ergo Se-*
neca tria illa genera statuum ita describit. Frustretur Seneca,
nos liberi simus; et nisi fallor, non ii sumus quos Flores Sene-

Finally Aristotle says, in the third book of his *Politics:* "Of all royal powers that are governed by laws, that in the Spartan commonwealth seems to be most truly and properly royal." All forms of kingly government, however, he says, were ac-
5 cording to laws, but one which he calls παμβασιλείαν, or Absolute Monarchy, and he does not mention that this existed anywhere. Aristotle, then, thought such a kingdom as that of the Spartans to be and deserve the name of a kingdom *par excellence,* and consequently could not deny that such a king
10 as theirs, though the people were above him, none the less was, and was to be called, *par excellence* a king. Now since authors so many and great do upon their faith and credit warrant unto the king that both the name and the substance of his royalty shall be unimpaired, and vouch it safe, even
15 where the supreme power, though generally unused, yet for times of need is kept by the people in their own possession; do you cease with so petty a mind to fear so much for the State of Grammar—of Words, to wit—that rather than the public weal of your word-list should be disturbed, or suffer
20 aught of harm, you would willingly betray the liberty and common weal of mankind. And for the future know that words are subordinate to things, not things to words. By this means you will have more discernment, and not run on "into the infinite and undefined" as you fear!
25 "In vain then does Seneca," you say, "thus describe those three forms of government." Let Seneca describe in vain, so we enjoy our liberty; and if I mistake not, we are not the sort of men to be enslaved by Seneca's Flowers. Yet Seneca, though

cæ in servitutem reducant. Seneca autem, si summam in uno potestatem esse dicit, *populi* tamen *eam* dicit *esse,* commissam videlicet regi ad salutem omnium, non ad perniciem; nec mancipio, sed usu duntaxat à populo datam. *Non jam ergo*
5 *per Deum reges regnant, sed per populum.* Quasi verò Deus non ita regat populum, ut cui Deus vult, regnum tradat populus; cum in ipsis institutionibus Imperator Justinianus palàm agnoscat, exinde Cæsares regnâsse, ex quo *lege regiâ populus iis et in eos omne imperium suum, et potestatem concessit.* Sed
10 quousque ista recoquemus, quæ jam toties refutavimus? Rursùs, quod ingenium tuum importunum et agreste, mores odiosissimos indicat, id nostra repub. quæ ad te nihil pertinet, alienigena et peregrinus curiosum te infers. Accede igitur, ut te tanto ardelione dignum est, cum insigni solœcismo. *Quic-*
15 *quid,* inquis, *illi perditi homines dicunt, ad populum decipiendum pertinent.* O scelerate! hoccine erat, quòd deminutus capite Grammaticus in nostram rempub. te ingerere cupiebas, ut solœcismis nos tuis et barbarismis oppleres? Verum tu dic populum quo modo decepimus? *Forma regiminis quam in-*
20 *troduxere non popularis est, sed militaris.* Ista scilicet grex ille perfugarum mercedulâ conductum jussit te scribere: non tibi igitur, qui ea blatis, quorum nihil intelligis, sed iis qui te pre-

he says that the sovereign power resides in a single person,
says withal that "the power is the people's," and by them
given to the king in trust for the welfare of the whole, not for
their ruin and destruction, and that the people have not given
5 him a property in it, but the use of it. "Kings at this rate,"
you say, "do not reign by God but by the people." As if God
did not so overrule the people that they give the kingdom to
whom God wills. The Emperor Justinian in his Institutes
themselves openly acknowledges that the Caesars' reign be-
10 gan when "by the Lex Regia the people granted unto them
and vested in them all their own power and authority."

But how long shall I keep warming over and over again
that stuff of yours which I have so often rejected and refuted?
Now once more you push yourself—and it is a thing which
15 reveals your boorish unmannerly nature and odious ways—
you, a foreign-born outsider, push yourself inquisitively into
our state affairs, which are none of yours! Come on, then, with
an egregious solecism, worthy of such a busybody. "Every
single thing," quotha, "every single thing that those despera-
20 does say, are only to deceive the people." Rascal! was it for this
that you, an outlawed grammarian, were so forward to intermeddle with the affairs of our government—that you might
stuff us with your solecisms and barbarisms? But say, how
have we deceived the people? "The form of government
25 which they have set up is not popular, but military." This is
what that gang of renegades hired you—and hired you cheap
—to write; so that I shall not trouble myself to answer you,
who babble what you know nothing of, but I will answer

tio conduxerunt respondebitur. Quis *ordinem procerum è*
Parlamento ejecit? an populus? Immo populus; eoque facto
servitutis jugum à cervicibus suis haud ferendum dejecit. Ipsi
milites, à quibus hoc factum dicis, non exteri, sed cives, et
5 magna pars populi fuere; idque cætero ferè consentiente populo et cupiente, nec sine Parlamenti etiam authoritate fecerunt. *An populus,* inquis, *plebeium ordinem domûs inferi-*
oris mutilavit, alios fugando, &c. Populus inquam; quod
enim Senatûs pars potior, id est sanior, fecit, in quo vera po-
10 puli potestas residebat, quid ni id populum fecisse dicam?
Quid si servire, quid si vænum rempub. dare, in Senatu plures
maluerint, annon id impedire, et libertatem retinere, si in
manu est suâ, paucioribus licebit? *At duces hoc fecerunt cum*
militibus suis. Habenda igitur gratia est ducibus, quòd operas
15 et tabernarios Londinenses qui paulò antè, veluti fæx illa Clo-
diana, ipsam curiam obsederant, ferocientes repulerint, reipub. non defuerint. Tùne idcirco jus Parlamenti primarium
ac proprium, ut libertati imprimis populi sive pace sive bello
prospiciat, *militarem dominationem* appellabis? Verùm hoc
20 à perduellibus dici, qui tibi ista dictârunt, non est mirum;
sic enim perditissima olim Antoniorum factio Senatum Romanum contra hostes patriæ ad saga euntem, *Castra Pompeii*

them that hired you. Who "excluded the Lords from Parliament—was it the people?" Ay, it was the people; and in so doing they threw an intolerable yoke of slavery from off their necks. Those very soldiers who you say did it were not
5 foreigners, but our own countrymen, and a great part of the people, and they did it with the consent and at the desire of almost all the rest of the people, and not without the authority of Parliament itself. "Was it the people that maimed the House of Commons by driving away some of the members,
10 etc.?" Yes, I say, it was the people. For whatever the better, that is, the sounder, part of the legislature did, in which the true power of the people resided, why may not the people be said to have done it? What if the majority of the legislature should choose to be slaves, or to set the government to sale—
15 ought not the minority prevent this, and keep their liberty, if it be in their power? "But the officers of the army with their soldiers did it." And thanks are due those officers for that they failed not the state, but repelled the riotous workmen and shopkeepers of London, who, like that rabble that ap-
20 peared for Clodius, had but a little before beset the very parliament house. The original and proper right of Parliament to look out before all else for the people's liberty both in peace and in war—is this what you therefore call "a military despotism"? It is no wonder indeed that the trai-
25 tors who dictated these passages to you should talk in this strain, for so did that profligate crew of Antony and his adherents use to call the Roman Senate when they took arms against the enemies of their country, "Pompey's Camp." And

appellare solebat. Jam verò fortissimo nostri exercitûs ductori Cromuello, quòd is amicorum læto agmine stipatus, non sine favore populi secundo, votis etiam bonorum omnium prosequentibus, in bellum Hibernicum Deo gratissimum proficisceretur, invidisse tuos gaudeo; auditis enim postea tot ejus victoriis, jam arbitror eos livore contabuisse. Multa prætereo quæ de Romanis militibus prolixè nugaris: quod sequitur à veritate remotissimum esse quis non videt? *Populi,* inquis, *potestas esse desinit ubi regis esse incipit.* Quo tandem jure? cùm satis constet, omnes ferè ubique gentium reges sub certis conditionibus traditum sibi regnum à populo accipere: quibus si rex non steterit, cur illa potestas, quæ fiduciaria tantùm fuit, ad populum redire non debeat, tam à rege quàm à consule, vel ab alio quovis magistratu, tu velim doceas: nam quòd *salutem reipub. id* aïs *postulare,* ineptias dicis; cùm salutis ratio eadem omninò sit, sive à rege, sive ab optimatibus, sive à triumviris imperio sibi tradito perperam utentibus *potestas illa ad populum revertatur;* posse autem à magistratibus quibuscunque præterquam à rege solo ad populum reverti ipse concedis. Sanè si neque regi, neque ullis magistratibus imperium in se populus mentis compos dederit, nisi tantummodò communis omnium salutis causâ, nihil potest obstare quo minùs ob causas planè contrarias ne interitus omnium sequatur,

now I am glad that they of your party looked grudgingly upon Cromwell, that most valiant general of our army, for undertaking the Irish campaign (so acceptable to Almighty God), surrounded with a joyful crowd of his friends, and 5 followed up by the well-wishes of the people and the prayers of all good men; for I question not but at the news of his many victories there they are by this time rotted with spite.

I pass by your quantities of long-winded nonsense about the Roman soldiers. What follows is most notoriously false: 10 "Power ceases to belong to a people," you say, "where it begins to belong to a king." By what law or right is that? For it is very certain that kings in general, throughout the world, receive from the people an authority entrusted to them subject to certain conditions; which if the king abide not 15 by, pray tell us why that power, which was but a trust, should not return to the people, as well from a king as from a consul or any other officer of government. For what you say about "the public safety requiring it" is not to the point; the requirements of safety are identical whether "that power re- 20 verts to the people" from a King, or from an Aristocracy, or from a Triumvirate, in case any of them abuse the power entrusted to them; and yet you yourself grant that it may so revert from officers of every sort, a king only excepted. Cer- tainly, if no people in their right wits ever gave power over 25 themselves either to a king or to any magistrates for any other purpose than the common good of all, there can be no reason why, for exactly the inverse purpose, to prevent the utter ruin of them all, they may not take back again the power they

haud secus regi quàm aliis magistratibus, quod dedit imperium adimere possit: quid quòd uni etiam faciliùs quàm pluribus ademerit? et potestatem in se plusquam fiduciariam
cuiquam mortalium tradere summæ esset insaniæ: neque cre-
5 dibile est ullum ab orbe terrarum condito populum, qui quidem suæ spontis esset, adeò miserè desipuisse, ut vel omnem
prorsus potestatem ab se alienaret, aut suis magistratibus con-
creditam sine causis gravissimis ad se revocaret. Quod si dis-
cordiæ, si bella intestina indè oriantur, regium certè jus nul-
10 lum indè oritur illius potestatis per vim retinendæ, quam populus suam sibi vendicat. Ex quo efficitur, quod ad prudentiam populi, non ad jus regis referendum est, quódque nos non
negamus, *rectorem non facilè mutandum esse:* nunquam ergo
aut nulla prorsus de causa, nullo modo sequitur: neque tu
15 adhuc quicquam allegâsti, neque jus ullum regis expromsisti,
quo minùs liceat consentienti populo, regem haud idoneum
regno privare; siquidem id, quod etiam in Gallia tua sæpiùs
factum est, sine tumultu ac civili bello fieri possit. Cùm itaque
salus populi suprema lex sit, non salus tyranni, ac proinde
20 populo in tyrannum, non tyranno in populum prodesse debeat, tu, qui tam sanctam legem, tam augustam tuis præstigiis
pervertere es ausus, qui legem inter homines supremam, et
populo maximè salutarem ad tyrannorum duntaxat impunitatem valere voluisti, tu inquam scito, quandoquidem Angli

gave, and this as well from a king as from other magistrates;
nay, and it may with far greater ease be taken from one than
from many. And to commit to any mortal creature a power
over themselves on any other terms than upon trust were
5 extreme madness; nor is it credible that any people since the
creation of the world, who had freedom of will, were ever so
miserably silly as either to part with the power absolutely and
entirely, or, having once entrusted it to their magistrates, to
recall it unto themselves without weightiest reasons. But
10 though dissensions, though civil wars, arise thence, surely no
royal right arises thence to withhold by force of arms that
power which the people reclaims unto itself for its own.

Whence it follows that what you say, and we do not deny,
that "the ruler ought not lightly to be changed," is true with
15 respect to the people's prudence, not the king's right; but it
nowise follows that therefore a ruler ought not to be changed
ever or for any cause whatsoever. Nor have you hitherto adduced any reason, or produced any right of kings, which
ought to hinder the people, when they all concur, from depos-
20 ing an unfit king, provided it may be done, as it has been often
done in your own country of France, without tumult or civil
war. Since therefore the safety of the people, not the safety of
a tyrant, is the supreme law, and consequently should advantage the people against a tyrant, and not a tyrant against the
25 people; you that have dared invert so sacred and so glorious a
law with your jugglings, you who would make this supreme
law, which of all laws is most beneficial to mankind, serve
only for the impunity of tyrants; let me tell you (since to you

Enthusiastæ, et *Enthei,* et *Vates* toties tibi sumus, me vate scito,
Deum tibi atque homines tanti piaculi ultores imminere:
quanquam universum genus humanum subjicere tyrannis, id
est, quantum in te fuit, ad bestias damnare, hoc ipsum scelus
5 tam immane sua partim in te ultio est, suis te furiis quocunque
fugis terrarum, atque oberras, vel, citiùs vel feriùs insequetur;
et pejore etiam eâ, quam nunc insanis, insaniâ agitabit. Venio
nunc ad alterum argumentum tuum, prioris haud dissimile;
si populo resumere liceret potestatem suam, *Nihil tum esset*
10 *discriminis inter popularem et regalem statum, nisi quòd in*
hoc singuli rectores constituuntur, in illo plures: quid si nihil
aliud interesset, nunquid indè respub. detrimenti caperet?
Ecce autem aliæ differentiæ à temetipso allatæ, *temporis* nimirum *et successionis; cùm populares magistratus annui ferè*
15 *sint,* reges, nisi quid committant, perpetui; et in eadem plerunque familia. Differant ergo inter se aut non differant, de
istis enim minutiis nihil laboro, in hoc certè conveniunt, quod
utrobique populus quoties id interest reipub. potest quam
alteri potestatem salutis publicæ causâ tradiderat, eam ad se
20 rursus nec injuriâ eandem ob causam revocare. *At lege regia*

we Englishmen so often are "Enthusiasts," "Inspired," and "Prophets") let me, I say, be so far a prophet as to tell you that the vengeance of God and man hangs over your head for so horrid a crime; although your casting down the whole
5 human race under the feet of tyrants, which is naught else than, as far as in you lies, condemning them to be thrown to the beasts of the amphitheatre,—this monstrous wickedness is itself part of its own vengeance upon you; and whithersoever on earth you flee, and wheresoever you wander, will
10 pursue you with its furies soon or late, and drive and harass you with madness yet worse than now you rave with.

I come now to your second argument, which is not unlike the first. If the people may resume their power, "there would be no difference," say you, "betwixt a democracy and
15 a kingdom; but that in a kingdom the appointed governor is one man and in a democracy many." And what if that were true—would the state take any harm of it? But here are some other differences which you yourself bring forward, of "time and succession," to be sure, for "the magistrates in a democ-
20 racy are generally chosen yearly," whereas kings, if they behave themselves well, are perpetual; and in most kingdoms there is a succession in the same family. But let them differ from one another, or not differ, I regard not those trifles: in this they surely agree, that in either a democracy or a king-
25 dom, when the public good requires it, that power which the people had entrusted to another for the public safety may for the same reason, and without violation of right or law, be recalled by the people unto itself.

Romæ sic appellata, de qua in institutis, populus Romanus principi et in eum omne imperium suum, et potestatem concessit. Nempe vi Cæsarum coactus, qui honesto legis titulo suam tantummodo violentiam sanxerunt; de quo suprà, id
5 quod ipsi jurisconsulti in hunc locum non dissimulant. Quod igitur legitimè, et volente populo concessum non est, id revocabile quin sit non dubitamus. Veruntamen rationi maximè consentaneum est, populum Romanum non aliam potestatem transtulisse in principem, atque priùs concesserat suis magi-
10 stratibus; id est imperium legitimum et revocabile, non tyrannicum et absurdum; quocirca et consularem, et tribunitiam potestatem Cæsares recepere; dictatoriam nemo post Julium; populum in Circo adorare etiam solebant, ut ex Tacito et Claudiano suprà meminimus. Verùm ut *multi olim privati*
15 *se in servitutem alteri vendiderunt, sic potest populus universus.* O equitem ergastularium et mangonem, patriæ etiam tuæ æternum opprobrium! quem servitutis tam fœdum procuratorem ac lenonem publicum etiam servitia infima cujusvis catastæ detestari atque conspuere deberent! Sanè si po-
20 pulus hunc in modum se regibus mancipâsset, possent et reges eundem populum alteri cuivis domino mancipare, aut pretio addicere; et tamen constat regem ne patrimonium quidem coronæ posse alienare. Qui igitur coronæ, quod aïunt, et patri-

"According to the Lex Regia, however, or royal law, so called by the Romans, which is treated in the Institutes, the people of Rome granted all their power and authority to and for the chief of state." Certainly—upon compulsion by the
5 Caesars, who under the honorable pretence of law ratified what was merely their own violence. But of this we have spoken before; and their own lawyers, commenting upon this passage in the Institutes, do not disguise the fact. Doubtless therefore what was not granted by right law or by true con-
10 sent of the people is revocable. But most reasonable it is to suppose that the people of Rome transferred no other power to the prince than they had before granted to their own magistrates, that is a power to govern according to law, and a power revocable, not unreasonable or tyrannical. Hence it was that
15 the Caesars took over the powers of the Consuls, and of the Tribunes of the People, but after Julius not one pretended to those of a Dictator; in the Circus they used even to adore the people, as I mentioned before, quoting Tacitus and Claudian.

But "as heretofore many a private person has sold himself
20 into slavery to another, so may a whole nation." Jailbird knight from the slaves' prison-house! Slave dealer thyself! Everlasting reproach even to thy native country! The most degraded band of slaves exposed for sale at the block ought to abhor and spit upon so foul a slave-procurer, such a public
25 pander! Certainly if a people had so enslaved themselves to kings, then might kings turn them over to any other master you like, or put them up for sale; and yet certain it is that kings cannot so much as alienate the demesnes of the crown. He then who holds as a grant from the people only the use and

monii regii usum fructum solùm à populo concessum habet,
is populi ipsius manceps erit? Non si pertusis auribus utrisque
perforatus eques, non si gypsatis pedibus prostares, tam esses
omnium servorum vilissimus, quam nunc es, hujus tam pu-
5 dendæ author sententiæ. Perge pœnas tuorum scelerum invitus, quod nunc facis, de temetipso sumere. Multa postremò
de jure belli balbutis, quæ hic locum non habent; nam neque
Carolus nos bello vicit; et majores ejus, tametsi maximè vicis-
sent, isti tamen juri sæpius renuntiaverant; nec verò tam un-
10 quam victi fuimus, ut nos in eorum nomen, illi in nostras
leges non vicissim jurarent; quas cùm Carolus insigniter vio-
lâsset, vel olim victorem, vel nunc regem perjurum priùs ab
ipso lacessiti armis debellavimus: ex tua autem sententia *quod
armis quæritur, transit in ejus dominium qui acquisivit.* Sis
15 itaque deinceps hac in parte quàm voles verbosus, sis quod in
Solino dudùm fuisti, exercitator Plinianus, blateronum omnium verbosissimus, quicquid exinde argutaris, quicquid turbas, quicquid rabbinicaris, quicquid rauces ad finem usque
hujus capitis, id totum non jam pro rege devicto, sed pro nobis
20 divinâ ope victoribus contra regem desudare te scias.

enjoyment of the crown (as the phrase is) and of the royal
demesne, shall he be owner, as if by purchase, of the people
itself? Though you stood forward, a riddled knight with both
ears bored and gypsum-whitened feet, exposed for sale, you
5 would not be so much the most contemptible of slaves as now
you are, being the author of such a shameful doctrine.

Go on and punish yourself against your will for your
rogueries, as now you do. Toward the last you stammer out
quantities of things about the right of war and conquest,
10 which have no place here. For on the one hand never did
Charles conquer us (and for his ancestors, though it were
never so much granted that they did, yet have they again
and again renounced their title as conquerors), nor on the
other hand were we ever so conquered but that as we swore
15 allegiance to them, so they swore to maintain our laws. When
Charles had notoriously violated these, and had first provoked us, we subdued him by force, take him in what capac-
ity you will, as formerly king conqueror or as now king
perjurer. But according to your own opinion, "Whatever is
20 acquired by war becomes the property of him that has acquired it." And so in this your argument begin again and be
as wordy as you will, be what you were not long ago upon
Solinus, a Plinian carping controversialist, of all babblers the
wordiest:—whatever you chatter next, whatever uproar you
25 make, whatever you quote from the rabbins, however you
shout yourself hoarse even to the end of this chapter, be assured that in the sweat of your brow you have been doing it
all, not for the conquered king, but for us, by God's help his
conquerors.

CAPUT VII.

PROPTER duo incommoda sanè maxima, et pro tuo pondere gravissima, potestatem populi esse regiâ majorem proximo capite negâsti: quippe, si concederes, quærendum regi aliud nomen esset, translato in populum regis vocabulo; et partitiones quædam politicæ conturbarentur: quorum alterum vocabularii dispendium foret; alterum, tuorum Crux politicorum. Ad ea sic à nobis responsum est, ut primum salutis et libertatis nostræ, deinde etiam nomenclaturæ tuæ et politices habita nonnulla ratio esset. Nunc *aliis rationibus evincendum esse* aïs, *regem à sibi subjectis judicari non posse, quarum hæc erit maximè potens et valida, quòd rex parem in suo regno non habeat.* Quid aïs? non habet rex in suo regno parem? quid ergo illi duodecim vetustissimi Franciæ Pares? an Turpini fabulæ sunt et nugæ? an frustra et ad ludibrium sic nominati? Cave istam viris Galliæ Principibus contumeliam dixeris. An quia inter se pares? quasi verò nobilitatis totius Gallicæ duodecim tantùm inter se pares esse; aut dicendos idcirco Franciæ Pares existimandum sit. Quòd nisi revera sint regis Franciæ Pares, proptereà quòd cum eo

CHAPTER VII.

TO avoid two great inconveniences, and, considering your own weight, very weighty ones indeed, you denied in the foregoing chapter that the people's power was greater than the king's; for if you granted that,
5 then kings must look about for some other name, the appellation "king" being turned over to the people, and certain classifications in your system of politics would be confounded. The first of these consequences would spoil your dictionary, and the second be the death of your Politics. To these I have
10 answered in such wise that a certain consideration might be given first to our own safety and liberty, and after even to your terminology and Politics! Now, say you, " 'Tis to be proved by other arguments that a king cannot be judged by his own subjects; of which arguments this shall be the most
15 powerful and most convincing, that a king hath no peer in his kingdom." What? A king hath no peer in his kingdom? What then is the meaning of those old Twelve Peers of France? Are they fables and trumpery stuff of Turpin's invention? Are they called so in vain and in mockery? Have
20 a care how you insult those Princes and Paladins of France! Or is it because they are equal among themselves? As if, forsooth, it were thinkable that of the whole French nobility only twelve were each other's peers, or that this were a reason for calling them Peers of *France!* Nay, if they are not in very
25 truth the Peers of the *King* of France, and this because with him they govern the State by equal right and by conference

rempub. pari jure atque consilio administrent, vide ne in
Franciæ regno potiùs quàm in nostra repub. quod unicum
tuâ interest, glossario illudatur. Age verò, fac planum, non
esse regi in regno suo parem. *Quia,* inquis, *populus Romanus*
5 *post reges exactos, duos constituit Consules, non unum; ut si*
unus peccaret, coërceri à collega posset. Vix fingi quicquam
potuit ineptius: cur igitur unus duntaxat Consulum fasces
apud se habuit, non uterque, ad alterutrum coërcendum alter
datus erat? quid si etiam uterque contra rempub. conjurâsset,
10 an meliore loco res fuisset, quàm si collegam alteri nullum
dedissent? Constat autem et ambos Consules et Magistratus
omnes obtemperare Senatui semper debuisse, quoties id è
repub. esse, patribus et plebi visum est. Hujus rei Marcum
Tullium in oratione pro Sestio locupletissimum testem habeo:
15 à quo simul brevissimam Romanæ civitatis descriptionem accipe; quam is et *sapientissime constitutam,* et omnes bonos
cives nôsse eam oportere dicebat, quod idem et nos dicimus.
Majores nostri cùm regum potestatem non tulissent, ita magi-
stratus annuos creaverunt, ut consilium Senatus reipub. præ-
20 *ponerent sempiternum: deligerentur autem in id consilium*
ab universo populo; aditúsque in illum summum ordinem

with him as his equals—look to it lest the dictionary, which is the only thing you are concerned for, be more mocked in the Kingdom of France than in the Commonwealth of England!

But go to, let us hear your demonstration that a king has no
5 peer in his own kingdom. "Because," you say, "the people of Rome, when they had banished their kings, appointed not one, but two Consuls, that if one of them should transgress, he might be checked by his colleague." A sillier argument could hardly have been invented: how came it to pass then
10 that but one of the Consuls kept the Fasces, and not both, if each had been appointed to check the other? And what if both had conspired against the commonwealth, would the case have been better than if the Romans had not given one Consul a colleague? What is certain, however, is that the
15 Consuls both, and all other magistrates, were bound to obey the Senate, whenever the Senate and the people decided that the interest of the commonwealth so required. For this I have abundant authority in Marcus Tullius's oration for Sestius. Listen at the same time to his concise account of the Roman
20 constitution, which, he always said, was "very wisely framed," and that it behooved all good citizens to be well acquainted with it. And so say I.

"Our ancestors, when they had thrown off the power of the kings, created offices to last one year, but in such wise that
25 over the commonwealth they set the deliberative assembly of the Senate to last forever; that members, however, were to be elected into this assembly by the people as a whole; and that entrance into that exalted body should stand open to the in-

omnium civium industriæ ac virtuti pateret: Senatum reipub.
custodem, præsidem, propugnatorem collocaverunt: Hujus
ordinis auctoritate uti magistratus, et quasi ministros gravis-
simi consilii esse voluerunt. Exemplo illustri esse poterunt
5 Decemviri; qui cùm potestate consulari, et summâ præditi
essent, eos tamen omnes simul, etiam renitentes, patrum authoritas in ordinem coëgit; Consules etiam nonnullos, antequam magistratum deposuerant, hostes judicatos et contra eos
sumpta arma esse legimus: hostilia enim facientem, esse con-
10 sulem nemo putabat. Sic bellum contra Antonium Consulem
Senatûs authoritate est gestum: in quo victus pœnas capitis
dedisset, nisi Octavianus Cæsar regnum affectans evertendæ
reipub. consilium cum eo iniisset. Jam quòd *hoc proprium*
esse aïs *Majestatis regalis, ut imperium penès unicum sit,* haud
15 minùs lubricum est, et à te quidem ipso statim refellitur:
Judices, enim *Hebræorum et singuli, et toto vitæ spatio im-*
perium obtinebant; Scriptura quoque reges eos vocat; et
tamen à Synedrio magno judicabantur. Ita fit, dum dixisse
omnia vis videri, ut nihil ferè nisi pugnantia loquaris. Quæro
20 deinde qualem tu formam regiminis esse dicas, cùm Romanum imperium duo simul trésve imperatores habuerunt; an

dustry and worth of all citizens. They stationed the Senate as
the guardian, protector, and champion of the State. This
body's authority it was that they would have the magistrates
employ, and would have them be, as it were, servants of this
5 most weighty assembly."

The Decemvirs may serve as a shining example: though
they were invested with the power of Consuls, and were the
chief magistrates, yet the authority of the Senate reduced
them all together and at once to order, against their strug-
10 gles. Nay, we read that some Consuls, before they laid down
their office, had been declared public enemies, and arms taken
up against them; for in those days no man accounted him a
Consul who carried on open war against his country. So, by
authority of the Senate, war was waged against Antony,
15 though a Consul; in which being worsted he would have
been put to death, but that Octavianus Caesar, grasping after
empire, joined with him in a conspiracy to subvert the commonwealth.

Your assertion that "it is a property peculiar to kingly
20 majesty that the power resides in a single person" is not less
slippery, and is at once contradicted by yourself. "The Hebrew judges," you say, "ruled as long as they lived, and there
was but one of them at a time: the Scripture also calls them
kings; and yet they were accountable to the Sanhedrim." So
25 it happens that while wishing to be thought to have said all
that can be said, you say hardly anything but contradictions.
Then I ask what kind of government you call it when sometimes two, sometimes three emperors at once held the Roman

imperatores tibi, id est reges, an optimates, an triumviri videntur fuisse? An verò dices Romanum imperium sub Antonino et Vero, sub Diocletiano et Maximiano, sub Constantino et Licinio, non unum imperium fuisse? Jam ista tua

5 *statuum tria genera* tuis ipsius argutiis periclitantur, si reges isti non fuere: si fuere, non est ergo proprium imperii regii, ut penès unicum sit. *Alter,* inquis, *horum si delinquat, potest alter de eo referre ad populum vel ad senatum, ut accusetur et condemnetur.* Annon ergo judicat vel populus vel Senatus ad

10 quos alter ille refert? Si quid igitur ipse tribuis tibi, collega opus non erat ad judicandum collegam. Heu te defensorem, nisi execrabilis potiùs esses, planè miserandum! undiquaque ictibus adeò opportunum, ut si fortè per lusum destinare quis vellet, quovis te loco punctim ferire, vix esse credo ubi temere

15 possit aberrare. *Ridiculum* esse statuis, *regem in se judices dare velle à quibus capite damnaretur.* Atqui ego non ridiculum sed optimum tibi oppono imperatorem Trajanum; qui præfectum prætorio Saburanum, cum ei insigne potestatis, uti mos erat, pugionem daret, crebrò sic monuit. *Accipe hunc*

20 *gladium pro me, si rectè agam; sin aliter, in me magis, quòd moderatorem omnium vel errare minùs fas sit.* Hæc Dion et Aurelius Victor. Vides ut judicem in se statuerit imperator

Empire? Do you reckon them to have been emperors, that is, kings, or members of an aristocracy, or a triumvirate? Or will you say that the Roman Empire under Antoninus and Verus, under Diocletian and Maximian, under Constantine
5 and Licinius, was not one empire? If these were not kings, your "three forms of government" are endangered by your own cleverness; if they were kings, then it is not an essential property of royal power to reside in a single person. "If one of these offend," say you, "then may the other report upon
10 him to the people, or to the Senate, that he may be accused and condemned." And is it not an act of judging that is performed by the Senate and the people, to whom that second colleague reports? So that if you give any weight to your own statement, there was no need of a second colleague to judge
15 the first. Alas, what a defender!—really to be pitied if you were not rather to be cursed! You lie every way so open to blows that if one were minded for sport's sake to thrust at any part of you, he could hardly miss, were his aim never so ill.

You call it "ridiculous that a king should be supposed
20 willing to appoint judges empowered to condemn him to death." But against you I cite the nowise ridiculous but most excellent Emperor Trajan, who when, as the custom was, he delivered to Saburanus, Captain of the Praetorian Guard, the dagger which was the badge of his office, frequently thus ad-
25 monished him: "Take this sword, and use it for me, if I do as I ought; if otherwise, against me; because for the governor and guide of all to go astray is especially unlawful." This Dion and Aurelius Victor say of him. You see here that an admirable

egregius quamvis non parem. Hoc idem Tiberius per simula-
tionem et vaniloquentiam fortasse dixisset; Trajanum autem
virum optimum et sanctissimum non id ex animo dixisse quod
verum, quod jus et fas esse sentiebat, scelestus penè sit qui arbi-
5 tretur. Quanto justiùs ergo Senatui, cùm viribus superior potuerit non parere, planè ex officii ratione paruit; et jure superiorem est fassus. De quo Plinius in Panegyrico: *Senatus ut*
susciperes quartum Consulatum et rogavit et jussit; imperii
hoc verbum, non adulationis esse, obsequio tuo crede: et
10 paulò pòst, *hæc nempe intentio tua ut libertatem revoces ac*
reducas. Quod Trajanus de se, idem Senatus de Trajano sensit,
suámque authoritatem revera esse supremam; nam qui imperatorem jubere potuit, potuit eundem et judicare. Sic Marcus Aurelius imperator, cùm præfectus Syriæ Cassius regnum
15 ei eripere conaretur, obtulit se in judicium vel Senatui vel
Populo Romano; paratus regno cedere, siquidem iis ita videretur. Jam verò quis rectiùs aut meliùs de jure regio existi-
mare et statuere queat, quàm ex ore ipso regum optimorum?
Profectò jure naturali rex quisque bonus vel senatum vel po-
20 pulum habet sibi semper et parem et superiorem: Tyrannus
autem cùm naturâ infimus omnium sit, nemo non illi par
atque superior existimandus est, quicunque viribus plus valet.

emperor appointed one, though not his peer, to be his judge. Tiberius perhaps might have said such words as these out of vanity and hypocrisy; but it is almost a crime to imagine that Trajan, a man most virtuous and blameless, did not speak in 5 all sincerity what he thought true and right and just. Superior to the Senate in power, he might have refused them obedience; how much the more righteous was it that he actually did obey them purely out of consideration for his duty, and acknowledge that they were by law set above him. Pliny tells 10 us in his Panegyric: "The Senate both desired and commanded you to be Consul a fourth time; this, you may trust your own submissiveness, is no word of flattery, but of command"; and a little after: "What you strive for is this,— namely, to recall and restore our liberty." And what Trajan 15 thought of himself, the Senate thought of Trajan, and were of opinion that their authority was indeed supreme, for they who might command their emperor might judge him. So the emperor Marcus Aurelius, when Cassius governor of Syria endeavored to get the empire from him, submitted himself 20 to the judgment of either the Senate or the Roman people, and declared himself ready to lay down the government if they would have it so. How indeed could anyone appraise and determine the right of kings better or more truly than out of the very mouths of the best kings?

25 Indeed by the law of nature every good king always accounts the senate or the people not only his peers but his betters. But a tyrant being by nature inferior to all men, whoever is stronger than he ought to be accounted equal and superior

Quemadmodum enim à vi olim ad leges duce naturâ deventum est, ita, ubi leges pro nihilo habentur, necessariò, eâdem etiam duce, ad vim est redeundum. *Hoc sentire,* inquit Cicero pro Sestio, *prudentiæ est; facere, fortitudinis; et sentire verò* 5 *et facere, perfectæ cumulatæque virtutis.* Maneat hoc igitur in natura, nullis parasitorum artibus concutiendum, rege sive bono, sive malo, vel senatum vel populum esse superiorem. Quod et ipse confiteris, cùm potestatem regiam à populo in regem transiisse dicis. Quam enim regi potestatem dedit, eam 10 naturâ, ac virtute quadam, vel, ut ita dicam, virtualiter, etiam cum alteri dederit, tamen in se habet: Etenim quæ causæ naturales isto modo per eminentiam quandam quidvis efficiunt, plus semper suæ retinent virtutis quàm impertiunt; nec impertiendo se exhauriunt. Vides, quò propiùs ad naturam acce- 15 dimus, eò evidentiùs potestatem populi supra regiam eminere. Illud etiam constat, populum, modò id ei liberum sit, potestatem regi suam simpliciter et mancipio nunquam dare, neque naturâ posse dare; sed tantùm salutis et libertatis publicæ causâ, quam cùm rex procurare destiterit, intelligitur popu- 20 lum nihil dedisse; quia certo fini tantummodò dedit, monente

to him. For even as nature of old taught men from force and violence to betake themselves to law, so wherever the law is set at naught, the same dictate of nature must necessarily prompt us to betake ourselves to force again. "To be con-
5 vinced of this," says Cicero *pro Sestio,* "is the part of wisdom; to practice it, the part of courage; but both to think and do it too belongs to manly excellence accomplished in full measure." Let this stand then as a settled maxim of the law of nature, never to be shaken by any tricks or sleights of kings'
10 toadies, that the senate or the people are superior to kings good or bad. This is what yourself do in effect confess, when you tell us that the authority of kings was derived from the people. For that power which they gave the king, they do yet, by nature and a sort of virtue, or, as I may say, *virtually,* even
15 though they have given it to the other party, hold in themselves; for whatever natural causes produce any effect in such outstanding degree still retain more of their own virtue than they impart; nor do they, by imparting to others, exhaust themselves. You see, the closer we approach nature, the more
20 evidently does the people's power stand out above that of the king.

And this is likewise certain, that the people, so the choice be but left free to them, never grant their power to a king in absolute and unconditional ownership, nor by nature can do
25 so; but only for the public safety and liberty, which when the king ceases to take care of, then it is understood that the people have given him nothing at all: for, being warned by nature herself, they gave it him for a certain purpose only; so that if

ipsâ naturâ; quem finem si neque natura, neque populus asse-
quitur, non erit magis ratum quod dedit, quàm pactum quodvis aut fœdus irritum. His rationibus firmissimè probatur superiorem rege esse populum; unde argumentum hoc tuum
5 *maximè potens et validum, non posse regem judicari, quia*
parem in suo regno non habet, nec superiorem, diluitur. Id
enim assumis quod nullo modo concedimus. *In populari*
statu, inquis, *Magistratus à populo positus ab eodem ob cri-*
men plecti potest; In statu Aristocratico optimates, ab iis quos
10 *habent collegas; sed pro monstro est, ut rex in regno suo coga-*
tur causam capitis dicere. Quid nunc aliud concludis quàm
miserrimos esse omnium et stultissimos, qui regem sibi constituunt? Sed quamobrem, quæso, non poterit populus tam
regem punire reum, quàm popularem Magistratum, aut opti-
15 mates? An putas omnes populos qui sub regibus vivunt,
amore servitutis usque eò deperiisse, ut, liberi cùm essent,
servire maluerint, séque omnes, séque totos in unius dominium viri sæpe mali, sæpe stulti ita tradere, ut contra dominum, si sors ferat, immanissimum, nullum in legibus, nullum
20 in natura ipsa præsidium salutis, aut perfugium sibi reliquerint? cur ergo regibus primò regnum ineuntibus conditiones
ferunt, cur leges etiam dant regnandi, an ut sperni se eò magis

neither nature nor the people can attain this, then their gift
or grant will be no more valid than any other void covenant or
agreement. These reasons establish unshakably the people's
superiority to the king; and so your "most powerful and con-
5 vincing argument that a king cannot be judged by his people,
because in his kingdom he has no peer or superior" melts
away. For you take for granted that which we do not grant
by any means.

   "In a democracy," you say, "the magistrates, being ap-
10 pointed by the people, may likewise be punished by the people
for crime; in an aristocracy the nobles may be punished by
their colleagues; but it is monstrous that a king in his own
kingdom should be forced to plead for his life." What can
you conclude but that they who set up a king over them are
15 the most wretched and foolish of mankind? But pray what
is the reason why the people may not punish a guilty king
as well as a popularly appointed magistracy or the nobility?
Do you think that all peoples who live under kings were so
desperately in love with slavery that when they were free they
20 chose vassalage, and to put themselves all and entirely under
the despotism of one man—often an evil man, often a fool—
and all this in such wise that against a most outrageous tyrant,
if such fall to their lot, they have not left themselves in the
laws or in nature herself any protection whatever for their
25 safety, or asylum for themselves? Why then do they tender
conditions to their kings when these first come to the throne,
and even prescribe laws for them to govern by? Is it that they
may suffer themselves to be the more trampled upon and

atque irrideri paterentur? adeóne populum universum se abjicere, se deserere, sibi deesse, spem omnem in uno homine,
eoque fere vanissimo, collocare? cur item jurant reges nihil se
contra legem facturos? ut discant nempe miseri mortales suo
5 maximo malo, solis licere regibus impunè pejerare. Id quod
hæc tua nefanda consectaria demonstrant. *Si rex qui eligitur,
aliqua vel cum sacramento promiserit, quæ nisi promisisset,
fortasse nec sumptus esset, si stare nolit conventis, à populo
judicari non potest. Immò si subditis suis juraverit in elec-*
10 *tione, se secundùm leges regni justitiam administraturum, et
nisi id faciat, eos sacramento fidelitatis fore solutos, et facto
ipso abiturum esse potestate, à Deo non ab hominibus pœna
in fallentem exposcenda est.* Descripsi hæc, non ob elegan-
tiam, sunt enim incultissima, nec quod ampliùs refutationis
15 indigeant, etenim ipsa se refutant, se explodunt, se damnant
apertissima falsitate sua, atque turpitudine; sed eò feci, ut ob
merita tua egregia commendarem te regibus: qui inter officia
aulæ tam multa aliquem dignitatis locum, aut munus idoneum tibi prospiciant: cum enim alii sint à rationibus, alii à
20 poculis, alii a ferculis, alii à voluptatibus, tu iis commodissimè
sanè eris à perjuriis; tu regiæ non elegantiæ, ut Petronius ille,

laughed to scorn? Would a whole people ever so vilify themselves, so forsake their own interest, and fail their own cause,
as to place all their hopes in one man, usually a most empty
insubstantial one? Why, likewise, do kings swear an oath
5 not to act anything contrary to law? In order, of course, that
wretched mortals may learn to their deep sorrow that only
kings may perjure themselves with impunity! This is the
plain import of your wicked conclusions: "If a king that is
elected promise even upon oath any thing which if he had not
10 promised perhaps they would not have chosen him, yet if he
refuse to abide by the agreement he cannot be judged by the
people. Nay, though at his election he have sworn to his subjects that he will administer justice according to the laws of
the realm, and that if he do not they shall be discharged of their
15 oath of allegiance and he shall *ipso facto* abdicate, yet if he
break his oath it is God and not man that must exact the penalty." I have transcribed these lines, not for their elegance,
for they are barbarously expressed, nor because I think there
needs any additional answer to them, for they answer them-
20 selves—they explode and damn themselves—by their bare-
faced falsehood and loathsomeness, but to recommend you
to kings for your distinguished merits, in order that among
so many places as there are at court they may procure for you
some preferment or office that may be fit for you. Some are
25 Chancellors of the Exchequer, some are cup-bearers, some
seneschals and stewards, some Masters of the Revels: you
will most fittingly be their Master of the Perjuries. You shall
not be, like the famous Petronius, Master of the Royal Lit-

nam inscitus nimiùm es, sed perfidiæ summus arbiter eris.
Verùm ut summam in te stultitiam summâ improbitate con-
junctam esse omnes fateantur, expendamus paulo accuratiùs
præclara illa, quæ proximè affirmâsti: *Rex,* inquis, *etsi sub-*
5 *ditis juraverit in electione, se secundùm leges regnaturum,* et
ni faciat, *eos sacramento fidelitatis solutos fore, et se facto ipso*
abiturum potestate, abdicari tamen aut puniri ab iis non poterit. Quî minùs, quæso, rex quàm popularis magistratus?
quia in eo regimine populus non omnem transfundit potesta-
10 tem suam ad magistratum. An hic igitur in regem, cui regnum in se non diutius tradunt, quàm id benè gesserit? Tam
itaque rex juratus in leges, reus abjici aut puniri poterit, quàm
popularis magistratus. Nam argumento illo Pancratico omnis
in regem translatæ potestatis, ampliùs uti non potes, quod tuis
15 ipse machinis imprudens arietâsti. Cognoscite nunc *aliam*
potentissimam et invictam ejus rationem cur subditi regem
judicare nequeant, *quia legibus solutus est, quia leges solus*
rex omnes fert; quæ cum falsissima esse jam toties probave-
rim, hæc etiam invicta tua ratio cum priore ad nihilum recidit.
20 Cæterùm rex ob delicta quævis privata, utpote stuprum, adulterium, et similia, si interdum non plectitur, non tam justitiâ

erary Graces—you are too ignorant for that—but you shall
be Lord High Master of the Royal Treacheries.

Yet, that all men may acknowledge how in you extreme
folly is joined with extreme knavery, let us weigh a little more
5 carefully those brilliant propositions which you have just asserted. "A king," say you, "though at his election he have
sworn to his subjects that he will govern according to law,"
and that if he do not "they shall be discharged of their oath of
allegiance, and he shall *ipso facto* abdicate," yet cannot be de-
10 posed or punished by them. Why not a king, pray, as well as
a magistrate in a democracy? Because in a democracy the
people do not transfer all their power to the magistrate. But
do they then vest it all in a king, to whom they convey royal
power over themselves for no longer than he uses it well?
15 Therefore a king sworn to observe the laws, may, if he transgress them, be punished and deposed as well as a democratic
magistrate. So you can make no more use of your all-powerful
argument that the entire power has been transferred to the
king, for it is hoist with your own petard.

20   Hear now another "most powerful and invincible reason
why subjects" cannot judge their king, viz. "because he is
bound by no law, being himself the sole lawgiver." But as I
have so often proved this to be utterly false, even this invincible argument of yours, as well as the former, comes to noth-
25 ing. For the rest, if a king is sometimes left unpunished for
personal and private crimes, as fornication, adultery, and the
like, this is not because the people feel that he ought not in
justice be punished, but because they are long-suffering—

quàm patientia populi id accidit, ne plus turbarum ex morte
regis, et rerum mutatione populo eveniat, quàm boni ex uno
atque altero vindicato. Ex quo verò omnibus gravis et intole-
randus esse incipit, tum quidem, quoquo possunt modo, judicatum vel injudicatum omnes nationes tyrannum occidere fas
esse semper credidere. Unde Marcus Tullius in secunda Philippica de Cæsaris interfectoribus, *Hi primi cum gladiis non
in regnum appetentem, sed in regnantem impetum fecerunt:
quod cum ipsum factum per se præclarum atque divinum est,
tum est positum ad imitandum.* Quàm hujus tu dissimilis!
*Homicidium, adulterium, injuria, non hæc crimina regia
sunt, sed privata.* Euge parasite, lenones jam omnes et pro-
pudia aulica hac voce demeruisti; O quàm lepidè simul et pa-
rasitaris, et eâdem operâ lenocinaris! *Rex adulter benè potest
regnare, et homicida, ideóque vitâ privari non debet, quia cum
vita regno quoque exueretur; at nunquam hoc fuit probatum
legibus divinis aut humanis, ut duplex vindicta de uno crimine sumeretur.* Os impurum et infame! eadem ratione nec
populares magistratus, nec optimates, ne duplici pœnâ affice-
rentur, ne judex quidem, aut senator flagitiosus pœnas capite
ullas persolvere debebit; cum vita enim et ipsi suo magistratu
privarentur. Ut potestatem, sic majestatem etiam populo adi-

lest they be more hurt through disturbances occasioned by
the king's death and the change of state, than profited by the
vindication of individual rights. But when he begins to
be injurious and insufferable to everybody, then indeed all
5 nations have believed it lawful to slay the tyrant any how,
condemned or uncondemned. Hence Marcus Tullius in his
Second Philippic says of those that killed Caesar: "They were
the first that ran through with their swords, not a man who
affected to be king, but one who was actually settled in the
10 government; which, as it was a glorious and godlike action,
so it is set before us for our imitation." How unlike are you to
him!

"Murder, adultery, injustice, are not regal and public, but
private and personal crimes." Well said, toady! you have
15 obliged all pimps and profligates at court by this expression.
How charmingly by a single act do you play at once both
parasite and pimp! "A king that is an adulterer or a murderer
may yet govern well, and consequently ought not to be put to
death, for with his life he must lose his kingdom; and it was
20 never approved by God's laws or man's that for one and the
same crime a man was to be punished twice." Shameless disreputable foulmouth! By the same reason the magistrates in
a democracy or in an aristocracy ought never to be put to
death, for fear of double punishment, nor any corrupt judge
25 or senator, for with their lives they must lose their magistracy too.

As you have endeavored to take all power out of the people's hands, and vest it in the king, so you would all majesty

mere et in regem conferre studes; vicariam si vis et translati-
tiam, primariam certè non potes, uti nec potestatem. *Crimen,*
inquis, *majestatis non potest committere rex adversùs popu-*
lum suum; potest autem populus adversùs regem. Et tamen
5 rex propter populum duntaxat rex est, non populus propter
regem. Populus igitur universus aut pars major plus semper
rege debet posse: negas, et calculos ponis; *plus potest quàm*
singuli, bini, terni, deni, centeni, milleni, decies milleni. Esto.
Plus quàm dimidia pars populi. Non repugno. *Quid si alte-*
10 *rius dimidiæ pars altera accedat, annon adhuc plus poterit?*
Minime. Progredere; quid aufers abacum, peritissime Lo-
gista, an progressionem Arithmeticam non calles? Vertit rationes, et *annon rex cum optimatibus plus potestatis habeat,*
quærit; iterum nego, Vertumne, si pro optimatibus proceres
15 intelligas; quoniam accidere potest, ut nemo inter eos optima-
tis nomine sit dignus: fit etiam sæpiùs, ut multo plures de
plebe sint, qui virtute et sapientiâ proceres antecellant; quibus
cùm pars populi major vel potior accedit, eos universi populi
instar esse haud verear dicere. *At si plus quàm universi non*
20 *potest, ergo rex erit tantùm singulorum, non omnium univer-*
sim sumptorum; rectè; nisi ipsi voluerint. Rationes jam sub-

too: a delegated transferred majesty if you will, but surely not
their original primary majesty, any more than their original
primary power. "A king," you say, "cannot commit treason
against his people, but a people can against their king." And
5 yet a king is what he is for the people only, not the people for
him. Hence I infer that the whole body of the people, or a
majority of them, must needs have greater power than the
king. This you deny, and begin to cast up accounts. "He has
more power than any one, than any two, than any three, than
10 any ten, than any hundred, than any thousand, than any ten
thousand." So be it. "More power than half the people." I
will not deny that. "Add now half of the other half, will he
not have more power than all those?" By no means!

Go on, o skilful logician, why do you take away the count-
15 ing-board; do you not understand arithmetical progression?
He begins to reckon after another manner, and asks "whether
the king together with the nobility have not more power"?
No, good Master Chapman Chop-and-Change, I deny that
too, if by the nobility you mean the Lords only, because it may
20 happen that among them there may be not one man deserving
the name of noble: for it often falls out that among the Commons there are many far better and wiser men than among
the Lords. When the majority or the better part of the people
joins these, I should not scruple to say that they represent and
25 stand for the whole people. "But if the king is not superior
in power to all the people together, he is then king but of
single persons, not of all taken together." True; no more he
is, unless they are content he should be. Now balance your

ducito; comperies te imperitè supputando sortem perdidisse.
Dicunt Angli penès populum jus majestatis ex origine et
natura residere; hoc verò est omnium statuum eversionem in-
ducere. Etiámne Aristocratiæ, et Democratiæ? Credibile
5 sanè narras: quid si etiam Gynæcocratiæ, sub quo statu ferunt
te domi propemodùm vapulare, annon bearent te Angli, O
perpusilli homo animi? sed hoc frustra speraveris; æquissimè
enim est comparatum, ut qui tyrannidem foris imponere omnibus cupias, ipse domi tuæ servitutem servias turpissimam, et
10 minimè virilem. *Doceamus te oportet,* inquis, *quid nomine*
populi intelligi velimus. Permulta sunt, quæ te doceri potiùs
oporteret; nam quæ te propiùs attingunt, videris ea penitùs
nescire, et præter literulas nihil unquam didicisse, ne percipere quidem potuisse. Hoc tamen scire te putas, nos populi
15 nomine plebem solùm intelligere quòd *optimatum consessum*
abrogavimus. At illud est ipsum quod demonstrat nos populi
vocabulo omnes ordinis cujuscunque cives comprehendere;
qui unam tantummodo populi curiam supremam stabilivi-
mus, in qua etiam proceres, ut pars populi, non pro sese qui-
20 dem solis, ut antea, sed pro iis municipiis, à quibus electi fuerint, suffragia ferendi legitimum jus habent. Inveheris deinde

accounts, and you will find that by miscasting you have lost your principal.

"The English say that the right of majesty by its origin and its nature resides in the people; this would indeed bring on the overthrow of all states." What, of an aristocracy and of a democracy? But you say well, after all, for what if it should overthrow a gynaecocracy too, under which state, they say, you go near to being beaten at home? Would not the English do you a kindness in that, Master Faint-heart? But there is no hope for that; for it is most justly so ordered that since you would impose tyranny upon all mankind abroad, you yourself should live in a shameful impotent unmanly slavery at home.

"It behooves us English to tell you," you say, "what we mean by the word People." There are a great many things which it would more behoove you to be told; for of things that more immediately concern you, you seem altogether ignorant, and never to have learnt or even been able to understand more than the alphabet. But this you suppose you know, that by the word people we mean the common people only, because we "have abolished the House of Lords." And yet this is the very thing that shows that under the word people we comprehend all our citizens, of what order and degree soever; in that we have established a single supreme Commons' House only, in which the lords also have by law the right to vote as a part of the people, not in their own right as they did before, but as representing those constituencies by which they have been chosen.

in plebem, *cæcam* eam et *brutam, regendi artem non habere,*
nîl plebe ventosius, vanius, levius, mobilius; Conveniunt in te
optimè hæc omnia; et de infima quidem plebe sunt etiam vera,
de media non item; quo ex numero prudentissimi fere sunt
5 viri, et rerum peritissimi: cæteros hinc luxus et opulentia,
inde egestas et inopia à virtute et civilis prudentiæ studio plerunque avertit. *Plures* nunc esse *modos* asseris *regum consti-*
tuendorum, qui nihil populo debent hoc nomine, et imprimis
illi, *qui regnum habent hæreditarium.* At verò servæ sint istæ
10 nationes oportet, et ad servitutem natæ, quæ talem agnoscant
dominum, cui se sine assensu suo hæreditate obvenisse cre-
dant: pro civibus certè, aut ingenuis et liberis haberi non possunt; nec rempub. habere ullam censendæ; quinimmò inter
facultates, et possessiones quasi heri sui, et herilis filii nume-
15 randæ sunt: nam quod ad jus dominii, quid distent à servi-
tiis et pecoribus non video. Secundò, *qui armis sibi regnum*
fecit, populum, inquis, *non potest authorem agnoscere im-*
perii prolati vel usurpati. At nobis non de victore, sed de subacto rege sermo nunc est; quid victor possit, aliàs disputabi-

Then you inveigh against the common people as being "blind and dull, ignorant of the art of governing"; you say there is "nothing more empty and changeable than they, nothing more fickle and excitable." All which is very true
5 of yourself, and it is true likewise of the rabble, but not of the middle sort, amongst whom the wisest men and most skilful in affairs are generally found; the rest are most commonly diverted, on the one hand by luxury and wealth, on the other by want and poverty, from achieving excellence, and from
10 the study of laws and government.

"There are many ways" now, you say, "by which kings are established, so as not to be beholden to the people at all on that score," and first "those who hold their kingdom by inheritance." But those nations must certainly be slaves, and
15 born to slavery, who acknowledge a lord and master so absolute that they believe themselves to have fallen to his lot by inheritance, without any consent of their own. Surely they cannot be held to be citizens, or freemen, or freeborn, nor are they to be accounted as having a body politic, but must be
20 reckoned among the goods and chattels, estates and properties of their owner and his son and heir; for as to ownership I see no difference betwixt them and slaves or cattle. Secondly, you say: "He that carves out a kingdom with his sword cannot acknowledge the people as the originator of the
25 power he has extended or usurped." But what we are talking about now is not a conquering king, but a conquered king; what a conqueror may do, we will discourse elsewhere; do you keep to your subject.

mus, tu hoc age. Quod autem regi jus patrisfamilias antiquum toties attribuis, ut inde *absolutæ potestatis in regibus*
exemplum petas, dissimillimum id esse jam sæpiùs ostendi:
Aristoteles etiam ille quem crepas vel initio politicorum, si
5 legisses, idem te docuisset: ubi aït malè eos judicare, qui inter
patremfamilias et regem parùm interesse existimant; *regnum*
enim à familia, non numero solùm, sed specie differre. Postquam enim pagi in oppida et urbes crevere, evanuit paulatim
jus illud regale familiæ, et agnosci desitum est. Hinc scribit
10 Diodorus, lib. 1. regna antiquitùs dari non regum filiis, sed iis
quorum maxima in populum beneficia extiterunt. Et Justi-
nus, *Principio rerum, gentium, nationúmque imperium penès*
reges erat; quos ad fastigium hujus majestatis, non ambitio
popularis, sed spectata inter bonos moderatio provehebat.
15 Unde perspicuum est, in ipso gentium principio, imperium
paternum et hæreditarium virtuti, et populari statim juri ces-
sisse. Quæ origo imperii regii et ratio et causa maximè naturalis est. Ob eam enim ipsam causam primò homines in unum
convenere, non ut unus omnes insultaret, sed ut quocunque
20 alterum lædente, ne lex deesset, neve judex inter homines,
quo læsus aut defendatur aut saltem vindicetur. Dispersos

Whereas you repeatedly ascribe to kings the ancient right of the paterfamilias, in order to fetch thence "a model of the unlimited power of kings," I have shown already over and over that there is no likeness at all betwixt them. And that
5 very Aristotle whom you keep prating about would have taught you as much even at the beginning of his *Politics,* if you had read it. There he says that they judge amiss who think there is but little difference betwixt a king and the head of a household: "For a kingdom is different from a household,
10 not in number only, but in kind." For when villages grew to be towns and cities, that right of the king as head of the household vanished by degrees, and was recognized no more. Hence Diodorus in his first book says that anciently kingdoms were transmitted not to the former kings' sons, but to those
15 whose services to the people were most eminent. And Justin says: "Originally the government of peoples and races was by kings, who were exalted to that pinnacle of majesty, not by soliciting the people's support, but for a moderation well-regarded among good men."
20 Whence it is manifest that in the very beginning of nations, paternal and hereditary government was soon replaced by personal worth and the people's right. This is the most natural reason and cause, and was the true rise of royal power. For it was for this very reason that at first men entered into
25 societies: not that any one might insult over all the rest, but that in case any should injure another, law might not be wanting, and a judge between man and man, whereby the injured might be protected or at least avenged. When men

olim homines et dispalatos disertus aliquis, et sapiens ad vitam civilem traduxit; tu *hoc maximè consilio,* inquis, *ut in congregatos imperium haberet.* Nimbrotum fortasse intelligis, qui tyrannorum primus fuisse dicitur: vel hæc tua solius malitia est, quæ in illos olim magnos et excelsi animi viros cadere non potuit, tuum solius commentum, à nemine, quod sciam, ante te traditum; cum utilitatem et salutem generis humani, non sua commoda, suúmque dominatum respexisse illos primos urbium conditores, antiquorum omnium monumentis proditum sit. Unum præterire non possum, quo tu veluti emblemate quodam exornare credo cætera hujus capitis voluisti: si *consulem,* inquis, *in judicium venire oportuisset, priusquam magistratu abisset, dictator ad hoc creandus fuisset,* cum initio dixeris, *ideo collegam ei fuisse datum.* Sic tua semper inter se congruunt, et quid de quaque re dicas, quidve scribas, quàm nullius momenti sit, paginis ferè singulis declarant. *Sub antiquis regibus Anglo-saxonicis plebem,* aïs, *ad comitia regni nunquam vocari solitam esse.* Si quis nostrorum hoc affirmâsset, possem eum haud multo negotio erroris arguere; tuâ istâ peregrinâ affirmatione res nostras hallucinante minùs mo-

were at first scattered asunder and straying about, some wise
and eloquent man brought them over into civil life; "chiefly,"
say you, "that when he had got them gathered together he
might exercise dominion over them." Perhaps you meant this
of Nimrod, who is said to have been the first tyrant, or else
it is your own wickedness only, which could have no appli-
cation to those great and high-souled men of yore—a mere
fiction of yours, not asserted, as far as I know, by anyone
before you. For it is delivered by the memorials of all the
ancients that those first founders of cities had in view not any
profit or power of their own, but the advantage and safety of
mankind.

One thing I cannot pass by, with which I suppose you intended to decorate the rest of this chapter as with some motto
in mosaic inlay. "If a Consul," say you, "had been required
to come to trial while still in office, there must have been a
Dictator created for that purpose;" though at the beginning
you had said that "for that very purpose the Consul's colleague was provided." Just so your statements always agree
with one another, and reveal on almost every page how whatever you say or write upon any subject is of no weight or importance. "Under the ancient Anglo-Saxon kings," you say,
"it was never the custom to call the people to the national
councils." If any of our own countrymen had asserted such a
thing, I could without much trouble have convinced him that
he was in error. But I am not so much concerned at this assertion of yours, which wanders about in foreign parts, and
wanders in its mind too about our affairs. This in effect is

veor. Et de communi regum jure quæ habuisti hæc ferè sunt. Reliqua multa, nam et sæpissimè devius esse soles, prætermitto, vel quæ fundamento nituntur nullo, vel quæ extra causam posita sunt: Non enim id operam do, ut tibi par esse lo-
5 quacitate videar.

CAPUT VIII.

SI de communi regum jure, Salmasi, quæ sentires, ea sine contumelia cujusquam protulisses, quamvis in hac rerum apud Anglos mutatione, tamen, cùm libertate scribendi uterere tuâ, neque erat cur quisquam Anglorum tibi
10 succenseret, neque in asserendâ, quam tueris, sententiâ minus effecisses. Nam si hoc et Mosis et Christi præceptum est, *Omnes regibus suis tam bonis quàm malis subjici, sive Hispanos, sive Gallos, sive Italos, sive Germanos, sive Anglos, sive Scotos,* quod suprà (p. 127.) affirmabas, quid attinebat te
15 exterum et ignotum jura nostra balbutire, eáque velle nobis è cathedra quasi schedulas tuas, et miscellanea prælegere, quæ utcunque legibus divinis debere cedere multis antea verbis docueras. Nunc satis constat non tam tuopte ingenio ad causam regiam adjecisse te animum, quàm partim pretio, pro
20 ejus qui te conduxit copia, maximo, partim spe præmii cujus-

all you say of the right of kings in general. The many things that remain—for you much too often digress—I omit: things that either rest on no foundation or are nothing to the purpose; for it is not my design to be thought your equal in talkativeness.

CHAPTER VIII.

IF YOU had published your own opinion, Salmasius, concerning the right of kings in general, without insulting anyone, albeit amid this revolution in England, yet while you did but use your own liberty to write, there was no reason why any Englishman should be displeased with you, nor would you have been less successful in establishing the opinion you maintain. For if it be a positive command both of Moses and of Christ "That all men whatsoever, whether Spaniards, French, Italians, Germans, English, or Scots, should be subject to their kings, whether good or bad," as you asserted before (page 127), what business had you, a foreigner, and unknown, to babble about our *laws,* and read us professorial lectures out of them as if they were your own papers and miscellanies, when all the while you had taught us already in a great many words that our laws, be they how they will, ought to give way to the laws of God?

But now it is apparent that you have undertaken the defence of this royal cause not so much out of your own inclination as because you were hired, partly for payment—and a good round payment too, considering your employer's finances,—and partly by hope of some greater reward hereafter;

dam majoris conductum fuisse, ut Anglos vicinorum nemini
molestos, rerum tantummodò suarum arbitros libello infami
lacerares. Hoc nisi esset, quenquámne tantâ credibile est impudentiâ esse aut insaniâ, ut longinquus et extraneus immer-
5 gere se gratis in res nostras, ad partes etiam se adjungere non
dubitaret? Nam quid tuâ malùm refert, quid rerum Angli
inter se gerant? Quid tibi vis, Ole, quid tibi quæris? nihilne
domi habes quod ad te pertineat? Utinam eadem haberes quæ
habuit ille notissimus in epigrammate Olus; et fortasse habes;
10 dignus profectò es. An uxor tua stimulatrix illa, quæ ut in
gratiam exulis Caroli hæc scriberes etiam currentem incitâsse
fertur, ampliores fortè in Anglia professiones, et honoraria
nescio quæ, redeunte Carolo, ominata tibi est? At scitote fœmina Virque, non esse locum in Anglia neque lupo neque
15 Lupi Domino. Unde mirum non est te toties in molossos
nostros tantam rabiem effudisse. Quin redis ad illustres illos
in Gallia titulos tuos, et imprimis ad famelicum illum Lupi
dominatum, deinde ad consistorium illud regis Christianis-
simi sacrum; nimis longo intervallo consiliarius peregrè abes
20 à patriâ. Verùm illa, quod planè video, neque te desiderat
neque consilia tua; ne cùm redires quidem paucis abhinc annis, et culinam Cardinalitiam olfacere et sectari cœpisses: Sapit
mehercule, sapit, téque oberrare semivirum Gallum cum

hired, I say, to rend and tear with your disreputable book the English, who trouble none of their neighbors, and meddle with their own matters only. Were it not so, is it credible that any man should be so shameless and so mad as not to hesitate,

5 though he be a stranger far away, to plunge into our affairs for nothing, and even attach himself to a party? What the devil is it to you what the English do amongst themselves? What would you have, Olus? what do you mean? Have you no concerns of your own at home? I wish you had the same

10 concerns that the much celebrated Olus had in the Epigram; and perhaps so you have; you thoroughly deserve them. Or did that hotspur your wife, who is said to have spurred you— willing horse!—to write all this stuff to please the exiled Charles,—did she bode you some more profitable professor-

15 ship in England, and God knows what fees, at Charles's return? But assure yourselves, *Madame la femme et Monsieur le mari,* that England has no place for a wolf or for the Seigneur of a wolf. No wonder, then, that you have so often spit so much venom at our English mastiffs! It were better

20 for you to return to those illustrious titles of yours in France: first to that hungerstarved Seigneurie of St. Loup, and next to that *sacré* Council of the Most Christian King; you are too far abroad from your own country for a counsellor. But I see full well that France desires not either you or your counsel,

25 and did not, even when you were back a few years ago, and were beginning to smell out and hunt after a Cardinal's kitchen. She is right, by my troth, she is right, and can willingly allow you, you French capon, with your mankind wife

uxore viro, et refertissimis inaniarum scriniis facilè sinit; donec stipem sive equiti grammatistæ, sive illustri Hippocritico satis largam alicubi gentium inveneris; si cui fert animus regi vel civitati, doctorem erraticum et venalem mercede maximâ 5 liceri. Sed eccum tibi licitatorem; vendibilis necne sis, et quanti, jam statim videbimus. *Pertendunt,* inquis, *Parricidæ, regni Anglicani statum mixtum esse, non merè regium.* Pertendit idem sub Eduardo Sexto Smithus noster, juris consultus idem bonus, et politicus, quem fuisse parricidam non 10 dices, ejus libri ferè initio, quem de repub. Anglicanâ scripsit; neque id de nostrâ solùm, sed de omni penè repub. idque ex Aristotelis sententiâ verum esse affirmat; neque aliter ullam rempub. stare posse. At enim quasi piaculum esse crederes quicquam dicere sine repugnantiis, ad priores illas et jam tri15 tissimas fœdè revolveris. *Nullam gentem* aïs *esse nec fuisse unquam quæ regis appellatione non intellexerit eam potestatem quæ solo Deo minor est, quæque solum Deum judicem haberet;* et tamen paulo post fateris, *nomen regis datum vel olim fuisse ejusmodi potestatibus et magistratibus qui plenum* 20 *et liberum jus non haberent, sed à populi nutu dependens,* ut *sufetes Carthaginiensium, judices Hebræorum, reges Lacedæmoniorum,* et postremo *Aragonensium.* Satisne bellè tibi constas? Tum quinque monarchiæ species ex Aristotele re-

and your desks chock-full of emptiness, to wander about, till somewhere in creation you light upon a dole bountiful enough for a grammarian-cavalier or illustrious hippo-critic,—always supposing any king or state has a mind to bid highest for a

5 vagabond pedant that is on sale. But here am I that will bid for you; whether you are a merchantable commodity or not, and what you are worth, we shall see at once.

You say: "The parricides assert that the kingdom of England is of a composite kind, not purely royal." In the time

10 of Edward the Sixth, Sir Thomas Smith, a countryman of ours, a good lawyer and statesman, whom you will not call a parricide, asserts the same thing near the beginning of his book on the commonwealth of England. He states that it is true not of our government only, but of almost all others—this upon

15 the opinion of Aristotle; and that otherwise no government can subsist. But as if you thought it a sin to say anything without unsaying it, you repeat your former threadbare contradictions. You say: "There neither is nor ever was any nation that did not understand by the name of king that

20 power which is inferior to God alone, and which has God for its sole judge." And yet, a little after, you confess that "The name of king was formerly given to such powers and magistrates as had not a full and unlimited right, but one depending upon the people's will," for example "the sufetes of the

25 Carthaginians, the judges of the Hebrews, the kings of the Lacedaemonians," and, lastly, "of Aragon." Isn't this a pretty piece of self-consistency?

Then you muster out of Aristotle five several sorts of

censes, quarum una tantùm jus illud obtinuit quod tu regibus
commune omnibus esse dicis. De qua haud semel jam dictum
est, nullum ejus exemplum vel ab Aristotele allatum, vel usquam extitisse: Quatuor reliquas, et legitimas, et legibus fuisse
5 minores dilucidè ostendit. Primum horum erat regnum Laconicum, et maximè quidem ejus sententiâ regnum, eorum
quatuor quæ legitima erant. Secundum erat Barbaricum,
hoc solo diuturnum quia legitimum, et volente populo: nolente autem, omnis rex continuò non erit rex sed tyrannus, si
10 invito populo regnum retinuerit, eodem teste Aristotele. l. 5.
Idem de tertia regum specie dicendum est, quos ille Æsymne-
tas vocat, electos à populo, et ad certum plerunque tempus,
certásque causas, quales ferè apud Romanos fuere Dictatores.
Quarta species eorum est, qui Heroïcis temporibus regnabant,
15 quibus ob egregia merita regnum ultro à populo delatum erat,
sed legitimum tamen; neque verò hi nisi volente populo regnum tenebant, nec aliâ re magis differre has quatuor regni
species à tyrannide aït, quàm quòd illic volente, hîc invito populo regnetur. Quinta denique regni species, quæ παμβασιλεία
20 dicitur, et est cum summa potestate, quale tu jus regum omnium esse vis, à philosopho planè damnatur, ut neque utile,
neque justum, neque naturale, nisi sit ut populus ferre possit

monarchies, only one of which possessed that right which
you say is common to all kings. Concerning this I have said
already more than once that no instance of it, either cited by
Aristotle or anywhere else, has existed. The other four king-
5 ships, he clearly shows, were limited by laws, and subject to
them. The first of these was that of the Lacedaemonians,
which of the four limited monarchies did in his opinion best
deserve the name of kingship. The second, of a kind foreign
to the Greeks, was lasting only in that it was limited, and that
10 the people willingly submitted to it; for according to Aristotle's own opinion in his fifth book, once the people are unwilling, whatever king retains the throne against their will,
will instantly be no king, but a tyrant. The same is to be said
of his third sort of kings, which he calls Aesymnetes, who
15 were chosen by the people, most commonly for a certain time
only, and for certain purposes; such, or nearly such, were
the Roman dictators. The fourth is the kind that reigned
in the heroic days, upon whom for their extraordinary merits
the people of their own accord conferred the government,
20 but yet limited; nor yet did these retain the throne unless
the people were willing. And these four sorts of kingship, he
says, differ from tyranny in no respect more than in this: that
these governments are with the consent of the people, and
tyranny against their will. The fifth sort of royal government,
25 finally, called παμβασιλεία, and endowed with the supreme
power, which you pretend to be the right of all kings, is
utterly condemned by the philosopher, as neither profitable
nor just nor natural—unless some people should be able to

istiusmodi regnum, iisque deferat qui virtute aliis omnibus longè prælucent. Hæc tertio politicorum, cuivis obvia sunt. Verùm tu, credo, ut vel semel ingeniosus et floridus esse viderere, *has quinque monarchiæ species quinque zonis* mundi assimilare gestiebas; *Inter duo extrema potentiæ regalis tres aliæ species interpositæ magis temperatæ videntur, ut inter zonas torridam et frigidam, quæ mediæ jacent.* Festivum caput! quàm pulchras nobis similitudines concinnare semper soles! Tu igitur, quò regnum *absolutæ potestatis* ipse damnas, ad zonam frigidam hinc ocyùs amolire; quæ post adventum illic tuum plus duplo frigebit: nos interim à te novo Archimede sphæram illam, quam describis, mirabilem expectamus, in qua duæ sint extremæ zonæ, una torrida, altera frigida, tres mediæ temperatæ. *Reges,* inquis, *Lacedæmoniorum in vincula conjici fas erat, morte multari fas non erat.* Quare? an quia damnatum capite Agidem lictores et peregrini milites rei novitate perculsi, regem ducere ad mortem non esse fas existimabant? Et populus quidem Spartanus ejus mortem ægrè tulit, non quòd rex capitali supplicio affectus fuerit, sed quòd bonus, et popularis, factione divitum judicio illo circumventus esset. Sic itaque Plutarchus, *primus rex Agis ab ephoris est morte multatus;* quibus verbis non quid fas, sed quid

endure a government of this kind, and withal should confer
it upon such as outshine all others in virtue. These things lie
open and accessible to anyone in the third book of the *Politics*.

But you, that for once in your life you might appear witty
5 and florid, I suppose, pleased yourself by likening "these five
sorts of monarchy to the five zones" of the world. "Between
the two extremes of royal power three more temperate kinds
appear to be interposed, even as those which lie in the midst
between the torrid and the frigid zones." Pretty wit! what
10 lovely comparisons you always make us! Away with you,
doublequick, whither you banish "absolute monarchy," to
the frigid zone, which after your arrival will be more than
doubly frigid. Meanwhile we await from you, our modern
Archimedes, that wondrous globe which you describe, in
15 which there be two extreme zones, one torrid and the other
frigid, and three temperate ones between.

"The kings of the Lacedaemonians," you say, "might lawfully be imprisoned, but it was not lawful to put them to
death." Why not? Is it because the officers of justice and
20 some foreign soldiers, being surprised at the novelty of the
thing, thought it not lawful to lead King Agis to his execution,
though condemned to die? Yea, even the Spartan people
took his death ill, not because it was a king that was condemned to die, but because he was a good man and beloved
25 by them, and had been hunted to his death by a faction of
wealthy men. Says Plutarch: "Agis was the first king that
was put to death by the ephors"; in which words he tells us
only what actually was done, not what lawfully might be

factum sit, tantummodò narrat. Nam qui regem in jus ducere, vel etiam in vincula possunt, illos non posse eundem
supplicio ultimo afficere, puerile est credere. Accingeris jam
tandem ad jus regum Anglicorum. *Rex,* inquis, *in Anglia*
unus semper fuit. Hoc eo dicis, quia modò dixeras, *rex non*
est nisi unus sit et unicus. Quod si ita est, aliquot sanè quos
credebam Angliæ reges fuisse, non erant: Nam ut multos
omittam Saxonicorum, qui consortes imperii vel filios vel
fratres habuere, constat Henricum Secundum è stirpe Nor-
manica cum filio regnâsse. *Ostendant,* inquis, *aliquod reg-*
num sub unius imperio, cui non potestas absoluta adjuncta
fuerit, in quibusdam tamen magis remissa, in aliis magis
intenta. Ostende tu potestatem absolutam remissam, asine;
annon absoluta est summa? Quomodo ergo summa et remissa
simul erit? quoscunque fateberis reges cum remissa potestate
esse, eos non esse cum absoluta facilè vincam, inferiores proinde esse populo naturâ libero, qui et suus ipse legislator est,
et potestatem regiam vel intendere, vel remittere potest. Britannia, an tota olim regibus paruerit, incertum: Verisimilius
est, prout tempora ferebant, nunc hanc nunc illam reipub. formam adhibuisse. Hinc Tacitus, *Britanni olim regibus parebant,*

done. For it were childish to imagine that they who may lawfully bring a king to trial, and imprison him, may not also lawfully put him to death.

At last you gird yourself up to tackle the law of English kings. "In England," you say, "there was always one king at a time." This you say because you had said before that "unless a king be sole in the government, he cannot be a king." If so, some who I used to think had been kings of England were not really kings; for—to omit many of our Saxon kings, who had either sons or brothers partners with them in the government—it is not disputed that King Henry II, of the Norman stock, reigned jointly with his son.

"Let them show," say you, "any kingdom under the government of a single person who has not absolute power, in some kingdoms, however, more loosened, in others more tightened." Ass, do you show us any absolute power that is loosened; is not that power that is absolute the supreme power? How can it then be both supreme and loosened? Whatsoever kings you shall acknowledge to be invested with a loosened power, those I will clearly prove to have no absolute power; and consequently to be inferior to a people free by nature, which, as it is its own lawmaker, can loosen or tighten the power of the king.

Whether the whole of Britain was anciently governed by kings or no is uncertain; it is most likely that they employed now one form of government, now another, according to the exigencies of the time. Whence Tacitus says: "The Britons anciently were under kings; now their chiefs distract them

nunc per principes factionibus et studiis trahuntur. Deserti
à Romanis, quadraginta circiter annos sine regibus fuere:
regnum itaque *perpetuum,* quod affirmas, antiquitùs non
fuit; fuisse autem hæreditarium præcisè nego; quod et regum
5 series, et mos creandi eorum demonstrat: disertis enim verbis
petuntur populi suffragia. Postquam enim rex consuetum
juramentum dedit, accedens archiepiscopus ad quatuor partes
exstructi suggesti, toties rogat populum universum his verbis,
consentire vultis de habendo ipsum regem? planè ac si Ro-
10 mano more dixisset, vultis, jubetis hunc regnare? quod opus
non foret, si regnum jure esset hæreditarium; verùm apud
reges usurpatio pro jure sæpissimè obtinet. Tu Caroli bello
toties victi jus regium jure belli fundare adniteris: Gulielmus
scilicet cognomento *conquæstor* nos subjugavit. At sciunt qui
15 in nostra historia peregrini non sunt, Anglorum opes uno illo
prælio Hastingensi non adeò attritas fuisse, quin bellum facilè
instaurare potuissent. Sed regem accipere, quàm victorem et
tyrannum pati malebant. Dant itaque jusjurandum Gulielmo, se fidem ei servaturos; dat pariter Gulielmus juramentum
20 illis, admotus altari, se omnia, quæ par est bonum regem, iis
esse vicissim præstiturum. Cum falleret fidem, et rursus Angli
arma caperent, diffisus ipse suis viribus juravit denuò, tactis

into parties and factions." When the Romans left them, they were about forty years without kings; that "perpetual kingship" which you allege had therefore no existence in ancient times. I positively assert that their kingship was not heredi-
5 tary, which is evident both from the succession of their kings, and from their way of creating them; for the approval of the people is asked in express words. When the king has taken the accustomed oath, the archbishop, stepping to the four sides of the platform erected for the purpose, asks the body
10 of the people four several times in these words, "Will ye consent to have this man your king?" Just as if he said, Roman fashion, "Do ye desire, do ye command, this man to reign?" Which would be needless if the kingdom were by law hereditary.

15 But with kings usurpation passes very frequently for **law** and right. You strive to ground Charles's royal right, who was so often conquered himself, upon the right of conquest. William, surnamed "the Conqueror," forsooth, subdued us. But they who are not strangers to our history know full well
20 that the strength of the English nation was not so broken in that one fight at Hastings but that they might easily have renewed the war. Yet they chose rather to accept a king than to endure a conqueror and a tyrant: they swear therefore to William to be his liegemen, and he likewise swears to them
25 at the altar to conduct himself towards them in all respects as a good king ought. When he broke his word, and the English betook themselves again to their arms, William, mistrusting his strength, renewed upon the Gospels his oath to keep the

Evangeliis, antiquas se leges Angliæ observaturum. Si postea
igitur Anglos miserè afflixit, non id jure belli, sed jure perjurii fecit. Certum est præterea jam multis ab hinc seculis
victos et victores in unam gentem coaluisse; ut jus illud belli,
5 si quod unquam fuit, antiquari jam diu necesse sit. Ipsius
verba morientis quæ ex libro Cadomensi fide dignissimo de-
scripta reddimus, omnem dubitationem tollunt. *Neminem,*
inquit, *Anglici regni constituo hæredem.* Qua voce jus illud
belli, simúlque illud hæreditarium, cum ipso mortuo Guli-
10 elmo conclamatum atque sepultum est. Video nunc aliquam
te in aula dignitatem, quod prædixi fore, esse adeptum, summus nimirum aulicæ astutiæ quæstor regius et procurator es
factus. Unde hoc quod sequitur videris ex officio scribere,
Vir magnifice. *Siquis prædecessorum regum factionibus pro-*
15 *cerum, vel seditionibus plebis coactus, aliquid de suo jure*
remiserit, id non potest successori obesse, quin id iterum sibi
vindicet. Rectè mones: itaque si quo tempore majores nostri
aliquid de jure suo per ignaviam amisere, an id oberit nobis,
eorum posteris? Pro se illi quidem servitutem spondere, si
20 vellent, pro nobis certè non poterant; quibus idem semper
jus erit nosmet liberandi, quod illis erat in servitutem se cuilibet tradendi. Miraris *quid faciat,* ut *rex Britanniæ hodie*

ancient laws of England. Therefore, if after that he miserably oppressed the English, he did it not by right of conquest, but by right of perjury. Besides, it is certain that many ages ago the conquerors and conquered coalesced into one and the same people; so that that right of conquest, if any such there ever were, must needs have been long ago barred by antiquity. His own words at his death, which I report as transcribed from the Caen Book—a thoroughly trustworthy document—remove all doubt. "I appoint no man," says he, "heir of the kingdom of England." By which words that right of conquest and that right of inheritance were at once and together officially bewailed as dead, and buried together with the dead Conqueror.

I see now that you have got a place at court, as I foretold: you are become High Treasurer and Steward of Court Craft; and the following passage you seem to write as if by virtue of your office, magnificent Sir. "If any among preceding kings, being thereunto compelled by factions of great men or seditions among the common people, have remitted somewhat of his right, that cannot hinder a successor from reclaiming it unto himself." A proper reminder! If therefore at any time our ancestors have through neglect lost any thing that was their right, will that hinder us their posterity? If they were willing to promise for themselves to be slaves, they could make no such promise for us, who shall always retain the same right of setting ourselves free that they had of enslaving themselves to any whomsoever.

You wonder "how it comes to pass that a king of Great

debeat haberi pro magistratu tantùm regni, qui autem alia
regna in Christianitate obtinent, plenâ et liberâ potestate pol-
leant. De Scotia remitto te ad Buchananum; de Gallia etiam
tua, ubi hospes esse videris, ad Francogalliam Hotomani, et
5 Girardum Franciæ Historicum; de cæteris ad alios, quorum
nulli quod sciam Independentes erant: ex quibus de jure regio
longè alia poteras didicisse, quàm quæ doces. Cùm jure belli
tyrannidem regibus Angliæ asserere nequiveris, facis jam
periculum in jure parasitico. Edicunt reges se regnare *Dei*
10 *gratiâ:* quid si Deos se esse edixissent? te credo flaminem facilè
erant habituri; sic Pontifex Cantuariensis *Dei providentiâ*
archiepiscopari præ se tulit. Túne istâ fatuitate Papam non vis
esse regem in Ecclesia, ut regem constituere plusquam Papam
in repub. possis? At in regni statutis appellatur *Rex Dominus*
15 *noster.* Mirus tu quidem statutorum nostrorum nomenculator
repentè evasisti; nescis tamen multos dici dominos qui non
sunt; nescis quàm iniquum sit ex titulis honorariis, ne dicam
adulatoriis, de jure et veritate rerum statuere. Eodem refer
quod *Parlamentum regis* dicitur: nam et frænum regis voca-

Britain must nowadays be looked upon as merely a magistrate of the kingdom, whereas they who govern other kingdoms in Christendom wield plenary and unlimited authority." For Scotland I refer you to Buchanan; for your native
5 France (where you seem a stranger), to Hotman's *Franco-
Gallia* and Gerard the historian of France: for the rest, to
other authors, of whom none as far as I know were Independents: out of whom you might have learned concerning
the right of kings a quite other lesson than what you teach.

10   Not being able to claim for the kings of England a tyrannical power by right of conquest, you now make trial by right
of toadyism. Kings proclaim openly, you say, that they reign
"by the Grace of God." What of it? What if they were to
proclaim that they *are* Gods? They might, I believe, easily
15 get you for a priest! So the Pontiff of Canterbury made public
pretence to archbishop it "by the Providence of God." Are
you such a fool that you refuse to acknowledge the Pope as
king in the Church in order to establish the king a more than
Pope in the State? But in the statutes of the realm, you say,
20 the king is called "our Lord the king." Flunkey, doorkeeper
slave at the king's levee, you are turned out on a sudden mar-
velous skilled in the names in our statutes that you call out to
your royal owner! But what you know not is that many are
called lords who are not lords; you know not how unfair it
25 is to determine of the right and truth of things from titles of
honor, not to say of flattery. Make the same inference from
the Parliament's being called "the King's Parliament"; for
it is called the king's bridle too, and the king is not on that

tur; adeóque non magis rex Parlamenti est dominus, quàm equus est sui dominus fræni. At *cur non regis Parlamentum, cum ab eo convocetur?* Dicam tibi; quia convocatur etiam senatus à Consule, neque propterea dominus illius concilii 5 erat. Quod itaque rex Parlamentum convocat, id facit pro officio suo ac munere quod à populo accepit, ut etiam quos convocat, eos de arduis regni negotiis consuleret, non de suis: aut siqua dici sua possunt, de iis postremo semper loco agi solitum erat; ad arbitrium etiam Parlamenti, non suum. Nec 10 verò ignorant, quorum id interest scire, Parlamentum sive vocatum, sive non vocatum, bis intra vertentem annum antiquitùs ex lege potuisse convenire. At *regis etiam leges nuncupantur.* Sunt istæ quidem ad regem phaleræ; rex autem Angliæ legem ferre per se potest nullam; neque enim ad leges 15 ferendas, sed ad custodiendas à populo latas constitutus erat. Túque hic fateris *congregari* idcirco *Parlamentum ut leges conderet.* Quapropter et lex Terræ vocatur, et lex populi: Unde Ethelstanus rex in præfatione legum, ubi omnes alloquitur, *vobis,* inquit, *lege vestrâ* omnia largitus sum: et in 20 formula juramenti quo reges Angliæ antequam crearentur obstringere se solebant, sic populus à rege stipulatur. *Concedis justas leges quas vulgus elegerit?* respondet rex, *concedo.*

account any more master of his Parliament than a horse is master of his bridle. But "why is it not a fair inference that Parliament is the king's, since he summons it?" I will tell you. The Roman Senate's being summoned by a Consul did

5 not make him master of that assembly either. And so, too, when the king summons Parliament, he does it by virtue and in discharge of his duty and of the office which he has received from the people, that he may advise even with them he summons, about the difficult business of the kingdom, not

10 his own; or if any can be called his own, this they have always been wont to move last, and not at the king's pleasure, but even at the pleasure of Parliament. And they whom it concerns to know this, know very well that Parliament anciently might by law meet twice in the course of a year, whether sum-

15 moned or not. But "the laws too are called the king's laws." These phrases, to be sure, are trappings and gewgaws for a king, but a king of England can of himself make no law, for he was appointed not to make laws, but to keep the laws which the people have made.

20 And you yourself here admit that "Parliament meets to make laws." Wherefore the law is also called the Law of the Land, and the Common Law. Whence king Aethelstan in the Preamble to his laws, speaking to all the people, says: I have bestowed all things "upon you according to your own law."

25 And in the form of the oath whereby the kings of England were wont to bind themselves before they were made kings, the people formally demand of them: "Do you grant those just laws which the people shall choose?" The king answers,

Erras etiam tota Anglia, qui *regem quo tempore Parlamen-*
tum non habetur, plenè planéque totum regni statum regio
jure gubernare aïs. Nam neque de bello, neque de pace quod
magni sit momenti, quicquam decernere, ne in jure quidem
5 dicundo curiarum decretis intercedere potest. Jurant itaque
judices nihil se in judiciis exercendis nisi ex lege facturos,
etiamsi rex ipse dicto, aut mandato, vel etiam literis proprio
annulo obsignatis aliter imperaret. Hinc sæpius in nostro jure
rex *infans* dicitur; nec sua jura aut dignitates, nisi pueri aut
10 pupilli in modum, possidere. Spec. Just. c. 4. sect. 22. hinc
etiam illud apud nos crebrò dici solitum, *rex non potest facere*
injuriam. Quod tu hoc modo sceleratè interpretaris, *non est*
injuria quam facit rex, quia in eo non punitur. Admirabilem
hominis impudentiam et improbitatem vel hoc solo interpre-
15 tamento quis non perspiciat? *Capitis est imperare,* inquis,
non membrorum; rex Parlamenti caput est. Siccine nugarere,
si cor tibi saperet? erras iterum (sed quis finis errorum est
tuorum) in quo regis consiliarios à Parlamenti ordinibus non
distinguis; nam neque illos quidem omnes, horum verò nullos
20 reliquis non probatos eligere debebat rex; in plebeium autem

"I grant." And when you say: "While Parliament is not in session, the king governs the whole state of the kingdom fully and entirely by royal right," you again stray wide of the truth by the length and breadth of all England. For he can deter-
5 mine nothing of much moment with respect to either peace or war; nor even in administering justice can he interfere with the decisions of the courts. It is on this account the judges swear that in performing their judicial functions they will do nothing but according to law, even though the king himself
10 by word, or injunction, yes, or letter under his own seal, should command otherwise. Hence it is that the king is often said in our law to be "an infant," and to possess his rights and dignities only as a child or a ward does his: see the *Mirror of Justices,* Chapter 4, Section 22. Hence too that common say-
15 ing amongst us, "The king can do no wrong"; which you interpret in this rascally fashion: "That is no wrong which the king does, because he is not liable to be punished for it." From this single interpretation would not anyone see through the man's astonishing impudence and villainy?
20   "It belongs to the head," you say, "to command, and not to the members; the king is the head of the parliament." Would you argue so flippantly if you were wise in heart or had any gust or savor of wit?

You are mistaken again (but there is no end of your mis-
25 takes) in not distinguishing the king's Councillors from the Houses of Parliament; for the king was so bound that he might choose not even all of his Council, and none to be of the House of Lords unless approved by the rest, while as for

ordinem ut quenquam eligeret, id sibi ne sumebat quidem unquam. Quibus id muneris populus delegabat, per municipia singuli suffragiis omnium eligebantur; notissima loquor, eoque brevior sum. *Falsum* autem *esse* aïs, *quod sanctæ*
5 *Independentiæ cultores asserunt, Parlamentum à populo fuisse institutum.* Video jam quid sit cur papatum tanto impetu evertere contendas: alium ipse papatum in alvo, quod aïunt, gestas: quid enim aliud uxor uxoris, lupus ex lupa gravidus, nisi aut portentum, aut papatum aliquem novum parturire
10 debebas? Certè Papa germanus quasi jam esses, sanctos et sanctas pro arbitrio facis; reges etiam omni peccato absolvis, et, quasi strato jam hoste papa, ejus exuviis opimum te ornas. Verùm, quia papa nondum per te planè cecidit, dum libri illius tui *de Primatu,* secunda et tertia, et fortasse quarta et
15 quinta pars prodierit, qui multos mortales tædio priùs enecabit, quàm tu papam eo libro subegeris, sit satis interea, quæso, ad Antipapatum saltem posse adscendere; est altera, quam tu, præter illam Independentiam abs te irrisam, sanctorum in numerum seriò retulisti, Tyrannis regia: sanctæ ergo
20 Tyrannidis regiæ tu Pontifex eris Maximus; et nequid desit tibi ad Papales titulos, *Servus etiam servorum* eris, non Dei sed aulæ; quoniam illa Chenaani maledictio adhæsisse tibi ad præcordia videtur. *Bestiam* appellas *populum.* Quid interim

choosing anyone to the House of Commons, he never so much
as pretended to it. They whom the people appointed to that
service were chosen severally for their respective constituencies
by the votes of all; I speak now of things universally known,
and therefore I am the shorter. But you say: "It is false that
Parliament was instituted by the people, as the worshippers
of Saint Independency assert." Now I see why you strive
with so much violence to subvert the papacy: you carry another papacy in your belly, as we say. For what else should
you be in labor of, you wife of your wife, you he-wolf preg-
nant by a she-wolf, but either a monster or some new sort
of papacy? At least you make he-saints and she-saints at your
pleasure, as if you were a genuine Pope; you absolve kings
too, of sin; and as if you had laid low the Pope your enemy,
you deck and enrich yourself with his spoils. But whereas you
have not yet quite prostrated the Pope till the second and third
and perhaps the fourth and fifth part of your book *de Primatu*
come out, and whereas this will bore many poor mortals to
death ere you shall put down the Pope by it, let it suffice you
in the meantime, I beseech you, to climb up to only an Anti-
papacy. For besides that Independency that you deride, there
is another she-saint that you have canonized in good earnest,
that is, Royal Tyranny; you shall therefore be Supreme Pontiff
of Saint Tyranny Royal; and that you may want none of the
Papal titles, you shall be even "a Servant of the Servants," not
of God, but of the court; for that curse pronounced upon
Canaan seems to stick as close to you as your shirt.

You call the people "a beast." What are you then yourself?

es ipse? Non enim sacrum illud consistorium, neque sanctus ille Lupus te dominum suum aut populo exemerit aut vulgo; neque effecerit, quin sicuti es, teterrima ipse bestia sis. Certè libri sacri prophetici magnorum regum monarchiam et do-

5 minationem immanis Bestiæ nomine ac specie adumbrare solent. *Sub regibus ante Guilielmum,* inquis, *nulla Parlamenti mentio exstat.* De vocabulo Gallicano altercari non libet: res semper fuit: et Saxonicis temporibus *Concilium Sapientum* vocari solitum concedis. Sapientes autem tam sunt

10 plebis, quàm procerum ex numero. At *in statuto Mertonensi, vigesimo Hen. Tertii comitum et Baronum tantum fit mentio.* Ita te semper nomina decipiunt, qui tantùm in nominibus ætatem omnem contrivisti; nobis enim satis constat, et Quinque-portuum curatores, et decuriones urbicos, nonnun-

15 quam et mercatores illo seculo baronum nomine appellatos fuisse; neque dubium omnino est, quin Parlamenti quosque Senatores quantumvis plebeios, ætas illa jure multò potiore barones nuncupaverit: nam et anno ejusdem regis quinquagesimo secundo tam nobiles, quàm plebeios fuisse convocatos,

20 Marlbrigii statutum, sicut et reliqua fere statuta omnia disertis verbis testantur: quos etiam plebeios, comitatuum magnates Edouardus tertius in præfatione Statuti Stapli, quam perdoctè pro me recitas, vocavit; eos nimirum *qui de singulis*

For neither that Sacré Council nor your Holy Wolf can exempt you, its Sire and Seigneur, from being one of the people, nay, of the rabble rout; nor can make you other than the loathsome beast you are. Indeed the Prophets in Holy Scrip-
5 ture shadow forth to us the monarchy and dominion of great kings by the name and under the figure of a great beast.

You say: "There is no mention of a Parliament held under the kings before William." It is not worth while to quibble about a French word; the thing was always in being, and you
10 yourself admit that in Saxon times it used to be called "Concilium Sapientum," Witena-gemot, or Meeting of the Wise Men. And there are wise men among the common people as well as among the nobility. But "in the statute of Merton, in the twentieth of Henry the Third, mention is made of earls
15 and Barons only." Thus you are always imposed upon by words, who yet have frittered away your whole life in nothing else but words. For we know very well that in that age the word Baron was applied not only to the Wardens of the Cinque Ports, and to members from cities, but sometimes
20 even to tradesmen; and doubtless all members of Parliament, though commoners never so much, might then with all the greater reason be called Barons. For the Statute of Marl-bridge and most of the other statutes declare in express words that in the fifty-second year of the same king the commoners
25 as well as the lords were summoned. These commoners King Edward the Third, in the Preamble of the Statute Staple, as you very learnedly quote it for me, calls "Comitatuum Magnates," the great men of the counties, those, to wit, "that had

civitatibus pro toto comitatu venerant; qui quidem plebeium ordinem constituebant, neque erant proceres, aut esse poterant: Tradit etiam liber statutis illis vetustior, qui inscribitur, *Modus habendi Parlamenta,* licere regi cum plebe sola Parla-
5 mentum habere, legésque ferre, quamvis Comites et Episcopi non adsint; non itidem licere regi cum comitibus et episcopis, si plebs non aderit. Hujus rei ratio quoque adjicitur; quia cum nondum Comites aut episcopi constituti essent, Reges cum populo tamen Parlamenta, et Concilia peragebant: deinde
10 comites pro se tantùm veniunt; plebeii pro suo quisque municipio. Ex quo iste ordo universi populi nomine adesse intelligitur; eóque nomine et potiorem, et nobiliorem ordine patricio, omnique ex parte anteponendum esse. Sed *judicandi potestas,* inquis, *penès domum plebeiam nunquam fuit.* Ne-
15 que penès regem Angliæ fuit unquam: illud tamen memineris, principio omnem potestatem à populo fluxisse, et etiamnum proficisci. Quod et Marcus Tullius de lege Agraria pulcherrimè ostendit. *Cùm omnes potestates, imperia, curationes ab universo populo proficisci convenit, tum eas profectò maxi-*
20 *mè, quæ constituuntur ad populi fructum aliquem, et commodum; in quo et universi deligant quem populo maximè consulturum putent, et unusquisque studio et suffragio suo viam sibi ad beneficium impetrandum munire possit.* Vides Parla-

come out of the several cities to serve the whole county." And
these it was that constituted the House of Commons, and
neither were lords, nor could be. Again, a book more ancient
than those statutes, called *Modus habendi Parlamenta,* or *The*
5 *Manner of Holding Parliaments,* tells us that the King and the
Commons may hold a Parliament and enact laws though
the Earls and the Bishops are absent, but that the King with
the Earls and the Bishops cannot do so in the absence of the
Commons. And there is a reason given for it, viz., that before
10 any Earls or Bishops were made, kings yet held Parliaments
and Councils with their people; then, too, the Earls serve
for themselves only, the Commons each for his constituency.
Therefore the Commons are felt to be present in the name of
the whole nation, and in that name to be more powerful and
15 more noble than the Lords, and altogether to be preferred.

But "the power of judicature," you say, "never was vested
in the House of Commons." Nor was it ever vested in the
King of England. Remember, though, that originally all
power proceeded, and yet does proceed from the people.
20 Which Marcus Tullius excellently well shows in his oration
Of the Agrarian Law: "As it is fitting that all powers, authorities, and commissions proceed from the people as a whole,
this is especially true of those which are ordained and appointed for the people's benefit and interest. In such a case
25 on the one hand the people as a whole pick out whoever they
think will best advance their interests, and on the other hand
each individual by electioneering and by his vote may pave
the way to receiving the appointment."

mentorum veram originem, illis Saxonicis archivis longè
vetustiorem. Dum in hac luce veritatis et sapientiæ versari
licebit, frustra nobis obscuriorum ætatum tenebras offundere
conaris. Quod non eò dici â me quisquam existimet, quasi
5 ego de authoritate et prudentiâ majorum nostrorum detrahi
quicquam velim; qui in legibus bonis ferendis plus sanè præ-
stiterunt, quàm vel illa secula, vel illorum ingenium et cultus
tulisse videatur: et quamvis leges rarò non bonas irrogarent,
ignorantiæ tamen, et imbecillitatis humanæ sibi conscii, hoc
10 veluti fundamentum legum omnium posteris tradi voluerunt,
quod et nostri Jurisperiti omnes agnoscunt, ut si qua lex aut
consuetudo legi divinæ aut naturali, aut rationi denique re-
pugnaret, ea ne pro lege sancitâ habeatur. Unde tu, etiamsi
edictum fortasse aliquod aut statutum in jure nostro, quo regi
15 tyrannica potestas attribuatur, invenire posses, id, cùm et
divinæ voluntati, et naturæ, et rationi contrarium sit, intelli-
gito, ex generali et primariâ ista lege nostra quam attuli, re-
scindi apud nos, et ratum non esse; verùm tu jus nullum tale
regium apud nos invenies. Cum enim judicandi potestas pri-
20 mitùs in ipso populo fuisse constet, Anglos autem eam ab se in
regem nullâ lege regia unquam transtulisse, (neminem enim
judicare aut solet aut potest rex Angliæ, nisi per leges provisas
jam et approbatas, Fleta l. 1. c. 17.) sequitur eandem adhuc
integram atque totam in populo sitam esse; nam parium do-

Here you see the true origin of Parliaments—one much more ancient than the Saxon chronicles. Whilst we may dwell in such a light of truth and wisdom, you labor in vain to spread around us the gloom of the Dark Ages. Let no one think I say this as if I would derogate in the least from the authority and prudence of our ancestors, who certainly went further in the enacting of good laws than either those ages or their own wit and learning seem to have been capable of. And though they seldom imposed laws that were not good, yet, being conscious of the ignorance and infirmity of human nature, they chose to hand down to posterity as the foundation of all laws, this principle, which likewise all our lawyers recognize: that if any law or custom be contrary to the law of God or of nature, or, in fine, to reason, it shall not be held a valid law. Whence you may learn that even though you shall perchance succeed in finding in our law some proclamation or statute whereby tyrannical power is ascribed to the king, yet this, since it would be repugnant to the will of God, to nature, and to reason, is repealed among us by that general and primary law of ours which I have cited, and is null and void. But indeed you will find in our law no such right of kings. Since it is plain therefore that the power of judicature was originally in the people themselves, and that the English never did by any Lex Regia part with it to the king (for the kings of England neither use to judge any man, nor can do it, otherwise than according to laws already provided and approved: Fleta, Book 1, Chap. 17), it follows that this power remains yet whole and entire in the people themselves. For that it was

mui aut nunquam traditam, aut recuperari jure posse non negabis. At, *regis est,* inquis, *de vico municipium,* de eo *civitatem facere, ergo illos creat qui constituunt domum inferiorem.* At inquam, oppida et municipia regibus antiquiora

5 sunt; etiam in agris populus est populus. Jam Anglicismis tuis magnoperè delectamur; *County Court, The Turn, Hundreda;* mirâ nempe docilitate centenos Jacobæos tuos Anglicè numerare didicisti.

> *Quis expedivit* Salmasio suam Hundredam,
> 10 Picámque *docuit nostra verba conari?*
> *Magister artis venter,* et Jacobæi
> Centum, exulantis viscera marsupii regis.
> *Quod si dolosi spes refulserit nummi,*
> Ipse Antichristi qui modò primatum Papæ
> 15 Minatus uno est dissipare sufflatu,
> *Cantabit* ultrò Cardinalitium *melos.*

Longam deinde de comitibus et Baronibus dissertationem subtexis; ut ostendas regem esse eorum omnium creatorem, quod facilè concedimus, eóque nomine regibus plerunque servie-

20 bant; ideóque ne gentis liberæ deinceps judices essent, rectè providimus. *Potestatem convocandi Parlamentum quoties*

either never conveyed away to the House of Peers, or if it were, that it may be recovered from them again by law, you yourself will not deny.

But "it is in the king's power," you say, "to make a village 5 into a borough, and that into a city, and consequently the king does appoint those that constitute the Lower House." But I say towns and boroughs are more ancient than kings, and the people are the people, though they should live in the open fields.

10   And now we take huge delight in your Anglicisms, "County Court," "The Turn," "Hundred": you have learnt with amazing docility to count your hundred Jacobuses in English!

> "Who provided" Salmasius with his *Hundred,*
> 15   And "taught the magpie to attempt our words?
> His Master of Arts was his guts," and Jacobuses
> One *Hundred,* the guts of the exiled king's money-bag.
> "For if the hope of treacherous coin shall gleam,"
> The very man who but now threatened to puff away
> 20   With a single breath the Primacy of the Pope as Antichrist
> Will of his own accord "sing a tune" to praise a Cardinal.

Next you subjoin a long discourse of the Earls and the Barons, to show that the king created them all; which we readily grant, and for that reason they were most commonly 25 at the king's beck; wherefore we have done well to take care that for the future they shall not be judges of a free people. You affirm that "the power of calling parliaments as often as

libet, et quando vult dissolvendi ex omni temporis memoria penès regem esse affirmas. Tibine igitur balatroni mercenario et peregrino, perfugarum dictata exscribenti, an disertis legum nostrarum verbis fides habenda sit, infrà videbimus. *At,* 5 inquis, *reges Angliæ Parlamento majus imperium habuisse alio argumento probatur, eóque invincibili; regis potestas perpetua est et ordinaria, quæ per se sine Parlamento regnum administrat; Parlamenti extraordinaria est authoritas, et ad certas tantùm res, nec sine rege quicquam validi statuere* 10 *idonea.* Ubinam dicamus vim magnam latere hujus argumenti? an in *ordinaria et perpetuâ?* Atqui minores multi magistratus habent potestatem ordinariam et perpetuam, quos Irenarchas vocamus; an summam ergo habent? suprà etiam dixi potestatem regi idcirco traditam à populo fuisse, ut videret 15 authoritate sibi commissâ ne quid contra legem fiat; útque leges custodiret nostras, non ut nobis imponeret suas: regis proinde potestatem nisi in regni curiis et per eas, esse nullam: imo populi potiùs ordinaria est omnis, qui per duodecim viros de omnibus judicat. Atque hinc est quòd interrogatus in 20 curiâ reus, *Cui te permittis judicandum?* respondet semper ex more atque lege, *Deo et populo,* non Deo et regi, aut regis vicario. Parlamenti autem authoritas, quæ re et veritate, sum-

he pleases, and of dissolving them when he pleases, has belonged to the king time out of mind." Whether you, mercenary foreign buffoon, who transcribe what some fugitives
dictate to you, or the explicit words of our own laws are more
5 to be trusted in this matter, we shall inquire hereafter. "But,"
say you, "there is another argument, and an invincible one,
to prove the power of the kings of England superior to that
of the Parliament. The king's power is continuous and of
course, and by itself administers the government without the
10 Parliament; that of the Parliament is out of course, and limited to particulars only, and incapable of enacting anything
valid without the king." Where should I say the great force
of this argument lies hid? In the words "of course and continuous"? Why, many inferior magistrates, whom we call
15 justices of the peace, have a power of course and continuous.
Have they therefore the supreme power? And I have said
already that the king's power was committed to him by the
people for the definite purpose that by the authority entrusted
to him he should see that nothing were done contrary to law,
20 and that he might watch over our laws, not lay his own upon
us; and consequently that the king has no power but in and
through the courts of the realm; nay, all the ordinary power
is rather the people's, who determine all controversies themselves by juries of twelve men. And hence it is, that when a
25 defendant is asked in court, "How will you be tried?" he
answers always, according to law and custom, "By God and
my country"—not by God and the King or the King's deputy.
But the authority of the Parliament, which indeed and in

ma populi potestas in illum senatum collata est, si extraordinaria est dicenda, id tantùm propter ejus eminentiam dicitur;
alioqui, ut notum est, ipsi ordines appellantur, non extra ordinem ergó; et si non actu, quod aïunt, virtute tamen perpe-
5 tuum habent in omnes curias et potestates ordinarias jus atque
authoritatem; idque sine rege. Offendunt nunc limatulas,
opinor, aures tuas nostrorum barbaræ locutiones: cujus ego si
vacaret, aut operæ pretium esset, tot barbarismos hoc uno
libro notare possem, quot si pro merito lueres, profectò omnes
10 puerorum ferulas in te frangi oporteret, nec tot aureos tibi
dari, quot illi quondam pessimo poëtæ; colaphos longè plures.
Prodigium esse aïs, *omnibus portentis opinionum monstro-*
sius, quod fanatici personam regis à potestate ejus sejungant.
Equidem dicta singulorum non præstitero; personam autem
15 si pro homine vis dici, separari à potestate ejus nec absurdè
posse Chrysostomus haud fanaticus docere te potuit; qui præceptum Apostoli de potestatibus ita explanat, ut potestatem
ibi et rem, non hominem intelligi asserat. Quidni dicam regem, qui contra leges quid facit, id agere ut privatum vel ty-
20 rannum, non ut regem legitimâ potestate præditum? Tu si

truth is the supreme power of the people committed to that senate, this power, I say, if it may be called extraordinary, out of order, or out of course, must be so called by reason of its eminence only. And another reason: our Estates in Parliament, as everybody knows, are called *Orders,* and therefore cannot properly be said to be out of order; and they have a continuous control and authority, if not in act, or actually, as the phrase goes, yet potentially and virtually, over all courts and ordinary powers,—and this without the king.

And now it seems our barbarous terms grate upon your critical ears, forsooth! whereas, if I had leisure, or it were worth the trouble, I could reckon up so many barbarisms of yours in this one book that if you were to be whipped for them as you deserve, all schoolboys' ferules must surely be broken upon you; nor would you receive so many pieces of gold as that worst of poets did aforetime, but many more boxes on the ear. You say: "It is a prodigy more monstrous than all the most absurd opinions in the world put together, that the madmen should make a distinction betwixt the king's person and his power." I will not quote what every author has said upon this subject; but if by *person* you mean the *man,* then Chrysostom, who was no madman, might have taught you that the person might without absurdity be distinguished from the power; for he explains the apostle's command to be subject to the higher powers, as meant of the thing, the power itself, and not of the man. And why may not I say that a king who acts any thing contrary to law, acts so far forth as a private person or a tyrant, and not as a king invested with

uno in homine posse plures esse personas, eásque ab ipso homine, sensu et cogitatione separabiles non intelligis, et sensus
communis et latinitatis planè expers es. Sed hoc eò dicis, ut
reges peccato omni absolvas, utque erepto Papæ primatu in-
5   dutum te esse existimemus: *Rex,* inquis, *non posse peccare*
intelligitur, quia peccatum ejus pœna non consequitur. Quisquis ergo non punitur, non peccat; non furtum sed pœna facit
furem: Salmasius Grammaticus non facit solœcismos, quia
manum ferulæ subduxit; post eversum à te Papam sint isti sanè
10   Pontificatûs tui canones, vel certè indulgentiæ tuæ, sive sanctæ Tyrannidis, sive sanctæ Servitutis Pontifex dici mavis. Congesta in extremo capite maledicta tua in *Anglicanæ reipub. et*
Ecclesiæ statum prætereo: hoc enim habent tui similes, homo
contemptissime; ut quidque plurimâ dignum est laude, id
15   solent per calumniam maximè vituperare. Sed de jure regio
apud nos, seu potiùs de jure populi in regem ne quid temere
affirmâsse videar, proferre ex ipsis monumentis non gravabor,
quamvis pauca quidem de multis, ea tamen quibus liquidò
satis constabit, Anglos ex lege et instituto, et more etiam ma-
20   jorum suorum, regem nuper judicavisse. Post Romanorum

legal authority? If you do not know that there may be in one
and the same man more persons or capacities than one, and
that those capacities may in thought and conception be severed
from the man himself, you are altogether ignorant both of
5 Latinity and of common sense. But this you say to absolve
kings from all sin, and to make us believe that you are invested
with that Primacy you have snatched from the Pope.

"The king," you say, "is supposed incapable of crime, because no punishment follows upon any crime of his." Who-
10 ever therefore is not punished offends not: it is not the theft
but the punishment that makes the thief! Salmasius the
Grammarian commits no solecisms now, because he has
pulled his hand from under the ferule! When you have over-
thrown the Pope, let these, then, be the canons of your pon-
15 tificate, or at least your indulgences, whether you shall choose
to be called the High Priest of Saint Tyranny, or of St.
Slavery.—I pass by the foul abusive language which at the
last of your chapter you have heaped upon "the state of the
English Commonwealth and Church"; it is common to such
20 as you, contemptible varlet, to rail most at those things that
are most praiseworthy.

But that I may not seem to have asserted anything rashly
concerning the right of the king among us, or rather concerning the people's right over the king, I will not grudge the
25 task to cite from our records themselves a few things indeed
of many, yet such as will make it evident that the English
lately tried their king according to the settled laws of the
realm and the customs of their ancestors. After the Romans

ex insula discessum sui juris Britanni circiter annos 40. sine regibus fuere; quos primos creârunt, eorum nonnullos supplicio affecere. Britannos ob id Gildas, longe alio, atque tu facis, nomine reprehendit; nempe non quòd reges necavissent, 5 sed quòd injudicatos, vel ut ejus verbis utar, *non pro veri examinatione*. Vortigernus ob incestas cum filia nuptias, teste Nennio historicorum nostrorum post Gildam antiquissimo, damnatur *à beato Germano, et omni concilio Britonum,* ejúsque filio Guorthemiro regnum traditur. Haud multò hæc 10 post Augustini obitum gesta sunt: unde vanitas tua facilè redarguitur, qui suprà asseruisti, primum omnium Papam, et nominatim Zachariam docuisse, judicari reges posse. Circa annum Christi 600. Morcantius, qui tunc temporis in Cambria regnabat, propter cædem patrui ab Oudoceo Landaviæ 15 Episcopo in exilium damnatur; quamquam is exilii sententiam latifundiis quibusdam ecclesiæ donatis redemit. Ad Saxones jam veniamus; quorum jura cum reperiantur, facta prætermittam. Saxones Germanis oriundos memineris; qui nec infinitam aut liberam potestatem regibus dedere, et de 20 rebus majoribus consultare omnes solebant; ex quibus intelligere est, Parlamentum, si solum nomen excipias, etiam apud Saxonum majores summâ authoritate viguisse. Et ab iis quidem Concilium Sapientum passim nominatur ab ipsis usque Ethelberti temporibus, quem *decreta judiciorum juxta ex-*

quitted this island, the Britons for about forty years were *sui juris,* and without kings; of those whom they first set up, some they put to death. Gildas reprehends them for that, upon a very different ground from yours,—not for killing
5 their kings, but for killing them without trial, or, to use his own words, "without an inquiry into the truth." Vortigern, as Nennius informs us, the most ancient of all historians next to Gildas, was for his incestuous marriage with his own daughter condemned "by St. Germain and a general council
10 of the Britons," and his son Vortimer set up in his stead. This came to pass not long after St. Augustine's death; which easily disproves your unfounded statement that it was a Pope, namely Zachary, who first asserted the lawfulness of judging kings. About the year of our Lord 600, Morcantius, who
15 then reigned in Wales, was by Oudoceus, bishop of Llandaff, condemned to exile for the murder of his uncle, though he bought off the sentence by bestowing certain landed estates upon the church.

  Come we now to the Saxons; since their laws are extant I
20 shall quote none of their deeds. Remember that the Saxons were sprung from Germans, who never gave their kings absolute or unlimited power, and who used to hold a council of the whole tribe upon the more weighty affairs of government; whence we may perceive that Parliament, the name itself only
25 excepted, flourished in high authority even among the ancestors of the Saxons. By these it is called, in fact, Council of the Wise Men, all the way from those very times down to the time of Ethelbert, who, says Bede, "with a Council of Wise

empla Romanorum cum Concilio Sapientum constituisse
memorat Beda. Sic Edwinus Northanymbrorum, Inas occi-
dentalium Saxonum rex, *habito cum sapientibus et Seniori-*
bus concilio, novas leges promulgavit: alias Aluredus edidit
5 *ex concilio* item *prudentissimorum; atque iis,* inquit, *omnibus*
placuit edici earum observationes. His atque aliis multis hujusmodi locis luce clarius est, delectos etiam ex plebe conciliis
maximis interfuisse; nisi siquis Proceres solos sapientes esse
arbitratur. Extat etiam apud nos perantiquus legum liber
10 cui titulus *Speculum Justiciariorum,* in quo traditur primos
Saxones, post Britanniam subactam, cùm reges crearent, ab
iis jusjurandum exigere consuevisse, se, ut quemvis alium è
populo, legibus ac judiciis subjectos fore: cap. 1. sect. 2.
ibidem aït jus esse et æquum ut rex suos in Parlamento habeat
15 pares, qui de injuriis quas vel rex vel regina, fecerit, cogno-
scerent; regnante Aluredo sancitum legibus fuisse, ut singulis
annis Parlamentum bis Londini, vel eo sæpiùs, si opus esset,
haberetur. Quæ lex cùm pessimo juris neglectu in desuetudinem abiisset, duabus sub Edouardo Tertio sanctionibus re-
20 novata est. In alio etiam antiquo manuscripto, qui Modus
Parlamenti inscribitur, hæc legimus; si rex Parlamentum
prius dimiserit, quàm ea omnia transigantur quorum causa
concilium indictum erat, perjurii reus erit; et juramentum
illud quod regnum initurus dederat, violâsse censebitur.
25 Quomodo enim, quod juratus est, justas leges concedit, quas
populus elegerit, si earum eligendi facultatem petenti populo

Men made decrees patterned upon those of the Romans." So Edwin king of the Northumbrians, and Ina king of the West Saxons, made new laws, "having held a Council with their wise men and the elders of the people." Other laws king Alfred likewise promulgated "from an assemblage of his wisest men," and he says: "All of these decreed their observance." From these and many other like passages it is clear as day that chosen men, even from amongst the common people, were members of the supreme councils—unless we must believe that no men but the nobility are wise.

We have likewise a very ancient law-book, called the *Mirror of Justices,* in which we are told that the early Saxons, when they had subdued Britain and set up kings, required an oath of them to submit to the judgment of the law as much as any of their subjects, Chap. 1, Sect. 2. In the same place it is said that it is but just and right that the king have his peers in Parliament to take cognizance of wrongs done by the king or the queen; and that a law made in king Alfred's time required Parliament to be holden twice a year at London, or oftener if need were: which law, when through neglect it grew into disuse, was renewed by two re-enactments in King Edward III's time. And in another ancient manuscript, called *The Manner of Parliament,* we read: "If the king shall dissolve Parliament before it have disposed of all those things wherefore the council was summoned, he is guilty of perjury, and shall be deemed to have broken his coronation oath." For how does he grant, as he is sworn to do, those good laws which the people chose, if he hinders the people from choos-

non dat, vel rariùs Parlamentum convocando, vel citiùs di-
mittendo quàm res populi ferunt? Jus autem illud jurandum,
quo rex Angliæ se obligat, nostri jurisperiti pro sanctissimâ
lege semper habuere. Quod autem maximis reipub. periculis
5 remedium inveniri potest (qui solus convocandi Parlamenti
finis erat) si conventus ille magnus, et augustissimus ad regis
libitum stultissimi sæpe et pervicacissimi dissolvetur? Posse
à Parlamento abesse, proculdubiò minus est, quàm Parlamentum dissolvere: at rex per leges nostras illo Modorum libro
10 traditas, abesse à Parlamento, nisi planè ægrotaret, neque potuit, neque debuit: et ne tum quidem nisi inspecto ejus corpore à duodecim regni paribus, qui de adversa regis valetu-
dine testimonium perhibere in senatu possent: soléntne servi
cum domino sic agere? Contrà verò plebeius ordo, sine quo
15 Parlamentum haberi non potest, etiam à rege convocatus
potuit non adesse, et secessione factâ, de repub. malè gestâ
cum rege expostulare: quod et prædictus liber testatur. Verùm, quod caput est, inter leges Edouardi regis vulgò Con-
fessoris, una est eximia, quæ de regis officio tractat; cui rex
20 officio si desit, *nomen regis in eo non constabit.* Hoc quid
esset, ne non satis intelligeretur, Chilperici Francorum regis
exemplum subnectit, cui idcircò regnum à Populo abrogatum
erat. Puniri autem malum regem ex legis hujus sententia
oportere, significabat ille S. Edouardi gladius cui nomen Cur-

ing them, either by summoning Parliaments seldomer, or by dissolving them sooner, than the people's business requires? That oath which the kings of England take at their coronation has always been looked upon by our lawyers as a most
5 sacred law. And what remedy can be found for greatest dangers to the state (which is the very end of summoning Parliaments) if that great and august assembly may be dissolved at the pleasure (oftentimes) of a silly and headstrong king?

To absent himself from Parliament is certainly less than to
10 dissolve it; and yet by our laws, as the aforementioned *Manner* reports them, the King neither can nor ought to absent himself from Parliament unless he be quite ill, nor even then unless his body have been inspected by twelve peers of the realm, who may present in Parliament the evidence of his
15 indisposition. Do slaves behave thus to a master? On the other hand the House of Commons, without which Parliament cannot be held, may, though summoned by the King, absent itself, and, having withdrawn, expostulate with the king concerning maladministration, as the same book has it.
20 But—and this is the greatest thing of all—among the laws of King Edward commonly called the Confessor there is a very excellent law relating to the kingly duty: which if the king do not discharge as he ought, then, says the law, "he shall not retain the name of king." Lest these words should
25 not be sufficiently understood, it subjoins the example of Chilperic king of the Franks, whom the people for that cause deposed. That by this law a wicked king is liable to punishment was betokened by that sword of Saint Edward, called

tana erat, quem in regum creatione et pompâ gestare Comes
Palatii solebat; *in signum,* inquit noster Matthæus Paris,
quòd et regem, si oberret, habeat de jure potestatem cohi-
bendi: gladio autem nemo ferè nisi capite punitur. Hanc

5 legem, cum aliis boni illius Edouardi, Gulielmus ipse conquæstor anno regni quarto ratam habuit: et frequentissimo
Anglorum Concilio prope Verulamium religiosissimè juratus
confirmavit: quo facto non solùm jus omne belli, si quod in
nos habuit, ipse extinxit, sed etiam hujus legis judicio atque

10 sententiæ se subjecit. Ejus etiam filius Henricus cùm in
omnes Edouardi leges, tùm in hanc quoque juravit; atque iis
duntaxat conditionibus, vivente adhuc fratre Roberto natu
majore, in regem est electus. Jurârunt eadem omnes deinceps
reges, antequam insignia regni acciperent. Hinc celebris ille

15 et antiquus noster jurisconsultus Bractonus. l. 1. c. 8. *Non*
est rex, ubi dominatur voluntas, et non lex. Et. l. 3. c. 9. *rex*
est dum benè regit; tyrannus, dum populum sibi creditum
violentâ opprimit dominatione. Et ibidem, *exercere debet rex*
potestatem juris, ut vicarius et minister Dei: potestas autem

20 *injuriæ diaboli est, non Dei: cum declinat ad injuriam rex,*
diaboli minister est. Eadem ferme habet vetustus alter ju-

Curtana, which the Earl Palatine used to carry in the proces-
sion at a coronation, "in token," says our historian Matthew
Paris, "that he has authority by law to restrain and control
even the king if he go astray": but punishment with a sword is
5 hardly other than capital. This law, together with the other
laws of good King Edward, did William the Conqueror himself ratify in the fourth year of his reign, and in a very full
council of the English held at Verulam did with a most solemn
oath confirm. By so doing he not only extinguished his right of
10 conquest, if he ever had any over us, but even subjected himself to judgment according to the tenor of this very law. His
son Henry also swore to the observance of king Edward's
laws—this among the rest, and upon those terms only was he
chosen king while his elder brother Robert was alive. The
15 same oath was taken by all succeeding kings before they
were crowned. Hence, saith our ancient and famous lawyer
Bracton, in his first book, Chapter viii,

> "There is no king in the case
> Where will rules and law takes not place."

20 And in his third book, Chapter ix. "A king is a king so long
as he rules well; he becomes a tyrant when he crushes with
despotic violence the people that are trusted to his charge."
And in the same chapter, "The king ought to use the power
of law and right as God's servant and vicegerent; the power
25 to do wrong is the Devil's, and not God's; when the king turns
aside to do wrong, he is the servant of the Devil." Almost
these very words hath another ancient lawyer, the author of

risconsultus, libri illius author qui Fleta inscribitur, memor nempe uterque et legis illius Eduardinæ verè quidem regiæ, et regulæ illius in jure nostro primariæ à me suprà dictæ, qua nihil Dei legibus et rationi contrarium haberi pro lege potest; 5 uti nec tyrannus pro rege, nec minister diaboli pro ministro Dei. Cùm itaque lex maximè ratio recta sit, siquidem regi, siquidem Dei ministro obediendum est, eâdem prorsùs et ratione et lege, tyranno et diaboli ministro erit resistendum. Et quoniam de nomine sæpius quàm de re ambigitur, tradunt 10 iidem, regem Angliæ, etiamsi nomen regis nondum perdiderit, judicari tamen, ut quilibet è vulgo, et posse et debere. Bracton. l. 1. c. 8. Fleta. l. 1. c. 17. *Non debet esse rege major quisquam in exhibitione juris; minimus autem esse debet in judicio suscipiendo, si peccat;* alii legunt, *si petat.* Judicari 15 igitur cùm debeat rex noster, sive tyranni sub nomine, sive regis, quos habeat item judices legitimos dictu difficile non debet esse. Eosdem consulere authores haud pejus erit. Bracton. l. 2. c. 16. Fleta. l. 1. c. 17. *In populo regendo rex habet superiores, legem, per quam factus est, rex, et curiam suam,* 20 *videlicet Comites et Barones: Comites dicuntur quasi socii regis; et qui habet socium, habet magistrum; et ideò si rex*

the famous book called "Fleta." Both of them in fact remembered that true *Lex Regia,* that truly royal law of King Edward, as well as that fundamental maxim in our law which
I mentioned before, by which nothing that is contrary to the
5 laws of God and to reason can be accounted a law, any more
than a tyrant can be said to be a king, or a servant of the
Devil a servant of God. Since therefore the law is right reason
above all else, then if we are bound to obey a king and a
servant of God, by the very same reason and the very same law
10 we ought to resist a tyrant and a servant of the Devil.

Now because controversies arise oftener about names than
about things, the same authors tell us that a king of England,
though he have not yet lost the name of king, yet can be
judged and ought to be judged like anyone of the common
15 people. Bracton, Book I, Chapter viii; Fleta, Book I, Chap.
xvii: "No man ought to be greater than the king in the administration of justice; but he himself ought to be as little as
the least in receiving justice, if he offends." Others read: "if
he require."

20 Since our king therefore is liable to be judged, whether by
the name of tyrant or of king, it ought not be difficult to say
who are his lawful judges. Nor will it be amiss to consult the
same authors upon that point. Bracton, Book II, Chap. xvi;
Fleta, Book I, Chap. xvii: "The king has his superiors in the
25 government: the law, which made him king, and his court, to
wit, the Earls and the Barons. *Comites* (earls) are as much
as to say the king's fellows; and he that has a fellow has a
master; and therefore, if the king will be without a bridle,

fuerit sine fræno, id est sine lege, debent ei frænum ponere.
Baronum autem nomine plebeium ordinem comprehendi
supra ostendimus; quin et Pares etiam Parlamenti eosdem
fuisse dictos, libri legum nostrarum antiqui passim tradunt:
5 et imprimis liber ille cui titulus, Parlamenti modus; *Eligentur*
inquit *de omnibus regni paribus* 25, quorum erunt *quinque*
milites, quinque cives id est urbium delegati, *quinque muni-*
cipes: et duo milites pro comitatu majorem vocem habent in
concedendo et contradicendo quàm major comes Angliæ; et
10 meritò quidem; illi enim pro tota aliqua provincia, aut municipio suffragia ferunt, isti pro se quisque duntaxat. Comites
autem illos *Codicillares,* quos vocas, et *rescriptitios,* cùm feudales jam nulli sint, ad judicandum regem à quo creabantur
minimè omnium idoneos esse, quis non videt? Cùm itaque
15 jus nostrum sit, ut est in illo speculo antiquo, regem habere
pares, qui in Parlamento cognoscant et judicent, *si quid rex*
in aliquem populi sui peccaverit, si notissimum sit licere apud
nos cuivis è populo in minoribus quibusque curiis injuriarum
actionem regi intendere, quantò justius est, quantóque magis
20 necessarium, si rex in universos peccaverit, ut habeat qui eum
non refrænare solùm et coërcere, sed judicare et punire possint. Pessimè enim et ridiculè institutam esse eam necesse est
rempub. in qua de minimis regum injuriis etiam privato cuivis
cautum sit, de maximis nihil in commune provisum, nihil de

that is, lawless, they ought to bridle him." That the Commons
are comprehended in the word Barons has been shown already; nay, our old law-books tell us quite generally that they
were called Peers of Parliament: the *Manner of Parliament,*
5 especially, says: "From all the peers of the realm there shall
be chosen five and twenty," of whom there shall be "five
knights, five citizens," that is, representatives of cities, "and
five burgesses. Two knights of the shire, furthermore, have a
greater vote in granting and rejecting than the greatest Earl
10 of England." And it is but reasonable they should, for they
vote for some whole county or borough or other constituency,
the Earls for themselves only. And who can fail to see that
those Earls "by Patent" as you call them, and Earls "by Writ,"
since we have now none that hold by ancient feudal tenure,
15 are less fit than anyone else to try the king who conferred
their honors upon them? Since therefore by our law, as appears by that old book, *The Mirror,* the king has his peers,
who in Parliament have cognizance and jurisdiction "if the
king have done wrong to any of his people"; and if it is noto-
20 rious, as it is, that any individual subject may even in inferior
courts sue the king for damages, how much more just, how
much more necessary is it that if the king have done wrong
to his whole people, there should be such as have authority
not only to bridle him and keep him within bounds, but to
25 judge and punish him? For that government must needs be
very ill and very ridiculously constituted, in which remedy is
provided for even private persons in case of the least injuries
done by the king, and no remedy, no redress for the greatest,

salute omnium, quo minùs liceat ei universos sine lege perdere, qui ne unum quidem lædere per legem poterat. Comites
autem esse regis judices, cum ostensum sit neque decere neque
expedire, sequitur judicium illud totum ad plebeium ordi-
5 nem, qui et Pares regni, et Barones, et populi totius potestate
sibi delegatâ præditi sunt, jure optimo pertinere. Cum enim
(ut in nostro jure scriptum est, quod suprà attuli) plebs sola
cum rege sine comitibus aut episcopis Parlamentum constituat, quia rex cum sola plebe, etiam ante comites aut episco-
10 pos natos, Parlamenta peragere solebat, eâdem prorsus ratione
plebs sola supremam et sine rege, et regem ipsum judicandi
potestatem habebit, quòd etiam ante ullum regem creatum,
ipsa universi populi nomine concilia et parlamenta peragere,
judicare, ferre leges, ipsa reges creare solita erat; non ut po-
15 pulo dominarentur, sed ut rem populi administrarent. Quem
si rex contrà injuriis afficere, et servitute opprimere conatus
fuerit, ex ipsa legis nostræ sententia nomen regis in eo non
constat, rex non est; quòd si rex non sit, quid est quod ei pares
ampliùs quæramus? Tyrannum enim jam re ipsa ab omnibus

no care taken for the safety of the whole; no provision made but that the king, who by law could not hurt even one of his subjects, may, without any law to the contrary, ruin all of them together!

5   Yet since I have shown that it is neither fit nor proper for the Earls to be the king's judges, it follows that that jurisdiction does wholly, and by the best possible right, belong to the Commons, who are Peers of the realm, and Barons as well, and are vested with the power and authority of all the
10 people committed to them. Now as we find it expressly written in our law, which I have already cited, that the Commons alone, together with the king, made a good Parliament without the Lords or the Bishops, because Kings used to hold Parliaments with their Commons alone before either Lords or
15 Bishops came into existence; by the very same reason the Commons apart shall have a power that is sovereign, and independent of the king, and capable of judging the king himself; because before there ever was a king, they in the name of the whole body of the nation had been wont to hold Councils and
20 Parliaments, to judge, to pass laws, yea to make kings: not that these might lord it over the people, but that they might manage the people's business. But if the king instead shall try to do them wrong and crush them into servitude, then by the express tenor of our law the name of king remains not in him;
25 he is no king; and if he be no king, why should we have his Peers far to seek? For being then by all good men adjudged already and actually a tyrant, there are none but who are

bonis judicatum nulli non satis pares atque idonei sunt, qui
supplicio mactandum esse pro tribunali judicent. Hæc cùm
ita sint, tot testimoniis, tot legibus prolatis, abundè hoc demùm, quod erat propositum, evicisse arbitror, cùm judicare
5 regem penès plebem jure optimo sit, cúmque plebs regem de
repub. déque ecclesia, sine spe ulla sanitatis, pessimè meritum
supplicio ultimo affecerit, rectè atque ordine, exque repub.
suáque fide, dignitate, legibus denique patriis fecisse. Neque
possum hìc non gratulari mihi de majoribus nostris, qui non
10 minore prudentiâ ac libertate, quàm Romani olim, aut Græcorum præstantissimi, hanc rempub. instituerunt; neque poterunt illi, siquid nostrarum rerum sentiunt, non sibi etiam
gratulari de posteris suis; qui tam sapienter institutam, tantâ
libertate fundatam ab impotenti regis dominatione, cùm re-
15 dacti penè in servitutem essent, tam fortiter, támque prudenter vindicârunt.

CAPUT IX.

SATIS jam arbitror palàm esse, regem Angliæ etiam
Anglorum legibus judicari posse; suos habere judices
legitimos, quod erat probandum. Quid tu porro? (nam
20 quæ tua repetis, ad ea non repetam mea) *ex rebus nunc ipsis
propter quas comitia indici solent, proclive,* inquis, *est osten-*

Peers good enough for him, and a court capable enough to
pronounce sentence of death upon him.

These things being so, I think that by means of the many
authorities and laws which have been cited I have sufficiently
5 proved what I undertook, to wit, that since authority to try the
King is by very good right lodged with the Commons, and
since they have actually put the king to death for the mischief
which without any hope of amendment he had done both in
church and in state,—in view of all this, they have acted
10 justly and regularly, for the interest of the State, and in the
discharge of their trust, in a manner becoming their dignity,
and, finally, according to the law of the land. And here I
cannot but congratulate myself upon our ancestors, who
founded this State with no less prudence and liberty than did
15 the most excellent of the ancient Romans or Grecians; and
they likewise, if they have any knowledge of our affairs, cannot but congratulate themselves upon their posterity, who,
when almost reduced to slavery, yet with such wisdom and
courage reclaimed that state, so wisely founded upon so much
20 liberty, from a king's outrageous despotism.

CHAPTER IX.

I THINK it by this time sufficiently evident that the king
of England may be judged even by the laws of England,
and that he has his lawful judges; which was the thing
to be proved. How do you go on?—for to your mere repe-
25 titions I shall not repeat my answers. "Now even from the
very business for which Parliaments are wont to be sum-

dere regem esse supra Parlamentum. Sit sanè proclive quantum voles, in quo præcipitem te dari jam statim senties. *Parlamentum, inquis, congregari solet ad majoris momenti negotia in quibus regni salus et populi versatur.* Si rex Parla-

5 mentum convocat ad procurandas res populi, non suas, neque id nisi assensu eorum atque arbitrio quos convocat, quid aliud est, obsecro, nisi minister populi et procurator? cùm, sine suffragiis eorum quos populus mittit, ne tantillum quidem, neque de aliis, neque de seipso decernere possit. Quod etiam

10 argumento est, officium esse regis, toties Parlamentum convocare, quoties populus id petit: quandoquidem et res populi, non regis, iis comitiis tractantur, idque populi arbitrio. Quamvis enim regis quoque assensus honoris causâ peti soleret, quem in rebus minoris momenti ad privatorum duntaxat

15 commoda spectantibus poterat non præbere, poterat pro illa formula dicere, *rex deliberabit,* de iis tamen, quæ ad salutem omnium communem et libertatem pertinebant, prorsus abnuere nullo modo poterat, cùm id et contra juramentum regium esset, quo veluti lege firmissimâ tenebatur, et contra

20 præcipuum magnæ Chartæ articulum, c. 29. *Non negabimus, non differemus cuiquam jus aut justitiam.* Non negabit rex

moned, it appears that the king is above the Parliament. The way to this demonstration," you say, "slopes down steep and easy ahead." Let it slope as steep as you will, for you shall instantly feel yourself hurled down it headlong. "The Par-
5 liament," you say, "is wont to be assembled upon affairs of uncommon weight, wherein the safety of the realm and of the people is concerned." If therefore the king call Parliament to attend to the people's business, not his own, nor to settle even that but by the consent and at the discretion of those he
10 has called, what is he more than the people's servant and agent? For without the suffrages of them that are delegated by the people he cannot resolve the least thing with relation either to others or even to himself. Which also goes to show that it is the king's duty to call Parliaments whenever and as
15 often as the people ask, since it is the people's business, and not the king's, that is to be treated of by that assembly, and to be ordered as the people wish.

For although the king's assent also were asked customarily out of respect, and although in lesser matters, concerning the
20 welfare of private persons only, he might refuse it, and use that form, "The king will advise," yet in affairs that con- cerned the public safety and the liberty of all the people he had no negative voice whatsoever; for this would have been both against his coronation oath, which was as binding upon
25 him as the most rigorous law, and against the chief article of Magna Charta, chap. 29: "We will not refuse, nor will we delay, right and justice to any man." Shall it be out of the king's power to refuse right and justice, and shall it therefore

jus aut justitiam, negabit ergo justas leges? non cuiquam,
an ergo omnibus? ne in ulla quidem Curiâ minori, num ergò
in Senatu supremo? an verò rex ullus tantum sibi arrogabit,
ut quid justum sit, quid utile, se unum universo populo scire
5 meliùs existimet? Cùm *ad hoc creatus et electus sit, ut justitiam faciat universis,* Bracton. l. 3. c. 9. per eas nimirum leges
quas vulgus elegerit. Unde illud in archivis nostris 7 H. 4.
Rot. Parl. num. 59. *non est ulla regis prærogativa, quæ ex
justitia et æquitate quicquam derogat.* Et reges olim acta Par-
10 lamenti confirmare recusantes, Chartam videlicet magnam
et hujusmodi alia, majores nostri sæpenumerò armis coëgerunt; neque propterea minùs valere illas leges, aut minùs legitimas esse jurisperiti nostri statuunt; quandoquidem assen-
sum rex iis decretis coactus præbuit, quibus jure atque sponte
15 assentiri debebat. Tu dum contendis aliarum etiam gentium
reges in potestate vel Synedrii vel Senatus, vel Concilii sui
æquè fuisse, non nos in servitutem, sed illas in libertatem
asseris: in quo idem facere pergis quod ab initio fecisti, quódque faciunt pragmaticorum stultissimi, ut incauti seipsos in
20 lite sæpiùs contra veniant. At nos scilicet fatemur *regem, ubicunque absit, in Parlamento tamen censeri præsentem vi potes-*

be in his power to refuse the enacting of just laws? Shall it be out of his power to refuse justice to any man, and shall it therefore be in his power to refuse it to all men? Shall it be out of his power to refuse it in any inferior court, and therefore be 5 in his power to refuse it in the highest court of all? Or can any king be so arrogant as to suppose that he—one person— knows what is just and profitable better than the whole body of the people? Especially, since "he is created and chosen for this very end and purpose, to do justice to all," as Bracton says, 10 lib. iii. c. 9—that is, according to those laws which "the people" have chosen. Hence this passage in our records, 7 H. IV, Rot. Parl. num. 59: "There is no royal prerogative that derogates aught from justice and equity." And formerly when kings have refused to confirm Acts of Parliament, to wit, 15 Magna Charta, and others the like, our ancestors often have brought them to it by force of arms; nor yet are our lawyers of opinion that those acts are on that account any less valid, or any less the law of the land, since the king was forced to assent to decrees which he ought in justice to have assented to volun- 20 tarily. Again, while striving to prove that kings of other nations have been as much under the power of their Sanhedrim or Senate or Council as our kings were, you do not argue us into slavery, but them into liberty. In which you keep on doing over again what you have done from the very beginning 25 of your discourse, and what incompetent practitioners do— argue unawares against their own side of the case.

We grant, you think, that "the king, wherever he absent himself, yet is supposed still to be present in his Parliament by

tatis: ergò quodcunque illic agitur à rege ipso actum intelligi.
Tum quasi bolum aliquem nactus esses aut mercedulam, illorum recordatione Caroleorum delinitus, *accipimus,* inquis,
quod dant: accipe igitur, quo dignus es, magnum malum;
5 non enim damus, quod sperabas, inde sequi *curiam illam non
alia potiri potestate quàm à rege delegata.* Si enim dicitur,
potestas regis, quæcunque ea sit, à Parlamento abesse non
potest, an suprema continuò dicitur? annon potiùs transferri
in Parlamentum potestas regia videtur, útque minor majore
10 contineri? sanè si Parlamentum potest, nolente et invito rege,
acta ejus et privilegia quibusvis data revocare atque rescindere,
si ipsius regis prærogativas, prout videtur, circumscribere, si
proventus ejus annuos et impensas aulæ, si famulitium ipsum,
si totam denique rem domesticam regis moderari, si vel inti-
15 mos ejus consiliarios atque amicos amovere, vel etiam è sinu
abripere ad supplicium potest, si cuivis denique de plebe à
rege ad Parlamentum quacunque de re provocatio est lege
data, non itidem à Parlamento ad regem, quæ omnia et posse
fieri, et fuisse sæpiùs facta, cum monumenta publica, tum
20 legum nostrarum consultissimi testantur, neminem esse arbitror, modò mens ei sana sit, qui Parlamentum supra regem
esse non fateatur. Nam in interregno etiam Parlamentum

virtue of his power, insomuch that whatever is transacted
there is supposed to be done by the king himself." Then as if
you had made a great haul, or, for that matter, a pittance
either, and tickled as you are with the remembrance of your
5 gold-pieces from Charles, "We take," you say, "what they
give us." Take what you deserve, then, a malediction. For
we grant not what you were hoping we granted, viz., that
thence this follows: "That court possesses no other power
than is delegated from the king." For if it is said that the
10 king's power, be it what it will, cannot be absent from Parliament, is it necessarily and immediately said that that power is
supreme? Does not the royal power rather appear to be transferred to Parliament, and, as a lesser, to be comprised in its
greater? Certainly, if Parliament may rescind the king's acts
15 without his consent and against his refusal, and revoke privileges granted by him to whomsoever; if they may set bounds
to the king's own prerogative, as they see cause; if they may
regulate his yearly revenue, and the expenses of his court, his
very retinue, and, in sum, all the concerns of his household;
20 if they may remove even his bosom friends and counsellors,
nay, pluck them from his lap to the scaffold; finally, if unto
any soever of the people there is granted by law an appeal in
any cause from the king to Parliament, but not so from Parliament to the king—all of which both our public records and
25 the most learned of our lawyers assure us not only can be
done, but have been frequently done—I suppose no man in
his right wits but will confess Parliament to be above the King.
Even in an interregnum the authority of the Parliament is in

viget; et quod historiis nostris testatissimum est, nullâ hære-
ditatis ratione habitâ, sæpè, quem sibi visum est, suffragiis
liberrimis regem creavit. Ut summatim dicam quod res est,
Parlamentum est supremum gentis Concilium, ad hoc ipsum
5 à Populo planè libero constitutum, et potestate plena instruc-
tum, ut de summis rebus in commune consulat; rex ideo erat
creatus, ut de consilio et sententia illorum Ordinum consulta
omnia exequenda curaret. Quod cùm Parlamentum ipsum
edicto nuper suo publicè declararet, neque enim pro æquitate
10 sua recusabat vel externis gentibus actionum suarum rationem
ultrò ac sponte reddere, ecce tibi è gurgustio nullius homo authoritatis, aut fidei, aut rei, Burgundus iste Verna, qui summum Angliæ Senatum, jus patrium atque suum scripto asse-
rentem, *detestandæ et horribilis imposturæ* insimulet. Patriam
15 mehercule tuam pudebit, verbero, se tantæ impudentiæ ho-
muncionem genuisse. Sed habes fortasse quæ salutariter
monitos nos velis; agedum, auscultamus. *Quas,* inquis, *leges
sancire potest Parlamentum, in quo nec præsulum ordo com-
paret?* Túne ergo, furiose, præsules ex ecclesia extirpatum
20 ibas, ut in Parlamenta induceres? O hominem impium, et

being, and—than which nothing is more clearly attested in our histories—they have often, without any regard to hereditary descent, appointed by free choice whomever they pleased to be king.

5   To sum up the whole truth, Parliament is the supreme council of the nation, constituted and appointed by an absolutely free people, and armed with ample power and authority, for this end and purpose: viz., to consult together upon the most weighty affairs; the king was created to take care
10 that there should be executed, obedient to their vote and resolution, all the acts and decrees of those Orders, Estates, or Houses.

Which things after the Parliament themselves had lately declared in a public edict of theirs,—for such is the justice of
15 their proceedings that of their own accord they have been willing to give an account of their actions,—look! here from his hovel appears this man of no standing or influence or property or credit, this home-born Burgundian slave, and accuses the supreme Senate of England, when it is asserting
20 by a public instrument its own and its country's right, "of a detestable and horrible imposture!" Your country shall be ashamed, you rascal, to have brought forth so prodigiously impudent a midget.

But perhaps you have somewhat to tell us that may be for
25 our good: go on, we are listening. "What laws," say you, "can be enacted by a Parliament in which not even the order of Bishops is present?" Did you then, you madman, go about to uproot the Bishops out of the Church, that you might trans-

Satanæ tradendum, quem neque ecclesia non ejicere hypocritam et atheum, neque ulla respub. recipere communem libertatis pestem atque labem deberet; quinetiam quod solo ex Evangelio probandum erat, id ex Aristotele et Hali-
5 carnassæo, deinde ex statutis papisticis pravissimorum temporum probare adnititur, regem Angliæ caput esse Anglicanæ Ecclesiæ, ut episcopos compransores suos et necessarios nuper factos, quos ipse Deus exturbavit, novos iterum prædones et tyrannos, pro virili sua parte, sanctæ Dei ecclesiæ imponat,
10 quorum universum ordinem, tanquam religioni Christianæ perniciosissimum, eradicandum esse stirpitùs, editis antea libris clamosè contenderat. Quis unquam Apostata, non dico à sua, quæ nulla certa est, sed à Christiana doctrina, quam ipse asseruerat, defectione tam fœda atque nefaria descivit? *Epis-*
15 *copis de medio sublatis, qui sub rege, et ex ejus arbitrio de causis ecclesiæ cognoscebant,* quæris *ad quos redibit ea cognitio.* O perditissime, verere tandem vel conscientiam tuam; memineris dum licet, nisi si hoc serò nimis te moneo, memineris quàm non impunè tibi erit, quàm inexpiabile demùm
20 sit, sanctum Dei Spiritum sic illudere. Collige te aliquando, et pone aliquem furori modum, ne te accensa ira numinis

plant them into Parliaments? A wicked wretch! who ought to be delivered over to Satan, and whom the church ought not fail to excommunicate as a hypocrite and an atheist, and no civil society of men to take in, being a common plague-sore to the liberty of mankind. Nay, and besides he struggles to prove out of Aristotle and Dionysius of Halicarnassus, and next from papistical statutes of the most corrupt ages, that the King of England is the head of the Church of England, a thing not to be proved at all if it be not proved from the Gospel:—all this to the end that he may once more, as far as in him lies, set up over God's holy Church those bishops, grown of late his intimates and boon-companions, whom God himself thrust out; set up them, I say, to be robbers and tyrants anew, whose whole order, as in his formerly published books he had noisily maintained, ought to be exterminated root and branch as the bane of the Christian religion. What apostate did ever so shamefully and wickedly desert as this man has done, I do not say his own doctrine, for he has none that is settled, but the Christian doctrine which he had formerly asserted?

"The Bishops being removed, who under the king and by his permission had jurisdiction of ecclesiastical causes, upon whom," ask you, "will that jurisdiction devolve?" O villain! have some regard at least to your own conscience; remember before it be too late, unless indeed this admonition of mine be already too late, remember that this mocking of God's Holy Ghost is the unpardonable sin, and will not be left unpunished. Stop at last, and set bounds to your madness, lest the wrath of God that you have provoked lay hold

repentè corripiat; qui Christi gregem, unctosque Dei minimè
tangendos, iis hostibus et sævissimis tyrannis obterendos iterum et persultandos tradere cupis, à quibus elata modò et
mirifica Dei manus eos liberavit; túque ipse, nescio eorúmne
5 ad fructum ullum, an ad perniciem et obdurationem tuam,
liberandos esse docuisti. Quod si jus nullum dominandi in
ecclesiam est episcopis, certè multo minùs est regibus; quicquid hominum statuta edicunt. Sciunt enim qui labris ali-
quanto plusquam primoribus Evangelium gustârunt, ecclesiæ
10 gubernationem divinam esse totam ac spiritualem, non civilem. *In secularibus* autem, quòd aïs *supremam jurisdictionem
habuisse regem Angliæ,* id falsum esse jura nostra ubertim
declarant. Curias omnes ubi judicia exercentur, non rex,
sed Parlamenti authoritas vel constituit, vel tollit; in quibus
15 tamen minimo cuivis è plebe licebat regem in jus vocare;
neque rarò judices contra regem pronuntiare solebant; id
si rex vel interdicto, vel mandato, vel scriptis literis impedire conaretur, ex juramento et lege non parebant judices, sed ejusmodi mandata rejiciebant, et pro nihilo ha-
20 bebant: non poterat rex quenquam in vincula conjicere,
aut ullius bona in publicum addicere; poterat neminem
supplicio punire, nisi in aliquam curiam priùs citatum, ubi
non rex, sed consueti judices sententias tulere; idque sæpe,

upon you suddenly,—you that are fain to deliver Christ's
flock, and God's untouchable anointed, to be crushed and
trampled again by those same enemies and cruel tyrants from
whom God's wonder-working hand did lately stretch out and
5 set them free. Yes, and from whom you yourself maintained
that they ought to be set free, I know not whether for any good
of theirs, or to the hardening of your own heart and the fur-
thering of your own damnation. If the bishops have no right
to lord it over the church, certainly much less have kings,
10 whatever human statutes may be to the contrary. For they
that have tasted the Gospel more than lip-deep know that the
government of the church is altogether divine and spiritual,
not civil.

Whereas you say that "in secular affairs, the king of Eng-
15 land has always had the highest jurisdiction," our laws do
abundantly show this to be false. Our courts of justice are
erected and suppressed, not by the King's authority, but by
that of the Parliament, and yet in them the meanest subject
might go to law with the King. Nor did the judges seldom
20 give judgment against him, which if the King should endeavor to obstruct by any prohibition, charge, or letter, the
judges were bound by law and by their oaths not to obey him,
but rejected such charges, and held them for naught. The
king could not imprison any man, or seize his estate as for-
25 feited; he could not inflict the penalty of death upon any man
who had not first been summoned to appear in some court
where not the king but the ordinary judges gave sentence; and
this, frequently, as I have said, against the king. Hence our

ut suprà dixi, contra regem. Hinc noster Bractonus l. 3. c. 9.
regia potestas juris est, non injuriæ; et nihil aliud potest
rex, nisi id solùm quod de jure potest. Aliud tibi suggerunt
Causidici tui, qui nuper solum verterunt; ex statutis nempe
5 quibusdam haud antiquis sub Edouardo Quarto, Henrico
Septimo, Edouardo Sexto promulgatis: neque viderunt,
quamcunque regi potestatem statuta illa concedunt, eam à
Parlamento concessam esse omnem et quasi precariam, quam
et eadem authoritas poterit revocare. Cur sic passus es nasuto
10 tibi imponi, ut quo maximè argumento regis potestatem ex
decretis Parlamenti pendere demonstratur, eo absolutam esse
et supremam probare te crederes? Nam et monumenta nostra
sanctiora testantur, reges nostros non hæreditati, non armis,
non successioni; sed populo suam omnem potestatem debere.
15 Talis potestas regia Henrico Quarto, talis ante eum Richardo
Secundo à plebeio ordine concessa legitur; Rot. Parlament. 1
Hen. 4. num. 108, haud secùs atque rex aliquis præsidibus
suis præfecturas et provincias édicto et diplomate solet concedere. Id nempe literis publicis consignari disertè jussit
20 Communium Domus, *concessisse se regi Richardo, ut tali*
bonâ libertate frueretur, *qualem ante eum reges Angliæ ha-*
buere; quâ cum rex ille *contra fidem Sacramenti sui* ad eversionem legum abuteretur, ab iisdem orbatus regno est. Iidem

Bracton, book 3, ch. 9: "The royal power is a power according to law, not a power to do wrong; and the king cannot do anything else than what he can do lawfully." Those pettifoggers you have consulted, men that have lately fled their country,
5 insinuate something else to you—something, to be sure, based upon certain statutes, not very ancient ones, made in the reigns of Edward IV, Henry VII, and Edward VI. But they overlooked the fact that what power soever those statutes granted the king was granted all by Parliament—begged for as a
10 favor, so to speak—and revocable by the same power that conferred it. How could sagacious you let yourself be so put upon that you thought you were proving the king's power to be absolute and supreme by the very argument which most convincingly proves that it depends upon Acts of Parliament?
15 Also our records of great authority declare that our kings owe all their power, not to any right of inheritance, of conquest, or of succession, but to the people. So in the Parliament Rolls of the first of Henry IV, number 108, we read that such a kingly power was granted by the Commons to Henry IV,
20 and before him to Richard II, just as any king customarily grants to his commissioners their governorships and official charges by edict and patent. Thus the House of Commons ordered expressly to be entered upon record "that they had granted to King Richard" to use "the same good liberty that
25 the Kings of England before him had." And because that king abused it to the subversion of the laws, and "contrary to his oath at his coronation," he was by these same Commons bereft of his kingdom. The Commons, as also appears by the

etiam, quod et eadem rotula testatur, in Parlamento edicunt, se prudentiâ et moderatione Henrici Quarti confisos, *velle ac jubere ut in eadem magnâ libertate regiâ sit quam ejus progenitores obtinuere.* Illa autem nisi fiduciaria planè fuisset,

5 quemadmodum hæc fuit, necesse est profectò et Parlamenti illius ordines, qui concederent quod suum non erat, ineptos ac vanos, et reges illos qui, quod suum jam erat, concessum ab aliis voluerint accipere, et sibi et posteris injurios nimis fuisse: quorum utrumvis credibile non est. *Tertia pars,* inquis, *regiæ*

10 *potestatis versatur circa militiam; hanc partem reges Angliæ sine pari et æmulo tractârunt.* Neque hoc veriùs quàm cætera quæ perfugarum fide scripsisti. Primùm enim pacis et belli arbitrium penès magnum regni senatum semper fuisse, et historiæ passim nostræ, et exterorum, quotquot res nostras paulo

15 accuratiùs attigere, testantur. Sancti etiam Edouardi leges, in quas jurare nostri reges tenebantur, certissimam fidem faciunt, capite de Heretochiis, *fuisse quasdam potestates per provincias et singulos comitatus regni constitutas, qui Heretoches vocabantur, latinè ductores exercitus,* qui provincialibus copiis

20 præerant, non *ad honorem coronæ* solùm, sed *ad utilitatem regni.* Isti vero eligebantur *per commune concilium, et per singulos comitatus in pleno conventu populari, sicut et vicecomites eligi debent.* Ex quo facilè perspicitur, et copias regni

same Roll, publish in Parliament that, having confidence in the prudence and moderation of Henry IV, "they will and enact that he be in the same great royal liberty that his ancestors possessed." Had the former, however, been other than
5 wholly a trust, as the latter was, then indeed not only must those Houses of Parliament have been foolish and vain to grant what was none of their own, but those Kings too that were willing to receive as a grant from others what was already theirs, must have been too injurious both to themselves and to
10 their posterity; neither of which can be believed.

"A third portion of the royal power," say you, "concerns the forces; this portion the kings of England have handled without peer or competitor." This is no truer than the rest that you have written in reliance upon what the renegades told
15 you. In the first place, both our own histories and those of foreigners that have been in the least exact touching our affairs declare that the making of peace and war always did belong to the Great Council of the realm. And the laws of St. Edward, which our kings are bound to swear that they will
20 maintain, put this beyond dispute in the chapter "De Heretochiis," viz. "That there were certain officers appointed in every province and county of the realm, that were called Heretochs, in Latin *ductores exercitus,* commanders of the army," that were to command the forces of the several counties, not
25 "for the honor of the crown" only, but "for the good of the realm." And they were chosen "by the common council, and by the several counties in full public assemblies of the inhabitants, as sheriffs ought to be chosen." Whence it is evident that

et copiarum ductores in potestate populi, non regis et antiquitùs fuisse, et esse oportere: illámque legem æquissimam nostro
in regno haud minùs valuisse, quàm olim in populari Romanorum statu valuit. De qua et M. Tullium audire non abs re
5 fuerit. Philipp. 10. *Omnes legiones, omnes copiæ quæ ubique*
sunt, Populi R. sunt. Neque enim legiones, quæ Antonium
Consulem reliquerunt, Antonii potiùs quàm reipub. fuisse
dicuntur. Sancti autem Edouardi legem illam, cum aliis illius
legibus Guilielmus ille conquæstor dictus, populo sic volente
10 ac jubente, juratus confirmavit; sed et hanc insuper adjecit,
c. 56. *Omnes civitates, burgos, castella, singulis noctibus ita*
custodiri, prout vicecomes, et Aldermanni, cæteríque præpo-
siti per commune concilium ad utilitatem regni meliùs provi-
debunt; et lege 62, *ideo castella, burgi, civitates ædificatæ sunt*
15 *ad tuitionem gentium et populorum regni, idcirco et obser-*
vari debent cum omni libertate, integritate, et ratione. Quid
ergo? custodientur arces et oppida in pace contra fures et
maleficos non nisi per commune Concilium ejusdem loci, non
custodientur in maximo belli metu contra hostes sive externos
20 sive intestinos per commune concilium totius gentis? sanè
illud nisi concedatur, neque *libertas*, neque *integritas*, nec
ratio denique in iis custodiendis ulla esse poterit; neque earum
rerum quicquam assequemur, quarum causâ fundari primùm

the forces of the kingdom, and the commanders of those
forces, were anciently, and ought to be still, not at the king's
command, but at the people's; and that this most just law obtained in this our kingdom no less than heretofore it did in
5 the Roman republic. Concerning which it will not be amiss
to hear what Cicero says, *Philipp*. 10: "All the legions, all the
forces, wheresoever they are, belong to the Roman people.
For not even those legions that deserted Antony when he was
Consul are said to have belonged to Antony rather than to the
10 Commonwealth." That law of St. Edward, together with the
rest of his laws, did William, called the Conqueror, at the
desire and command of the people, confirm by oath, yes and
added over and above, chap. 56: "All cities, boroughs, and
castles to be so guarded every night, as the Sheriff, the Alder-
15 men, and the other officers placed in command by the Common Council shall think meet for the safety of the realm."
And in the 62d law, "Castles, boroughs, and cities were built
for the protection of the folks and peoples of the realm, and
therefore ought to be maintained free, entire, and unimpaired,
20 by all ways and means." How then? Shall towns and places
of strength in times of peace be guarded against thieves and
evildoers no otherwise than by the Common Council of each
place; and shall they not be defended in dangerous times of
war, against enemies both domestic and foreign, by the Com-
25 mon Council of the whole nation? If this be not granted, they
surely cannot be guarded and maintained "free" or "unimpaired" or "by all ways and means"; nor shall we obtain any
of those ends for which the law itself tells us that towns and

urbes et arces lex ipsa dicit. Majores certè nostri quidvis potiùs regi quàm sua arma et oppidorum præsidia tradere solebant; idem esse rati acsi libertatem ipsi suam ferocitati regum
et impotentiæ proditum irent. Cujus rei exempla in historiis
5 nostris uberrima cùm sint, et jam notissima, inserere huic loco
supervacaneum esset. At *protectionem rex debet subditis;*
quomodo eos protegere poterit, nisi arma virósque habeat in
sua potestate? At, inquam, habebat hæc omnia ad utilitatem
regni, ut dictum est, non ad civium interitum et regni disper-
10 ditionem: quod et Henrici tertii temporibus, prudenter Leo-
nardus quidam vir doctus in episcoporum conventu respondit
Rustando Papæ nuntio et regis procuratori: *omnes ecclesiæ*
sunt Domini Papæ, ut omnia principis esse dicimus, ad tuiti-
onem, non ad fruitionem vel proprietatem, quod aïunt; ad
15 defensionem, *non ad dispersionem:* Eadem et prædictæ legis
Edouardi sententia erat; quid est hoc aliud nisi potestate fiduciaria, non absoluta? qualem cùm imperator bellicus ferè
habeat, id est delegatam, non planè propriam, non eò segniùs
populum, à quo eligitur, sive domi sive militiæ defendere
20 solet. Frustra autem Parlamenta, et impari sane congressu de
legibus Sancti Edouardi et libertate olim cum regibus con-
tendissent, si penès regem solùm arma esse oportere existi-

fortresses are founded in the first place. Indeed our ancestors were willing to put anything into the king's power rather than their arms and the garrisons of their towns; conceiving that that would be as if they went about to hand over their 5 liberty to the unrestrained cruelty of their kings. Of which there are so very many instances in our histories, and those so generally known, that it would be superfluous to mention any of them here.

But "the king owes protection to his subjects; and how can 10 he protect them unless he have men and arms at command?" But, say I, he had all this for the good of the kingdom, as has been said, not for the destruction of his people and the ruin of the realm. In Henry III's time, one Leonard, a learned man, in an assembly of the Bishops, wisely answered Rustand, the 15 Pope's Nuncio and the king's Chancellor, in these words: "All churches belong to My Lord the Pope, as we say all things belong to a prince, for protection, not for his use and enjoyment or his property," as the phrase is; for defence, "not for destruction." The aforementioned law of St. Edward is to the 20 same purpose; and what is this but a power in trust—not a power absolute? Now, though the commander of an army in the field has much this same sort of power—delegated, that is, and not absolutely his own—yet he is generally none the slower to defend both at home and abroad the people that 25 chose him. Vainly had our Parliaments contended of old with our kings about liberty and St. Edward's laws, and surely it had been an unequal match, had they been of opinion that the power of the sword must belong to the king alone; for how

mâssent; nam et leges quamlibet iniquas ipse dare si voluisset, frustra se *Chartâ* quantumvis *Magnâ* contra ferrum defendissent. *At quid proderit,* inquis, *Parlamento militiæ magisterium habere, cùm ne teruncium quidem ad eam sustinen-*
5 *dam queat, nolente rege, de populo cogere.* Ne sit ea tibi cura: primùm enim hoc falsò ponis, Parlamenti ordines *non posse sine rege tributa populo imponere,* à quo et ipsi missi sunt, et cujus causam suscipiunt. Deinde non potest te fugere tam sedulum de alienis rebus percontatorem, sua sponte populum,
10 vasis aureis atque argenteis conflatis, magnam vim pecuniæ in hoc bellum contra regem impendisse. Amplissimos exinde regum nostrorum annuos reditus recenses; nîl nisi *millies quingenties quadragies* crepas; *ex patrimonio regis maximas largitiones* fieri solitas ab iis *regibus qui liberalitatis laudibus*
15 *emicuerunt,* avidus audieras: hac te illecebrâ veluti Bileamum illum infamem proditores patriæ ad suam causam perduxere; ut Dei populo maledicere, et divinis judiciis obstrepere auderes. Stulte, quid tandem regi injusto ac violento tam immensæ opes profuere? Quid etiam tibi? ad quem nihil pror-
20 sus eorum, quæ spe ingenti devoraveras, pervenisse audio,

unjust laws soever the king would have imposed upon them, in vain would they have defended themselves against his sword by a "Charter," however "Great"!

But, you ask, "What shall it profit Parliament to have com-
5 mand of the forces, since towards the maintenance of them they cannot without the king's assent raise a farthing from the people?" Let not that trouble you! In the first place you go upon the false supposition that the Estates in Parliament "cannot without the king's assent impose taxes upon the
10 people"—the very people who send them, and whose side they are taking! In the next place it cannot have escaped you —so busy an inquirer into other people's business—that the people by melting down their gold and silver vessels raised a great sum of money of their own accord toward the carrying
15 on of this war against the king.

Then you recount the large annual revenues of our kings; you rattle on about nothing less than "five hundred and forty thousands"; you have heard, and greedily, that "those of our kings that have been eminent for their bounty and liberality"
20 have used to give "large boons out of their own patrimony." Greedily you heard this; it was by this allurement that those traitors to their country enticed you to their side, as the wicked Balaam was enticed of old, so that you dared to curse the people of God and to clamor against the divine judgments.
25 Fool! what, pray, did such boundless wealth profit that unjust and violent king? What did it profit you? For I hear that nothing whatever of all you had been devouring with your huge expectations did reach you, beyond that one paltry purse

præter unam illam crumenulam vitreis globulis vermicula-
tam, et centum aureolis confertam. Cape istam Balaame,
quam adamâsti, iniquitatis mercedem, ac fruere. Pergis enim
desipere: *Erectio standardi,* id est *vexilli, ad Regem solum*
5 *pertinet.* Quapropter? quia

—*Belli signum Laurenti Turnus ab arce*
Extulit.

Túne verò nescis, Grammatice, hoc idem cujusvis imperatoris bellici munus esse? At *aït Aristoteles, necesse est regi*
10 *præsidium adsistere, quo leges tueri possit; ergò oportet regem*
plus armis posse quàm populum universum. Tales hic homo
consequentias torquere solet, quales Ocnus funes apud inferos;
quæ nulli sunt usui, nisi ut comedantur ab asinis: aliud enim
est præsidium à populo datum, aliud armorum omnium po-
15 testas, quam Aristoteles hoc ipso, quem protulisti, loco à regibus abjudicat. Oportet, inquit, habeat rex tantam circa se
manum armatorum, *quanta singulis vel compluribus fortior*
sit, populo verò minor; εἶναι δὲ τοσαύτην ἰσχὺν ὥστε ἑκάστου
μὲν καὶ ἑνὸς καὶ συμπλειόνων κρείττω, τοῦ δὲ πλήθους ἥττω.
20 Polit. l. 3. c. 11. Alioqui sanè, sub specie tuendi, possit statim
et populum et leges sibi subjicere. Hoc autem rex et tyrannus
interest; rex à senatu et populo volente, ac libente, quod satis
est præsidii circa se habet contra hostes, et seditiosos: Tyran-

wrought with glass beads and stuffed with a hundred gold pieces. Balaam, take your wages of unrighteousness that you loved, and much good may it do you!

You go on playing the fool. "The setting up of the stand-
5 ard," that is, "of the signal of battle, is a prerogative that belongs to the king only." Why? Why because

> "Turnus set up an ensign of war on the top of the tower of Laurentum."

Do you really not know, Grammarian, that this very thing is
10 the office of any commander of an army in the field? But "Aristotle says that the king must always have a guard to help him defend the laws, and therefore it behooves the king to have greater military strength than the whole body of the people." This man twists conclusions as Ocnus does ropes in
15 Hell; which are of no use but to be eaten by asses. For a guard given by the people is one thing, and the control of all the forces is quite another thing; the latter, Aristotle judges, in the very passage which you have cited, should not belong to kings. It behooves the king, says he, to have so many armed
20 men about him "as to make him stronger than any one man, or many men together, but not stronger than the people." *Pol.* Book 3, ch. 11. Else, under show of protecting them, he could subject both people and laws to himself. This indeed is the difference betwixt a king and a tyrant: a king, by con-
25 sent of the senate and the people, has about him a sufficient guard against public enemies and seditious persons. A tyrant, against the will of the senate and the people, strives to get as

nus invito senatu ac populo, vel hostium, vel perditorum
civium præsidium sibi quàm maximum comparare studet,
contra senatum ipsum et populum. Concessit itaque Parlamentum regi, ut alia omnia, sic *standardi erectionem;* non ut
5 infesta patriæ signa inferret, sed ut populum contra eos defenderet, quos Parlamentum hostes judicâsset; si secus fecisset,
ipse hostis judicandus erat: cum juxta ipsam Sancti Edouardi,
vel quod sanctius est, ipsam naturæ legem, nomen regis perdiderit. Unde in prædictâ Philippicâ, *amittit is omne exerci-*
10 *tûs et imperii jus, qui eo imperio et exercitu rempub. op-*
pugnat. Neque licebat regi *feudales* illos *equites* ad *bellum*
evocare, quod Parlamenti authoritas non decrevisset; id quod
ex statutis pluribus manifestum est. Idem de vectigalibus et
censu navali censendum; quem imperare civibus sine sena-
15 tusconsulto fas regi non erat: atque ita gravissimi legum nostrarum interpretes annis abhinc plus minus duodecim, tum
cùm adhuc firmissimum erat regium imperium, publicè sta-
tuerunt. Sic diu ante eos Fortescutius Henrici Sexti cancellarius
juris nostri consultissimus; rex Angliæ, inquit, neque leges
20 mutare potest, neque tributa, nolente populo, imponere. Sed
nec probaverit quisquam ullis testimoniis antiquorum *regni*
Angliæ statum merè esse *regalem. Habet rex,* inquit Bractonus, *jurisdictionem super omnes.* Id est in curiâ; ubi regis

great a guard as he can, either of public enemies, or of profligate subjects, against the senate and the people. Parliament therefore granted the king, as they granted whatever he had besides, the "setting up of the standard"; not that he might
5 give hostile signals to attack his own people, but that he might defend them against such as the Parliament should declare enemies to the state. If he acted otherwise, he was to be accounted an enemy himself, for according to that same law of St. Edward, or, what is more sacred, the very law of nature, he
10 lost the name of king. Whence Cicero in his *Philippic* aforesaid: "He who attacks the state with an army and his official powers forfeits all right to the command and to his office."

As for "tenants by knight-service," the King was not allowed to summon them to a war which the authority of Par-
15 liament had not resolved upon; as is evident from many statutes. The same is true of Tonnage and Poundage and Ship Money; these the king could not exact from his subjects without an Act of Parliament; as was publicly resolved by the ablest of our lawyers about twelve years ago, when the king's
20 authority was at its height. And, long before them, Fortescue, an eminent lawyer, and chancellor to Henry the Sixth, was of the same opinion. The king of England, says he, can neither alter the laws, nor lay taxes without the people's consent.

Nor can any testimonies be brought from antiquity to prove
25 "the government of the realm of England an unmixed monarchy." "The king," says Bracton, "has jurisdiction over all his subjects"; that is, in his courts of justice, where justice is administered in the king's name indeed, but according to our

quidem nomine, nostris autem legibus jus redditur. *Omnis sub rege est;* id est singuli: atque ita se explicat ipse Bractonus locis à me suprà citatis. Ad ea quae restant, ubi eundem volvis lapidem, in quo vales ipsum, credo, Sisyphum delassare, ex

5 suprà dictis abunde respondetur. De cætero, si quando Parlamenta suum regibus bonis obsequium amplissimis verbis citra assentationem et servitutem detulere, id quasi eodem modo tyrannis delatum esset, intelligi, aut populo fraudi esse non debet; neque enim justo obsequio libertas imminuitur. Quod

10 autem ex Edouardo Coco et aliis citas, *Angliæ regnum absolutum est imperium,* id est si ad ullum regem externum, aut Cæsarem respicias; vel, ut Cambdenus aït, *quia in imperii clientela non est:* alioqui adjicit uterque imperium hoc consistere non *ex rege* solo, sed *ex corpore politico.* Unde Forte-

15 scutius, de laud. legum Angl. c. 9. *rex,* inquit. *Angliæ* populum gubernat *non merâ potestate regiâ, sed politicâ; populus enim iis legibus gubernatur quas* ipse fert. Externos hoc etiam scriptores non latebat. Hinc Philippus Cominæus author gravissimus commentariorum quinto; *inter omnia orbis terræ*

20 *regna, quorum ego notitiam habeo, non est meâ quidem sententiâ, ubi publicum moderatiùs tractetur, neque ubi regi minus liceat in populum, quàm in Anglia.* Postremò *ridicu-*

own laws. "Everyone is subject to the king"—that is, every private individual; and so Bracton explains himself in the passages that I cited before.

What follows is but turning the same stone over and over
5 again—a sport at which I believe you able to tire out Sisyphus himself—and is sufficiently answered by what has been said already. For the rest, if our Parliaments have sometimes offered deference to good kings with expressions as generous as they could be this side of flattery and servility, this should
10 not be understood as offered in like measure to tyrants, or in prejudice of the people; for liberty is not impaired by proper deference. As for what you cite out of Sir Edward Coke and others, "that the realm of England is an absolute power," so it is with regard to any foreign king, or to the Emperor, or,
15 as Camden says, "because it is not among the dependents of the Empire": but each of them adds, besides, that this power dwells not "in the king" alone, but "in the body politic." Whence Fortescue says, *de Laud. Leg. Ang.* ch. 9: "The king of England" governs his people "not by an unmixed royal
20 power, but by the power of a State; for the English people is governed by those laws which" it makes. Foreign authors were not ignorant of this: hence Philippe de Comines, a weighty authority, says in the Fifth Book of his Commentaries: "Of all the kingdoms of the earth that I have any
25 knowledge of, I think there is none where government is carried on under more restraint, or where the king is allowed less power against his people, than in England."

Finally you say: "Ridiculous is the argument they adduce

lum est, inquis, *argumentum, quod afferunt, regna ante reges fuisse, quasi dicas lucem ante solem extitisse.* At nos, ô bone vir, non regna, sed populum ante reges fuisse dicimus. Quem interim te magis quam teipsum ridiculum dicam, qui lucem ante solem extitisse, quasi ridiculum, neges. Ita dum in alienis curiosus esse vis, elementa dedidicisti. Miraris denique, *eos qui regem in comitiis regni viderunt solio sedentem, sub aureo et serico cælo, potuisse in dubium vocare utrùm penès regem an penès Parlamentum majestas sit.* Incredulos profectò homines narras, quos tam lucidum argumentum è *cælo,* præsertim *aureo et serico,* petitum nihil moverit. Quod tu cœlum aureum homo Stoïcus adeò es religiosè et unicè contemplatus, ut et cœli Mosaïci et Aristotelici oblitus esse penitus videare: cùm in illo *lucem ante solem extitisse* negaveris, in hoc tres Zonas temperatas esse suprà docueris. Quot Zonas in illo regis aureo et serico cœlo observaveris, nescio: hoc scio, te Zonam unam centum stellis aureis bene temperatam ex illa tua cœlesti contemplatione abstulisse.

—that kingdoms existed before kings; which is as much as to say there was light before the sun was created." But, my good Sir, we do not say that kingdoms, but that the people, were before kings. In the mean time, whom shall I call more
5 ridiculous than you, in denying (as if *it* were ridiculous) that light came into being before the sun? Thus while you would be inquisitive in other men's matters you have unlearned your very rudiments! You wonder, in the last place, "how they that have seen the King at a session of Parliament sitting upon
10 his throne under the golden and silken heaven of his canopy of state, should so much as make a question whether the majesty resided in him or in the Parliament." Hard of belief indeed are they, whom so brilliant an argument, prayed down from "heaven," especially a "golden and silken heaven," can-
15 not convince. Which golden heaven, you, like a Stoic, have so devoutly and singly gazed upon, that you seem to have quite forgot the heaven of Moses and the heaven of Aristotle; for you have denied that in Moses's heaven "there was any light before the sun"; and in Aristotle's you have exhibited three
20 temperate zones. How many zones you observed in that golden and silken heaven of the king's I know not, but so much I know: you got one money-belt—one zone well tempered with an hundred golden stars—by this your heavenly contemplation!

CAPUT X.

CUM hæc omnis controversia de jure, sive generatim regio, sive separatim regis Angliæ, obstinatis partium contentionibus, quàm ipsa rei natura difficilior facta sit, spero, qui studium veritatis factionibus anteponunt, 5 iis ea me ex lege Dei, juréque gentium, ex institutis denique patriis, copiosè attulisse, quæ regem Angliæ judicari posse, atque etiam capite puniri indubitatum reliquerint. Cùm cæteris, quorum animos aut superstitio occupavit, aut mentis aciem anticipata regii splendoris admiratio ita perstrinxit, ut nihil in 10 virtute ac libertate vera illustre ac splendidum videre possint, sive ratione et argumentis pugnemus, sive exemplis, frustra contendimus. Tu verò, Salmasi, ut reliqua omnia, ita hoc etiam absurdè admodum facere videris, qui cùm omnes independentes omnibus probris onerare non desinas, regem ipsum 15 quem defendis, maximè omnium independentem fuisse statuis: neque *regnum populo, sed generi debuisse:* deinde quem *capitis causam dicere coactum* initio graviter dolebas, eum nunc *inauditum periisse* quereris. At verò totam causæ dictionem ejus, fide summa Gallicè editam, inspicere si libet, per-

CHAPTER X.

SINCE this whole controversy, whether concerning the right of kings in general, or that of the king of England in particular, has been rendered more difficult by partisan obstinacy than by the nature of the thing itself, I

5 hope that for those who prefer the pursuit of truth before the interest of faction I have produced out of the law of God, the laws of nations, and the municipal laws of my own country, such abundance of proofs as shall leave it beyond question that a king of England may be brought to trial and put to

10 death. With the rest, whose minds fanaticism possesses wholly, or whose wit has been so blunted by premature admiration of royal splendor that they can see nothing glorious or magnificent in true magnanimity and liberty—with these whether we strive either by reason and arguments or by ex-

15 amples, we strive in vain.

In fact, Salmasius, absurdly as you seem to do all else, you seem to fill up the measure of absurdity in this, that while you cannot give over heaping all manner of abuse upon all Independents, you assert that the very king you defend was the

20 most Independent of all, for that he did not "owe his sovereignty to the people, but to his descent."

Next, whereas in the beginning of your book you vehemently bewailed him for being "forced to plead for his life," now you complain "that he perished unheard." But if you

25 have a mind to look into his whole defence, which is very correctly published in French, it may be you will be of another

suasum tibi aliud fortasse erit. Carolo certè cùm per aliquot dies continuos amplissima loquendi facta copia esset, non ille quidem est eâ usus ad objecta sibi crimina diluendum, sed ad judicium illud ac judices omnino rejiciendum. Qui autem reus aut tacet, aut aliena semper respondet, eum non est injuria, si manifestus criminum sit, vel inauditum condemnari. Carolum si *mortem* aïs *planè egisse vitæ respondentem,* assentior: si dicis piè et sanctè et *securè* vitam finiisse, scito aviam ejus Mariam, infamem fœminam, pari in speciem pietate, sanctitate, constantia in pegmate occubuisse: ne animi præsentiæ, quæ in morte quibusvis è vulgo maleficis permagna sæpè est, nimium tribuas: sæpè desperatio aut obfirmatus animus fortitudinis quandam speciem et quasi personam induit, sæpè stupor tranquillitatis: videri se bonos, intrepidos, innocentes, interdum et sanctos pessimi quique non minùs in morte quàm in vita cupiunt; inque ipsa scelerum suorum capitali pœnâ solent ultimam simulationis suæ et fraudum, quàm possunt speciosissimè, pompam ducere; et, quod poëtæ aut histriones consueverunt insulsissimi, plausum in ipso exitu ambitiosissimè captare. Nunc *ad istam quæstionem pervenisse te* aïs, *quâ tractandum est quinam fuerint illius regiæ condemnationis præcipui authores.* Cum de te potiùs

opinion. Whereas Charles certainly was afforded for some
days together the fullest opportunity to say what he could for
himself, he made no use of it—not he—to clear himself of the
crimes laid to his charge, but utterly to spurn his judges and
5 their jurisdiction. Now whenever the accused either is mute,
or always says nothing to the purpose, then, if his guilt is evident beyond all doubt, there is no injustice in condemning
him even unheard.

If you say that Charles "died a death fully answerable to
10 his life," I agree with you; if you say that he died piously,
holily, and "composedly," remember that his grandmother
Mary, an infamous woman, died on the scaffold with as much
outward show of piety, holiness, and constancy as he did. And
lest you should ascribe too much to that very strong impres-
15 sion of courage which any common malefactors often give at
their death, let me tell you that despair or a hardened heart
many times puts on a certain look and mask, as it were, of
fortitude, and stupidity many times a show of tranquillity of
mind. The worst of men desire to appear good, undaunted,
20 innocent, and sometimes holy, not only in their life, but at
their death as well. In going to their death for very villainies,
they are wont to make a last parade of their hypocrisy and de-
ception as handsomely as they can, and, as is the way of foolish poets or stageplayers, hanker after applause even when
25 the play is over.

Now you say you are "come to that part of the inquiry
where you must discuss who were the chief movers of the
king's condemnation." Whereas it ought rather to be in-

inquirendum sit, quomodo tu, homo exterus, et Gallicanus erro, ad quæstionem de rebus nostris, tibi tam alienis, habendam perveneris? quo pretio emptus? verùm de eo satis constat. Te verò percontantem de rebus nostris quis demùm docuit? 5 ipsi nimirum perfugæ, et perduelles patriæ, qui te hominem vanissimum nacti, mercede ad maledicendum facilè adduxerunt. Data deinde tibi est aliqua aut furibundi cujuspiam sacellani semipapistæ, aut servientis aulici de statu rerum scriptiuncula; eam ut latinè verteres negotium tibi dabatur: 10 hinc istæ narrationes confectæ, quas, si videtur, paulùm excutiamus. *In hanc condemnationem non centena millesima pars populi consensit.* Quid ergo cæteri, qui sese nolentibus tantum facinus fieri sunt passi? an stipites, an trunci hominum, an verò quales illi in scena Virgiliana ignavissimi,

15   *Purpurea intexti tollunt aulæa Britanni?*

Non enim veros tu quidem Britannos, sed pictos nescio quos, vel etiam acu pictos videris mihi velle dicere. Cùm itaque incredibile sit gentem bellicosam à tam paucis, iisque infimis de plebe sua, sub jugum mitti, quod in narratione tua primum 20 occurrit, id esse falsissimum apparet. *Ordo ecclesiasticus erat ab ipso senatu ejectus.* Eo miserior itaque tua est insania, nec-

quired into how you, a foreigner and a French vagabond,
came to hold an inquiry into our affairs, so strange to you?
And bought with what price? That, however, is well enough
known. But who at last satisfied your curiosity about our af-
5 fairs? Even those deserters and traitors to their country that
got hold of your eminent emptiness and easily hired you to
speak ill of us. Then there was handed you some paltry account of the state of our affairs, written either by some crazy
half papist chaplain or by some cringing courtier, and you
10 were given the job of turning it into Latin. Out of that you
took those made-up stories of yours, which, if you please, we
will examine a little.

"Not the hundred thousandth part of the people consented
to this sentence of condemnation." What were the rest of the
15 people then, that suffered so great a deed to be done against
their will? Were they stocks and stones, were they mere
trunks of men only, or such utterly inert creatures as those in
Virgil's tapestry?

Britons interwove hold up the purple hangings.

20 For methinks you mean to describe no true Britons, but some
sort of painted Picts, or even gentlemen embroidered in
needlework! Since therefore it is a thing incredible that a
warlike nation should be subdued by so few, and these of the
dregs of the people, which is the first thing that occurs in your
25 narrative, that is manifestly quite false.

"The Lords Spiritual were turned out by the Parliament
itself." The more deplorable is your madness therefore—for

dum enim te sentis insanire, qui eos è Parlamento quereris
ejectos, quos tute ex ecclesia ejiciendos esse, libro longissimo
scribis. *Senatûs alter ordo qui in proceribus consistebat, ducibus, comitibus, vicecomitibus, statione sua dejectus est.* Et
5 meritò; à nullo enim municipio missi pro se tantùm sedebant,
nihil juris in populum habebant, juri tamen ejus et libertati,
suo quodam instituto, adversari in plerisque consueverant:
erant à rege constituti, ejus comites, et famuli, et quasi umbræ,
quo amoto, ipsos necesse est ad plebem, unde orti sunt, redigi.
10 *Una et deterrima portio Parlamenti potestatem sibi vindicare
non debuit reges judicandi.* At plebeius ordo, quod te suprâ
docui, non solùm Parlamenti pars erat potissima, etiam sub
regibus, sed per se ipse Parlamentum omnibus numeris absolutum et legitimum, etiam sine Comitibus, nedum Ecclesi-
15 asticis, constituebat. Atqui *ne tota quidem hæc ipsa pars ad
sententiam de regis capite ferenda admissa est.* Pars illa
nempe non admissa, quem verbo regem, re hostem toties judi-
caverat, ad eum animis atque consiliis palàm defecerat. Parlamenti ordines Anglicani cum iis qui à Scotiæ itidem Parla-
20 mento missi erant legati, idibus Januarii 1645. rescripserant

you are not yet sensible that you rave—to complain that Parliament turned out those who, as you yourself say in a lengthy book, ought to be turned out of the Church. "A second Estate of Parliament, to wit, the Lords Temporal, consisting of dukes, earls, and viscounts, was cast down from its place." And deservedly, for, not being returned by any constituency, they represented themselves only. They had no right over the people, but by a sort of old-established custom of their own used for the most part to oppose the people's rights and liberties. Created by the king, they were his companions, his servants, and, as it were, his shadows; and, the king once got rid of, they must needs be reduced to the body of the people, from whom they rose.

"One part of the Parliament, and that the worst of all, ought not to have assumed unto itself that power of judging kings." But I have shown you already that the House of Commons was not only the chief part of our Parliament, even while we had kings, but made in and by itself a Parliament in all respects perfect and lawful, even without the Lords Temporal, much more the Lords Spiritual. But "not even the whole House of Commons itself was admitted to vote at the king's trial." True, for the part that was not admitted had in sentiment and counsel openly revolted to Charles—to one whom, though they deemed him their king in words, they had yet in their deeds so often deemed an enemy. The Estates of the Parliament of England, and the deputies sent from the Parliament of Scotland, had written to the king on the 13th of January, 1645, in answer to his request for a deceitful truce

regi, dolosas inducias et habenda secum Londini colloquia petenti, non posse se eum in urbem admittere, donec is de bello civili tribus jam regnis ejus operâ excitato, de cædibus tot civium ejus jussu factis reipub. satisfecisset; déque pace firma

5 atque sincerâ iis conditionibus cavisset, quas ei utriusque regni Parlamenta et tulerant sæpiùs, et latura essent: ipse è contrario postulata eorum æquissima jam septies humillimè oblata, responsionibus aut surdis repudiaverat, aut ambiguis eluserat. Ordines tandem post tot annorum patientiam ut ne fraudu-

10 lentus rex, quam debellare rempub. in acie non valebat, eam in vinculis per dilationes everteret, et jucundissimum ex nostris dissidiis fructum capiens, de victoribus etiam suis restitutus hostis inspiratum sibi triumphum ageret, decernunt, se regis deinceps rationem non habituros; nullas se ei postula-

15 tionesampliùs esse missuros, aut ab eo accepturos. Post hæc tamen decreta reperti sunt ex ipso Ordinum numero, qui invictissimi exercitûs odio, cujus maximis rebus gestis invidebant, quémque post ingentia merita, dimittere cum ignominia cupiebant, ministris aliquot seditiosis, quibus miserè servie-

20 bant, morem gerentes, tempusque sibi opportunum nacti, cùm eorum multi, quos à se longè dissentire sciebant, ad sedandos Presbyterianorum gliscentes jam tumultus, missi ab

and for a conference with them at London, that they could
not admit him into the City till he had made satisfaction to
the state for the civil war that he had raised in the three kingdoms, and for the deaths of so many of his subjects slain by his
5 order, and till he had in writing provided and taken order for
a true and firm peace upon such terms as the Parliaments of
both kingdoms had offered him so often already, and should
offer him again. He for his part had either rejected their very
just requests by answering that he refused to listen, or by
10 ambiguous answers had evaded them, though most humbly
presented to him seven times over. After so many years'
patience, the Houses at last, lest the deceitful king, even in
prison, should by his temporizings ruin that Commonwealth
which he had not the strength to subdue in the field, and
15 by gathering the sweet fruit of our divisions be restored,
though a public enemy, and triumph unexpectedly over his
conquerors,—this to prevent, the Houses resolve that for
the future they will pay no attention to the king, send him
no more requests, and receive no more from him. After this
20 resolution there were yet found even some members of Parliament who hated that invincible army, envied its glorious
deeds, and, after it had deserved so well of the nation, desired
to disband it in disgrace. They were under the thumb of a
certain number of seditious ministers, by whom they were
25 governed like miserable slaves. They found their opportunity
when many whom they knew to be far otherwise minded than
themselves were absent in the provinces, sent by the House
itself to put down the Presbyterian rising which had already

ipso ordine, in provinciis abessent, mira levitate, ne dicam perfidiâ, decernunt, inveteratum hostem, verbotenùs duntaxat regem, nulla penè ab eo satisfactione priùs accepta, aut cautione facta, ad urbem esse reducendum; in summam dignitatem atque imperium æquè esse restituendum, ac si de repub. preclarè meritus esset. Ita religioni, libertati, fœderi denique illi à se toties jactato regem anteponebant. Quid illi interea qui integri tam pestifera agitari consilia videbant? An ideo deesse patriæ, saluti suorum non prospicere debuerant, eo quod istius mali contagio in ipsorum Ordinem penetraverat? At quis istos exclusit malè sanos? *Exercitus,* inquis, *Anglicanus,* id est, non externorum, sed fortissimorum et fidissimorum civium; quorum tribuni plerique, Senatores ipsi erant, quos illi boni exclusi patriâ ipsâ excludendos, et in Hiberniam procul ablegandos esse censuerant; Scoti interim dubia jam fide quatuor Angliæ provincias suis finibus proximas magnis copiis insidebant; firmissima earum regionum oppida præsidiis tenebant; regem ipsum in custodia habebant: ipsi etiam factiones suorum atque tumultus, Parlamento ipsi plusquam minaces, et in urbe et in agris passim fovebant, qui tumultus paulò pòst in bellum non civile solùm, sed et Scoticum illud

begun to spread. With a strange levity, not to say perfidy, they vote that that inveterate enemy of the state, king in name only, though he had given scarce any security or satisfaction, should be brought back to the City and restored to his throne
5 and sovereignty, exactly as if he had deserved excellently well of the nation. So that they preferred the king before their religion, their liberty, and that Covenant of theirs which so often they had vaunted. Meantime what of those who were sound themselves, and saw such pestilent councils on foot?
10 Ought they to have been wanting to their country, and have failed to provide for the safety of their countrymen, because the infection had spread even into their own House?

But who excluded those unsound members? "The English army," you say. So it was not an army of foreigners, but of
15 most valiant and faithful citizens, officered for the most part by the very members of Parliament whom those excluded Honorable Members had thought fit to exclude from their very country, and send far away into Ireland! The Scots, meanwhile, acting in what had by now become very dubious
20 good faith, were occupying with large forces the four English counties nearest their border, were keeping garrisons in the strongest towns of those parts, and were holding the king himself in custody. They also encouraged here and there in both city and country factions and uprisings of their own
25 countrymen, which were more than threatening to Parliament, and which soon after broke out into not only our Civil War but the Scottish War as well.

If it has been always counted praiseworthy in private men

erupêre. Quòd si privatis etiam consiliis aut armis subvenire reipublicæ laudatissimum semper fuit, non est certè cur exercitus reprehendi possit, qui Parlamenti authoritate ad urbem accersitus imperata fecit; et regiorum factionem atque tumultum ipsi curiæ sæpiùs minitantem facilè compressit. In id autem discrimen adducta res erat, ut aut nos ab illis, aut illos à nobis opprimi necesse esset. Stabant ab illis Londinensium plerique institores atque opifices, et ministrorum factiosissimi quique; à nobis exercitus magna fide, modestiâ, virtute cognitus. Per hos cùm retinere libertatem, reipub. salutem liceret, an hæc omnia per ignaviam et stultitiam prodenda fuisse censes? Debellati regiarum partium duces arma quidem inviti, animum hostilem non deposuerant: omnibus belli renovandi occasionibus intenti ad urbem se receperant. Cum his, quamvis inimicissimis, Presbyteriani, postquam non permitti sibi in omnes tam civilem quàm ecclesiasticam dominationem viderunt, clandestina consilia, et prioribus tum dictis tum factis indignissima consociare cœperant: eóque acerbitatis processere, ut mallent se regi denuò mancipare, quàm fratres suos in partem illam libertatis, quam et ipsi sibi suo sanguine acquisiverant, admittere; mallent tyrannum tot civium cruore perfusum, irâ in superstites, et conceptâ jam ultione ardentem rursus experiri dominum, quàm fratres, et amicissi-

to succour the state by advice or arms, there surely is no reason
why our army can be blamed, who being by authority of Parliament summoned to the City, obeyed orders, and quelled
with ease an uprising of the royalist faction which more than
5 once threatened the House itself. Things had been brought to
such a pass indeed, that of necessity either we must be crushed
by them, or they by us. On their side were most of the London
hucksters and handicraftsmen, and generally the most fac-
tious of the ministers; on ours an army known for its great
10 loyalty, moderation, and courage. It being in our power by
their means to keep the liberty, the safety, of our state, do you
think that all ought to have been surrendered and betrayed by
negligence and folly?

The leaders of the Royalist party, when subdued, had un-
15 willingly laid down their arms indeed, but not their hatred;
and they had flocked to town, watching all opportunities of
renewing the war. With these men (though their greatest
enemies) the Presbyterians, seeing themselves not admitted
to civil as well as ecclesiastical despotism over everybody, had
20 begun to make common cause, secret and most unworthy of
what they had formerly both said and done. They went on to
such a degree of bitterness that they would rather enthral
themselves to the king again than admit their own brethren to
that portion of liberty which they too had purchased with their
25 own blood, and would rather try being lorded over once more
by a tyrant dyed in the gore of so many of his own subjects,
and burning with rage and with the vengeance he already
imagined against the survivors, than endure their brethren

mos æquo jure ferre sibi pares. Soli Independentes qui vocan-
tur, et ad ultimum sibi constare, et suâ uti victoriâ sciebant:
qui ex rege hostem se fecerat, eum ex hoste regem esse amplius, sapienter, meo quidem judicio, nolebant: neque pacem
5 idcircò non volebant, sed involutum pacis nomine aut bellum
novum, aut æternam servitutem prudentes metuebant. Exercitum autem nostrum quo prolixiùs infamare possis, narrationem quandam rerum nostrarum inconditam et strigosam
exordiris: in qua tametsi multa falsa, multa frivola reperio,
10 multa abs te vitio data, quæ laudi ducenda essent, huic tamen
alteram ex adverso narrationem opponere nihil arbitror atti-
nere. Rationibus enim hîc non narrationibus certatur; atque
illis utrobique, non his fides habebitur. Et sanè sunt ejusmodi
res istæ, ut nisi justa historia dici pro dignitate nequeant.
15 Melius itaque puto, quod de Carthagine Sallustius, silere tantis de rebus, quàm parùm dicere. neque committam ut non
solùm virorum illustrium, sed Dei præcipuè maximi laudes,
in hac rerum serie mirabili sæpissimè iterandas, tuis hoc libro
intexam opprobriis. Ea igitur duntaxat, quæ argumenti ha-
20 bere speciem videntur, pro more decerpam. *Anglos et Scotos*

and friends to share and share alike with them. Only those
who are called Independents knew from first to last how to be
true to their cause, and what use to make of their victory. They
would not—and wisely, in my opinion—that he who when
5 he was king had made himself the state's enemy should
ever, from being the state's enemy, be king any more; nor
were they on this account averse to peace, but they very prudently dreaded either new war or perpetual slavery wrapped
up in the name of peace.

10 To slander our army the more fully, you begin a dry disorderly narrative of our affairs; in which though I find many
things false, many things frivolous, many things laid to our
charge which ought rather to be credited in our praise, yet I
think it will be to no purpose for me to set over against it
15 another narration from the opposite side. For our contest is
by reasonings, not by narrations, and both sides will believe
the former, but not the latter. And indeed the nature of the
things themselves is such that for their weight and worth they
cannot be related as they deserve but in a right history; so that
20 I think it better, as Sallust said of Carthage, rather to say
nothing at all about things of such weight and importance
than to say too little. Nor will I so much offend as to interweave in my book the praises not of great men only, but above
all of Almighty God, which in this wonderful course of affairs
25 ought to be most often repeated, to interweave these, I say,
amongst your slanders and reproaches. I will therefore, as is
my wont, pick out only such things as seem to have any color
of argument.

quòd aïs *solenni conventione promisisse, se regis majestatem conservaturos,* omittis quibus id conditionibus promiserint; si salvâ nimirum religione et libertate id fieri posset: quibus utrisque ad extremum usque spiritum iniquus adeò et insidi-
5 osus rex iste erat, ut, vivente illo, et religionem periclitaturam, et libertatem interituram esse facilè appareret. Sed redis jam ad illos regii supplicii authores. *Si res ipsa ponderibus suis, et momentis rectè æstimetur, exitus facti nefandi ita Independentibus imputari debet, ut principii et progressûs gloriam*
10 *Presbyteriani sibi possent vindicare.* Audite Presbyteriani, ecquid nunc juvat, ecquid confert ad innocentiæ et fidelitatis opinionem vestræ, quòd à rege puniendo abhorrere tantoperè videremini? Vos isto regis actore verbosissimo, accusatore vestro, *plusquam dimidium itineris confecistis;* vos *ad quar-*
15 *tum actum et ultra in dramate hoc desultando frigultientes spectati estis;* At interim reconditissimæ homo eloquentiæ, quos tam laboriosè accusas, cur tam facilè imitaris, *spectatus* toties in hac regia defensione *desultando* ipse *frigultiens?* vos *meritò regis occisi crimine notari debetis; ut qui viam ad ip-*
20 *sum occidendum munistis;* vos *nefariam illam securim cervicibus ejus inflixistis, non alii.* Væ vobis imprimis, si un-

You say: "The English and the Scots by solemn covenant promised to preserve the majesty of the king." But you omit upon what terms they promised it—to wit, if it might consist with the safety of their religion and their liberty; to both of which that king was so hostile and treacherous, even unto his last breath, that it was evident their religion would be endangered, and their liberty would perish if he lived.

But now you come back to the movers of the king's execution: "If the thing be considered according to the influences that decided it, the conclusion of this abominable action must be imputed to the Independents in such a way that the Presbyterians may justly claim the glory of its beginning and progress." Hark, ye Presbyterians, how does it help, how does it profit your reputation for innocence and loyalty that ye seemed so much to abhor putting the king to death? According to this everlasting talkative advocate of the king, your accuser, ye "went more than half-way"; "to the fourth act and beyond ye were beheld twittering and stammering while ye turned this tragedy into a circus feat of jumping or straddling two horses at once." But meanwhile, o wielder of farfetched rhetoric, why imitate so readily those whom you accuse so toilsomely—being yourself so often "beheld" in this *Royal Defence* "twittering and stammering" while you "straddle two horses at once!"

But, once more, O Presbyterians! ye "may justly be charged with the crime of killing the king, since ye paved the way to killing the same." "Ye, and no others, struck the accursed axe upon his neck." Woe to you before all others, if ever

quam stirps Caroli regnum posthac in Anglos recuperabit: in vos, mihi credite, cudetur hæc faba. Sed Deo vota persolvite, fratres diligite liberatores vestros, qui illam calamitatem, atque certam perniciem ab invitis etiam vobis hactenus prohi-
5 buere. Postulamini vos item, quòd *aliquot annos antè per varias petitiones jus regis imminuere moliti estis, quòd voces contumeliosas regi illis ipsis libellis quos nomine Senatús regi porrexistis, insertas publicâstis;* videlicet *in illa declaratione dominorum et communium, Maii 26. 1642. apertè quid sen-*
10 *sistis de regis authoritate aliquot perduellionem spirantibus et insanis positionibus fassi estis. Hullæ oppidi portas Hothamus, tali mandato à senatu accepto, venienti regis occlusit; vos quid rex pati posset, hoc primo rebellionis experimento cognoscere concupivistis.* Quid hoc dici potuit accommoda-
15 tiùs ad conciliandos inter se Anglorum animos, atque à rege penitùs abalienandos? Cum intelligere hinc possint, si rex revertatur, se non solùm regis mortem, sed etiam petitiones quondam suas, et frequentissimi Parlamenti acta de liturgia et episcopis abolendis, de triennali Parlamento, et quæcunque
20 summo populi consensu ac plausu sancita sunt, tanquam seditiosas atque *insanas Presbyterianorum positiones* luituros. Sed repentè mutat animum homo levissimus; et quod modo *rem ipsam rectè æstimanti* sibi videbatur solis Presbyterianis deberi, id nunc *rem* eandem *ab alto revolventi* Independenti-

Charles's stock recover the crown of England; upon my word, ye are like to pay the piper! But make your prayers to God, and love your brethren your deliverers, who have hitherto kept that calamity and sure destruction from you, though
5 against your wills. Ye are accused likewise for that "some years ago ye endeavored by sundry petitions to lessen the king's authority; that in the very papers ye presented to the king in the name of Parliament, ye inserted and published some expressions abusive of the king": to wit, "in that Decla-
10 ration of the Lords and Commons of the 26th of May, 1642, ye declared openly, in some mad proposals that breathed rebellion, what ye thought of the king's authority. Hotham, by order of Parliament, shut the gates of Hull against the king": ye "aimed by this first act of rebellion to make trial how much
15 the king would bear." What could be said more perfectly adapted to reconcile the minds of all Englishmen to one another, and estrange them wholly from the king? For hereby they may understand that if ever the king come back, they shall be punished not only for his father's death, but for peti-
20 tions they made long ago, and Acts passed in full Parliament for putting down the Bishops and the Book of Common Prayer, and for the Triennial Parliament, and what was else enacted with the people's fullest consent and applause—all these as seditious and "mad proposals of the Presbyterians"!
25   But this slight fickle fellow changes his mind all of a sudden; and what but of late "when he reckoned the thing itself aright" he thought was due wholly to the Presbyterians, this, now that "he turns over from on high" the very same "thing,"

bus totum deberi videtur. Modò Presbyterianos *vi apertâ atque armis contra regem grassatos esse,* eúmque ab iis *bello victum, captum, in carcerem conjectum* affirmabat, nunc omnem *hanc rebellionis doctrinam* Independentium esse scribit.
5 O hominis fidem et constantiam! quid aliam jam opus est narrationem comparare contra tuam, quæ ipsa sibi tam turpiter decoxit? Verùm de te siquis dubitat, albúsne an ater homo sis, tua legat quæ sequuntur. *Tempus est,* inquis, *pandere unde et quando proruperit inimica regibus secta: belli*
10 *isti sanè Puritani sub regno Elisabethæ prodire tenebris Orci, et Ecclesiam inde turbare primum cœperunt, imo rempub. ipsam: non enim sunt minores reipub. pestes quàm ecclesiæ.* Nunc te verè Balamum vox ipsa sonat; ubi enim virus omne acerbitatis evomere cupiebas, ibi insciens atque invitus bene-
15 dixisti. Hoc enim tota Anglia notissimum est, si qui ad exemplum ecclesiarum vel Gallicarum vel Germanicarum, ut quasque reformatiores esse judicabant, puriorem cultus divini rationem sequi studebant, quam penè omnem Episcopi nostri cæremoniis et superstitionibus contaminaverant, si qui tan-
20 dem pietate erga Deum, aut vitæ integritate cæteris præstabant, eos ab Episcoporum fautoribus Puritanos fuisse nominatos. Hi sunt quorum doctrinam regibus inimicam esse cla-

he thinks is due wholly to the Independents. A moment ago
he was averring that the Presbyterians "advanced against the
king with overt force of arms," and that by them the king was
"defeated, taken, and put in prison." Now he says this whole
5 "theory of rebellion" belongs to the Independents. Such trust-
worthiness and consistency in the man! What need is there
now of a counter-narrative to this of yours, that has so shamefully failed to meet its own obligations?

But if anyone should question whether you are an honest
10 man or a knave, let him read these following lines of yours:
"It is time to explain whence and at what time this sect of
enemies to kingship first broke out. Why truly these charm-
ing Puritans began in Queen Elizabeth's time to issue forth
out of the darkness of Hell, and thenceforward to disturb the
15 Church, yea and the State itself too; for they are no less plagues
to the State than to the Church." Now your very speech be-
wrays you right Balaam; for where you designed to vomit out
all the venom of your bitterness, there unwittingly and against
your will you have pronounced a blessing. For it is notorious
20 throughout all England that if any endeavored, after the
pattern of those churches, whether French or German, which
they accounted more truly reformed, to follow a purer type
of divine service, which our Bishops had almost universally
defiled with their ceremonies and superstitions, or if any, in
25 fine, excelled the rest either in piety toward God or in purity
of conduct, such persons were by the Bishops' party termed
Puritans. These are they whose principles you so loudly declare to be unfriendly to kings; nor are they alone in this, for

mitas; neque hi solùm, nam *plerique reformatorum,* inquis, *qui in alios disciplinæ ejus articulos non jurârunt, hunc tamen unum videntur approbâsse, qui regiæ adversatur dominationi.* Ita Independentes, dum gravissimè insectaris, laudas; qui eos

5 ab integerrima Christianorum familia deducis; et quam doctrinam Independentium esse propriam ubique asseris, eam nunc *reformatorum plerosque approbâsse* confiteris; usque eò demùm audaciæ, impietatis, apostasiæ provectus es, ut etiam Episcopos, quos tanquam pestes et Antichristos ex Ec-

10 clesia radicitùs evellendos, atque exterminandos esse nuper docuisti, eos nunc *à rege tuendos fuisse* affirmas, ne quid *Sacramento* scilicet *inaugurationis derogatum iret.* Nihil est ulterius jam sceleris aut infamiæ quò possis procedere, quàm, quod solum superest, ut reformatam, quam polluis, religio-

15 nem quamprimùm ejures. Quòd autem nos aïs *omnes sectas et hæreses tolerare,* id noli accusare; quamdiu te impium, qui Christianorum sanctissimos, et plerosque etiam reformatos tibi adversos *è tenebris orci prodire* audes dicere, te vanum, mendacem, et conductitium calumniatorem, te denique Apo-

20 statam ecclesia tamen toleret. Tuas autem exinde sycophantias, quibus magnam reliqui capitis partem insumis, et quæ monstrosa dogmata Independentibus, ad cumulandam iis invidiam, affingis, quidni omittam? cùm neque ad causam hanc regiam omninò pertineant, et ea ferè sint quæ risum po-

25 tius aut contemptum cujusvis quàm refutationem mereantur.

"the majority of Protestants, who have not adopted the rest of their principles," you say, "yet seem to have approved of this only, which opposes royal despotism." So that while you inveigh bitterly against the Independents, you praise them in
5 deriving their descent from the most pure and uncorrupted family of Christians; and a principle which you everywhere affirm to be peculiar to the Independents, you now confess that "the majority of Protestants have approved." Nay, you are arrived to that degree of temerity, impiety, and apostasy,
10 that even the Bishops, who, you formerly maintained, ought to be uprooted out of the church, as so many plagues and Antichrists, you now aver "ought to have been protected by the king" in order not to "impair his coronation oath"! Beyond your present villainy and shame there is no step you can
15 take but one alone—to abjure as soon as possible the Reformed religion which you taint with your presence. Whereas you say we "tolerate all sects and heresies," you ought not to find fault with us for that as long as the Church tolerates you, impious wretch and empty-headed lying slanderer for hire,
20 you Apostate who have the impudence to say that the most saintly Christians, and even the majority of Protestants—a majority which happens to be opposed to you—issue forth out of the darkness of Hell!

Why should I not pass by the telltale rascalities upon which
25 you spend a great part of the rest of your chapter, and those prodigious tenets that you ascribe to the Independents, to render them odious? For they concern not at all this disputed question about kings, and are for the most part such as deserve anybody's laughter or contempt rather than refutation.

CAPUT XI.

AD undecimum hoc caput videre mihi, Salmasi, quamvis nullo cum pudore, cum aliqua tamen conscientia futilitatis tuæ accessisse. Cùm enim hoc loco
perquirendum tibi proposueris *quâ authoritate* pronuntiatum
5 de rege fuerit, subjungis quod à te nemo expectabat, *frustra
id quæri;* scilicet *quæstioni huic vix locum reliquit qualitas
hominum qui id fecere.* Cùm igitur, quàm es importunitatis
et impudentiæ in hac causa suscipienda compertus, tam sis
nunc etiam loquacitatis tibi conscius, eo à me brevius respon-
10 sum feres. Quærenti jam tibi *quâ authoritate* ordo plebeius
vel judicavit ipse regem, vel aliis id judicium delegavit, respondeo supremâ: supremam quemadmodum habuerit, do-
cebunt te ea quæ tunc à me dicta sunt, cùm te suprà, hac ipsa
de re gnaviter ineptientem redarguerem. Quòd si tibi saltem
15 crederes, posse te ullo tempore quod satis est dicere, non
eadem toties cantare odiosissimè soleres. Aliis autem delegare
suam judicandi potestatem ordo plebeius eadem sanè ratione
potuit, qua tu regem, qui et ipse omnem potestatem à populo
accepit, eandem aliis delegare potuisse dicis. Unde in illa
20 *solenni conventione,* quam nobis objecisti, cùm Angliæ tum

CHAPTER XI

YOU seem to me to approach this eleventh chapter, Salmasius, though still unashamed, yet with some sense of your inefficiency. For whereas you proposed to yourself to inquire in this place "by what authority" sen-
5 tence was given against the king, you add immediately something which nobody expected of you, that "it is in vain to make any such inquiry," to wit, because "the quality of the persons that did it leaves hardly any room for such a question." And therefore as the conviction of meddlesomeness
10 and impudence of which you have been found guilty in the undertaking of this cause is now matched by your present guilty consciousness of your own impertinent garrulity, I shall give you the shorter answer. To your question then "by what authority" the House of Commons either condemned
15 the king themselves, or delegated that power to others, I answer: "the highest in the land." How they came to have the highest authority, you may learn from what I said before, when I was refuting your persistent nonsense upon this very subject; for if you believed yourself capable of ever saying the
20 sufficient and satisfactory thing, you would not have the habit of so often and so tediously repeating the same old singsong. And the House of Commons might delegate their judicial power in the same way in which you say the king, who himself likewise received all he had from the people, may dele-
25 gate his. Hence in that Solemn League and Covenant that you have brought against us, the Estates of England and

Scotiæ summi ordines religiosè profitentur ac spondent, ea se supplicia de perduellibus esse sumpturos, *quibus utrisque gentis potestas judiciaria suprema, aut qui ab ea delegatam potestatem accepturi erant,* plectendos judicassent. Audis hìc

5 utriusque gentis Senatum unâ voce testantem se posse suam authoritatem judiciariam, quam *supremam* ipsi vocant, aliis delegare: vanam ergo et frivolam de ista potestatis delegatione controversiam moves. At *cum his,* inquis, *judicibus è domo inferiori selectis juncti etiam judices fuere ex cohortibus mili-*

10 *taribus sumpti; nunquam autem militum fuit civem judicare.* Paucissimis te retundam; non enim de cive nunc, sed de hoste memineris nos loqui: quem si imperator bellicus cum tribunis militaribus suis, bello captum, et è vestigio, si ita videretur, occidendum, pro tribunali judicare voluerit, an quicquam

15 præter jus belli aut morem censebitur fecisse? qui autem hostis reipublicæ, et bello captus est, ne pro cive quidem is, nedum pro rege in ea repub. haberi potest. Hanc ipsa lex Regis Eduardi sacrosancta sententiam tulit; quæ negat malum regem aut esse regem, aut oportere regis nomine appellari. Ad illud

20 autem quod aïs non *integram* plebis domum, sed *mancam et mutilam de regis capite judicâsse,* sic habeto; eorum, qui regem plectendum esse censebant, longè majorem fuisse numerum, quàm qui res quascunque in Parlamento transigere, etiam per absentiam cæterorum, ex lege debebant; qui cùm

Scotland solemnly protest and engage to each other to punish traitors in such manner as "the supreme judicatories of both Kingdoms respectively, or others having power from them for that effect, shall judge convenient." Now you hear the Parliaments of both nations with one voice bearing witness that they may delegate their judicial power, which they call "supreme"; so that the controversy you raise about delegating this power is vain and frivolous.

"But," you say, "with those judges that were chosen from the lower House were joined even judges from the army; soldiers never, though, had a right to sit in judgment upon a citizen." I will turn the edge of your argument in a very few words; for remember that we are not now talking of a citizen, but of an enemy. Suppose such an enemy taken prisoner, and to be dispatched at once if duly sentenced; now if the commander of the army with his officers should decide to try him before a Court Martial, would he be deemed to have done aught contrary to martial law and custom? An enemy to a state, made a prisoner of war, cannot be looked upon to be so much as a citizen in that state, much less a king. This is the purport of the sacred law of St. Edward, which declares that a bad king neither is a king, nor ought to be called a king.

To your objection that it was "not a whole" House of Commons, but a house "maimed and mutilated, that tried and condemned the king," take this answer. The number of them who gave their votes for putting the king to death was far greater than is lawfully necessary—even in the absence of the rest—to transact any business whatsoever in Parliament.

suo vitio atque culpâ abessent (defectio enim animorum ad communem hostem pessima absentia erat) nullam iis, qui in fide permanserant, afferre moram conservandæ reipub. poterant; quam vacillantem, et ad servitutem atque interitum prope redactam, populus universus eorum fidei, prudentiæ, fortitudini primò commiserat. Atque illi quidem strenuè rem gessere; exulcerati regis impotentiæ, furori, insidiis sese objecere; omnium libertati atque saluti suam posthabuere; omnia antehac Parlamenta, omnes majores suos prudentiâ, magnanimitate, constantia supergressi. Hos tamen populi magna pars, quamvis omnem illis fidem, operam, atque auxilium pollicita, ingratis animis in ipso cursu deseruit. Pars hæc servitutem et pacem cum ignavia atque luxuria ullis conditionibus volebat; pars altera tamen libertatem poscebat, pacem non nisi firmam atque honestam. Quid hìc ageret Senatus? partem hanc sanam, et sibi et patriæ fidelem defenderet, an desertricem illam sequeretur? Scio quid agere oportuisse dices; non enim Eurylochus, sed Elpenor es, id est vile animal Circéum, porcus immundus, turpissima servitute etiam sub fœmina assuetus; unde nullum gustum virtutis, et quæ ex ea nascitur, libertatis habes; omnes esse servos cupis, quòd nihil

Now since they were absent through their own fault, nay guilt (for their hearts' desertion to the common enemy was the worst sort of absence) they could not delay the rest, who had continued faithful to the cause, in the work of preserving 5 the state, which, when it was tottering and almost quite reduced to slavery and utter ruin, the whole body of the people had before all else committed to their fidelity, prudence, and courage. And they acted their parts like men; they set themselves against the unruly wilfulness, the rage, the secret de10 signs of an embittered king; they held the common liberty and safety before their own; they outdid all former Parliaments, they outdid all their ancestors, in wisdom, magnanimity, and steadfastness to their cause. Yet a great part of the people, though it had promised full fidelity, support, and 15 assistance, did ungratefully desert these men in the midst of their undertaking. This part was for slavery and peace, with sloth and luxury, upon any terms; the other part, however, kept demanding liberty, and no peace but what was sure and honorable. What was the Parliament to do now? 20 Ought it to have defended the part that remained sound and faithful to it and to the country, or to have sided with the one that deserted both? I know what you will say it ought to have done, for you are not Eurylochus, but Elpenor, a miserable Circean beast, a filthy swine, accustomed to foulest slavery 25 even under a woman; so that you have not the least relish of manliness or of the liberty which is born of it. You would have all men slaves, because you feel not in your heart aught

in tuo pectore generosum aut liberum sentis, nihil non ignobile atque servile aut loqueris aut spiras. Injicis porrò scrupu-
lum quòd *et Scotiæ rex erat, de quo statuimus,* quasi idcirco
in Anglia impune quidvis illi facere liceret. Ut hoc caput
5 denique præ cæteris elumbe atque aridum aliquo saltem facetè
dicto queas concludere, *duæ,* inquis, *sunt voculæ iisdem ac
totidem elementis constantes, solo literarum situ differentes,
sed immane quantum significatione differentes, Vis, et Jus.*
Minimè profectò mirum est, te trium literarum hominem tam
10 scitam ex tribus literis argutiolam exculpere potuisse; hoc
magis mirandum est quod toto libro asseris, duas res tam inter
se cæteroqui *differentes,* in regibus unum atque idem esse.
Quæ enim vis est unquam à regibus facta, quam non jus
regium tu esse affirmaveris? Hæc sunt quæ novem paginis
15 bene longis responsione digna animadvertere potui; cætera
sunt ea, quæ aut identidem repetita haud semel refutavimus,
aut ad hanc causam disceptandam nullum habent momen-
tum. Itaque solito nunc brevior si sum, id non meæ diligentiæ,
quam in hoc summo tædio languescere non patior, sed tuæ
20 loquacitati, rerum et rationum tam cassæ atque inani, imputandum erit.

magnanimous or free; you say nothing, you breathe nothing, but what is mean and servile.

You raise another scruple, to wit, "that he whom we condemned was the king of Scotland too." As if he might there
5 fore do what he would in England! But that you may conclude this chapter, which of all others is the most dry and doddering, at least with some witty quirk, "There are two little words," you say, "consisting of the same letters and the same number of them, and differing only in the position of
10 them, but differing enormously in meaning, to wit, VIS and IVS (might and right)." Of course it is no great wonder that you, being a man of three letters (*fur,* a thief), should make such a clever little quibble upon three letters; much more wonderful is this which you affirm throughout your book:
15 that two things "differing" so much in all other respects should yet be one and the same thing in kings. For did kings ever perpetrate a royal violence which you do not affirm to be their royal right?

In nine long, long pages these are the matters that I could
20 observe worth answering. The rest are either matters which, having been again and again repeated, have been more than once refuted, or matters which have no bearing upon this discussion. So that my more than usual brevity should not be counted against my diligence, which, though I be irked in the
25 extreme, I let not slack, but against your everlasting talk, so void and vacant of matter and sense.

emplo suis vehementissimè nocuit; secundo loco, quod temporis libidinibus et rebus ludicris impendit, quod erat plurimum, id totum reipub. quam susceperat gubernandam, subduxit; postremò immensas opes, innumerabilem pecuniam
5 non suam, sed publicam luxu domestico dilapidavit. Itaque
domi rex malus primùm esse cœpit. Verùm ad ea potiùs
crimina *quæ malè regnando commisisse arguitur transeamus.*
Hic doles *tyrannum* eum, *proditorem,* et *homicidam* fuisse
judicatum. Id non injuriâ factum demonstrabitur. Tyran-
10 num autem priùs, non ex vulgi opinione, sed ex Aristotelis et
doctorum omnium judicio definiamus. Tyrannus est qui
suam duntaxat, non populi utilitatem spectat. Ita Aristoteles
ethicorum decimo, et alibi, ita alii plerique. Suáne commoda
an populi spectârit Carolus, pauca hæc de multis, quæ tan-
15 tummodò perstringam, testimonio erunt. Cùm aulæ sumptibus patrimonium et proventus regii non sufficerent, imponit
gravissima populo tributa; iisque absumptis nova excogitavit;
non ut rempub. vel augeret, vel ornaret, vel defenderet, sed ut
populi non unius opes vel unam in domum importatas ipse
20 sibi congereret, vel una in domo dissiparet. Hunc in modum sine lege cùm incredibilem pecuniam corrasisset, quod

example; in the second place, all the time—and it was very much—that he spent upon his lusts and sports, he stole away from the State which he had undertaken to govern; lastly, he squandered away upon the luxury of his household boundless
5 wealth, uncounted sums of money which were not his own but the public revenue of the nation. So it was in his private life at home that he first began to be an ill king.

But let us rather "pass over to those crimes that he is charged with having committed in misgoverning." Here you lament
10 his being condemned as "a tyrant, a traitor, and a murderer." That in this he was not wronged shall now be shown. First, however, let us define a tyrant, not according to the notions of the crowd, but according to the judgment of Aristotle and of all learned men. A tyrant is one who regards his own wel-
15 fare and profit only, and not that of the people. So Aristotle defines one in the tenth book of his *Ethics,* and elsewhere, and so do many others. Whether Charles regarded his own advantage or the people's, these things, which I shall only touch upon, and which are only a few out of many, will serve to
20 show.

When his crown property and royal revenue could not defray the expenses of the court, he laid very heavy taxes upon the people, and having squandered these, invented new ones —not for the benefit, honor, or defence of the state, but that
25 he might hoard up in one house, or in one house fritter away, the riches of nations more than one. When in this fashion he had unlawfully scraped together an incredible amount, he attempted either wholly to do away with Parliament, which

unicum sciebat sibi fræno fore, Parlamentum aut funditus abolere, aut convocatum haud sæpius quàm id suis rationibus con-
duceret, sibi soli reddere obnoxium conatus est. Quo fræno
sibi detracto, aliud ipse populo frænum injecit: Germanos
5 equites, pedites Hibernos per urbes, pérque oppida quasi in
præsidiis, cùm bellum esset nullum, collocandos curavit: pa-
rúmne tibi adhuc tyrannus videtur? In quo etiam, ut in aliis
multis rebus, quod suprà per occasionem abs te datam ostendi
(quanquam tu Carolum Neroni crudelissimo conferri indig-
10 naris) Neroni perquàm similis erat: nam et Senatum ille è
repub. se sublaturum persæpe erat minatus. Interea consci-
entiis religiosorum hominum supra modum gravis, ad cære-
monias quosdam et superstitiosos cultus, quos è medio pa-
pismo in ecclesiam reduxerat, omnes adigebat; renuentes aut
15 exilio aut carcere multabat; Scotos bis eam ob causam bello
adortus est. Huc usque *simplici* saltem *vice* nomen tyranni
commeruisse videatur. Nunc cur adjectum in accusatione proditoris nomen fuerit exponam. Cùm huic Parlamento sæpiùs
pollicitis, edictis, execrationibus confirmâsset, se nihil contra
20 rempub. moliri, eodem ipso tempore aut papistarum delectus
in Hibernia habebat, aut legatis ad regem Daniæ clanculum
missis, arma, equos, auxilium disertè contra Parlamentum
petebat, aut exercitum nunc Anglorum nunc Scotorum pretio

he knew was the only thing that could bridle him, or to summon it no oftener than suited his convenience, and to make it
accountable to himself alone. This bridle being once cast off
himself, himself put another bridle upon the people: he had
5 German horse and Irish foot stationed in many towns and
cities as if to garrison them, though in time of peace. Do you
think he does not begin to look like a tyrant? In this very
thing, as in many others which I have exhibited above upon
occasion given me by you—in this, I say, though you scorn to
10 have Charles compared with so cruel a tyrant as Nero, he re-
sembled him extremely, for Nero likewise often threatened to
abolish the Senate.

Meanwhile the king bore extremely hard upon the con-
sciences of godly men, and compelled all to use certain cere-
15 monies and superstitious worships which he had brought back
into the Church again from the midst of popery. Them that
would not conform he banished or imprisoned; and he made
war upon the Scots twice for no other cause than that. So far
he may seem to have surely deserved the name of tyrant at
20 least "once over."

Now I will tell you why the word traitor was put into his
indictment. While he had again and again assured this Parliament by promises, by proclamations, by imprecatory oaths,
that he had no design against the state, at that very time either
25 he was recruiting levies of Papists in Ireland, or by secret
embassy to the king of Denmark he was begging arms, horses,
and troops, expressly against the Parliament, or he was en-
deavoring to raise an army, first of Englishmen, and then of

sollicitabat; illis Urbem Londinum diripiendam, his quatuor
provincias Aquilonares Scotorum ditioni adjungendas promisit si sibi ad Parlamentum quoquo modo tollendum com-
modare suam operam vellent. Cùm hæc non succederent,
5 cuidam Dillonio perduelli dat secretiora ad Hibernos mandata, quibus juberentur omnes Anglos ejus insulæ colonos
repentino impetu adoriri. Hæc ferè proditionum ejus monumenta sunt, non vanis rumoribus collecta, sed ipsis literis
ipsius manu subscriptis atque signatis comperta. Homicidam
10 denique fuisse, cujus acceptis mandatis Hiberni arma ceperint,
ad quinquies centena millia Anglorum in summa pace nihil
tale metuentium exquisitis cruciatibus occiderint, qui etiam
ipse tantum reliquis duobus regnis bellum civile conflârit,
neminem puto negaturum. Addo enim quod in illo Vectensi
15 colloquio hujus belli et culpam et crimen rex palam in se
suscepit, eóque omni Parlamentum notissimâ confessione suâ
liberavit. Habes nunc breviter quamobrem rex Carolus et tyrannus et proditor et Homicida judicatus fuerit. At *cur non
prius,* inquis, neque in illo *solenni fœdere,* neque postea cum
20 dedititius esset, vel *à Presbyterianis* vel ab *Independentibus*
sic judicatus est, sed potiùs, *ut regem decuit accipi, omni reve-
rentiâ est exceptus?* Vel hoc solo argumento persuaderi cuivis
intelligenti queat, non nisi serò tandem, et postquam omnia
sustinuerant, omnia tentaverant, omnia perpessi erant, delibe-

Scots, by bribes. To the English he promised the plunder of
the City of London; to the Scots, that he would annex the four
northern counties to Scotland, if they would but help him get
rid of the Parliament by any means soever. These projects not
5 succeeding, he gave one Dillon, a traitor, secret instructions
to the Irish to fall suddenly upon all the English colonists in
Ireland. These are the proofs of his treasons, and they are not
gathered out of idle reports, but are certainties found in letters
under his own hand and seal.

10   Finally, I suppose no man will withhold the name of murderer from him by whose order the Irish took arms and put to
death with most exquisite torments five hundred thousand
English, who in a time of profound peace apprehended nothing of the kind; nor will any man, I suppose, deny that he
15 who raised so great a civil war in the other two kingdoms was
a murderer. I add that at the conference held in the Isle of
Wight the king openly took upon himself the guilt of this war
and the blame for it, and in his confession known of all men
cleared the Parliament. Thus you have in short why King
20 Charles was adjudged a tyrant, a traitor, and a murderer.

      But you ask "why was he not so adjudged before by either
the Presbyterians or the Independents," either in that "Solemn League and Covenant," or afterwards when he was surrendered, but rather "was received as became a king to be
25 received, with all reverence?" This very point is sufficient to
convince any man of good understanding that only at long
last, and after they had borne all things, and tried all things,
and steadfastly endured all things, were the Estates resolved

ratum Ordinibus fuisse regem abjicere. Tu id solus malitiosè nimis in invidiam rapis, quod summam eorum patientiam, æquanimitatem, moderationem, fastúsque regii tolerantiam nimis fortasse longam apud omnes bonos testabitur. At

5 *mense Augusto qui præcessit ejus supplicium, domus Communium quæ sola jam tum regnabat et Independentibus erat obnoxia, scripsit literas ad Scotos, quibus testabatur nunquam sibi in animo fuisse mutare statum qui huc usque in Anglia obtinuerat sub Rege, domo Dominorum et Communium.*

10 Vide jam quàm non doctrinæ Independentium abrogatio regis attribuenda sit. Qui suam dissimulare doctrinam non solent, etiam potiti rerum profitentur *nunquam sibi in animo fuisse statum regni mutare.* Quod si id postmodum in mentem venit, quod in animo non fuit, cur non licebat quod rectius, et è repub.

15 magis esse videbatur, id potissimum sequi? præsertim cùm Carolus neque exorari, neque flecti ullo modo potuerit, ut justissimis eorum postulatis, quæque semper eadem ab initio obtulerant, assentiretur. Quas initio de religione, quas de jure suo sententias perversissimas tuebatur, nobisque adeò calami-

20 tosas, in iisdem permanebat: ab illo Carolo nihil mutatus, qui et pace et bello tanta nobis omnibus mala intulerat. Siquid est assensus, id et invitè facere, et quamprimùm sui juris

to depose the king. That which to all good men will evidence
their extreme patience, calmness, self-control, and perhaps
overlong forbearance with the king's pride, you alone maliciously seize upon as a reproach.

5   But "in the month of August before the king suffered, the
House of Commons, which already ruled alone and was con-
trolled by the Independents, wrote a letter to the Scots pro-
testing that it had never had in mind an alteration of the form
of government which had obtained so long in England under
10 King, Lords, and Commons." See now how little the deposing of the king is to be ascribed to the principles of the
Independents! They, who are not wont to dissemble their
principles, profess even then, when they have the sole man-
agement of affairs, that they "had never had in mind an
15 alteration of the form of government." But if a thing which
at first they had not in mind afterwards came into their mind,
why might they not take the course which seemed to lead
straighter to the common weal? Especially when they found
that Charles could not possibly be entreated or anywise moved
20 to assent to those just demands which they presented, and
which were always the same from the beginning. Those
froward opinions with respect to religion and his own right
which he had all along maintained, and which were so destructive to us, in these he persisted, nothing changed from
25 that too-well-known Charles who both in peace and in war
had done us all so much mischief. If he assented to anything,
he gave intimations not obscure both that he did it against his
will, and that as soon as he should have his own way he would

fuisset, pro nihilo se habiturum haud obscuris indiciis significabat: idem apertè filius, abductâ secum per eos dies classis parte, scripto edito; idem ipse per literas ad suos quosdam in urbe declarabat. Interea cum Hibernis Anglorum hostibus immanissimis, reclamante Parlamento, fœdis conditionibus occultè pacem coagmentaverat, Anglos ad repetita inutiliter colloquia et pacem quoties invitabat, toties contra eos omni studio bellum coquebat. Hic illi quibus concredita respub. erat, quò se verterent? an commissam sibi nostram omnium salutem in manus hosti acerbissimo traderent? An alterum belli propè internecini septennium, nequid pejus ominemur, gerendum nobis iterum, et exantlandum relinquerent? Deus meliorem illis mentem injecit, ut prioribus de rege non movendo cogitationibus, non enim ad decreta pervenerant, rempub. religionem, libertatem ex ipso illo fœdere solenni anteponerent; quæ quidem stante rege constare non posse, tardiùs illi quidem quàm oportuit, sed aliquando tamen viderunt. Sanè Parlamento nunquam non liberum atque integrum esse debet, ex re nata quàm optimè reipub. consulere; neque ita se prioribus addicere sententiis, ut religio sit in posterum, etiamsi Deus mentem et facultatem dederit, vel sibi vel reipub.

hold it null and void. The same thing his son openly declared
by a published writing, when in those days he ran away with
part of the fleet, and so did the king himself by letter to certain of his party in town.

5   In the mean time, against the open disapprobation of Parliament, he had in secret struck up a peace upon base dishon-
orable terms with the Irish, our most savage and inhuman
enemies; but whenever he invited the English to negotiations
for peace—which he kept asking for, and which were always
10 bootless—at those very times he was making every effort to
prepare for war against them. In this situation, which way
should they turn who were charged with the common weal?
The safety of us all, with which they were entrusted—should
they betray it to our most bitter adversary? Should they leave
15 us another seven years of almost exterminating war to bear
again to the bitter end, not to forebode worse? God gave them
a better mind, to prefer, pursuant to that Solemn League and
Covenant, the common weal, and religion, and liberty, before
their former thoughts of not dethroning the king (for they
20 had not come to a vote); all which they saw—later indeed
than behooved them, but still some time!—could not stand
firm if and while the king stood. Surely Parliament ought
never to be otherwise than entirely free and uncommitted, to
provide in the best possible way for the good of the nation as
25 occasion requires, nor so bound to their former opinions as to
scruple to change—though God have given them the understanding and the means—to wiser ones thereafter for their
own or the nation's good.

plus sapere. At *Scoti non idem sentiunt, quinimo ad filium Carolum scribentes, sacratissimum regem appellant parentem ejus, et sacerrimum facinus quo necatus est.* Cave plura de Scotis, quos non novisti; nos novimus, cùm eundem regem *sacerrimum,* et homicidam et proditorem; facinus quo tyrannus necaretur *sacratissimum* appellarent. Nunc regi quam dicam scripsimus, quasi parùm commodè scriptam cavillaris, et *quid opus fuerit ad elogium illud tyranni addere proditoris et homicidæ titulos,* quæris; *cùm tyranni appellatio omnia mala comprehendat:* tum quis tyrannus sit grammaticè et glossematicè etiam doces. Aufer nugas istas literator, quas una Aristotelis definitio modò allata nullo negotio difflabit; quæque te doctorem docebit, nomen tyranni, quoniam tuâ nihil interest præter nomina intelligere, posse citra proditionem et homicidium stare. Atqui *leges Anglicanæ non dicunt proditionis crimen regem incurrere si procuraverit seditionem contra se vel populum suum.* Neque dicunt, inquam, Parlamentum læsæ Majestatis reum esse, si malum regem tollat, aut unquam fuisse, cum sæpius olim sustulerit: posse autem regem suam majestatem lædere atque minuere, immò amittere, clarâ voce testantur. Quod enim in illa lege Sancti Edouardi legitur, *nomen regis perdere,* nihil aliud est quàm regio munere ac dignitate privari; quod accidit Chilperico Franciæ regi, cujus ex-

But "the Scots are of another opinion; for in a letter to the younger Charles they call his father a most sacred king, and the putting him to death a most execrable villainy." Take care to say no more of the Scots, whom you know not; we know
5 them, and know the time when they called that very king a "most execrable" murderer and traitor; and the putting the tyrant to death a "most sacred" deed.

Then you pick holes in the sentence we drew up against the king, as not being properly drafted, and you ask "why we
10 needed to add to the count of tyrant the titles of traitor and murderer, since the name tyrant includes all evils," and then you actually explain to us grammatically and lexicographically what a tyrant is! Off with your trifles, pedant, which that definition of Aristotle's that has lately been cited will alone
15 easily blow away, and teach you, teacher, that the word *tyrant* (for you care not to understand aught but words) may well fall short of treason and murder.

But "the laws of England do not declare it treason or lese-majesty in the king to stir up sedition against himself or his
20 people." Nor, say I, do they declare that Parliament can be guilty of lese-majesty, or hurting majesty, in deposing a bad king, or ever was guilty, though it has often deposed one in times past; but our laws do plainly declare that a king may indeed hurt his own majesty, and diminish it, yes and wholly
25 lose it. For that expression in the law of St. Edward, of "losing the name of king," signifies neither more nor less than being deprived of the kingly office and dignity; as befel Chilperic king of France, whose example the law itself mentions

emplum illustrandæ rei causâ eodem loco lex ipsa ponit. Committi autem summam perduellionem tam in regnum, quàm in regem non est apud nos jurisperitus qui inficias ire possit. Provoco ad ipsum, quem profers Glanvillanum. *Siquis ali-*
5 *quid fecerit in mortem regis, vel seditionem regni, crimen proditionis esse.* Sic illa machinatio quâ Papistæ quidam Parlamenti curiam cum ipsis Ordinibus uno ictu pulveris nitrati in auras disjicere parabant, non in regem solùm, sed in Parlamentum et regnum, ab ipso Jacobo et utraque Ordinum domo
10 *summa proditio* judicata est. Quid plura attinet in re tam evidenti, quæ tamen facilè possem, statuta nostra allegare? cùm ridiculum planè sit et ratione ipsa abhorrens, committi perduellionem in regem posse, in populum non posse, propter quem et cujus gratiâ, cujus, ut ita dicam, bonâ veniâ, rex est id quod
15 est. Frustra igitur tot statuta nostra deblateras, frustra in vetustis legum Anglicarum libris angis te atque maceras; ad quas vel ratas vel irritas habendas Parlamenti authoritas semper valuit; cujus etiam solius est, quid sit perduellio, quid læsa majestas interpretari: quam majestatem nunquam sic à
20 populo in regem transiisse, ut non multo celsior atque augustior in Parlamento conspiciatur, jam sæpiùs ostendi. Te verò vappam et circulatorem Gallum jura nostra interpretantem quis ferat? Vos verò Anglorum perfugæ, tot episcopi, doc-

in the same passage for the sake of illustration. There is not a
lawyer amongst us who can deny that high treason may be
committed against the kingdom as well as against the king.
I appeal to Glanville himself, whom you cite: "If any man
5 attempt to put the king to death, or raise sedition in the realm,
it is high treason." Thus that machination whereby certain
Papists were making ready to blow up the Parliament-house
with the Estates themselves in a single explosion of gun-
powder was by King James himself and both Houses of Par-
10 liament adjudged to be "high treason" not against the King
only, but against the Parliament and the realm. Where the
truth is so clear, of what use is it to quote, as I yet could easily,
more of our precedents established? For the thing itself is
highly ridiculous, and contradictory to reason itself, that trea-
15 son can be committed against the king, and cannot be against
the people, on account of whom, for whose sake, by the grace
of whom, and by whose good leave, so to speak, the king is
what he is. So that you babble in vain over so many statutes
of ours; in vain you torment yourself and steep yourself in our
20 ancient law-books; for the laws themselves Parliament always
had power to confirm or repeal; and to Parliament alone it
belongs to declare what is treason, what lese-majesty. And I
have often shown that this majesty never has so far deserted
the people for the king, as not to be visibly more lofty and
25 august in Parliament.

Who can yet endure to hear such an inspid French mounte-
bank as you expound our laws? But you, English deserters!
so many bishops, doctors, and lawyers, who proclaim that all

tores, jurisconsulti, qui literaturam omnem et eruditionem vobiscum ex Anglia aufugisse prædicatis, adeóne ex vestro numero nullus causam regiam atque suam defendere satis strenuè satísque latinè scivit, gentibúsque exteris dijudican-
5 dam exponere, ut cerebrosus iste et crumenipeta Gallus mercede accersendus in partes necessariò esset, qui regis inopis, tot doctorum et sacerdotum infantiâ stipati, patrocinium susciperet? magnâ, mihi credite, infamiâ etiam hoc nomine apud exteras nationes flagrabitis; et meritò vos utique cecidisse
10 causâ omnes existimabunt, quam ne verbis quidem, nedum armis aut virtute sustinere valuistis. Sed ad te redeo, vir bone, dicendi perite, si tute modò ad te rediisti; nam stertentem te tam prope finem et de *morte* voluntaria nescio quid ab re somniculosè oscitantem offendo; tum statim negas *cadere in*
15 *regem suæ mentis compotem, ut populum seditionibus distrahat, exercitus suos hostibus debellandos tradat, ut factiones contra se suscitet.* Quæ omnia cùm et alii multi reges, et Carolus ipse fecerit, dubitare non potes, præsertim Stoïcus, quin ut omnes improbi, sic omnes quoque tyranni prorsus insaniant.
20 Flaccum audi.

> *Quem mala stultitia, et quæcunque inscitia veri*
> *Cæcum agit, insanum Chrysippi porticus et grex*
> *Autumat, hæc populos, hæc magnos formula reges,*
> *Excepto sapiente, tenet.* —

learning and literature is fled out of England with yourselves, did not one of you know how to defend the king's cause and his own with sufficient vigor and Latinity, and submit it to the judgment of other nations? Did you fall so far short that 5 this crackbrained purse-snatcher of a Frenchman must needs be fetched out for hire to take sides with you, and undertake the defence of a helpless poverty-stricken king, attended though he was with so much infantry of speechless priests and doctors? Even for this too, believe me, your dishonor will 10 blaze forth notorious among foreigners; and all men will consider that you deserved to fail at any rate in a cause which you availed not even to uphold by words, much less by force of arms and valor.

Now, goodman speechifier, I come to you again,—if at 15 least you are come to yourself again; for here, so near the end of your book, I catch you snoring, and sleepily yawning out an irrelevant something-or-other about voluntary death. Then you deny "that it can occur to a king in his right wits to embroil his people in seditions, betray his own forces to defeat 20 by enemies, and raise factions against himself." All which things having been done by many kings, and particularly by Charles himself, you can no longer doubt, especially being a Stoic, that, like all profligate villains, all tyrants too are downright mad. Hear what Flaccus says: "Whoever is led blindly 25 on by malign stupidity and by whatsoever ignorance of truth, him doth Chrysippus' porch and school account a madman. This saying comprises great kings, this whole nations, except the wise man only." So that if you would clear King Charles

Si igitur insani cujuspiam facti crimen à rege Carolo amovere cupis, debebis improbitatem ab eo priùs amovere quàm insaniam. At enim *rex non potuit proditionem in eos committere, qui vassalli ipsius et subjecti fuere.* Primùm, cum æquè atque
5 ulla gens hominum liberi simus, nullum barbarum morem fraudi nobis esse patiemur: fac deinde *vassallos* fuisse nos regis, ne sic quidem tyrannum perferre dominum necesse habuimus. Omnis ea subjectio, ut ipsæ leges nostræ loquuntur, *honesto et utili* definita est. Leg. Hen. 1. c. 55. Fidem eam
10 esse *mutuam* jurisconsulti omnes tradunt, si dominus *ligeam,* quod aïunt, *defensionem* præstiterit: sin è contrario nimiùm sævus fuerit, aut atrocem aliquam injuriam intulerit, *dissolvi et penitùs extingui omnem homagii connexionem.* Hæc ipsa Bractoni verba et Fletæ sunt. Unde vassallum est ubi lex ipsa
15 in dominum armat; eúmque singulari certamine à vassallo, si acciderit, interimendum tradit. Idem si universæ civitati aut nationi in tyrannum non licuerit, deterior liberorum hominum conditio quàm servorum erit. Nunc Caroli homicidia aliorum regum partim homicidiis, partim justè factis
20 excusare contendis. De laniena Hiberniensi *remittis lectorem ad opus illud regium Iconis Basilicæ;* et ego te remitto ad Iconoclastem. *Captam Rupellam,* proditos Rupellenses, *osten-*

from the imputation of acting like a madman, you must rid
him of wickedness first, before you can rid him of insanity.

But you say: "The king could not commit treason against
such as were his own vassals and subjects." In the first place,
5 since we are as free as any nation of mankind, we will not
endure any barbarous custom to our hurt. In the second place,
suppose we had been the king's "vassals"; even so we were
not bound to endure a tyrant to lord it over us. And as for our
being "subjects," all such subjection, as our own laws declare,
10 is limited to what is "honorable and beneficial." Leg. Hen. I.
Cap. 55. All our lawyers tell us that this engagement is
"mutual" upon condition that the lord shall give, as the phrase
goes, "liege protection and defense"; but if the lord be too
harsh to his tenant, and do him some cruel hurt, "all bond of
15 homage is dissolved and utterly extinguished." These are the
very words of Bracton and Fleta. Hence there are situations
in which the law itself arms the vassal against the lord, and
delivers the lord over to be killed, if it so fall out, by the vassal
in single combat. If a whole state or nation may not lawfully
20 do the same to a tyrant, the condition of freemen will be worse
than that of slaves.

Then you strive to excuse king Charles's murders, partly
by murders committed by other kings, and partly by instances
of right action on their part. For the matter of the Irish butch-
25 ery, you "refer the reader to the king's well-known work the
Eikon Basiliké," and *I* refer *you* to *Eikonoklastes.* "The taking of La Rochelle," the betrayal of its townsmen, "the making a show of assistance instead of giving it them," you will

tatam potiùs quàm datam opem, imputari Carolo non vis: imputetur nécne meritò, non habeo dicere; satis supérque ab eo peccatum est domi, ne externa persequi curem: omnes interim ecclesias Protestantium, quotquot ullo tempore se contra

5 reges religionis hostes armis defenderunt, eodem nomine rebellionis damnas. Quam contumeliam ab alumno suo sibi illatam quanti intersit ad disciplinam ecclesiasticam, suámque tuendam integritatem, non negligere, secum ipsi cogitent: nos etiam Anglos eâ expeditione proditos acerbè tulimus.

10 Qui enim regnum Angliæ in tyrannidem convertere diu meditatus erat, non, nisi extincto priùs militari civium robore ac flore, cogitata perficere se posse arbitrabatur. Aliud erat crimen regis quod ex jurejurando regibus regnum capessentibus dari solito verba quædam ejus jussu erasa fuerint,

15 antequam jurâsset. O facinus indignum et execrandum! impium qui fecit, quid dicam qui defendit? nam quæ potuit, per Deum immortalem, quæ perfidia, aut juris violatio esse major? quid illi sanctius post sacratissima religionis mysteria illo jurejurando esse debuit? Quis quæso sceleratior, ísne qui

20 in legem peccat, an qui legem ipsam uti secum unà peccare faciat dat operam? aut denique ipsam legem tollit ne peccâsse videatur? Agedum, jus hoc religiosissimè jurandum rex iste

not have laid at Charles's door, nor have I anything to say as
to whether it deserves to be; he did mischief enough and more
than enough at home, so that I need not take the trouble to
follow up his misdemeanors abroad. (But you in the mean
5 time would make out all the Protestant churches that have at
any time defended themselves by force of arms against kings
who were professed enemies of their religion, to have been
upon this one ground guilty of rebellion. Let these churches
themselves consider how important it is for the preservation
10 of ecclesiastical discipline and of their own integrity, not to
pass by this insult offered them by their own nursling and
disciple.) What troubles us most is that we English were betrayed in that expedition. He who had long designed to con-
vert the government of England into a tyranny thought he
15 could not accomplish his plan till the flower and strength of
his subjects' military power were cut off.

Another of the king's crimes was the causing some words
to be struck out of the usual coronation oath before he would
take it. Unworthy and abominable action! Him that did it I
20 call wicked; what shall I call him that defends it? For by the
eternal God, what breach of faith and violation of the laws
can possibly be greater? What ought to be more sacred to him,
next to the holy sacraments themselves, than that oath?
Which, pray, is guiltier, he that offends against the law, or he
25 that endeavors to make the law his accomplice in offending,
or rather, destroys the law that he may not seem to offend
against it? Look you: that oath, which he ought most scru-
pulously to have sworn to, this king of yours did violate; but

violavit; sed ne palàm tamen violâsse videretur, turpissimo
quodam adulterio per dolum corrupit; et ne pejerâsse diceretur, jus ipsum jurandum in perjurium vertit. Quid aliud
potuit sperari, nisi injustissimè, versutissimè, atque infelicis-
5 simè regnaturum esse eum, qui ab injuria tam detestanda auspicatus regnum est; jusque illud primum adulterare ausus,
quod solum impedimento sibi fore, ne jura omnia perverteret,
putabat. At enim *Sacramentum* illud, sic enim defendis, *non*
magis obligare reges potest, quàm leges; legibus autem se
10 *devinciri velle præ se ferunt, et secundùm eas vivere, cùm*
tamen re vera iis soluti sint. Quemquámne tam sacrilego,
támque incesto ore esse, ut sacramentum religiosissimum
tactis Evangeliis datum, quasi per se leviculum solvi sine causa
posse asserat? Te verò, scelus atque portentum, ipse Carolus
15 redarguit; qui cùm sacramentum illud non esse per se leve
quidpiam existimaret, idcirco ejus religionem aut subterfu-
gere, aut fallaciâ quavis eludere satius duxit, quàm apertè
violare; et corruptor jurisjurandi hujus et falsarius esse maluit,
quàm manifestè perjurus. At verò *jurat quidem rex populo*
20 *suo, ut populus vicissim regi, sed populus jurat regi fideli-*
tatem, non populo rex. Lepidum sanè hominis commentum!
annon qui juratus promittit atque spondet se quidpiam fideliter præstiturum, fidem suam iis obligat qui jusjurandum ab
eo exigunt? Rex sanè omnis ad præstanda ea quæ promittit,
25 et *fidelitatem,* et *obsequium,* et *obedientiam populo* jurat.
Hîc ad Gulielmum Conquæstorem recurris, qui ipse, non

that he might not seem openly to violate it, he craftily adulterated and foully corrupted it, and lest he might be said to have perjured himself, turned the very oath into a perjury. What else could be expected than that one who began his
5 reign with so detestable a wrong, and dared as a first step to adulterate that law which he thought his only hindrance from perverting all the laws, would rule most unrighteously, craftily, and disastrously? But that "Oath" (thus you justify him) "cannot bind kings more than do the laws; and kings pretend
10 that they will be bound by laws, and live according to them, though actually they are unbound by them." To think that anyone should express himself so impiously and sacrilegiously as to assert that a most solemn oath, sworn upon the Holy Evangelists, may without cause be unbound as if in itself it
15 were the merest trifle! Scoundrel, monster, you are refuted by Charles himself, who, thinking that oath no trifle, chose rather by stealth to evade, or by artifice to elude, its binding force, than openly to violate it, and chose rather to be a corrupter and falsifier of the oath, than visibly a perjurer.

20 "The king indeed swears to his people, as the people do to him; but the people swear fealty to the king, not the king to them." Pretty invention! Does not he that promises and engages under oath faithfully to perform something, bind his fidelity to them that require the oath of him? To the per-
25 formance of what he promises, every king does in fact swear to the people his "fealty, service, and obedience." Then you come back to William the Conqueror; yet even he was forced more than once to swear to perform not what was agreeable

quod sibi collibitum erat, sed quod populus ab eo et magnates postulabant, id omne haud semel jurare est coactus se præstiturum. Quòd si multi reges *coronam* solenni ritu non *accipiunt,* et proinde non jurant, et tamen regnant, idem de po-
5 pulo responderi potest; cujus pars magna fidelitatem nunquam juravit. Si rex ob eam causam solutus erit, erit et populus. Quæ autem pars populi jurabat, non regi solùm, sed regno et legibus jurabat, à quibus rex factus est, et quidem eatenus tantùm regi, quoad is leges observaret, *quas vulgus,* id est,
10 communitas sive plebeius ordo *elegerit.* Stultior enim sit, qui legum nostrarum loquelam ad puriorem semper latinitatem exigere velit. Hanc clausulam, *quas vulgus elegerit,* Carolus, antequam coronam acciperet, ex formula juramenti regii eradendam curavit. At, inquis, *sine regis assensu nullas leges*
15 *vulgus elegerit;* eóque nomine duo statura citas, unum Anni 37 Hen. 6. c. 15. alterum 13 Edouardi 4. c. 8. Tantum autem abest quo minùs eorum alterutrum in libro statutorum usquam appareat, ut annis abs te citatis, neuter eorum regum ullum omnino statutum promulgaverit. Tu fidem jam per-
20 fugarum, statuta tibi inaudita dictantium, elusus querere; dum alii tuam admirantur impudentiam simul et vanitatem, quem non est puditum iis in libris versatissimum videri velle, quos inspexisse nunquam, ne vidisse quidem tam manifestè

to him, but what the people and the great men of the realm demanded of him.

If many kings "receive the crown" without the usual solemnity, and accordingly reign without taking an oath, the
5 same thing may be said of the people, a great many of whom never have taken the oath of allegiance. If the king by not taking an oath be unbound, the people are so too. And that part of the people that swore, swore not to the king only, but to the realm and the laws by which the king came to his
10 crown, and to the king so far only as he should act according to those laws which "the common people," that is, the commonalty or House of Commons, "should choose." For it were folly always to wish to turn the phraseology of our laws into purer Latin. This clause, "which the commons shall choose,"
15 Charles before he was crowned procured to be razed out of the form of the royal oath. "But," say you, "without the king's assent the people can choose no laws"; and for this you cite two statutes, one 37 Henry VI, Chap. 15, and the other 13 Edward IV, Chap. 8. But either of the two is so far from
20 appearing in our statute-books, that in the years you mention neither of those kings enacted any statute at all! Now that you are fooled, go and complain of the bad faith of those renegades in dictating to you statutes that never were heard of; while other people stand astonished at the combination of
25 presumption with empty-headedness in you, who were not ashamed to pretend to be thoroughly versed in books which you have so clearly shown you have never looked into or so much as seen.

argueris. Clausula autem ista jurisjurandi, quam tu perfricti
oris balatro *commentitiam* audes dicere, *regis,* inquis, *defen-*
sores fieri posse aiunt, ut in aliquot antiquis exemplaribus ex-
titerit, *sed in desuetudinem abiisse, quòd commodam signifi-*
5 *cationem non haberet.* Verùm ob id ipsum majores nostri
illam clausulam in hoc regis jurejurando posuere, ut signifi-
cationem tyrannidi semper non commodam haberet. In desuetudinem autem si abierat, quod tamen falsissimum est,
quis neget multò meliori jure revocandam fuisse? frustrà, si
10 te audio: quippe *in regibus* mos ille *jurandi qui hodie receptus*
est, cæremonialis est tantùm. Atqui rex, cùm episcopos abo-
leri oportuit, per illud jus jurandum non licere sibi causatus
est: ita sacramentum illud sanctissimum, quoties ex usu est
regis, vel solidum quiddam et firmum erit, vel inane tantùm
15 et *cæremoniale.* Quod ego vos obtestor, Angli, etiam atque
etiam animadvertatis: et qualem estis regem habituri, si re-
dierit, vobiscum reputetis: non enim in mentem venisset unquam huic Grammatico sceleroso et extraneo de jure regis
Anglorum velle scribere, aut posse, nisi Carolus ille extorris,
20 paternâ disciplinâ imbutus, unàque illi monitores ejus profli-
gatissimi, quid hac de re scribi vellent omni studio suggessis-
sent. Dictabant huic illi, *totum Parlamentum proditionis in*
regem insimulari posse, vel ob hoc solum, quòd *sine assensu*

As for that clause in the coronation oath, which you, brazen-faced jack-pudding, dare to call "fictitious," you yourself say: "The king's defenders say that possibly" it may be extant in some ancient copies, "but that it fell into disuse be-
5 cause it had no satisfactory meaning." But precisely on this account did our ancestors put that clause into this oath, that it might have a meaning which would forever be *not* satisfactory to tyranny! If it had really fallen into disuse, however, which yet is utterly false, who would deny that there was the
10 greater need of reviving it? But even that would have been to no purpose, according to your doctrine; for that custom "of taking an oath, as kings nowadays generally use it, is only ceremonial." Yet the king, when it behooved him to put down the bishops, pretended that he could not do it by reason
15 of this same oath. Consequently that sacred solemn oath, according as it serves the king's turn or not, will be something genuine and immovable, or merely something empty and "ceremonial."

Englishmen, take notice of this, I adjure you, again and
20 again, and consider what manner of king ye are like to have, if he ever come back! For it would never have entered into this rascally foreign grammarian's head to wish to write, or to think himself able to write, of the law of the English crown, had not Charles's banished son, deep-dyed in his father's
25 teachings, together with those profligate prompters of his, eagerly supplied what they would have him write. 'Twas they dictated to him "that Parliament as a whole was liable to be charged with treason against the king" even for this alone,

regis declaravit omnes esse proditores qui arma contra Parla-
mentum Angliæ sumpserunt; vassallum scilicet regis esse
Parlamentum; jusjurandum verò regium *cæremoniale tan-*
tùm esse, quidni *vassallum* etiam? Ita neque legum ulla
5 sanctitas, neque sacramenti ulla fides, aut religio, quicquam
valebit ad cohibendam à vita atque fortunis vestrûm omnium
vel libidinem effrænati regis, vel ultionem exacerbati: qui ita
institutus à pueritia est, ut leges et religionem, ipsam denique
fidem vassallari sibi, et servire suis libitis arbitretur debere.
10 Quanto præstabilius esset, vobísque dignius, si opes, si libertatem, si pacem, si imperium vultis, à virtute, industria, prudentia, fortitudine vestra non dubitare petere hæc omnia,
quàm sub regio dominatu necquicquam sperare? Certè qui
sine rege ac domino parari hæc posse non putant, dici non
15 potest, quàm abjectè, quàm non honestè, non dico quàm
indignè de se ipsi statuant: quid enim aliud nisi se inertes,
imbecillos, mentis inopes atque consilii, corpore atque animo
ad servitutem natos fatentur esse? Et servitus quidem omnis
homini ingenuo turpis est; vobis autem post libertatem Deo
20 vindice, vestróque marte recuperatam, post tot fortia facinora, et exemplum in Regem potentissimum tam memorabile
editum, velle rursus ad servitutem, etiam præter fatum, redire, non modò turpissimum, sed et impium erit et sceleratum: párque vestrum scelus illorum sceleri erit, qui servitutis

that "without the king's assent it declared all to be traitors who have taken arms against the Parliament of England; for that Parliament is the king's vassal"; but that the king's coronation oath is "merely a matter of ceremony." Then why not

5 the vassal's oath too? So that no reverence for laws, no binding force of an oath, or scruple to break it, will avail to protect your lives and fortunes either from the cupidity of a king unbridled, or from the revenge of a king embittered, who from childhood has been taught to think that laws, religion,

10 nay, and his own promise, ought to be his vassals, and subject to his will and pleasure. If you desire riches, liberty, peace, and empire, how much more excellent, how much more becoming yourselves would it be, resolutely to seek all these by your own virtue, industry, prudence, and valor, than under

15 a royal despotism to hope for them in vain? They who think that these things cannot be compassed but under a king and lord—it cannot well be expressed how meanly, how dishonorably (I do not say how unworthily!) they think of themselves; for what do they other than confess that they them-

20 selves are lazy, weak, wanting in intelligence and prudence, and born to be slaves body and soul? All manner of slavery indeed is disgraceful to a man freeborn; but for you, after recovering your liberty with God to warrant and your own arms, after so many brave deeds done, and so notable an

25 example made of a most mighty and puissant king, for you to desire, against your very destiny, to return again into bondage, will be not only most shameful, but a thing sinful and wicked. And your wickedness will be like unto the wick-

olim Ægyptiacæ desiderio capti, multis tandem cladibus ac variis divinitùs absumpti, liberatori Deo pœnas tam servilis animi dedere. Quid tu interim, servitutis conciliator? *Potuit,* inquis, *rex proditionis et delictorum aliorum gratiam facere;*
5 *quod satis evincit legibus eum solutum fuisse.* Proditionis quidem, non quæ in regnum, sed quæ in se commissa erat, poterat rex, ut quivis alius, gratiam facere: poterat et quorundam aliorum fortasse maleficiorum, quanquam non id semper: an ideò qui maleficum servandi nonnunquam jus quoddam
10 habet, idem continuò omnes bonos perdendi jus ullum habebit? Citatus in curiam, eámque inferiorem, necesse non habet respondere, nisi per procuratorem, rex, uti nec de populo quidem ullus; an ideo in Parlamentum citatus ab universis non veniet? non ipse respondebit? *Conari* nos aïs *Batavorum*
15 *exemplo factum nostrum tueri,* atque hinc, stipendio scilicet metuens quo te Batavi luem atque pestem alunt, ne Anglos infamando etiam Batavos altores tuos infamâsse videaris, demonstrare cupis quàm *dissimile sit quod hi et quod illi fecerunt.* Quam ego collationem tuam, quanquam in ea quædam
20 sunt falsissima, alia, ne salario fortasse tuo non satis litares, palpum olent, omittam. Negant enim Angli opus sibi esse ut

edness of them who were seized with desire of their former Egyptian bondage, and were at length divinely cut off with many and divers destructions, paying to God their deliverer the penalty for so slavish a mind.

5   You who would persuade us to become slaves, meanwhile what say you? "The king," you say, "had power to pardon treason and other crimes; which sufficiently proves that the king himself was not bound by the laws." The king might indeed pardon treason, not against the kingdom, but against
10 himself, as anybody else may pardon a wrong done to himself; and he might perhaps pardon some other offenders, though not always. But does it follow that one who sometimes has some right to save an evildoer, shall therefore necessarily have any right whatever to destroy all good men? If
15 the king be impleaded in an inferior court, he, like any one of the people, to be sure, is not obliged to answer but by his attorney; shall he therefore, when summoned by all of his subjects to appear in Parliament, refuse to come—refuse to answer in person?

20 You say that we "endeavor to justify our action by the example of the Dutch"; and hence, fearing to lose the pay with which the Dutch support such a murrain and pest as you, you would fain show "how unlike are their actions and ours," lest in defaming the English you should appear also to defame
25 the Dutch who support you. I shall omit this comparison of yours, though some things in it are quite false, and other things reek flattery lest perchance you should not bring an acceptable offering unto your wages. For the English think

exterorum quorumvis exemplo facta sua tueantur. Habent leges, quas secuti sunt, patrias, hac in parte, sicubi terrarum aliæ sunt, optimas: habent quos imitentur, majores suos, viros fortissimos, qui immoderatis regum imperiis nunquam ces-
5 sere; multos eorum intolerantiùs se gerentes per supplicium necavere. In libertate sunt nati, sibi sufficiunt, quas volunt leges, possunt sibi ferre; unam præ cæteris colunt antiquissimam, à natura ipsa latam, quæ omnes leges, jus omne atque imperium civile non ad regum libidinem, sed ad bonorum
10 maximè civium salutem refert. Jam præter quisquilias et rudera superiorum capitum restare nihil video; quorum quidem acervum cùm satis magnum in fine congesseris, nescio quid aliud tibi volueris, nisi hujus tuæ fabricæ ruinam quasi præsagire. Tandem aliquando post immensam loquacitatem rivos
15 claudis; *Deum testatus te hanc causam tuendam suscepisse, non tantùm quia rogatus, sed quia meliorem nullam te potuisse defendere conscientia tibi suggessit.* Rogatus tu in res nostras tibi alienissimas, nobis non rogantibus, te interponas?
Tu populi Anglicani summos magistratus pro authoritate
20 próque imperio sibi commisso quod suum munus est in sua

they need not justify their actions by the example of any foreigners whatever. They have their laws of the land, which they have followed—laws which in this matter are the best in the world; they have for their imitation the examples of 5 their ancestors, great and gallant men who never gave way to the unrestrained power of kings, and who put many of them to death when their government became insupportable. They were born free; they stand in need of no other nation; they can make unto themselves what laws they desire. One 10 law in particular they venerate before the rest, a very ancient one enacted by nature itself, which measures all human laws, all civil right and government, not according to the lust of kings, but, above all else, according to the safety and welfare of good men.

15 Now I see nothing left over but rubbish and fragments of your earlier chapters; yet as you have raised an huge great heap of these at the end, I cannot imagine what other design you could have than to forebode the ruin of your whole fabric. At last after unmeasured talk you shut off the stream, "call 20 ing God to witness that you undertook the defence of this cause not only because you were asked, but because your conscience prompted you that you could defend no better cause." Merely because you were asked, would you intermeddle with our affairs, so utterly foreign to you, when we ourselves did 25 not ask you? Would you rend with insults undeserved, would you in a disreputable book libel and defame, the supreme magistracy of the English nation, when according to the authority and power to them entrusted they do but their duty within

ditione agentes, nullâ injuriâ lacessitus (neque enim natum te esse sciebant) indignissimis verborum contumeliis laceres, libróque infami edito proscindas? A quo autem rogatus? An ab uxore, credo, quæ jus regium, ut perhibent, in te exercet;
5 quæque tibi, quoties libet, ut illa Fulvia, cujus, ex epigrammate obscœno, centones modò consuisti (*p.* 320.) *aut* scribe *aut pugnemus* aït: unde tu, ne signa canerent, scribere malebas. An rogatus fortasse à Carolo minore, et perditissimo illo peregrinantium aulicorum grege, quasi alter Balaamus ab
10 altero Balacco Rege accersitus, ut jacentem regis causam, et malè pugnando amissam maledicendo erigere dignarere? Sic sanè fieri potuit; nisi quòd hujusmodi quiddam interfuit; ille enim vir sagax asino insidens locutuleio ad execrandum venit; tu asinus loquacissimus insessus à fœmina, et sanatis quos vul-
15 neraveras episcoporum capitibus obsitus, apocalypticæ illius bestiæ parvam quandam imaginem exprimere videris. Sed ferunt pœnituisse te hujus libri, pòst paulò quàm scripsisses. Benè profectò habet; tuam itaque ut testere omnibus pœnitentiam, nihil tibi priùs faciendum erit, quàm ut pro libro tam
20 longo unam tantummodò literam adhuc longam ex te facias. Sic enim pœnituit Iscarioten illum Judam cui similis es; ídque novit puer Carolus, qui crumenam idcircò tibi, insigne illud Judæ proditoris, dono misit, quòd primùm audierat, et postmodùm sciebat, te apostatam esse et Diabolum. Judas

their own jurisdiction—and all this without the least injury
or provocation from them, for they did not even know that
you were born? By whom, though, *were* you asked? By your
wife, I suppose, who, they say, exercises the royal right over
5 you, and, like the notorious Fulvia in the obscene epigram
from which a while ago (p. 320) you patched together a
cento, cries to you whenever she has a mind: "Either" *write*
"or we must fight!" Wherefore you preferred to write rather
than the trumpets should sound the charge! Or were you
10 asked by the younger Charles and that profligate crew of vagabond courtiers, like a second Balaam solicited by a second
King Balak, to deign to restore by curses and ill writing a
king's desperate cause that was lost by ill fighting? That may
well be, except there was something like this difference: when
15 *he* came to curse, he was a clever man sitting upon a talkative
little ass; you are a very talkative ass yourself, sat upon by a
woman, and being overgrown with the healed heads of the
bishops that heretofore you had wounded, you seem to present
a sort of miniature portrait of that beast in Revelation.
20 But they say that you repented yourself of this book a little
after you had written it. It is mighty well; and therefore to
witness your repentance unto all men, the first thing you
ought to do will be, instead of so long a book, to make only
just one proper long letter of yourself. For it was so Judas
25 Iscariot repented himself, whom you resemble. Young
Charles found it out too, and he sent you the purse, that badge
of traitor Judas, precisely because he had heard before, and
knew afterward by experience, that you were an apostate and

adversarium hunc vestrum ipsi refutetis; quod nulla alia ratione video posse fieri, nisi omnium maledicta vestris optime
factis exuperare perpetuò contendatis. Vota vestra et preces
ardentissimas Deus, cùm servitutis haud uno genere oppressi
5 ad eum confugistis, benignè exaudivit. Quæ duo in vita
hominum mala sanè maxima sunt, et virtuti damnosissima,
Tyrannis et Superstitio, iis vos gentium primos gloriosissimè
liberavit; eam animi magnitudinem vobis injecit, ut devictum
armis vestris et dedititium regem judicio inclyto judicare, et
10 condemnatum punire primi mortalium non dubitaretis. Post
hoc facinus tam illustre, nihil humile aut angustum, nihil non
magnum atque excelsum et cogitare et facere debebitis. Quam
laudem ut assequamini, hac sola incedendum est via, si ut
hostes bello domuistis, ita ambitionem, avaritiam, opes, et
15 secundarum rerum corruptelas, quæ subigunt cæteras gentes
hominum, ostenderitis posse vos etiam inermes media in pace
omnium mortalium fortissimè debellare; si, quam in repel-
lenda servitute fortitudinem præstitistis, eam in libertate conservanda justitiam, temperantiam, moderationem præstite-
20 ritis. His solis argumentis et testimoniis evincere potestis, non
esse vos illos, quos hic probris insequitur, *Perduelles, latrones,*
sicarios, parricidas, fanaticos; non vos ambitionis aut alieni

ye too, my countrymen, yourselves refute this adversary of
yours, which to do I see no other way than by striving con-
stantly to outdo all men's bad words by your own good deeds.
Your vows, your burning prayers, when, crushed beneath
5 more than one kind of slavery, ye fled to God for refuge, he
hath graciously heard and granted. Gloriously hath he delivered you before all other nations from what surely are the
two greatest mischiefs of this life, and most pernicious to virtue—Tyranny and Superstition; he hath inspired you with
10 the greatness of soul to be the first of mankind who, after having conquered their own king, and having him delivered into
their hands, have not hesitated to judge him with a judgment
that yet resounds in men's ears, and to condemn him, and
pursuant to that condemnation to put him to death. After so
15 glorious a deed, ye ought to think, ye ought to do, nothing
that is mean and petty, nothing but what is great and sublime.
This praise that ye may attain, there is but one path to tread:
as ye have subdued your enemies in the field, so ye shall prove
that unarmed and in the midst of peace ye of all mankind
20 have highest courage to subdue what conquers the rest of the
nations of men—faction, avarice, the temptations of riches,
and the corruptions that wait upon prosperity; and in maintaining your liberty shall show as great justice, temperance,
and moderation as ye have shown courage in freeing your-
25 selves from slavery. By these arguments and documents only
can ye prove ye are not such as this libeler reproaches you
with being—"Traitors, Robbers, Assassins, Parricides, Madmen"; that what ye did was not the slaughtering of a king

liberiùs, at certè in exemplo majore atque illustriore qui defenderit vix reperietur: ut si exempli tam ardui atque præclari facinus non sine divino instinctu tentatum tam prosperè atque confectum creditur, sit sanè cur eadem ope atque impulsu celebratum quoque idem his laudibus atque defensum videatur: id quod ab omnibus multo malim existimari, quàm aliam quamvis felicitatem vel ingenii vel judicii vel diligentiæ mihi tribui. Hoc tantùm, quemadmodum Consul ille Romanus, abiens magistratu juravit in concione rempub. atque illam urbem suâ unius operâ esse salvam, ita ego manum huic operi nunc ultimam imponens, Deum hominésque contestans ausim dicere, ea me demonstrâsse hoc libro, eáque ex summis cùm divinæ tum humanæ sapientiæ authoribus in medium protulisse, quibus et populum Anglicanum ad sempiternam posteritatis famam satis esse confidam in hac causa defensum, et plerosque mortales fœda sui juris ignorantia, falsáque specie religionis antea deceptos, nisi qui servire ipsi malint ac meruerint, satis esse liberatos. Atque illius quidem Consulis jusjurandum tale atque tantum populus Romanus universus illa in concione juratus ipse una voce et consensu approbavit: meam hanc persuasionem non meorum modò civium, sed exterorum etiam hominum quosque optimos haud tacita ubique gentium voce comprobare jamdudum intelligo.

freedom more freely than here it is defended, yet there shall hardly be found anyone who hath defended it in a greater and more glorious example. If, then, an action of example so high and illustrious is believed to have been as successfully accom-
5 plished as not without God's prompting undertaken, let this be reason good for thinking that in these my praises too it hath even by the same Might and Inspiration been glorified and defended. Indeed I had much rather all men thought so, than that any other success, whether of wit or judgment or industry,
10 were allowed me. Yet as that famous Roman Consul, upon re-tiring from office, swore in the popular assembly that the state and the city owed their safety to his single efforts, even so, as I now put the last touches to this work, so much only I dare assert, calling God and man to witness: that in this book I
15 have indicated and brought to light, from the highest authors of wisdom both divine and human, matters whereby, I trust, not only the English people has been adequately defended in this cause, to the everlasting reputation of its posterity, but numerous other human beings as well, hitherto deluded by
20 foul ignorance of their right and by false show of religion,— multitudes of men, I say, except such as themselves prefer and deserve to be slaves—have been quite set free. Now the oath of that Consul, great as were its claims, was in that same assembly ratified by oath of the whole Roman people with
25 one mind and one voice; this conviction of mine, I have long understood, is fully ratified by the most excellent not only of my fellow-citizens, but of foreigners too, with the loud voice of nations everywhere.

Quo ego fructu summo studiorum meorum, quem quidem in hac vita mihimet proposui, et gratus fruor, et id simul potissimum cogito, quî possim maximè non patriæ solùm, cui quod habui summum persolvi, verùm etiam quarumvis gentium hominibus totíque præsertim nomini Christiano testari, majora his quidem si possum assequi, potero autem si Deus dederit, eorum causa me cupere quidem interea ac meditari.

This my zealous labor's fruit—the highest that I for my part have set before me in this life—I gratefully enjoy; yet therewith too consider chief how I may bear best witness— not only to my own country, to which I have paid the highest 5 I possessed, but even to men of whatever nation, and to the cause of Christendom above all—that I am pursuing after yet greater things if my strength suffice (nay, it will if God grant), and for their sake meanwhile am taking thought, and studying to make ready.

NOTES

DEFENSIO PRIMA

THE editor has accepted the conclusions of F. F. Madan (*Milton, Salmasius, and Dugard,* Transactions of the Bibliographical Society IV (1923), pp. 119–145) in regard to the chronological order of the editions. In the preparation of the text chief use has been made of the third issue of the quarto first edition (1651: Madan no. 1), of the folio (*Editio emendatior,* 1651: Madan no. 2), and of the edition of 1658 (*Editio correctior et auctior, ab Autore denuo recognita,* 1658: Madan no. 14). The readings of the 1658 edition, which Milton designates as the final form of the work, have been printed unless there appeared to be excellent reasons for rejecting them. In cases of special difficulty the continental reprints which Madan numbers 3, 4, 5, 9, 12, and 13 have occasionally been consulted also.

Editions are designated in the critical notes by Madan's numbers. Unless otherwise stated, it is to be understood that the 1658 edition (Madan no. 14) has been followed. The very small number of emendations made by the editor are designated by his initials.

C. W. K.

TRANSLATOR'S NOTE

Masson (IV. 258, note), when introducing translated excerpts from the first *Defensio,* praises the translation by "Mr. Washington, of the Temple," published in 1692, as "faithful and good in the main." In practice, however, he finds it inadequate: "I have had it before me, and have taken phrases from

it, while translating the present and subsequent passages from the original."

The present translation originated in an attempt to render the Washington translation available by means of minor changes. As the work proceeded, such changes proved insufficient: strong reasons were found for disagreeing with Masson's praise and agreeing with his practice. The present translation, then, though retaining some of the phrases of the old, was made directly from Milton's Latin.

S. L. W.

PAGE 2

TITLE. Salmasii Defensionem] 1, 2 *Salmasii*, Defensionem —9 perstringam,] 1, 2 astringam, —10 esse:] 1, 2 esse; —15 parvas, neque vulgares; Regem] 1, 2 parvas neque vulgares, regem

PAGE 4

—18 perfunderet;] 1, 2 perfundere —19 vereretur?] C. W. K. vereretur? 1, 2, 14 vereretur. —20 prædico;] 1, 2 prædico? —21 Deum?] 1, 2 Deum.

PAGE 6

—1 efferentes,] 1, 2 attollentes, —4 Ducem] 1, 2 ducem —14 confidat] 1, 2 opinetur —19 gesserant,] 1, 2 gessere

PAGE 8

—10 facili nuper negotio] 1, 2 facili negotio nuper —12 redargui atque summovi,] 1, 2 redarguit atque summovit, —13 nunc] 1, 2 ego —15 et, quamvis] 1, 2 et quamvis —16 eâ tamen stipe] 1, 2 eâ stipe contentus, quam] 1, 2 contentus quam —18 sed etiam alienæ:] 1, 2 sed alienæ: —25 quamvis . . . partes,] 1, 2 quamvis alioqui regias secutus ipse partes,

PAGE 10

—2 quidem, qui] 1 quidem qui —4 more, (quandoquidem] 1, 2 more (quandoquidem —20 fuisset,] 1, 2 foret,

PAGE 12

—3 aggrediamur,] 1, 2 aggrediamur; —4 barbariem,] 1, 2 barbariem; —5 studia atque] 1, 2 studia, atque —8 imprimis, quid exponat, videamus:] 1, 2 imprimis videamus quid ait, —10 filium:] 1, 2 filium; —16 *Regiis*:] 1, 2 *Regiis*;

PAGE 14

—1 empta,] 1, 2 emta,   rege:] 1, 2 Rege: Non] 1, 2 non
—3 variatam;] 1, 2 variatam,   —7 Regis] 1, 2 regis   —9 operam,
et] 1, 2 operam et   —13 Regis] 1, 2 regis   —15 machæram
. . . quam] 1, 2 gladium multo longiorem eo quem   —22 mittam]
1, 2 apportem   —24 habeant] 1, 2 habent

PAGE 16

—2 barbarie] 1, 2 audaciâ   —5 simillimo, nullius,] 1, 2
simillimo nullius,   —7 excitâsse.] 1, 2 concitâsse.   —8 *Regis*]
1, 2 *regis*   —9 *Regis?*] 1, 2 *regis?*   —11 Regis] 1, 2 regis
—14 Regis,] 1, 2 regis,   Rex] 1, 2 rex   —18 Magistratibus]
1, 2 magistratibus   Rege] 1, 2 rege

PAGE 18

—7 reipublicæ] 1 reipub.   —8 reipublicæ] 1 reipub.   —11
vindices] 1, 2 Vindices   —12 illustrissimi . . . Ordines,] 1, 2
Illustrissimi Fœderatorum Ordines,   —20 fuisset,] 1, 2 foret,

PAGE 20

—2 Physici comas] 1, 2 Physici, comas   —5 indicare?] 1 indicare
2 indicare.   —10 jubeo,] 1, 2 jubeo

PAGE 22

—3 crebrius] 1, 2 frequentius   —6 sumpti] 1, 2 sumti
—21 moli tanta] 1, 2 mole tantum

PAGE 24

—6 accepturus] 1, 2 excepturus   sit:] 1, 2 sit;   —14 calumniæ
et] 1, 2 calumniæ, et   —21 *ecclesia*] 1, 2 *Ecclesia*

PAGE 26

—7 196.] 1, 2 169.   —13 *probabilis, cur*] 1, 2 *probabilis cur*

PAGE 28

—1 prodere?] 1, 2 prodere;   —8 nunc, et] 1, 2 nunc et
—14 redegisses,] 1, 2 redigere poteras,   —19 respublica] 1 Respub.
2 Respublica

PAGE 30

—13 majore] 1, 2 majori

PAGE 32

—3 dicis;] 1, 2 dicis,   —4 esses;] 1, 2 esses,   —6 *terræ
filii*] 1 *terræ filii*   2, 14 *terræ-filii*   —8 quid] 1, 2 quæ
—9 doceat:] 1, 2 doceat.   —12 promens.—] 1, 2 promens—
—18 vendendo quod] 1, 2 vendendo, quod

PAGE 34

—10 ecclesiam;] 1, 2 Ecclesiam;   —11 hinc] 1, 2 Hinc

PAGE 36

—3 rex] 1, 2 Rex   —7 hostes;] 1, 2 hostes: —8 Arsaci. Te]

1, 2 Arsaci: Te — 9 quæ tanta fiducia] 1, 2 quæ fiducia — 14 credam?] 1, 2 credam. — 18 *faciamus, quam*] 1, 2 *faciamus quam*

PAGE 38

— 6 dubites,] 1, 2 dubitas, — 10 removere] 1, 2 amovere — 15 suspicetur;] 1, 2 suspicaretur; — 18 ageres, quis,] 1 ageres quis,

PAGE 40

— 10 postera] 1, 2 proxima — 12 ut] 1, 2 si — 15 pervagari . . . sinant.] 1, 2 pervagari, quo velit, sinant. — 18 nos, quemadmodum] 1, 2 nos quemadmodum — 19 Caput I.] 1 Cap. I. — 20 superbiæ, Salmasi,] 1, 2 superbiæ Salmasi,

PAGE 42

— 4 duodecimâ, *Ornari*] 1, 2 duodecimâ *Ornari* — 10 potes, rhetoricis] 1 potes rhetoricis — 14 causidici] 1, 2 caussidici possis;] 1, 2 potes; 22 dicam] 1, 2 Dicam

PAGE 46

— 3 perdiderit?] 1, 2 perdiderit, — 5 æstimandum] 1 estimandum — 9 decennalem;] 1 decennalem,

PAGE 48

— 2 quam plurimos] 1, 2 quam plurimos 14 quamplurimos — 14 reorum, qui,] 1 reorum qui, — 15–18 Quæ ratio . . . fuisse creditur?] 2 Quæ ratio igitur animadvertendi in civem moderatior est habita, cur non eadem in regem quoque moderatior, et vel ipsi regi acceptior fuisse existimanda est? 1 AS 2, EXCEPT . . . existimanda est. — 22 faventem] 1, 2 amicam

PAGE 50

— 8 sit.] 1 sit? 2 sit: — 12 crediderim,] 1 crediderim; — 13 repeto,] 1 repeto; — 16 depoposcerit.] 1, 2 deposcebat. — 17 magistratum, sive] 1, 2 magistratum sive

PAGE 52

— 2 reddiderunt.] 1, 2 reddidere. — 9 rege] 1, 2 Rege

PAGE 54

— 16 publicam] 1, 2 Publicam — 20 conscriptos;] 1, 2 conscriptos:

PAGE 58

— 9 effudisset,] 1, 2 effuderit, 9–10 fuissent . . . eò] 1, 2 sint quæ chartâ illinantur; adeò

PAGE 60

— 2 docuerant;] 1, 2 docuerunt; — 3 destiterant,] 1, 2 destiterunt, — 7 sacerdotibus, quos] 1 sacerdotibus quos — 16 quod

inquies ambitione] 1 quod, inquies, ambitione —22 extirpari;]
1, 2 extirpari,

Page 62

—2 scio;] 1, 2 scio, —5 factiosis et] 1, 2 factiosis, et —12
curatores;] 1, 2 *curatores*. Apparat.] 1 Apparat: —17 feliciter;]
1 feliciter, —19 sis non] 1, 2 sis, non

Page 64

—3 est, superstitiosas] 1 est superstitiosas —7 *Christiani*]
1 *christiani* —8 fuissent,] 1, 2 essent, —11 transfuga;] 1, 2
transfuga, —15 nominabo, quoniam] 1 nominabo quoniam
—19 *sapientum, et*] 1, 2 *sapientium et* —20 *illustres?*] 1, 2
illustres.

Page 66

—5 assensus] 1, 2 assentitus —10 sunt, aboleret] 1, 2 sunt
aboleret —14 perlegisse;] 1, 2 perlegisse? —15 mendosum
crepas;] 1, 2 mendosum, crepas; —17 rixari, et] 1, 2 rixari et

Page 68

—2 nebulonem appellas,] 1 nebulonem palàm appellas, —2
Grammaticum] 1, 2 grammaticum —7 habeam, nam] 1, 2 habeam
(nam —9 esset; qui] 1, 2 esset) qui —10 quasi . . . cui]
1 ac si deo cuilibet 2 ac si Deo cuilibet —14 virtutem et] 1, 2
virtutem, et —21 doctrina,] 1, 2 doctrina;

Page 70

—1 Caput II.] 1 Cap. II. —4 *sentiant,*] 1, 2 *sentiant*; —6
retorquere.] 1, 2 affirmare. —10 testimoniis et] 1, 2 testimoniis,
et —12 barbariam] 1, 2 barbariem —15 quenquam] 1, 2
ullum 17–18 flagitia, . . . defenderit.] 1, 2 flagitia regum jura
esse asseverârit. —19 abhorruere;] 1 abhorruere,

Page 72

—2 ingenio atque animo] 1, 2 vernilitate —4 Caracalla, ab]
1 Caracalla ab —5 persuasus, non] 1 edoctus non 2 edoctus,
non —6 est, aut] 1 est aut —15 es?] 1, 2 es; —16
dejicere] 1, 2 projicere

Page 74

—2 qui, contrà] 1 qui contrà —3 Dionysius, ex] 1 Dionysius
ex —15 ferendi, neque] 1, 2 ferendi neque —19 statuerit.]
1, 2 statueret. —23 *dices, statuam*] 1, 2 *dices statuam*

Page 76

—3 fuisse vel] 1, 2 fuisse, vel —7 Deo] 1 deo —9 concesserit.] 1, 2 concederet. —11 justè;] 1, 2 justè, —13 ipsi]
1, 2 sibi —14 potuerit.] 1, 2 potuit.

PAGE 78

—1 anteponendus:] 1, 2 anteponendus.   lib. 4,] 1, 2 lib. 4.
—12 possit.] 1, 2 possit,   —13 etc;] 14 &c: 1, 2 &c.   —18
igitur, quid] 1, 2 igitur quid

PAGE 80

—5 quenquam] 1, 2 ullum   —9 videamus:] 1, 2 videamus.
etc:] 14 &c: 1, 2 &c.   —12 *ei, quid*] 1, 2 *ei quid*   —14
regis] 1, 2 sua   —18 Jos. I:] 1, 2 Jos. I.   —20 alioquin] 1, 2
Alioquin cap. 9:] 1, 2 cap. 9.   —23 *volet, faciet;*] 1, 2 *volet faciet,*

PAGE 82

—1 nimirum . . . authoritate] 1, 2 nimirum faciet authoritate
armatus;] 1, 2 armatus,   —4 *regis, ibi dominatio;*]   1, 2 *regis
ibi dominatio,*   *ei, quid*] 1, 2 *ei quid*   —6 fecisti, I Sam.]
1 fecisti. Sam.   2 fecisti. I Sam.   —7 pag. 49,] 1, 2 pag. 49.
—10 *insita*] 1, 2 *tacitâ*   —13 plurimùm damnosa] 1 plurimùm,
damnosa   —15 universus, quoties] 1 universus quoties   —20
grassetur, ita] 1, 2 grassetur ita

PAGE 84

—1 posthac] 1, 2 post hoc   —10 *teste*] 1, 2 *Teste*

PAGE 86

—affirmat:] 1, 2 affirmat.

PAGE 88

—3 causam] 1, 2 caussam   —4 demonstraret.] 1 demonstraret,
—14 indicaverat:] 1, 2 indicaverat.   —16 erat, sed] 1, 2 erat sed

PAGE 90

—2 causâ] 1, 2 caussâ   —5 potuisses,] 1, 2 potuisti,   —14
fatearis?] 1, 2 fatearis.

PAGE 92

—2 eorum] 1, 2 illorum   —3 expulerant?] 1, 2 expulerant.
—7 *pare*: Aliaque] 1, 2 *pare*; aliaque   —16 impellunt.] 1, 2
proturbant.

PAGE 94

—7 dicas,] 1, 2 dicis,   —12 94;] 1, 2 94.   —14 *statutum?*]
1, 2 *statutum.*   —16 docuerit,]   1, 2 doceret,   —19 quem
tu] 1, 2 quem, tu

PAGE 96

—3 introductum, non] 1, 2 introductum non   —7 recitem;]
1, 2 recitem,   —8 4.] 1, 2 4   —19 agat?] 1 agat,   —20
inimicum et] 1, 2 inimicum, et

PAGE 98

—2 postremò, *leges*] 1, 2 postremò *leges*   —11 pœnam] 1
pænam   —20 libuisset] 1, 2 libeat

PAGE 100

—3 rabbinos;] 1, 2 rabbinos,   —11 *Jehova*;] 1, 2 *Jehovah*;
—15 proculdubio] 1 procul dubio   —18 cætera] 1 cœtera
—21 accepimus;] 1, 2 accepimus,

PAGE 102

—13 Postbabylonicis] 1, 2 Post-babylonicis

PAGE 104

—18 abire et] 1, 2 abire, et   —19 Judæos et] 1, 2 Judæos, et

PAGE 106

—5 impius, iniquus,] 1, 2 impius, iniquus,   14 impius iniquus,
—13 Carolum IV. se] 1, 2 Carolum 4 se   —16 assequuntur?] 1, 2
assequuntur.   —18 Majestatis maxime] 1, 2 Majestatis maxime
—14 Majestatis, maxime   —19 Aristoteles, Polit.] 1, 2 Aristoteles
Polit.   —22 reipub.] 1 reipub:

PAGE 108

—2 proficiscens, accersivit] 1, 2 proficiscens accersivit   —6
inquis;] 1, 2 inquis,   —9 populus, refragante] 1, 2 populus
refragante   Deo, regem] 1, 2 deo regem   —13 David,] 1, 2
David?   —15 Sam. 5,] 1, 2 Sam. 5.   —16 Solomon,] 1, 2
Salomon,   —17 *Domini, et*] 1, 2 *Domini et*   *Par.*] 1, 2
Paralip.   —19 populum,] 1, 2 populum.

PAGE 110

—5 debuisti, vers. 11, 12. *Tua*] 1 potuisti v. 11, 12. *tua*   2 potuisti.
v. 11, 12. *tua*   —7 etc: diciturque] 1, 2 &c. Diciturque   —9
Deum] 1, 2 deum   esse cui] 1, 2 esse, cui   11–17 nam . . . Et]
OMITTED IN 1, 2   —17 certè] 1, 2 enim

PAGE 112

—3 *intuentur?*] 1, 2 *intuentur.*   —4 *quia . . . objiciant*:]
1, 2 IN ROMAN LETTERS   10 Horatii,] 1, 2 Horatii.

PAGE 114

—8 Evangelio] 1 evangelio   —10 gloriantur: ne] 1, 2 gloriantur. Ne   —19 certe, . . . loquitur;] 1, 2 certe quem citas de
αὐταρχία loquitur;

PAGE 116

—18 visa:] 1, 2 visa;   —18 *Judæorum*;] 1, 2 *Judæorum*,
addis, *Judæos*] 1, 2 addis *Judæos*

PAGE 118

—5 Psal. 17;] 1 Psal, 17.   2 Psal. 17.   —7 scripsisse cùm] 1, 2
scripsisse, cùm   —17 palmarium, *Tibi*] 1, 2 palmarium. *Tibi*   Ps.]
1, 2 Psal.

PAGE 120

—3 *peccavi*, proculdubio] 1 *peccavi* procul dubio   2 *peccavi* pro-

culdubio   —11 videatur, 2 Sam. 12,] 1 videatur. 2 Sam. 12.   2 videatur, 2 Sam. 12.   —12 numquis] 1, 2 an quis   —14 condemnaverat; v. 5,] 1, 2 condemnaverat. v. 5.   —18 pronuntiaverat, v. 13,] 1, 2 pronuntiaverat. v. 13.

PAGE 122

    —4 30 hæc] 1, 2 30. hæc   —6 42 Advocatum] 1, 2 42. Advocatum   —8 *est, sævitiam*] 1 est sævitiam   —9 *assueverant?*] 1, 2 *assueverant.*   —12 advocatus;] 1, 2 advocatus,   —23 tuam, et] 1, 2 tuam et   Apparat.] 1 Apparat:

PAGE 124

    —9 Affirmas p. 29,] 1, 2 Affirmas. p. 29.   —10 *gentes*;] 1, 2 *Gentes,*   —11 *Occidens*:] 1, 2 *occidens.*   At p. 43,] 1, 2 At. p. 43. —16 tibi,] 1, 2 tibi;

PAGE 126

    —23 secundus:] 1, 2 secundus;

PAGE 128

    —19 possit,] 1, 2 possit.   quanquam] 1, 2 quamquam

PAGE 130

    —1 Moses, Deut.] 1 Moses Deut.   —3 *Dei,*] 1 *dei.* 2 *Dei.* —10 dicis;] 1, 2 dicas;   Apparatu . . . 230,] 1, 2 apparatu in primatum, p. 230.   —13 idque, sicut] 1, 2 idque sicut   —15 sequitur, reges,] 1 sequitur reges,   —17 summo non] 1, 2 summo, non   —18 suum?] 1, 2 suum.   —20 *constituendo,*] 1, 2 *constituendo.*   —22 *regem:*] 1, 2 *regem*;

PAGE 132

    —1 p. 42,]   1, 2 p. 42.   —6 *Deus*] 1 *deus*   —7 impeditum;] 1, 2 impeditum: —8 Prophetam,] 1, 2 prophetam, Deum,] 1 deum,   —13 verbo, improbe,] 1, 2 verbo improbe,

PAGE 134

    —5 testatur Deus] 1, 2 testatur Deus 14 testatur. Deus   —6 petîssent: . . . *sed*] 1 petîssent. ver. 7 *Non te sed* 2 petîssent. ver. 7. *Non te sed*   —8 planè quasi] 1, 2 acsi   —13 19,] 1, 2 19. —14 *malis et*] 1, 2 *malis, et*   —15 *nobis*: . . . 12,] 1, 2 *nobis.* et cap. 12. 12.   —16 *vester*: . . . 17,] 1, 2 *vester.* et ver. 17. —17 *Jehova, petendo*] 1, 2 *Jehova petendo*   —18 rege, . . . 11;] 1, 2 rege, 13. 10. 11.

PAGE 136

    —6 13,] 1, 2 13.   —8 habuisset.] 1, 2 habuerat.   —11 fuit.] 1, 2 fuerit

PAGE 138

    —2 *p.*] 1, 2 *pag.*   —6 magistratus?] 1, 2 magistratus.   —14

suamet] 1, 2 suomet   opera] 1, 2 opere   —18 rex] 1, 2 *Rex*
—20 dubitaverint,] 1, 2 dubitârunt,

PAGE 140

—1 erat:] 1, 2 erat;   Jacobus, Darlii] 1, 2 Jacobus Darlii   —6
dictus;] 1, 2 dictus,   divinandum . . . reliquerit.] 1, 2 dubium sit.
—8 Solomone, quî] 1, 2 Solomone quî   —19 Bucchinghamio]
1 Bucchingamio   —21 Summo regni concilio] 1, 2 comitiis
—23 conventum] 1, 2 comitia

PAGE 142

—2 impendit;] 1, 2 impendit,   —3 est;] 1, 2 est,   —10
populo] 1, 2 populo   14 Populo   —16 Caput III.] 1 Cap. III.
—20 *possent*,] 1, 2 *possint*,

PAGE 144

—1 Lex,] 1, 2 lex,   —5 Dei] 1 dei   —8 civili:] 1, 2 civili;
—12 stabilivit,] 1, 2 stabiliret,   —13 subjecit?] 1, 2 subjiceret.
—17 7,] 1, 2 7.   —18 statuit:] 1, 2 statuit.   —22 confirmavit:]
1, 2 confirmavit.

PAGE 146

—9 17,] 1, 2 17.   —11 Ergo,] 1, 2 ergo,   —19 loquitur;]
1, 2 loquitur,

PAGE 148

—3 est, civibus] 1 est civibus   —7 est, fideles] 1 est fideles
Christianos] 1 christianos   —9 Christo, liberos] 1, 2 Christo
liberos   —10 Christianos:] 1 christianos: —15 nosset.] 1, 2
esset   —16 imponere, certè] 1, 2 imponere, certè   14 imponere
certè   —17 Christianos,] 1 christianos,

PAGE 150

—5 esset,] 1, 2 sit,   —11 *Cujus*,] 1 *cujus*,   —12 *Dei sunt
Deo*.] 1 *dei sunt deo*.   —18 hominis et] 1, 2 hominis, et   aspi-
ciens, interrogaret] 1, 2 aspiciens interrogaret   —20 Dei] 1 dei
Dei] 1 dei   —21 Deo] 1 deo

PAGE 152

—1 est, homini,] 1 est homini,   —2 piaculo et] 1, 2 piaculo, et
—3 Dei,] 1 dei,   —5 Deo] 1 deo   —7 Deo] 1 deo   —18
effigie] 1, 2 nomine

PAGE 154

—8 regio, sed] 1 regio sed   —12 Atque] 1, 2 Verùm   —18
Christianos] 1 christianos   —21 eas;] 1, 2 eas,

PAGE 156

—1 *servus*.] 1, 2 *servus*?   —6 cæci . . . tanquam] 1, 2 utì tu
soles, cæci atque inermes tanquam   —9 Deus] 1 deus   —12

Christianus] 1 christianus   populus more] 1 populus more   —16
vult (quis] 1, 2 vult, quis   —17 major?) esto] 1, 2 major, esto
primus] 1, 2 primus   —20 Christianum] 1 christianum

PAGE 158

—1 Christianos] 1 christianos   —3 Christianus] 1 christianus
—4 populo tamen superbè] 1 populo superbè   —6 lactantem:]
1, 2 lactantem.   nutricius] 1, 2 nutritius   —7 dominos, sed]
1 dominos sed   —12 Dei] 1 dei

PAGE 160

—1 domi Lyciscam] 1, 2 domi, ut ferunt, Lyciscam   tibi . . .
miserè] 1, 2 tibi miserè   —2 dominatur, . . . unde] 1, 2 dominatur;
cujus partim impulsu etiam scripsisse hæc diceris; unde   —13
Dominum;] 1 dominum,   2 Dominum,   —16 Dei.] 1 dei.
—17 dispersis atque] 1, 2 dispersis, atque

PAGE 162

—9 Dominum.] 1 dominum.   —10 Deo] 1 deo   —11
Dei.] 1 dei.   —14 addit, v. 16,] 1, 2 addit. v. 16   liberi;] 1, 2
liberi,   —21 Atqui] 1 At qui   ille, cui] 1 ille cui

PAGE 164

—6 Romanos: c. 13,] 1, 2 Romanos. c. 13.   —7 esto; non] 1,
2 esto, non   —8 Deo;] 1 deo,   2 Deo,   Deo] 1 deo   —14
est, quisque] 1, 2 est quisque   —17 induxisse, ut] 1 induxisse ut
—22 suscipienda;] 1, 2 suscipienda,

PAGE 166

—1 novatores, quasi] 1, 2 novatores quasi   —4 Apostoli,] 1
apostoli,   —7 Apostolo] 1 apostolo   fuerit, ex] 1, 2 fuerit ex
—8 scrutemur:] 1, 2 scrutemur.   —9 esto;] 1, 2 esto,   —17
appellat:] 1, 2 appellat.   —18 rationem:] 1, 2 rationem.   —19
κρατύνει;] 1, 2 κρατύνει.

PAGE 168

—9 Deo;] 1 deo;   —11 Deum] 1 deum   —12 Phil. 12,]
1, 2 Philip. 12.   12–14 nihil . . . contraria.] 1, 2 IN ROMAN LET-
TERS.   —14 Deo] 1 deo   —17 proculdubio] 1 procul dubio
—19 8,] 1, 2 8.   —20 principes, quos] 1, 2 principes quos   —21
Deum] 1 deum   22 Deum] 1 deum   —23 Deo] 1 deo

PAGE 170

—1 Nonnumquam] 1, 2 Aliquando   —3 4;] 1, 2 4.   Omnem;]
1, 2 omnem,   —5 dicitur;] 1, 2 dicitur,   13,] 1, 2 13.   —7
Quapropter] 1, 2 Propterea   —8 legitimas cujusmodi] 1, 2 legitimas, prout   —11 Deo] 1 deo   —13 Deo,] 1 deo,   —14
Chrysost.] 1, 2 Chrysostomus.   Deo] 1 deo   —23 Deo] 1 deo

PAGE 172

—10 Deo] 1 deo —15 *existunt*, reddi] 1, 2 *existunt* reddi
—17 'ἀπώλεσας·] ἀπώλεσας:

PAGE 174

—7 num] 1, 2 an —13 hortetur:] 1, 2 hortetur; —23 illa,
neque] 1 illa neque

PAGE 176

—14 *damus?*] 1, 2 *damus.*

PAGE 178

—4 deserto,] 1, 2 deserto; Dei] 1 dei

PAGE 180

—2 Deus] 1 deus —5 Deo] 1 deo Deo] 1 deo —7 Deus]
1 deus —10 Deo] 1 deo

PAGE 182

—2 Flacco;] 1, 2 Flacco, —6 *servire, nisi*] 1 *servire nisi*
—8 Populus] 1, 2 populus —11 Plancio;] 1, 2 Plancio, —22
tyrannum, plus] 1 *tyrannum plus simplici,* fuisse] 1 *simplici*
fuisse

PAGE 184

—3 Senatu;] 1, 2 Senatu, —10 debet?] 1, 2 debet. —13
Honorii:] 1, 2 *Honorii.*

PAGE 186

—17 alioquin] 1 alioqui —19 *intelligemus?*] 1, 2 *intelligemus.* —22 nonnulli, pro] 1 nonnulli pro

PAGE 188

—2 *pessimi:*] 1, 2 *pessimi;* —3 est;] 1, 2 est, —5 Paulus,
non] 1, 2 Paulus non —13 honestam mallet agere,] 1, 2 honestam
agere, —15–19 inhonestam? Audi . . . adhibeo; non] C. W. K.
inhonestam? 14 inhonestam. Audi . . . adhibeo; non 1, 2
inhonestam. Teipsum testem adhibebo, non —20 discors tibi,]
1, 2 fraudulentus,

PAGE 190

—7 editâ, p. 412;] 1, 2 editâ. p. 412. —9 vidimus, et] 1, 2
vidimus et —12 Scriptura] 1, 2 scriptura —16 Scriptura]
1 scriptura —18 Deus,] 1 deus,

PAGE 192

—7 quis iis] 1, 2 quis non iis

PAGE 194

—2 Imperatorem] 1, 2 imperatorem —5 *cognomen:*] 1, 2
Cognomen: —6 *Dei*] 1 *dei* —7 *cæterùm*] *Cæterùm Deus*]
1 *deus* —8 ibidem, *qui*] 1, 2 ibidem *qui Dominus*] 1, 2 *dominus*
—14 antea] 1, 2 priùs —20 Dei] 1 dei

PAGE 196

—4 plusquam] 1 plus quam   —11 *imperator, interiora*] 1, 2 *imperator interiora*

PAGE 198

—3 *Deo*] 1 *deo*   —4 *peccavisse;*] 1, 2 *peccavisse.*   —9 Deum] 1 deum   —13 Deum] 1 deum   —14 Deus] 1 deus —18 Deum] 1 deum   —22 Deus] 1 deus

PAGE 200

—16 barbariam] 1, 2 barbariem

PAGE 202

—13 addictissimum, nullius] 1, 2 addictissimum nullius   —16 mancipium nostrum] 1 mancipium, nostrum   —21 erat, tuae] 1 erat tuae

PAGE 204

—12 docuerint neque approbarint?] 1, 2 docuerunt neque approbârunt?   —14 dissentiant?] 1, 2 dissentiunt?   —15 *Deo*] 1 *deo*   —16 Deo] 1 deo   —17 *Deum*] 1 *deum*

PAGE 206

—4 Deus] 1 deus   54,] 1, 2 54.   —12 affirmas] 1 *affirmas constituti:*] 1, 2 *constituti.*   —13 Deo] 1 deo   —15 Deo] 1 deo

PAGE 208

—9 passus, æquissima] 1, 2 passus æquissimâ   —11 possit;] 1, 2 possit,   —13 Deus] 1, 2 deus   —21 Deus] 1 deus

PAGE 210

—2 ecclesia] 1, 2 Ecclesia   —6 ecclesia] 1, 2 Ecclesia   —7 ecclesiæ] c. w. k. ecclesiæ   1, 2 Ecclesiæ   14 ecclesia   —13 ecclesia] 1, 2 Ecclesiâ

PAGE 212

—1 Caput IV.] 1 Cap. IV.   —6 propellere] 1, 2 abigere

PAGE 214

—6 sapientissimi:] 1, 2 sapientissimi.   —20 reliquisse,] 1, 2 reliquisse;

PAGE 216

—11 Jerichunte] 1, 2 Hierichunte   —12 Dei] 1 dei   —16 Dei] 1 dei   —19 Dei] 1 dei   —20 legimus. *Clamârunt*] 1, 2 legimus, *clamârunt*

PAGE 218

—1 erat:] 1, 2 erat;   —5 *consul*] 1, 2 *Consul*   —13 suis, Jud. 15.] 1, 2 suis (Jud. 15.)   —16 Dei,] 1 dei,   —17 Deum] 1 deum   —21 *Dei.*] 1 *dei.*

PAGE 220

—2 Dei] 1 dei   —6 Deus] 1 deus   —8 44,] 1, 2 44.

Domini] 1 domini   —14 Domini.] 1 domini.   —15 105,]
2 105.   est, populum] 1 est populum   —18 Domini] 1 domini
—19 Domini] 1 domini   —22 Domini] 1 domini
PAGE 222
   —7 32,] 1, 2 32.   —10 meliore] 1, 2 meliori   —12 rex;]
1, 2 rex,
PAGE 224
   —1 Philistæis] 1, 2 Phelisthæis   —7 mendacissime?] 1, 2
mendacissime.   —17 Philistæos] 1 Phelisthæos   2 Philisthæos
PAGE 226
   —5 *Domini*] 1 *domini*   —9 Solomone, populus] 1, 2 Solomone
populus   —16 sibi, suadent,] 1, 2 sibi suadent,   —22 testatur:]
1, 2 testatur.
PAGE 228
   —9 regem;] 1, 2 regem,   Deus] 1 deus   —13 Deo;] 1, 2 Deo,
PAGE 230
   —1 quis] 1 Quis   —7 *fuit, et*] 1, 2 *fuit et*   —9 Dei] 1 dei
—21 *fuisse*. Anglos] 1, 2 *fuisse*. Primùm delirâsse te cùm hæc scriberes
planè video, neque mentis neque latinitatis compotem satis fuisse: deinde
Anglos
PAGE 232
   —3 quia is dereliquerat] 1, 2 quia dereliquerat   —4 Deum;]
1 deum;   —16 Deus] 1 deus   —19 Deus] 1 deus
PAGE 234
   —8 potuit, utpote fœmina;] 1, 2 potuit utpote fœmina,   —10–11
tyrannum: . . . fœmina.] 1, 2 tyrannum. Pares ergo jam sumus.
—15 *Deum*] 1 *deum*
PAGE 236
   —1 inferiorem.] 1, 2 inferiorem;   —11–12 virorum etiam regum
nomina] 1, 2 virorum nomina   —13–16 Davide, . . . justissimo]
1, 2 Davide, regem et prophetam religiosissimum cum superstitioso et
Christianæ doctrinæ vix initiato, sapientissimum cum stolido, fortissimum
cum imbelli, justissimum cum iniquissimo   —21 cætera dicam,
attrectare] 1, 2 dicam cætera, pertrectare   —23 ego quæ] 1 ego,
quæ
PAGE 238
   —21 ductus, mortem] 1, 2 ductus mortem
PAGE 240
   —2 Pharisæorum] 1, 2 pharisæorum   —4 habet:] 1, 2 habet;
PAGE 242
   —2 vi, (extraneorum] 1 vi, extraneorum   ducebat;) partim] 1
ducebat; partim

PAGE 244
—11 Cæsari et] 1, 2 Cæsari, et   —13 verba?] 1, 2 verba,
PAGE 246
—5 *interpositam.*] 1 *interposita.*   —7 accipe:] 1, 2 accipe;
—9 esse,] 1, 2 erit,   —22 *probatur?*] 1, 2 *probatur:*
PAGE 248
—2 loquatur;] 1, 2 loquatur,   —5 civilibus postmodùm] 1, 2
civilibus, postmodùm   prætulerit.] 1, 2 prætulit.   —9 movisse;]
1, 2 movisse,
PAGE 250
—14 Christianos, aut] 1, 2 Christianos aut   20 Deo] 1 deo
—23 Deo] 1 deo
PAGE 252
—11 puduerit?] 1, 2 puduit?
PAGE 254
—10 laudat:] 1, 2 laudat.   —15 *Dei*] 1 *dei*
PAGE 256
—10 commemoro:] 1, 2 memoro: —13 Christiani,] 1
christiani,   —17 Christianus] 1 christianus
PAGE 258
—9 Christianorum] 1 christianorum   —11 Pastores] 1, 2
pastores   —12 Patres,] 1, 2 patres,   —20 penè] 1, 2 pæne
PAGE 260
—3 sed vel] 1 sed, vel   —4 Christianorum] 1 christianorum
—11 Christianos cum Christianis,] 1 christianos cum christianis,   —16
si ita pronuntiavit] 1, 2 ista si dicat   —17 dixisse] 1, 2 dicere
—19–p. 262, 10. videatur: . . . sit. Quæ] 1, 2 videatur. Quæ
PAGE 262
—17 *Christianum,*] 1 *christianum,*
PAGE 264
—5 sua, *cap. 13.*] 1 sua *cap. 13,*
PAGE 266
—1 Nam] 1 *Nam*   —13 Caput V.] 1 Cap. V.   —14 Dei]
1 dei   —16 Dei] 1 dei   —18 sit,] 1, 2 sit;
PAGE 268
—1 Dei] 1 dei   —5 Græci, tum] 1 Græci tum   —7 quàm]
1, 2 sed   —22 *Prudentia;*] 1 *prudentia;*
PAGE 270
—12 potuissem,] 1, 2 potueram,
PAGE 272
—10–11 respiciat; . . . Jam] 1, 2 respiciat. Jam   —16 præcellit; cæteri] 1, 2 præcellit: Cæteri

Page 274

—2 rebus publicis] 1 rebuspublicis —3 habere, cùm] 1 habere. Cùm —9 Deo] 1 deo

Page 276

—8 inservires?] 1, 2 inservires. —11 invitus pérque] 1, 2 invitus, pérque —13 potest, ne] 1 potest ne —18 excitaveris?] c. w. k. excitaveris? 1, 2, 14 excitaveris.

Page 278

—2 dixisses,] 1, 2 dixeras, —2–3 *rationem, . . . æque*] 1 *rationem sive per plures sive per pauciores sive per unum æque* —4 *eam quæ*] 2 eam, quæ *exercetur, ex*] 1 *exercetur ex tribus, magis*] 1 *tribus magis* —5 aïs;] 1, 2 aïs, —14 *Dei*] 1 *dei* —17 Deo] 1 deo —18 Dei] 1 dei

Page 280

—2 cæterarum, . . . *respub.*] 1 cæterarum te teste *respub.* —6 nostra:] 1, 2 nostra;

Page 282

—1 *ratio postulat,*] 1, 2 *ratio naturalis postulat,* —22 recitata his] 1 recitata, his

Page 284

—1 *dissensiones,*] 1, 2 *dissentiones,* —2 *malum,* affirmabas,] 1 *malum affirmas,* 2 *malum,* affirmas, —5 deauratus, . . . seu] 1, 2 delinitus et deauratus in —8 erubescere;] 1, 2 erubescere, —22 perditam, quò] 1 perditam quo

Page 286

—2 Stoïcum] 1 stoïcum —3 tale, sat] 1 tale sat —9 *desolatæ:*] 1, 2 *desolatæ;* —23 num] 1, 2 an

Page 288

—1 num] 1, 2 an civili, quamvis] 1 civili quamvis truculentissimo, supersedendum,] 1 truculentissimo supersedendum, —2 num] 1, 2 an

Page 290

—2 Deo] 1 deo —3 Deus] 1 deus —19 inquis, *nusquam*] 1, 2 inquis *nusquam*

Page 292

—12 verùm] 1, 2 at enim —16 Triumphas;] 1, 2 Lætaris; —18 recito;] 1, 2 recito, —18–20 *tolerabant . . . poterant.*] 1, 2 in roman letters.

Page 294

—15 Ægyptii, *fideles,*] 1, 2 Ægyptii *fideles, extitere:*] 1, 2 *extitere;* —20 Cùm . . . desciscunt,] 1, 2 Quo occiso iterum fidem mutant,

PAGE 296

—1 Ocho rursus in] 1, 2 Ocho in   —20 Deum] 1 deum

PAGE 298

—4 *Jus*] 1, 2 *jus*   —8 Persarum, id] 1, 2 Persarum id

PAGE 300

—3 fateris] 1, 2, 14 *fateris*

PAGE 302

—5 pòst] 1, 2 postea   —22 *est*;] 1, 2 *est*,

PAGE 304

—1 *legitimus*;] 1, 2 *legitimus*,   —6 infra, ὁ] 1, 2 infra ὁ   —9 octava, Ἀρχὴ] 1, 2 octava ἀρχὴ   —23 *statuant*.] 1, 2 *statuunt*.

PAGE 306

—3 sexto,] 1, 2 6$^{to.}$ —9 poetas] 1, 2 Poëtas   —14 scito, (præcipitem] 1 scito, præcipitem   —15 perspicio) scito,] 1 perspicio, scito,   —16 poëtam] 1, 2 Poëtam   —19 poëtæ] 1, 2 Poëtæ cuique personæ maximè] 1, 2 cuique maximè   —21 se contulerant;] 1, 2 pervenerant;

PAGE 308

—14 *facerem*,] 1, 2 *faciam*,   20 lætantis,] 1, 2 lætantis.

PAGE 310

—24 *redduntur*.] 1, 2 *rependuntur*.

PAGE 312

—4 μόνῳ] 1 μόνω   —5 *soli*.] 1, 2 *solùm*.   —6 Antigone:] 1, 2 Antigone.   —10–p. 314, 14. nemo . . . hæc] 1, 2 nemo ignorat. Atque hæc

PAGE 314

—4 2. 13. 29] 1, 2, 14 23. l. 2.   —24 *libitum, Romanis*] 1 *libitum Romanis*   —26 legibus colluvies] 1, 2 legibus, colluvies

PAGE 316

—7 tandem, ut] 1, 2 tandem ut   —9 antea] 1, 2 priùs   —10 censuisset?] 1, 2 sensisset?   —12 regi] 1, 2 Regi   —24 etsi] 1, 2 quamvis

PAGE 318

—3 alia, quæ] 1 alia quæ   —7 solùm, aut] 1 solùm aut —13 *statu, nihil*] 1, 2 *statu nihil*   —15 regium:] 1, 2 regium;

PAGE 320

—1 Cæsaris, effectum] 1 Cæsaris effectum   —9 Deus] 1 deus

PAGE 322

—1–2 dignior, . . . superbire,] 1, 2 dignior es; quanquam tu hinc noli superbire,   —3 confero,] 1, 2 conferendum putem,   —5–6 solvendum . . . imponere] 1, 2 solvendum, imponere   —8 suum cod.] 1, 2 suum, cod.   —9 juris imperatorum] 1, 2 juris, impera-

torum   —15 *Omnia*] 1, 2 *omnia*   —22–p. 324, 17. Tarquinium
. . . *Sed*] 1, 2 Tarquinium expulerunt. Sed

PAGE 324
    —17–18 inquis, *Tarquinium expulerunt?*] 1, 2 inquis, *expulerunt*,
—21 mori, si modò] 1, 2 mori, modò   C.] 1, 2 Ca.   —22 illius]
1, 2 ejus

PAGE 326
    —2 secunda] 1, 2 2da —3 *boni, quantum*] 1 *boni quantum*
—5 infra,] 1, 2 infrà.   —16 Si] 1, 2 si   —23 Panegyrico:]
1, 2 Panegyrico.

PAGE 328
    —3 *Nemo*] 1, 2 *nemo*   —8 trucidaverit,] 1, 2 trucideraverit.
—17 mortuum et] 1, 2 mortuum tamen et

PAGE 330
    —2 consularis, cùm] 1 consularis cum   —8 et ut] 1, 2 et, ut

PAGE 332
    —6 *occiderit, præmium*] 1, 2 *occiderit præmium*   —11 Paucæ]
1, 2 paucæ

PAGE 336
    —2 nunc, hominum] 1 nunc hominum   —3 corruptissime, *ob*]
1 corruptissime *ob*   —6 luerunt] 1, 2 luent   —7 vellem:]
1, 2 vellem;   —20 inde statuere] 1, 2 colligere

PAGE 338
    —1 *eo, quo*] 1 *eo quo*

PAGE 340
    —5 *Galba, qui*] 1 *Galba qui*   —9 Trifurcifer!] 1, 2 Trifurci-
fer, vituperatio] 1, 2 vituperium   —14 sint?] 1, 2 sint.

PAGE 342
    —17 canem; te Sancti] 1, 2 canem, te S^{ti}

PAGE 344
    —9 possent?] 1, 2 poterant?   argumentari] 1, 2 ratiocinari

PAGE 346
    —11 Caput VI.] 1 Cap. VI.

PAGE 348
    —8 opporteret;] 1, 2 opporteret,   —13 Dei, aut] 1 Dei aut
—14 rebus;] 1, 2 rebus,   —16 libertate;] 1, 2 libertate:

PAGE 350
    —7 Euripides] 1 Euripedes   —19 *hic*;] 1, 2 *hic*,   —23
octava.] 1, 2 octava,

PAGE 352
    —6 tertio,] 1, 2 3^{tio},

PAGE 354

—5 *Deum*] 1 *deum*   Deus] 1 deus   —6 Deus] 1 deus —10 recoquemus,] 1, 2 recoquemus?   refutavimus?] 1, 2 refutavimus.

PAGE 356

—2 *Parlamento*] 1, 2 *parlamento*   —16 obsederant,] obsederant;

PAGE 358

—4 Deo] 1 deo

PAGE 362

—1 *Vates*] 1, 2 *vates*   —2 Deum] 1 deum   —9 *Nihil*] 1, 2 *nihil*   —11 *plures:*] 1 *plures.*   —13 temetipso] 1 temet ipso

PAGE 364

—1 usum fructum] 1 usumfructum   —3 prostares,] 1, 2 cursitares,   —8 vicit;] 1, 2 vicit,   tametsi] 1, 2 etsi

PAGE 368

—1 Caput VII.] 1 Cap. VII.   —6 foret;] 1, 2 foret,   —7 Crux] 1 crux   —13–14 duodecim . . . Pares?] 1 regis Franciæ duodecim vetustissimi Pares;   —14 an Turpini fabulæ] 1, 2 an fabulæ   —16–18 dixeris. . . . Quòd] 2 THE SAME EXCEPT duodenos INSTEAD OF duodecim   1 dixeris. Quòd   —19–p. 370, 1. regis . . . vide] 1 regis pares, ut nominantur, vide

PAGE 370

—13–p. 372, 4. plebi . . . poterunt] 1 plebi visum est. Illustri exemplo esse poterunt

PAGE 374

—5 tuis] 1, 2 tuismet   —16 ridiculum sed] 1, 2 ridiculum, sed —20 *agam;*] 1, 2 *agam,*

PAGE 376

—7 Panegyrico:] 1, 2 Panegyrico.   —9 *verbum, non*] 1 *verbum non*   —16 cedere, siquidem] 1 cedere siquidem   —18 optimorum?] 1, 2 optimorum.

PAGE 378

—9 dicis. Quam] 1, 2 dicis. Quam   —14 dicis Quam   —10 vel, ut] 1, 2 vel ut   dicam, virtualiter,] 1, 2 dicam virtualiter, —11 Etenim quæ] 1, 2 Quæ enim

PAGE 380

—2 natura, neque] 1 natura neque   —6 *judicari, quia*] 1 *judicari quia*   —11 *collegas;*] 1, 2 *collegas,*   —15 Magistratum,] 1, 2 magistratum,   —20 immanissimum, nullum] 1, 2 immanissimum nullum

Page 382

—20 poculis, . . . alii] 1, 2 poculis, alii   —21 elegantiæ, . . . nam] 1, 2 elegantiæ, nam

Page 384

—8 minùs, quæso, rex] 1, 2 minùs quæso rex   —10 regem,] 1, 2 regem?   —11 gesserit?] 1, 2 gesserit.   —21 interdum non] 1, 2 rarò

Page 386

—1 quàm patientia . . . ne] 1, 2 quàm æquitate id fit, ne   —7 interfectoribus,] 1, 2 interfectoribus.

Page 388

—7 ponis;] 1, 2 ponis,   —21 *sumptorum*;] 1, 2 *sumptorum*.

Page 390

—3 *residere*;] 1, 2 *residere*,

Page 394

—10 Diodorus, lib.] 1, 2 Diodorus. 1.

Page 398

—4 Non] 1, 2 non   —6 Caput VIII.] 1 Cap. VIII.   —12 *Omnes*] 1, 2 *omnes*   —13 *Italos, sive*] 1, 2 *Italos, sive*   —14 *Italos sive*   —20 ejus qui] 1, 2 ejus, qui   conduxit copia,] 1, 2 conduxit, copia,

Page 400

—6 refert, quid] 1 refert quid   —7 vis, Ole,] 1, 2 vis Ole, —8 pertineat?] 1, 2 pertinet?   —22 Sapit] 1, 2 sapit

Page 402

—8 Sexto] 1, 2 6to   —17 *Deo*] 1 *deo*   *Deum*] 1 *deum*

Page 404

—5 Quatuor] 1, 2 quatuor   —8 Barbaricum,] 1, 2 barbaricum,

Page 406

—8–9 concinnare semper soles!] 1, 2 semper concinnas!

Page 408

—7 Nam] 1, 2 nam   —9 Secundum] 1, 2 2dum   —11 *imperio, cui*] 1 *imperio cui*

Page 410

—13 Gulielmus] 1, 2 Guilielmus   —18 Gulielmo,] 1, 2 Guilielmo,   —19 Gulielmus] 1, 2 Guilielmus

Page 412

—9 Gulielmo] 1, 2 Guilielmo

Page 414

—3 Buchananum;] 1, 2 Buchananum,   —14 *Rex*] 1, 2 *rex*

PAGE 416

—3 *convocetur?*] 1, 2 *convocetur.*   tibi;] 1, 2 tibi,   —11 vocatum, bis] 1, 2 vocatum bis

PAGE 418

—1 qui] 1, 2, 14 *qui*   —16 *membrorum;*] 1, 2 *membrorum,*

PAGE 420

—10 debebas? Certe] c. w. к. debebas? Certe   14 debebas. Certe 1, 2 te oportebat? certe   —12 hoste papa, ejus] 1, 2 hoste, ejus —13 Verùm, quia] 1 Verùm quia   —17 saltem posse] 1, 2 saltem aliquem posse   —21 Dei sed] 1, 2 Dei, sed

PAGE 422

—3 quin sicuti] 1, 2 quin, sicuti   —11 *Tertii*] 1, 2 *3^{tii} Baronum*] 1, 2 *baronum*   —16 fuisse;] 1 fuisse,   —18 quinquagesimo secundo] 1 52.   2 52   —22 Edouardus] 1, 2 Edouardus   14 Edovardus

PAGE 424

—10 plebeii] 1, 2 plebeii   14 plebii   —17 Agraria] 1, 2 agraria

PAGE 426

—18 nos, et] 1 nos et   —21 transtulisse, (neminem] 1, 2 transtulisse, neminem   —23 approbatas,] 1, 2 approbatas: 17.) sequitur] 1, 2 17. sequitur

PAGE 428

—6 *County*] 1, 2 *Countie*   —20 essent, rectè] 1, 2 essent rectè —21 *Parlamentum*] 1, 2 *parlamentum*

PAGE 430

—5 *Parlamento*] 1, 2 *parlamento*   —8 *administrat;*] 1 *administrat*,   —20 *judicandum?* 1, 2 *judicandum;*   —21 Deo] 1 deo —22 authoritas, quæ] 1 authoritas quæ

PAGE 432

—14 præstitero;] 1, 2 præstitero:

PAGE 434

—8 furem:] 1, 2 furem;   —11 Congesta in extremo] 1, 2 Congesta extremo

PAGE 436

—2–3 nonnullos supplicio] 1, 2 nonnullos, supplicio   —3–5 Britannos . . . sed] 1, 2 Britannos eo nomine Gildas, contrà quam tu facis, reprehendit, non quòd reges necavere, sed   —23 nominatur ab ipsis usque] 1, 2 nominatur; ipsis

PAGE 438

—2 Beda. Sic] 1, 2 Beda; sic   —4 promulgavit:] 1, 2 promul-

gavit; —5 *concilio* item] 1 *concilio*, item —13 fore:] 1, 2 fore. —19 Tertio] 1, 2 3^{tio}

PAGE 440

—1 dat, vel] 1 dat vel —10 traditas, abesse] 1, 2 traditas abesse

PAGE 442

—5 Gulielmus] 1, 2 Guilielmus —16 *rex, ubi*] 1 *rex ubi voluntas, et*] 1 *voluntas et* —17 *regit;*] 1 *regit, tyrannus, dum*] 1 *tyrannus dum* —19 *Dei:*] 1 *dei:* —20 *Dei:*] 1 *dei:*

PAGE 444

—2 Eduardinæ verè] 1, 2 Edvardinæ, verè —4 Dei] 1 dei —6 Dei.] 1 dei. —7 Dei] 1 dei —14 *peccat;*] 1, 2 *peccat,* legunt, *si*] 1 legunt *si* —20 Comites] 1, 2 comites Comites] 1, 2 comites —21 regis;] 1, 2 regis,

PAGE 446

—6 *paribus* 25,] 1 *paribus.* 25. —10 quidem;] 1, 2 quidem,

PAGE 448

—5 Pares] 1, 2 pares —8 Parlamentum] 1, 2 parlamentum —10 Parlamenta] 1 parlamenta

PAGE 450

—17 Caput IX.] 1 Cap. IX. —19 legitimos,] 1, 2 legitimos;

PAGE 452

—18 poterat,] 1, 2 poterat; —21–p. 454, 1. rex jus aut justitiam,] 1, 2 rex justitiam,

PAGE 454

—2 ne . . . num] 1, 2 ne in Curiâ quidem ullâ minori, an —7 7 H.] 1, 2 7. H. —11–12 coëgerunt;] 1, 2 coëgere; —13 statuunt;] 1, 2 statuunt: —17–18 servitutem, . . . asseris:] 1, 2 servitutem asseris, sed eas in libertatem:

PAGE 458

—14 insimulet.] 1, 2 insimulat.

PAGE 460

—3–4 quinetiam . . . erat,] 1, 2 qui etiam quod nequit ex Evangelio, —9 imponat,] 1, 2 imponat; —20 Collige te] 1, 2 Subsiste

PAGE 462

—2 tangendos,] 1 tangendos; —4 liberavit;] 1, 2 liberavit

PAGE 464

—5 Quarto,] 1, 2 4to, —6 Septimo,] 1, 2 7^{timo}, Sexto] 1, 2 6to —8 precariam,] 1, 2 precariam; —15 Quarto,] 1, 2 quarto, —16 Secundo] 1, 2 secundo I Hen.] 1, 2 I. Hen. —17 108,] 1, 2 108.

PAGE 466

—2 Quarti] 1, 2 4ᵗⁱ   —8 voluerint] 1, 2 vellent   —14 exterorum, quotquot] 1 exterorum quotquot   —15 attigere, testantur.] 1 attigere testantur.   Edouardi] 1, 2 Edvardi

PAGE 468

—4 valuit.] 1, 2 valebat.   abs] 1 ab   —6 *legiones, quæ*] 1 *legiones quæ*

PAGE 470

—6 *subditis*;] 1, 2 *subditis*,   —12 nuntio et regis] 1, 2 nuntio et regis   14 nuntio regis   —15 Eadem] 1, 2 eadem   fiduciaria,] 1, 2 fiduciaria;

PAGE 472

—2 *Chartâ*] 1, 2 *chartâ*   *Magnâ*] 1, 2 *magnâ*   —12 recenses;] 1, 2 recenses: —17 Dei] 1 dei   —18 Stulte,] 1, 2 Stulte;

PAGE 474

—2 centum] 1, 2 centenis   —4 desipere:] 1, 2 desipere; *vexilli, ad Regem*] 1, 2 *vexilli ad regem*   —23 Tyrannus] 1, 2 tyrannus

PAGE 476

—6 judicâsset;] 1, 2 judicat;   —7 Sancti] 1, 2 Sᵗⁱ   —15 fas regi non erat:] 1, 2 rex non potuit: —18 Sexti] 1, 2 6ᵗⁱ —20 imponere. Sed] 1 imponere, sed

PAGE 478

—1 nomine, nostris] 1, 2 nomine nostris   —14 Fortescutius, de] 1 Fortescutius, Fortesc. de

PAGE 480

—4 magis quam teipsum ridiculum] 1, 2 magis ridiculum   —5 neges.] 1, 2 negas.   —10–11 *cœlo*, ... moverit.] 1, 2 cœlo ipso petitum nihil movit.   —12 Stoïcus] 1, 2 stoïcus   —14 *extitisse*] 1, 2 *exstitisse*

PAGE 482

—1 Caput X.] 1 Cap. X.   —5 Dei,] 1 dei,   —11 pugnemus,] 1, 2 agamus,

PAGE 484

—10 occubuisse:] 1, 2 occubuisse: 14 occubisse: —18 quod] 1, 2 veluti   —19 consueverunt insulsissimi,] 1, 2 deterrimi,

PAGE 486

—8 aulici de] 1, 2 aulici, de   —14 verò] 1, 2 forte   Virgiliana ignavissimi,] 1, 2 Virgiliana,

PAGE 488

—3 scribis.] 1, 2 scribis?   —5 meritò;] 1, 2 meritò,   —7 adversari] 1, 2 refragari   —9 ipsos] 1, 2 ipsi   redigi.] 1, 2 redigerentur.

Page 490
—6 ipse] 1, 2 ipse   14 ipsa   —14 habituros;] 1, 2 habituros,
—15 accepturos. Post] 1, 2 accepturos: post   —19 cupiebant,
ministris] 1, 2 cupiebant, et ministris   —20 tempusque sibi oppor-
tunum] 1, 2 opportunum sibi tempus
Page 492
—7 anteponebant.] 1, 2 præponebant.   —15 censuerant; Scoti]
1, 2 censuerant; dum Scoti   —17 insidebant;] 1 2 insidebant,
—18 tenebant;] 1, 2 tenebant,   habebant: ipsi] 1, 2 habebant: dum
ipsi   —20–21 qui tumultus paulò] 1 qui paulò
Page 494
—5 compressit.] 1, 2 compescuit.   —10 reipub.] c. w. k. reipub.
1, 2, 14 rempub.   —15 inimicissimis, Presbyteriani,] 1, 2 inimicissimis, quamvis sanguinem eorum avidè sitientibus, Presbyteriani,   —20
sibi suo] 1, 2 suo sibi
Page 496
—7 prolixiùs] 1, 2 fusiùs   —16 dicere.] 1 dicere:
Page 498
—2 promiserint;] 1, 2 promisere;   —16–18 *estis*; . . . vos]
1, 2 *estis*; vos
Page 500
—16 Cum] 1, 2 cum
Page 502
—20 Deum,] 1 deum,
Page 504
—7 usque eò] 1, 2 eò usque
Page 506
—1 Caput XI.] 1 Cap. XI.   —3 acessisse.] 1, 2 accedere.   —20
solenni conventione] 1, 2 in roman letters.
Page 508
—4 judicassent.] 1, 2 judicarent.
Page 512
—14 affirmaveris?] 1, 2 affirmasti?
Page 514
—1 Caput XII.] 1 Cap. XII.   —9 reservares,] 1, 2 reservares;
—13 *possunt*:] 1, 2 *possunt*;   —14 *versatur*;] 1, 2 *versatur*,
—16 tacuero:] 1, 2 tacebo:
Page 516
—19–20 importatas ipse sibi congereret,] 1, 2 congerendas inferret,
—21 incredibilem pecuniam corrasisset,] 1, 2 pervolaret omnia,
Page 518
—16 *simplici* saltem *vice*] 1, 2 in roman letters.

PAGE 520

—2–3 promisit si] 1, 2 promisit, si   —7 repentino impetu] 1, 2 repente armis   —12 etiam ipse tantum] 1, 2 etiam tantum

PAGE 522

—9 *Rege,*] 1, 2 *rege,*   *Dominorum*] 1, 2 *dominorum*

PAGE 524

—1 fuisset,] 1, 2 foret,   —3 scripto edito; idem] 1, 2 scripto, idem   —21 Deus . . . vel sibi vel] 1, 2 Deus dederit, vel sibi, vel

PAGE 526

—6 appellarent.] 1, 2 appellarent.   14 appellarunt.   —8 *elogium*] 1, 2 *Elogium*   —13 docebit, nomen] 1, 2 docebit nomen —21 Sancti] 1, 2 S^{ti}

PAGE 528

—7 Ordinibus] 1, 2 ordinibus   —9 Ordinum] 1, 2 ordinum —16 angis] 1, 2 exerces   maceras;] 1, 2 volutas;

PAGE 530

—2 vestro] 1, 2 vestrûm   —4 scivit,] 1, 2 sciebat,   —13 ab re somniculosè oscitantem] 1 ab re somniantem   2 abs re somniantem

PAGE 532

—7 necesse habuimus.] 1, 2 tenemur.

PAGE 534

—4 Protestantium,] 1, 2 protestantium,   —13 jurejurando regibus] 1, 2 jurejurando à regibus   —20 qui . . . peccare] 1, 2 qui secum legem ipsam ut peccare

PAGE 536

—6 ausus,] 1, 2 auderet,   —24 ad] 1, 2 quoad   —26 Gulielmum] 1, 2 Guilielmum

PAGE 538

—3 Quòd si] 1 Quòd, si   —16 37 Hen. . . . c. 8.] 1, 2 xxxij. Hen. 6. c. xv. alterum *decimo tertio,* Edouardi IV. c. VIII.   —18 neuter eorum regum] 1, 2 neque rex iste neque ille   —20 tibi inaudita dictantium,] 1, 2 tibi dictantium,   —22 est puditum] 1, 2 pudebat   —23 manifestè] 1, 2 facilè

PAGE 540

—1 Clausula autem ista] 1, 2 Clausulam autem istam   —10 audio:] 1, 2 audiam: —13 est: ita] 1, 2 est. Atque ita   —20 paternâ disciplinâ] 1, 2 disciplinâ patriâ

PAGE 542

—12 non dubitare] 1, 2 indubitanter   —13 necquicquam] 1, 2 incassùm   —17 inopes atque] 1, 2 inopes, atque   —18 servitutem natos fatentur] 1, 2 servitium natos, fatentur   —20 vindice,] 1, 2 vindice;   —21 Regem] 1, 2 regem   —23 erit et] 1, 2 erit, et

Page 544

—11 necesse non habet respondere,] 1, 2 respondere non tenetur, —12 rex, . . . an] 1 rex; an

Page 548

—12 hujusmodi quiddam] 1, 2 hoc ferè

Page 550

—6 extitisti,] 1, 2 fuisti,   —13 rabiem et] 1, 2 rabiem, et —16 juvante, videor] 1, 2 juvante videor   —23 Cives, adversarium] 1 Cives adversarium

Page 552

—4 oppressi ad] 1, 2 oppressi, ad   —5 exaudivit.] 1, 2 exaudiit. —7 Superstitio,] 1, 2 superstitio   gloriosissimè] 1, 2 gloriosè

Page 554

—4 ardentes,] 1, 2 accensos,   —14 faventem, præ] 1, 2 faventem et paternum, præ   —16 WHAT FOLLOWS (TO THE END OF THE WORK) IS FOUND ONLY IN 14.

COLUMBIA UNIVERSITY PRESS
Columbia University
New York

FOREIGN AGENT
OXFORD UNIVERSITY PRESS
Humphrey Milford
Amen House, London, E.C.